VISUAL QUICKSTART GUIDE

InDesign CS6

FOR WINDOWS AND MACINTOSH

SANDEE COHEN

Peachpit Press

Visual QuickStart Guide
InDesign cs6

Peachpit Press
1249 Eighth Street
Berkeley, CA 94710
phone 510 524 2178
fax 510 524 2221

Find us on the Web at www.peachpit.com.
To report errors, please send a note to errata@peachpit.com.

Copyright © 2012 by Sandee Cohen

Peachpit Press is a division of Pearson Education.

Editor: Becky Morgan
Production Editor: Becky Winter
Compositor & Interior Design: Sandee Cohen
Cover Design: RHDG/Riezebos Holzbaur, Peachpit Press
Logo Design: MINE (TM) www.minesf.com
Proofreader: Megan Tytler
Indexer: Jack Lewis

ISBN-10: 0321822536
ISBN-13: 9780321822536

0 9 8 7 6 5 4 3 2 1

Printed and bound in the United States of America

Introduction

Welcome to the *InDesign CS6 Visual QuickStart Guide*, my ninth version of the book. From its humble start, InDesign is now the primary application for desktop publishing and page layout. I feel very lucky to have been working with and teaching InDesign since its very first beta. In fact, this is the only third-party book that has had editions for all versions of InDesign.

Using This Book

If you have used any of the other Visual QuickStart Guides, you will find this book to be similar. Each chapter is divided into different sections that deal with a specific topic — usually a set of tools or similar commands. For instance, the chapter on text has sections on creating text frames, typing text, selecting text, and so on.

Each of the sections contains numbered exercises that show you how to perform a specific technique. As you work through the steps, you gain an understanding of the technique or feature. The illustrations help you judge if you are following the steps correctly.

I've also sprinkled sidebars, printed in colored boxes, throughout the chapters. Some of these sidebars give you a bit of history or background for a specific feature. Other times, I've written out humorous stories about desktop publishing. These sidebars are the same little stories and anecdotes I tell my students in the classes I teach.

Strictly speaking, you don't have to work through the book in the same order as it is printed. If you want to learn more about imported images, you can skip right over to that chapter.

However, the book is organized in the same order that I run my InDesign beginner classes. We start with the document setup, then move to basic text, color, and so on. It's just as if you were sitting in one of my classes. The only thing you won't see is a lunch break.

Instructions

You will find it easier to use this book once you understand the terms I am using. This is especially important since some other computer books use terms differently. Therefore, here are the terms I use in the book and explanations of what they mean.

Click refers to pressing down and releasing the mouse button on the Macintosh, or the left mouse button on Windows. You must release the mouse button or it is not a click.

Press means to hold down the mouse button, or a keyboard key.

Press and drag means to hold the mouse button down and then move the mouse. I also use the shorthand term **drag**.

Menu Commands

InDesign has menu commands that you follow to open dialog boxes, change artwork, and initiate certain actions. These menu commands are listed in bold type. The typical direction to choose a menu command might be written as **Object > Arrange > Bring to Front**. This means that you should first choose the Object menu, then choose the Arrange submenu, and then choose the Bring to Front command.

Modifier Keys

Modifier keys are always listed with the Macintosh key first and then the Windows key second. So the instruction "Hold the Cmd/Ctrl key" means hold the Cmd key on the Macintosh platform or the Ctrl key on the Windows platform. When the key is the same on both computers, such as the Shift key, only one key is listed.

Keyboard Shortcuts

You'll notice that I don't usually provide the keyboard shortcut for commands. For instance, I'll list the menu command for File > New, but not the keyboard shortcut Cmd/Ctrl-N.

While keyboard shortcuts help you work faster, you really don't have to start using them right away. In fact, you will most likely learn more about InDesign by using the menus. As you look for one command, you may see another feature that you would like to explore.

So don't worry about keyboard shortcuts as you start. Focus on the big picture.

My Thanks to:

Nancy Ruenzel, publisher of Peachpit Press.

Becky Morgan, my editor at Peachpit Press. Thanks for being so patient with me.

Becky Winter, for her eagle production eye and blazingly fast corrections.

The staff of Peachpit Press, all of whom make me proud to be a Peachpit author.

The **InDesign team** in Seattle, who has made InDesign my favorite program to use and to write about.

And a very special thanks to **David Lerner** of **Tekserve,** who has helped me keep my computers running in the middle of the book crunch. Tekserve (www.tekserve.com) is the best place to buy, fix, or enhance Macintosh computers.

Colophon

This book was created using InDesign CS5.5 running on a MacBook Pro and a Dell Vostro. Screen shots were taken using Snapz Pro X (Mac) and Snagit (Win). InDesign CS6 beta ran on the Macintosh OS X (Lion) and on Windows 7. Fonts are Myriad Pro from Adobe.

And Don't Forget...

Whether you're learning InDesign in a class or on your own, I hope this book helps you master the program.

Just don't forget to have fun!

Sandee Cohen

(Sandee@vectorbabe.com)
June, 2012

Table of Contents

Getting Started 1

One of the reasons why InDesign has become so popular is that it uses many of the same tools, panels, and onscreen elements that are found in Adobe Photoshop and Adobe Illustrator. This makes it very easy to use your knowledge of those programs to learn InDesign. With InDesign CS6, this synergy between all the programs is even stronger than ever before.

However, with every version of the Creative Suite, there are slight changes in how to work with the software. This chapter should help you pick up some power shortcuts in working with the interface.

Finally, this chapter contains a rundown of all the panels and tools in the program. This is an excellent way to quickly familiarize yourself with all the features of InDesign. As you read the descriptions of all the panels, you should get a better idea of the power of InDesign.

Working with Panels

Most of the commands and features that control InDesign are found in the onscreen panels. If you don't see a panel, you can open it by choosing it in the Window menu.

To open a panel:

Choose the panel from the Window menu or submenu. For instance, to open the Character panel go to the Window menu, then to the Type & Tables listing, and then choose Character from the submenu. This is written as **Window > Type & Tables > Character**.

To close a panel:

Click the close control in the panel's title bar. The close control for Windows panels is on the right of the title bar **A**. The close control for Macintosh panels is on the left of the title bar **B**.

You can also minimize a panel so that it only displays the panel tab **C**.

To minimize a panel display:

Click the minimize icon **B** to collapse the panel.

TIP Some panels need more than one click to minimize the display completely.

TIP If a panel does not contain all its controls, click the minimize icon to expand the panel. This can also be done by choosing the Show Options command from the panel menu.

Panels can also be displayed in an icon view. This view takes up less screen real estate.

To collapse a panel to the icon view:

Click the top gray bar of the panel to collapse the panel to the icon view **D**.

TIP Click the gray bar again to expand the panel out of the icon view.

A The **controls** for Windows panels.

B The **controls** for Macintosh panels.

C A **minimized panel**.

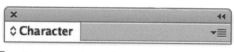

D A **panel in the icon display**.

E **Drag a panel in the icon view** to the left or right to show or hide the name of the panel.

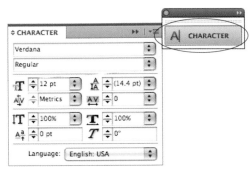

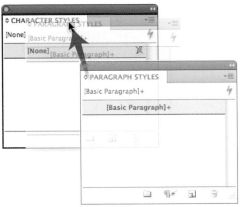

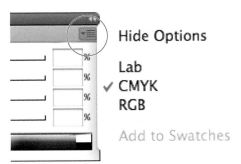

F Click the name of the panel or icon to open the **full panel display**.

G Click the **panel menu icon** to display the menu for a panel.

H Drag the panel tab into another panel area to **nest panels**.

To control the icon view of a panel:

Drag the icon panel to the left to display just the icon of the panel **F**. Or drag the icon panel to the right to display both the icon and the name of the panel.

The icon view allows you to open the panel in the full panel display.

To reveal the full panel from the icon view:

Click the name or the icon of the panel. The full panel appears next to the icon panel **F**.

TIP Click the icon panel name again, or another panel, to retract the full panel display.

Most panels contain a menu with additional commands.

To display the panel menus:

1. Click the panel menu icon to open the panel menu **G**.

2. Choose a command from the menu.

Another way to save screen space is to move one panel so that it is located within the boundaries of another. This is called *nesting*.

To nest panels:

1. Position the cursor over the panel tab.

2. Drag the tab so that the outline is inside another panel. A rectangular highlight inside the panel indicates that the two panels will be nested **H**.

3. Release the mouse button. The panel appears next to the other item.

To unnest panels:

1. Drag the panel tab so that the outline is completely outside the other panel.

2. Release the mouse button. The panel appears as a separate onscreen item.

Using Workspaces

I don't know any two InDesign users who agree as to how to arrange their panels. Although my panels may start out neatly arranged, within a short time I've got them scattered all over my screen — especially if I am demonstrating in front of a class.

Fortunately, you can arrange and save your panel arrangements into workspaces that you can call up at any time.

To save a custom workspace:

1. Arrange your panels as you want them to appear on the screen.

2. Choose **Window > Workspace > New Workspace**. The New Workspace dialog box appears .

3. Enter a name for the workspace.

4. Select the Capture options:

   - **Panel locations** remembers the positions of the panels.

   - **Menu Customisation** remembers the display of menus. *(See Chapter 21, "Customizing.")*

5. Click OK. The workspace appears alphabetically at the top of the Workspace menu.

To delete a workspace:

1. Choose **Window > Workspace > Delete Workspace**. The Delete Workspace dialog box appears .

2. Use the pop-up menu to choose the workspace you want to delete. Or choose All to delete all the custom workspaces.

3. Click the Delete button.

TIP You cannot delete any of the workspaces in brackets. These are the workspaces that ship with the application.

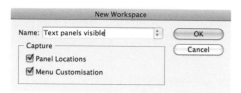

A The **New Workspace dialog box** lets you set a custom workspace configuration.

B The **Delete Workspace dialog box** lets you choose the workspace you want to delete.

```
    Text panels visible              Custom
    Working with color               workspaces

    [Advanced]
    [Book]
    [Digital Publishing]
 ✓  [Essentials]                     Default
    [Interactive for PDF]            workspaces
    [New in CS6]
    [Printing and Proofing]
    [Typography]

    Reset Essentials
    New Workspace...
    Delete Workspace...

    Show Full Menus
```

C The **Workspace menu** with the custom workspaces and default workspaces.

Suggestions for Using Workspaces

Workspaces save all the attributes, appearances, and positions of the panels. This means that you can have a workspace that closes all the panels except one or two that you want to use.

You can have workspaces that show just the panels that apply colors, gradients, and other object attributes. You can have other workspaces that show only the panels that you use for text. You can even have a workspace that puts all the panels on the left for left-handed users.

You can apply workspaces at any time as you are working — even with a document open. It's very soothing to see all your panels rearrange into orderly groups.

There is no direct route to edit a workspace, but you can modify it.

To modify a workspace:

1. Make the changes in the workspace.

2. Choose **Window > Workspace > New Workspace**. The New Workspace dialog box appears.

3. Name this new arrangement with the same name as the workspace you want to modify.

4. When asked if you want to replace the original workspace, say Yes.

Once you set up your workspaces, it is a joy to apply them as you work.

To apply a workspace:

Choose a workspace from the **Window > Workspace** menu **C**. The panels fly around into their designated spots.

TIP You can also apply workspaces using keyboard shortcuts. You can use the Keyboard Shortcuts dialog box (Edit > Keyboard Shortcuts) to set shortcuts for the first nine default workspaces and the first nine custom workspaces. *(See Chapter 21, "Customizing.")*

If you move items in a workspace, you have actually created a new version of that workspace. To go back to the original setting of the workspace, you need to reset the workspace.

To reset a workspace:

Choose **Window > Reset [name of workspace]**. This resets the captured elements of the workspace to the way they were when you first defined the workspace.

Using the Tools Panel

The Tools panel contains the tools for working in InDesign, as well as controls for applying the colors of fills and strokes. Some of the tools have fly-out panels that let you access the other tools in the category.

To choose a tool:

Click the tool in the Tools panel . Or tap one of the keyboard shortcuts for each of the tools.

> **TIP** Double-click the title bar on the Tools panel to change the Tools panel from single column to double column or horizontal column.

Tools and controls in the Tools panel that have a small triangle in their slot have other tools hidden in a fly-out panel.

To open the tools in the fly-out panels:

1. Press the fly-out triangle on the tool slot. The fly-out panel appears **B**.
2. Choose one of the tools listed in the fly-out panel.

To see the tool keyboard shortcuts:

Pause the cursor over the tool. The name of the tool and the keyboard shortcut appear **C**.

> **TIP** If you don't see the tool tip after pausing for a moment, make sure the Tool Tips control is turned on in the application preferences *(see Chapter 21, "Customizing")*.

> **TIP** You can change or add keyboard shortcuts for tools using the keyboard shortcut controls *(see Chapter 21, "Customizing")*.

Title bar

A The **Tools panel** at its default display.

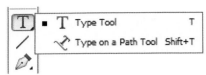

B The **fly-out panel** for the Type tools.

C Pause over a tool to see its **tool tip**.

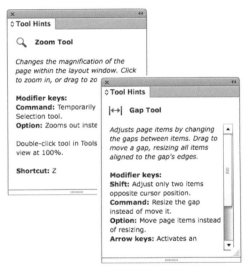

D Open the **Tool Hints panel** to read short descriptions of the functions and features of the selected tool.

Using the Tool Hints Panel

If Tool Tips aren't enough information on a certain tool, use the Tools Hints panel for more details without a trip to the Help menu.

Using the Tool Hints panel:

1. Select a tool in the Tools panel.

2. Choose **Window > Utilities > Tool Hints** to open the Tool Hints panel **D**. The panel displays the following:

   - The tool icon and name.

   - A description of the function.

   - Any modifier keys and how they affect the tool behavior.

   - The keyboard shortcut that accesses the tool.

TIP Move the mouse cursor over the Tool Hints panel to highlight the text in the panel. Right-click to copy the text from the panel. The text can be pasted into documents. (But that's *not* how I wrote this book.)

Using Contextual Menus

Contextual menus are menus that change depending on the type of object selected or where the mouse is positioned . The benefit is that you don't have to move all the way up to the menu bar to invoke a command.

To display contextual menus:

(Mac and Win) Click the right mouse button.

or

(Mac) Hold the Control key and click the mouse button.

TIP Watch for the Macintosh contextual menu cursor, which appears next to the arrow as you press the Control key.

Contextual cursor

Cut
Copy
Paste
Paste in Place

A The **contextual menu** changes depending on what type of object is selected.

Document Setup 2

Billions of years ago, when dinosaurs ruled the earth — or about 25 years ago, before the start of desktop publishing — people prepared documents for printing using pieces of stiff board. They marked up the boards with special blue pencils to indicate the edges of the pages. They drew marks that specified where the margins and columns should be and how the pages should be trimmed. This board, called a *mechanical,* was used as the layout for the document.

Unlike the board mechanicals of the past, InDesign documents are electronic layouts. Just as with the board mechanicals, you need to set the page sizes, margins, and column widths. But because you are using a computer rather than a pencil, you have additional controls for how the document is laid out.

Of course, changing an electronic layout takes far less time than it did with the board mechanicals that old dinosaurs like me used to use.

The Welcome Screen

How nice of InDesign to welcome you when you first launch the application. Rather than just close the Welcome Screen, take a look at its features because there are things that may be useful.

Using the Welcome Screen:

1. The Welcome Screen automatically appears when you first launch InDesign .

2. You can click one of the Welcome Screen features:
   - To create new documents or open sample templates, click one of the Create New commands B.
   - Use the Recent Items area to open InDesign documents that you have recently opened and saved C.
   - Click one of the choices in the Community area to open a Web browser and visit a site where you can get more information or support for working with InDesign D.

TIP Click the Don't Show Again checkbox to keep the Welcome Screen from opening.

Most people I know click the Don't Show Again box and never look at the Welcome Screen again. However, one day you may decide that you would like to investigate the Welcome Screen resources. Here's how to get the Welcome Screen back.

To reopen the Welcome Screen:

Choose **Help** > **Welcome Screen**. The Welcome Screen opens.

A   The **Welcome Screen** appears when you first launch InDesign.

Create New

B   The **Create New** commands in the Welcome Screen.

Open a Recent Item

C   The **Open a Recent Item** lists InDesign documents you have recently opened and saved.

Community

D   The **Community area** sends you to Web sites where you can get more information on InDesign.

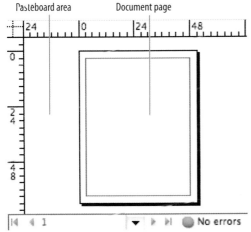

F Each **document page** is surrounded by the non-printing pasteboard area where you can store objects for later use.

E The **New Document dialog box** set for the basic layout options.

Setting Up Documents

When you create a new document, you have the opportunity to set many options in the New Document dialog box.

To set the basic options for a new document:

1. Choose **File > New > Document**. This opens the New Document dialog box E.

2. Set each of the document options below *(For details see "Setting the Layout Options" on page 13.)*:

   - Choose the Print, Web, or Digital Publishing from the Intent menu.
   - Enter the number of pages in the Number of Pages field.
   - Choose at what page number the document should start.
   - Check Facing Pages to set your document with left-hand and right-hand pages.
   - Check Primary Text Frame to make it easy to flow text onto pages. *(See Chapter 10, "Pages and Books," for more information on primary text frames.)*
   - Use the Page Size pop-up list to set the size of your page.
   - Set the Orientation to portrait or landscape.
   - Enter the size of the margins in the Margins fields.
   - Set the number of columns and the gutter width in the Columns Number and Gutter fields.

3. Click OK. The document appears in the window F.

TIP The pages are surrounded by an area called the pasteboard. Like a drawing table, you can set items there for later use. Items on the pasteboard do not print.

You can also set the advanced options for a document. The first is the area around the page, called a *bleed*. When you set a bleed, you define an area outside the trim of the page where objects will still print. The second area is called a *slug*. This is an area outside the page that may or may not print. Slugs are often used by advertising agencies to list insertion dates and the name of the product, manufacturer, and ad agency.

To set the advanced options for a new document:

1. Click the More Options button in the New Document dialog box. The advanced options for Bleed and Slug dimensions appear at the bottom of the dialog box.

2. Set the amounts for the size of the bleed area around the document 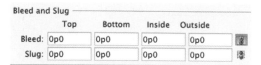.

3. Set the amounts for the size of the slug area around the document. The slug area is displayed outside the document trim **B**.

TIP Click the Fewer Options button to hide the Bleed and Slug dimensions.

TIP Click the Make Same Size icon **C** for the Bleed or Slug to automatically set all the dimensions to the same size.

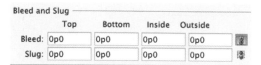

Bleed and Slug				
	Top	Bottom	Inside	Outside
Bleed:	0p0	0p0	0p0	0p0
Slug:	0p0	0p0	0p0	0p0

A Click the More Options button to reveal the **Bleed and Slug fields.**

B A document with **bleed and slug areas**.

C The **Make Same Size icon** forces all the fields to the same amount.

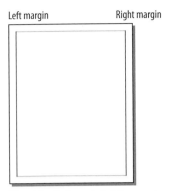

Left margin   Right margin

D The **left and right margins** on nonfacing pages.

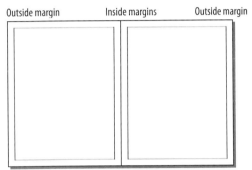

Outside margin   Inside margins   Outside margin

E The **outside and inside margins** on facing pages.

Setting the Layout Options

As you enter your settings in the New Document dialog box, you are actually making decisions as to the layout of your document.

The Intent menu refers to the final output of a document. The choices are Print, for ink on paper, Web, for online output, or Digital Publishing, for tablet applications.

Setting the output intent:

Choose Print, Web, or Digital Publishing from the Intent menu.

TIP The Web and Digital Publishing intents change the units of measurement into pixels and changes colors from CMYK to RGB.

Setting the number of pages:

Enter the total number of pages in the Number of Pages field.

TIP This doesn't mean you can't add or delete pages later. It just saves a step of adding them later on.

Setting the start page:

Use the Start Page # field to enter the number at which your document should start.

Facing pages refers to documents such as a book where pages on one side of its spine face the pages on the other side. (This is also called a *spread*.) Single pages, such as advertisements, have facing pages turned off.

To set facing pages:

With the Document Setup dialog box open, select the Facing Pages option. This changes the document from single page to facing pages D and E.

TIP When a document is set for facing pages, the names in the dialog box for the Left and Right margins change to Inside and Outside margins.

The page size is the size of the individual pages of the document.

To set the size of the page:

Choose one of the choices from the Page Size menu 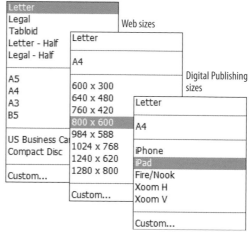:

TIP The A4, A3, A5, and B5 sizes are used primarily outside of the United States.

TIP The online and digital publishing sizes are set in pixel dimensions.

TIP If you change the values in the Width or the Height field, the Page Size automatically switches to the Custom setting.

The term *orientation* refers to how the page is positioned, either up and down or sideways.

To set the orientation:

Click the Portrait orientation to create a document where the width is always less than the height **B**.

Click the Landscape orientation to create a document where the width is always greater than the height **B**.

To set the margins:

1. Enter an amount for the Top and Bottom fields **C**.

2. If the document is set for facing pages, enter an amount for the Inside and Outside fields.

   If the document is not set for facing pages, enter an amount for the Left and Right margins **D**.

TIP When you finish typing in one of the fields, press the Tab key to jump to the next field.

TIP Click the Make Same Size icon in the Margins area to make all the margins the same size. When the icon displays a broken link, you can enter different sizes for each margin.

A The **Page Size menu** changes depending on the output intent that is chosen.

B The **Orientation controls** let you set the position of the page.

C The margin settings for a document with **facing pages**.

D The margin settings for a document with **nonfacing pages**.

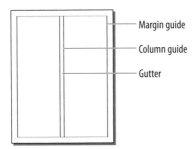

E The **column settings** let you set the number of columns and the amount of space for the gutter between the columns.

Margin guide
Column guide
Gutter

F A **two-column document** with margin, column, and gutter guidelines.

Setting Other Defaults

As you work in InDesign, you will discover other areas where you would like to set defaults. Perhaps you'd like certain colors to appear (or not appear) in each new document. Or you would like certain text options to appear automatically.

Just as you can set the Document Setup options with no document open, you can also set other defaults.

With no document open, go to the panels or preferences and set the controls to what you would like to have as a default.

You can also set visible guides for columns and the *gutters* (or spaces) between the columns.

To set the columns and gutters:

1. Click the field arrows or enter an amount for the number of columns **E**.

2. Click the field arrows or enter an amount for the gutter.

TIP The columns and gutters act as guidelines on your page **F**. You can still place text or graphics across or outside the columns or gutters.

TIP InDesign remembers the last new document settings and uses it for a new document.

You can also create the *default setting* for new documents.

To set the document defaults:

1. Close all InDesign documents, leaving just the application open.

2. Choose **File > Document Setup**. The Document Setup dialog box appears.

3. Make whatever changes you want to the options in the Document Setup dialog box.

4. Click OK. The settings you have chosen become the default for any new documents.

TIP Hold the Opt/Alt key as you open a new document to override the previously created document and go back to the default new document setting.

Changing Layout Options

When you start a new document, all the settings appear in one dialog box. However, after you begin working on the document you must use two separate controls to make changes to the document.

To change the document setup:

1. Choose **File** > **Document Setup** to open the Document Setup dialog box 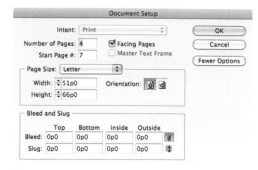.

2. Make whatever changes you want to the settings.

3. Click OK to apply the changes.

Although most of the layout options are in the Document Setup dialog box, the margins and columns are set separately.

To change the margins and columns:

1. Choose **Layout** > **Margins and Columns** to open the Margins and Columns dialog box **B**.

2. Make whatever changes you want to the following settings:
   - **Margins**
   - **Number of columns**
   - **Gutter** (the width of the space between the columns)

3. Click OK to apply the changes.

TIP Changing the margins and columns while on a page or spread changes the settings only for that page or spread. To change the settings for all the pages, you need to work with the master page. *(See Chapter 10, "Pages and Books," for more information on master pages.)*

A The **Document Setup dialog box** for an existing document.

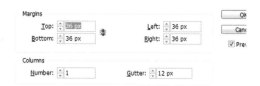

B The **Margins and Columns dialog box** for an existing document.

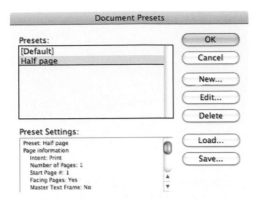

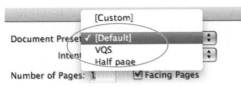

C The **Document Presets dialog box** lets you edit, delete, and create new document presets.

D You can apply presets using the **Document Preset menu** in the New Document dialog box.

Using the Document Presets

You may want to save all the settings for certain types of documents so they can easily be applied when you start new documents. For instance, my Visual QuickStart books require different settings from the handouts I use when teaching. Document presets make it easy to apply the different settings when I create new documents.

You can also use the Document Presets dialog box to create document presets without going through the New Document dialog box.

To create a new document preset:

1. Choose **File > Document Presets > Define**. This opens the Document Presets dialog box C.
2. Click the New button to open the New Document Presets dialog box.
3. Use the dialog box to name and set the options for the new preset.
4. Click OK to save the preset.

To delete a document preset:

1. Choose **File > Document Presets > Define**. This opens the Document Presets dialog box.
2. Choose the document preset that you want to delete.
3. Click the Delete button.

To apply a document preset:

Choose the document preset from the Document Preset menu in the New Document dialog box D.

Or choose **File > Document Presets** and then choose one of the presets listed in the menu. This opens the New Document dialog box with that preset chosen.

To edit a document preset:

1. Choose **File** > **Document Presets** > **Define**. This opens the Document Presets dialog box.

2. Select the document preset that you want to edit.

3. Click the Edit button. This opens the Edit Document Preset dialog box 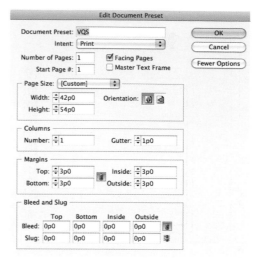.

4. Make whatever changes you want. Click OK to save the changes in the preset.

TIP You can edit the [Default] present, but you can't delete it.

You can also export document presets into a file that can be shared with others.

To export document presets:

1. Click the Save button in the Document Presets dialog box.

2. Name and save the document preset file.

You can also import document presets from others.

To import document presets:

1. Click the Load button in the Document Presets dialog box.

2. Navigate to find the document preset file.

3. Click the Open button. The document presets are imported into InDesign.

A Use the **Edit Document Preset dialog box** to make changes to the existing document presets.

Vertical ruler   Horizontal ruler

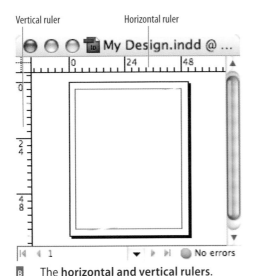

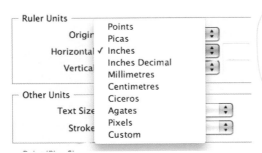

B   The **horizontal and vertical rulers**.

C   The choices for the ruler's
units of measurement.

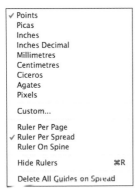

D   The contextual menu choices for the
ruler's **units of measurement**.

Using Document Rulers

Designers need to measure things on pages.
Rather than hold a ruler up to your monitor,
you can use InDesign's electronic rulers.

To show and hide the document rulers:

> To see the rulers along the top and left
> edges of the document window, choose
> **View** > **Show Rulers** ▣.
>
> *or*
>
> Choose **View** > **Hide Rulers**.

You can change the rulers to display different
units of measurement. This is helpful if you
receive instructions written in measurements
with which you are not familiar.

To change the unit of measurement:

1. Choose **Edit** > **Preferences** > **Units
   & Increments** (Win) or **InDesign** >
   Preferences > **Units & Increments** (Mac).
   This opens the Preferences Units &
   Increments dialog box.

2. For the Horizontal and Vertical settings,
   choose one of the measurements from
   the pop-up lists ▣.

3. If you choose Custom, enter the number
   of points for each unit on the ruler.

TIP   You can also change the units with the ruler
contextual menus ▣.

TIP   The Units & Increments preferences also let
you set your own value for the number of
points per inch.

The rulers start numbering at the top-left corner of the page. You may want to move this point, called a *zero point,* to a different position. This can help you judge how much space you have from one spot of the page to another.

To reposition the zero point:

1. Position the cursor over the zero point crosshairs at the upper-left corner of the rulers 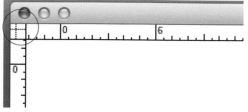.

2. Drag the zero point to the new position on the page **B**.

3. Release the mouse button to position the zero point.

TIP Double-click the zero point crosshairs in the corner of the rulers to reset the zero point to the upper-left corner.

If you are working on a project such as an advertising spread, it may be easier to position objects if the rulers continue across the *spine* of the pages. (The spine is where the pages of a book or magazine are bound together.)

To set the origin of the rulers:

1. Choose **Edit** > **Preferences** > **Units & Increments** (Win) or **InDesign** > **Preferences** > **Units & Increments** (Mac).

2. Set the Ruler Units Origin menu to one of the following:

   • **Ruler Per Page** sets individual rulers for each page.

   • **Ruler Per Spread** sets one ruler that crosses the spine.

   • **Ruler Per Spine** sets the ruler in negative numbers to the left of the spine and positive numbers to the right of the spine **C**.

TIP You can choose the same settings from the ruler contextual menu.

A The **zero point indicator** of the rulers.

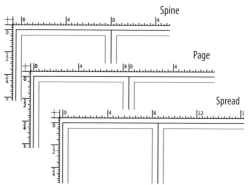

B You set the ruler's **zero point** by dragging the zero point indicator to a new position on the page.

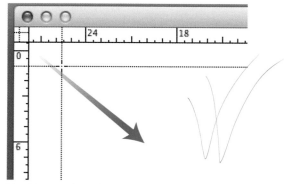

C You can control **whether the rulers reset for each spine or each page.** They can also be set to stay across a spread.

The **Page tool** in the Tools panel.

W: 51p0   Letter

H: 66p0

Liquid Layout Rule:
Controlled by Master

☑ Objects Move with Page

☐ Show Master Page Overlay

The **Page tool controls** in the Control panel.

The **Master overlay** can be displayed when the Page tool selects a page.

Using the Page Tool

Pages don't have to be the same size in a single document. Once you have created a page, you can use the Page tool to make that page a different size from the rest of the pages in the document. This makes it possible to combine the layouts for different sized items into a single document.

To change the size of a page:

1. Choose the Page tool from the Tools panel.

2. Click the page or pages that you want to customize. Use the Shift key to select pages in more than one spread.

3. Use the width and height fields in the Control panel to adjust the size of the pages or choose a size from the pull-down menu.

4. Choose one of the Liquid Layout rules to control how objects change their size as you change the size of the page. *(See Chapter 18, "Working with Layouts" for information on using Liquid Layout features.)*

5. Check Show Master Page Overlay to see the prefix and name of the master applied to a page. *(See Chapter 10, "Pages and Books" for how to work with master pages.)*

6. Check Objects Move with Page to have items on the page move as you rearrange pages. *(See the next exercise on how to move pages in a layout.)*

TIP You can also select pages in the Pages panel with the Page tool.

You can also use the Page tool to move pages up or down in a spread.

To move pages in a spread:

1. Select the Page tool from the Tools panel.

2. Position the Page tool over the page you want to move and drag up or down.

TIP The vertical area of the pasteboard expands as you drag a page beyond the top or bottom of the other page A.

TIP Custom-sized pages appear as different sizes on the artboard B. However, they do not appear with the same relationship in the Pages panel C.

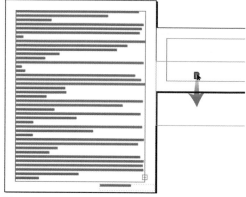

A Moving a page up or down next to another page.

B Two different sized pages as they appear on the artboard.

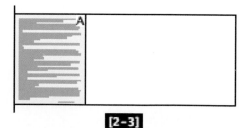

C Two different sized pages as they appear in the Pages panel.

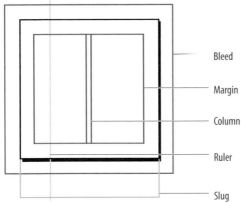

Bleed

Margin

Column

Ruler

Slug

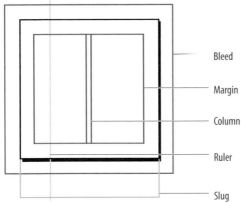

D Examples of the various types of **guides on a page**.

E The dialog box for the **guides preferences**.

Guides in Back turned on

Guides in Back turned off

F The **Guides in Back command** changes how guides are displayed as they pass through text and artwork.

Working with Guides

Guides are nonprinting lines that help you position objects. InDesign has many different types of guides that you can work with **D**.

- **Ruler Guides** can be positioned anywhere on the page or pasteboard.
- **Margin Guides** show the settings of the margins for the document.
- **Column Guides** show the column settings for a page or master page.
- **Bleed Guides** show the bleed area for the document.
- **Slug Guides** show the slug area for the document.
- **Smart Guides** appear as you create and move objects around a page. *(See the next section for working with Smart Guides.)*

InDesign gives you options for how to work with guides.

To change the guide preferences:

1. Choose **Edit** > **Preferences** > **Guides & Pasteboard** (Win) or **InDesign** > **Preferences** > **Guides & Pasteboard** (Mac) to open the Guides & Pasteboard Preferences **E**.

2. Use each of the menus to set the colors of the guides.

3. Check Guides in Back to position the guides behind text and graphics on the page **F**.

4. Enter an amount in the Snap to Zone field. This is the distance, in pixels, for how close an object must be before it will snap or jump to align with a guide.

To show or hide guides:

To see the margin, column, and ruler guides, choose **View > Grids & Guides > Show Guides**.

or

To hide the guides, choose **View > Grids & Guides > Hide Guides**.

Objects can be set to automatically snap to guides as you move them. This makes it easier to align objects to guides.

To make objects snap to guides:

Choose **View > Grids & Guides > Snap to Guides**.

TIP Choose the command again to turn off the feature.

There may be times when you want to move a column guide manually. This results in a custom guide setting.

To unlock and move column guides:

1. If **View > Grids & Guides > Lock Column Guides** is checked, choose the command to unlock the column guides.

2. Position the cursor over the guide you want to move.

3. Press the mouse button. The cursor turns into a two-headed arrow that indicates that the column has been selected **A**.

4. Drag the column guide to the new position.

TIP You cannot change the width of the gutter space between the columns by moving a column guide. But you can change it in the Margins and Columns dialog box.

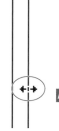

A The **two-headed arrow** indicates that a column guide can be moved.

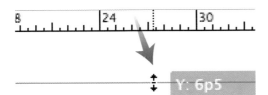

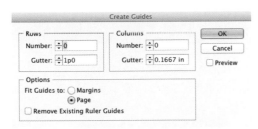

B You can **drag ruler guides** out from the horizontal ruler or vertical ruler.

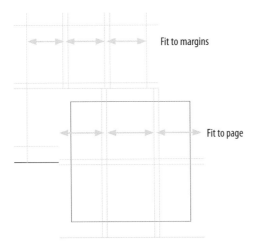

C The **Create Guides dialog box** lets you automatically add many guides on a page.

D Fit Guides to Margin spaces the guides equally inside the page margins. Fit Guides to Page spaces the guides equally inside the page trim.

Ruler guides are more flexible than margin or column guides and can be positioned anywhere on the page to help with object placement.

To create ruler guides:

1. Position the cursor over the horizontal or vertical ruler.

2. Press the mouse button. The cursor turns into a two-headed arrow.

3. Drag to pull the guide out onto the page **B**.

Rather than pulling guides out one at a time, you can also create a series of ruler guides in rows and columns.

To create rows and columns using guides:

1. Choose **Layout > Create Guides**. This opens the Create Guides dialog box **C**.

2. Enter the number of rows (horizontal guides) in the Rows Number field.

3. Enter the amount for the space between the rows in the Rows Gutter field.

4. Enter the number of columns (vertical guides) in the Columns Number field.

5. Enter the amount for the space between the columns in the Columns Gutter field.

6. Choose between Fit Guides to Margins or Fit Guides to Page **D**.

7. Check Remove Existing Ruler Guides to delete all the ruler guides that were previously on the page.

8. Click OK to apply the guides.

TIP Check Preview to see the guides on the page change as you enter the values within the dialog box.

TIP If you set the Number fields to zero for both the Rows and Columns, the Remove Existing Ruler Guides option deletes all the ruler guides on the page.

To reposition ruler guides:

1. Position the cursor over the guide you want to move.

2. Press the mouse button. The cursor turns into a two-headed arrow and the guide changes color. This indicates that the guide has been selected.

3. Drag the ruler guide to a new position.

You can manually move or delete guides.

To move existing ruler guides:

Use either of the Selection tools to drag the ruler guide to a new position .

To delete selected ruler guides:

1. Click the ruler guide with one of the Selection tools.

2. Press the Delete/Backspace key.

You can lock ruler guides so they don't move.

To lock guides:

Choose **View** > **Grids & Guides** > **Lock Guides**.

TIP Choose the command again to unlock the guides.

You can change the color of guides and set when they are visible.

To change the appearance of ruler guides:

1. Choose Layout > Ruler Guides to open the dialog box **B**.

2. Use the Color pop-up list to pick the color for the ruler guides.

3. Set a percentage for the View Threshold. This sets the magnification below which the guides are not displayed **C**.

TIP Increase the View Threshold if you have many guides on the page. This hides the guides at low magnifications and shows them at higher ones.

A Use **either of the Selection tools** to select a ruler guide.

B Use the **Ruler Guides dialog box** to change the color of the ruler guides. You can also set the threshold to determine at what magnification the guides are visible.

C A view threshold of 200% means the guides are visible only when the magnification is 200% or higher.

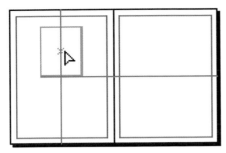

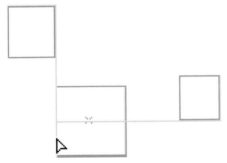

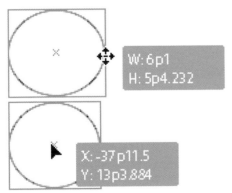

Using Smart Guides

Ruler guides are static elements that are always on the page. Smart Guides are dynamic elements that appear and disappear depending on what you are doing on the page. Smart Guides make it very easy to align objects to the center of a page.

To show or hide Smart Guides:

Choose **Window** > **Grids & Guides** > **Smart Guides**. This turns the Smart Guides on or off.

To align and center to the page using Smart Guides:

Drag an object near to where the center of the page is. A Smart Guide appears when the center of the object or edge of the object is centered to the page .

Smart Guides also appear when one object is near the center or edge of another.

To align and center to an object using Smart Guides:

Drag an object near to where the center or edge of another object is. A Smart Guide appears when the center of the object or edge of the object is centered to the other object .

Viewing Transformation Values

Transformation Values provide additional feedback as to the position and size of objects.

To view Transformation Values:

1. Choose **Preferences** > **Interface**.
2. Turn on Show Transformation Values. This adds an information label that provides the size or position of objects as they are moved or created 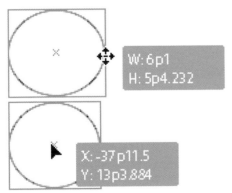.

D Two **Smart Guides** appear as an object is positioned at the center of a page.

E Smart Guides appear when an object is near the **edge or center of other objects**.

F The **Transformation Values** appear when an object is created (top) or moved (bottom).

Working with Document Grids

Ruler guides aren't the only way to align objects. The document grid can also be used as a structure for designing pages. The baseline grid is used to keep lines of text even.

To display the grids:

Choose **View > Grids & Guides > Show Document Grid**  or **View > Grids & Guides > Show Baseline Grid**.

To hide the grids:

Choose **View > Grids & Guides > Hide Document Grid** or **> Hide Baseline Grid**.

To change the grid appearance:

1. Choose **Edit > Preferences > Grids** (Win) or **InDesign > Preferences > Grids** (Mac) to open the preferences dialog box **B**.

2. Use the Color list to change the grid color.

3. Enter an amount in the Horizontal and Vertical Gridline Every fields to set the distance between the main gridlines.

4. Enter an amount in the Subdivisions field to create lighter gridlines between the main gridlines.

5. Enter an amount in the Start field to set where the baseline grid should start.

6. Use the Relative To list to position the start of the grid relative to the top of the page or the top margin.

7. Enter a percentage in the View Threshold field. This sets the lowest magnification at which the grid is visible.

8. Check Grids in Back to position the gridlines behind objects on the page.

To turn on Snap to Grid:

Choose **View > Grids & Guides > Snap to Document Grid**. If Snap to Document Grid is checked, the feature is already turned on.

A Choose **Show Document Grid** to see the horizontal and vertical gridlines.

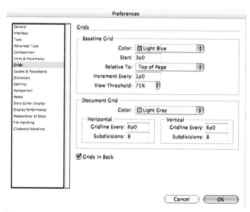

B The **Grids Preferences dialog box** lets you control the display and arrangement of the document grid.

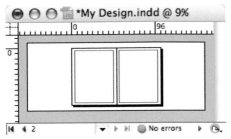

The **Entire Pasteboard command** shows the page as well as the pasteboard.

InDesign's "Smart" View Commands

If you have not used other page layout programs, you may not realize how smart some of InDesign's View commands are. These are the commands Fit Page in Window, Fit Spread in Window, and Entire Pasteboard.

In most other programs, if you choose the Fit Page in Window command, the magnification changes to show the entire page. If you then change the size of the window, the magnification is no longer the correct size to show the entire page.

InDesign, however, is much smarter. When you choose those three View commands, InDesign continues to display the entire page, spread, or pasteboard even if you resize the window. The magnification dynamically changes as you change the size of the window.

The command will stay active until you choose a new view or manually change the magnification. That's pretty smart!

Changing the Magnification

Magnification refers to the size of the document as it appears on your screen. InDesign gives you many ways to change the magnification setting. Some of the quickest and easiest ways to change the magnification settings are to use View commands.

TIP A small monitor forces you to use small magnifications to see the entire page. A larger monitor allows you to set its resolution so that it shows the entire page at magnifications that are easier to read.

To zoom with the View commands:

1. To increase the magnification, choose **View > Zoom In**.

2. To decrease the magnification, choose **View > Zoom Out**.

3. To see all of the current page, choose **View > Fit Page In Window**. This changes the magnification setting to whatever amount is necessary to see the entire page.

4. To see all of the current spread, choose **View > Fit Spread in Window**.

5. To see the document at 100% magnification, choose **View > Actual Size**.

6. To see the entire pasteboard area, choose **View > Entire Pasteboard** C.

InDesign lets you view the page with a wide range of magnification settings. You can select a specific magnification amount from the magnification list.

To use the magnification list:

1. Click the control in the Application bar to display the magnification list 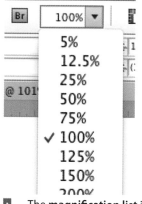.

2. Choose one of the magnifications in the list.

You can also view specific magnifications not in the list.

To enter a specific magnification amount:

1. Double-click or drag across the magnification shown in the Application bar.

2. Type a number between 5 and 4000.

TIP It is not necessary to type the % sign.

3. Press Return or Enter to apply the setting.

A The **magnification list** in the Application bar.

Magnification Shortcuts

Because the View commands are used so often, the keyboard shortcuts are listed here. You can also find these shortcuts displayed on the View menu.

Mac Commands

Zoom In	Cmd-=
Zoom Out	Cmd-hyphen
Fit Page in Window	Cmd-0
Fit Spread in Window	Cmd-Opt-0
Actual Size	Cmd-1

Windows Commands

Zoom In	Ctrl-=
Zoom Out	Ctrl-hyphen
Fit Page in Window	Ctrl-0
Fit Spread in Window	Ctrl-Alt-0
Actual Size	Ctrl-1

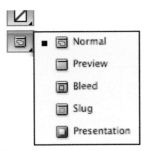

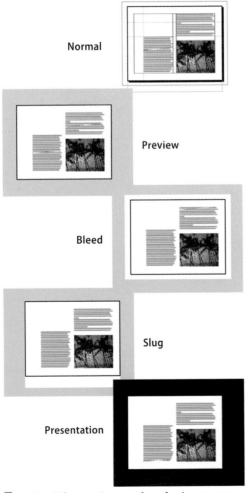

B Choose **one of the view modes** to see specific areas in a Preview Mode.

Normal

Preview

Bleed

Slug

Presentation

C The different **view modes** of a document.

View and Pasteboard Controls

As you work, you may want to view your document in different ways. The four view modes provide different ways of looking at your document.

To choose the four view modes:

Choose one of the view modes from the fly-out panel at the bottom of the Tools panel **B**.

- **Normal View mode** is the default view and shows you all the guides in the document as well as the pasteboard, bleed, and slug areas **C**.

- **Preview mode** shows only the area inside the page boundaries. All guides are automatically hidden. A gray background hides any objects on the pasteboard **C**.

- **Bleed mode** adds the area inside the bleed to the Preview Mode **C**.

- **Slug mode** adds the area inside the slug to the Preview Mode **C**.

- **Presentation mode** is similar to the Preview Mode except that the background is black. Also, you can use keyboard shortcuts to move through the document as a slide show **C**.

TIP The view controls are also in the Application bar.

The area above and below the document is controlled by the Minimum Vertical Offset. You can make that area larger.

To change the Minimum Vertical Offset:

1. Choose **Edit** > **Preferences** > **Guides & Pasteboard** (Win) to open the Guides & Pasteboard Preferences.

   or

2. Choose **InDesign** > **Preferences** > **Guides & Pasteboard** (Mac) to open the Guides & Pasteboard Preferences.

3. Enter an amount in the Horizontal Margins field **A**. This changes the pasteboard size to the left and right of the page **B**.

4. Enter an amount in the Vertical Margins field **A**. This changes the pasteboard size on the top and bottom of the page **B**.

Pasteboard Options
Horizontal Margins: 51p0   Vertical Margins: 6p0

A Use the **Margin control fields** to change the size of the pasteboard around the document.

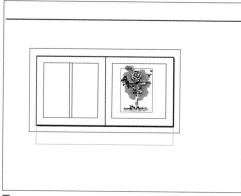

B The effects of changing the size of the Pasteboard Options.

Use the **Zoom tool** to change the magnification of the page.

D **Drag the Zoom tool diagonally** to magnify a specific area. The marquee indicates the area to be selected.

E The selected area fills the window after you release the mouse button.

Using the Zoom and Hand Tools

The Zoom tool lets you jump to a specific magnification and position on the page. The Hand tool moves the view to a new position.

To use the Zoom tool:

1. Click the Zoom tool in the Tools panel **C**. The cursor turns into a magnifying glass.

2. Click the Zoom tool on the area you want to zoom in on. Click as many times as is necessary to change the magnification.

TIP Press Cmd/Ctrl and Spacebar to access the Zoom tool without leaving the tool that is currently selected.

TIP Each click of the Zoom tool changes the magnification to the next setting in the magnification list.

TIP Press the Opt/Alt key while in the Zoom tool to decrease magnification. The icon changes from a plus sign (+) to a minus sign (−).

TIP Double-click the Zoom tool in the Tools panel to set the view to the actual size (100%).

A *marquee zoom* allows you to zoom quickly to a certain magnification and position.

To create a marquee zoom:

Drag the Zoom tool diagonally across the area you want to see. Release the mouse button to zoom in **D** and **E**.

You can also use the Hand tool (sometimes called the *Grabber* tool) to move around within the area of the document. This is more flexible than using the scrollbars, which only go up and down or left and right.

To use the Hand tool:

1. Click the Hand tool in the Tools panel .

2. Drag the Hand tool to move around the page.

TIP Double-click the Hand tool in the Tools panel to fit the entire page in the window.

A *power zoom* allows you to zoom out, move around, and then zoom back in on a document.

To create a power zoom:

1. With the Hand tool active, press down on the mouse button until you see two triangles appear inside the Hand. The screen zooms out and displays a red rectangle **B**.

2. With the mouse button still pressed, move the rectangle to a new position in the document.

3. Release the mouse button. The view snaps back to the original magnification before the power zoom.

If you want to become a true InDesign power user, you need to use keyboard shortcuts. One of the primary shortcuts you should learn is how to temporarily access the Hand tool without leaving the current tool.

To temporarily access the Hand tool:

Press the Opt/Alt plus Spacebar keys. This gives you the Hand tool in all situations.

TIP You can also access the Hand tool by pressing just the Opt/Alt key if you are working in a text frame.

A Use the **Hand tool** to move the page around the window.

B Use a **power zoom** to quickly zoom out, navigate around, and then zoom back in on a document.

Playing the Keyboard "Bass Notes"

I confess! I haven't chosen the Zoom or Hand tools in years. Rather than move the mouse all the way over to the Tools panel, I use the keyboard shortcuts.

On the Mac, I keep my fingers lightly resting on the Cmd, Opt, and Spacebar keys. By changing which keys are pressed, I alternate between the Zoom In, Zoom Out, and Hand tools.

On Windows, I do the same thing with the Ctrl, Alt, and Spacebar keys.

So, as my right hand moves the mouse around and taps other keys on the keyboard, my left hand is always playing the three bass notes of the keyboard.

Click to open   Click to close

C The **Split Window controller** at the bottom of the document window.

D The **Split Window controller** at the bottom of the document window.

Controlling Windows

The Split Window feature lets you view one document in two windows and control the display of multiple windows.

To see a document in two windows:

Click the Split Window controller at the bottom of the document window C. This creates a second window containing the document D.

TIP Drag the divider between the windows to change the size of the window.

If you have many documents open, you can quickly arrange them neatly.

To arrange multiple document windows:

Choose **Window > Arrange > Tile**. This changes the size of the windows and positions them so that all the documents are visible C.

or

Choose **Window > Arrange > Cascade**. This stacks all the open windows so that their title bars are visible.

Using the Application Bar

Another useful tool for working with documents is the Application bar.

To work with the Application bar:

On the Macintosh, choose **Window > Application bar**. The Application bar appears as one of the panels 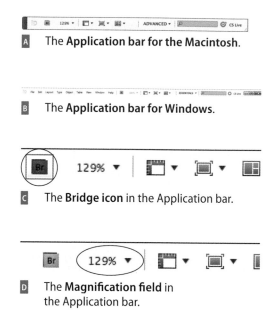.

or

On Windows the Application bar is always visible. The Application bar on Windows contains the menus for the application **B**.

The best part of the Application bar is that it combines many commands and features into a single area. Although these features are found elsewhere, having them in the Application bar makes them more convenient.

To open Adobe Bridge from the Application bar:

Click the Bridge icon to go to the Adobe Bridge application **C**.

To change the magnification from the Application bar:

Click the Magnification menu in the Application bar **D**.

To change the view options with the Application bar:

Click the View Options menu icon to hide or display any of the following **E**:

- Frame Edges
- Rulers
- Guides
- Smart Guides
- Baseline Grid
- Hidden Characters

A The **Application bar for the Macintosh**.

B The **Application bar for Windows**.

C The **Bridge icon** in the Application bar.

D The **Magnification field** in the Application bar.

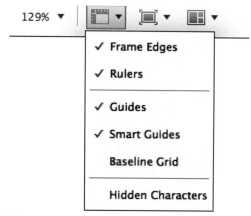

E The **View Options menu** in the Application bar.

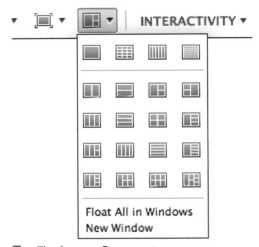

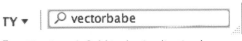

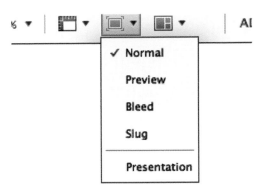

The **Screen mode menu** in the Application bar.

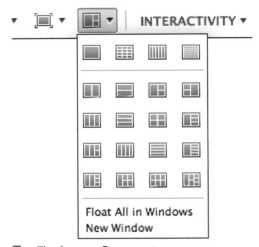

The **Arrange Documents menu** in the Application bar.

The **Workspace menu** in the Application bar.

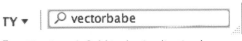

The **Search field** in the Application bar.

To change the view mode from the Application bar:

1. Click the Screen Mode menu in the Application bar **F**.
2. Choose to display the view mode options as described on page 31.

If you have many documents open, your screen may get cluttered. You can quickly arrange all the open documents using the Application bar.

To tile documents using the Application bar:

1. Click the Arrange Documents menu in the Application bar **G**.
2. Choose one of the tile options as shown by the graphic in the menu.

You can also change the workspace via the Application bar.

To change the workspace using the Application bar:

1. Click the Workspace menu in the Application bar **H**.
2. Choose one of the workspaces in the menu.

The Application bar also has an online connection to Adobe.com. This makes it easy to search for technical documents, support files, and other information.

To search Adobe.com using the Application bar:

1. Enter a search term in the Search field **I**.
2. Press Enter or Return. This opens the default browser and takes you to the Adobe.com Web site.

File Maintenance

After you work on a document for even a little while, you need to save your work to a hard drive or disk.

To save and name a file:

1. Choose **File > Save** or **File > Save As**. This opens the Save As dialog box

2. Choose a destination disk and folder for the file.

3. Use the File Name field (Win) or Save As field (Mac) to name the file.

4. Use the Save As Type menu (Win) or Format (Mac) menu **A** to choose one of the following:

   • InDesign CS6 document (indd) saves the file as a regular InDesign document.

   • InDesign CS6 template (indt) saves the file as a template.

TIP The template format saves the file so that each time it is opened, it opens as an untitled document. This protects the document from inadvertent changes.

   • InDesign CS4 or later (IDML) saves the file in a format that can be opened by InDesign CS4, CS5, or CS5.5.

5. Click Save to save the file and close the dialog box.

Save As: Chapter 2

Where: Desktop

Format ✓ InDesign CS6 document
InDesign CS6 template
ew Images   InDesign CS4 or later (IDML)

A The **Save As formats**.

The Three Different Save Commands

The first time you look under the File menu you may be a little confused by the three different commands for saving documents. What are the differences between Save, Save As, and Save a Copy?

The first time you save an untitled document, there is no difference between choosing **File > Save** and **File > Save As**. Both commands bring up the Save As dialog box.

Once you have named a file, the Save command adds new work to the file without changing the file's name. The Save As command will always open the dialog box where you can change the file's name or location.

I use the Save command almost all the time. That way I only have to remember one keystroke combination: Cmd/Ctrl-S. The only time I use the Save As command is if I want to change the name of a document or save it somewhere else.

The **File > Save A Copy** command is different. When you save a copy, you can save the file under a new name. However, unlike the Save As command, you continue to work on the file you were working on.

I use the Save a Copy command when I am about to do something strange or bizarre to my work. The Save a Copy command lets me create a version of the file that I know I can fall back on.

As you work, you may want to spin off a copy of your document under another name. The Save a Copy command makes this easy to do.

To create a copy of a document:

1. Choose **File > Save a Copy**. This opens the Save As dialog box.

2. Use the same steps as described in the two previous exercises to save the file.

3. Click Save. The copy of the document is saved while you can continue to work on your current file.

There may be times when you want to revert to the previously saved version of a document without saving any changes.

To go back to the saved version of a document:

Choose **File > Revert**. The file closes and then reopens to where it was when last saved.

To undo the steps you have done:

Choose **Edit > Undo [Action]**.

TIP Repeat this command as often as necessary.

To redo the steps you have done:

Choose **Edit > Redo [Action]**.

To close a document:

Choose **File > Close**.

or

Click the Close box or button in the document window.

It happens — someday, somehow your computer will crash, a blackout will hit the city, or you will be forced to restart the computer without saving your work. Fortunately, InDesign has an automatic recovery option that can save your work.

To recover a file:

1. Restart the computer after the crash or data loss.

2. Start InDesign. Any files that were open when the crash occurred will be automatically opened.

3. Choose **File > Save As** to save the file with a new name and destination.

TIP The restored data is a temporary version of the file and must be saved in order to ensure the integrity of the data.

InDesign gives you options for opening and closing files.

To open a file within InDesign:

1. Choose **File > Open**.

2. Use the navigation controls to select the file you want to open.

TIP You can also open a document by double-clicking its icon.

To open recently saved documents:

Choose **File > Open Recent** and then choose one of the files listed in the submenu.

TIP InDesign lists the ten last-opened documents in the submenu.

Opening QuarkXPress or PageMaker Files

InDesign can convert documents and templates from QuarkXPress 3.3 or 4.0, and Adobe PageMaker 6.5 (or later). Simply choose **File > Open** and choose the file. InDesign converts the file into a new InDesign document.

How good is the conversion? It's great for templates that consist of the layout without any text. All the master pages are converted along with the style sheets and colors. This lets you use your old templates to produce new work in InDesign.

Graphics that were pasted via the clipboard into QuarkXPress or PageMaker — and not placed using the Place or Get Picture commands — are not converted.

The conversion may change documents with lots of text. For instance, InDesign arranges type with a very sophisticated composition engine. This means that text could move to new lines when it appears in the InDesign document.

If you need to make just one or two small changes to an old document, you're better off opening the file in QuarkXPress or PageMaker and making the changes to the original files.

However, if you need to completely redo a document, export the text from the file, and then use InDesign to convert the template into an InDesign file. You can then use that template for all new documents.

What if you need to open QuarkXPress files greater than version 5 in InDesign? I suggest you investigate the product *Q2ID* from Markzware. It provides a conversion for those versions of QuarkXPress files.

Basic Text 3

When I started in advertising, back in the late seventies, setting type was a complicated process. First, the writer typed out the text on paper. The art director or typographer then marked up the copy with a red (sometimes blue) pencil to indicate the typeface, point size, leading, and so on.

Then, the copy was sent to a typesetting house where a typesetter retyped the text into a special typesetting machine. The text was printed onto special photographic paper and sent back the next morning. The copywriter then had to proof the text to make sure that there were no errors.

She might also have to cut some lines of text to fit the layout. Depending on how much text had to be cut, the art director would use a razor blade to delete the text, or the copy would be sent back to the typesetter.

That's why I am amazed every time I use a program such as InDesign to set text. I don't type the copy onto a piece of paper; I type to fit right onto my actual layout. I don't have to send the copy out overnight; it's right there on my computer screen. And I know that the only mistakes are the ones I make myself!

Creating Text Frames

InDesign holds text in objects called *frames*. Before you can start typing text, you need to create a text frame. The easiest way to do this is with the Type tool.

TIP You can resize or reshape text frames like you can other objects. *(See Chapter 4, "Working with Objects," for more details on creating and working with objects.)*

To create a text frame with the Type tool:

1. Click the Type tool in the Tools panel .
2. Move the cursor to the page. The cursor changes to the Type tool cursor ▣.
3. Drag diagonally to create the frame ▣.

TIP The frame starts from the horizontal line that intersects the text frame cursor.

4. Release the mouse button. The text frame appears with an insertion point that indicates you can type in the frame.

The Type tool will always create rectangular frames. However, you can use the frame tools to create other geometric shapes such as ellipses and polygons to hold text.

TIP The frame tools also let you use numerical settings to specify the exact dimensions of a frame.

To draw an elliptical frame:

1. Click the Ellipse tool in the Tools panel ▣.
2. Drag diagonally to create the ellipse ▣.
3. Release the mouse button when the ellipse is the correct size.
4. Click the Type tool inside the frame to convert it to a text frame.

Choose the **Type tool** in the Tools panel to work with text.

The cursor set to create a text frame.

Drag diagonally with the Type tool to create a text frame.

The Ellipse tool in the Tools panel.

Drag diagonally to create an ellipse.

Where are the Transformation Values Labels?

When you drag to create objects, you will see transformation value labels that appear next to the cursor.

Rather than show them in this chapter, I've turned the feature off so you can concentrate just on the objects being drawn.

The **Polygon tool** in the Tools panel.

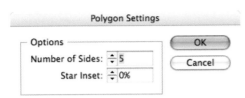

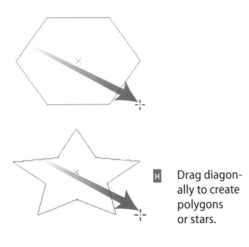

Use the **Polygon Settings dialog box** to change the shape and the number of sides of a polygon.

Drag diagonally to create polygons or stars.

The Polygon tool also lets you draw stars as well as ordinary polygons.

To draw a polygon frame:

1. Double-click the Polygon tool in the Tools panel F. This opens the Polygon Settings dialog box G.

2. Enter a number in the field for the number of sides.

3. Leave the Star Inset amount as 0%. If you increase the star inset, you create a star. (See the next exercise.)

4. Drag across the page to create the polygon H.

5. Release the mouse button when the polygon or star is the correct size.

6. Click the Type tool inside the frame to convert it to a text frame.

To create a star frame:

1. Double-click the Polygon tool in the Tools panel to open the Polygon Settings dialog box G.

2. Enter a number in the Number of Sides field for the number of outer points.

3. Enter a value for the Star Inset amount. The greater the amount, the sharper the points will be.

4. Drag to create the star H.

5. Release the mouse button when the star is the correct size.

6. Click the Type tool inside the frame to convert it to a text frame.

You can also create rectangular frames using the Rectangle tool.

To draw a rectangular frame:

1. Click the Rectangle tool in the Tools panel .

2. Drag diagonally to create the rectangle **B**.

3. Release the mouse button when the rectangle is the correct size.

4. Click the Type tool inside the frame to convert it to a text frame.

The Ellipse tool and the Rectangle tool let you numerically specify the frame size.

To set the size of a frame numerically:

1. Choose the Ellipse or Rectangle tool from the Tools panel.

2. Position the cursor where you want to create the frame.

3. Click. A dialog box appears **C**.

4. Set the Width and Height of the frame.

5. Click OK. The frame appears with its upper-left point where you first clicked.

TIP Hold the Opt/Alt key as you click to position the centerpoint of the frame at that point.

Frames created with the Ellipse, Polygon, and Rectangle tools must be converted before they can be used as text frames.

To convert unassigned frames:

1. Select the frame you want to convert.

2. Choose the Type tool and click inside the frame.

   or

   Choose **Object > Content > Text.** An insertion point appears indicating that you can begin typing.

A The **Rectangle tool** in the Tools panel.

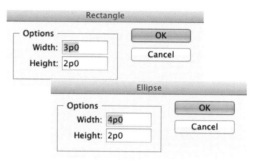

B Drag diagonally to create a rectangle.

C The **Ellipse and Rectangle dialog boxes** let you specify the width and height of a frame.

Tips for Drawing Frames

There are several keyboard shortcuts you can press as you draw frames:

Hold the **Shift key** to constrain the frame to a square, circle, or uniform polygon.

Hold the **Opt/Alt key** to draw the frame from the center outward.

Hold the **Spacebar** to reposition the frame as you draw.

Chapter 3 - How Dorothy Saved the Scarecrow

When Dorothy was left alone she began to feel

D   The **overset symbol** indicates that there is more text than will fit in the frame.

Chapter 3 - How Dorothy Saved the Scarecrow

When Dorothy was left alone she began to feel

E   The **blinking insertion point** indicates where text will be added.

Typing Text

The two most important parts of working with text are typing the text and then selecting it to make changes.

To type text:

1.   Click with the Type tool in a frame.

2.   Begin typing.

3.   Press Return to begin a new paragraph.

      or

      Press Shift-Return to begin a new line without starting a new paragraph. InDesign calls this a *Forced Line Break*. Others call it a *soft return*.

TIP   InDesign automatically wraps text within the text frame.

TIP   If the text frame is too small to display all the text, an overset symbol appears D. You can reshape the text frame or flow the text into a new frame to convert the overset text into visible text.

To add text into a passage you have already typed, you move the *insertion point* to where you want to place the new material. The point blinks to help you find it E.

To move the insertion point:

1.   Position the Type tool cursor where you want the insertion point.

2.   Click to set the insertion point.

To move the point using the keyboard:

1.   Use the arrow keys to move the insertion point left or right one character at a time or up and down one line at a time.

2.   Use the Cmd/Ctrl key with the arrow keys to move the insertion point one word or one paragraph at a time.

Selecting Text

The simplest way to select text is to use the mouse.

To select text using the mouse:

Press and drag across the text. The highlight indicates which text is being selected.

TIP You don't have to drag from left to right to select multiple lines. Simply drag down.

Like other programs, InDesign has special techniques to select words, lines, and paragraphs with the mouse.

To select a single word:

Double-click within a word to select it **A**.

TIP Although only the word is selected, if you hit the Delete key, the word and the space after it will be deleted.

To select a single line:

Triple-click within the line **B**.

TIP Turn on Triple Click to Select a Line in the Type preferences.

To select a paragraph:

If **Triple Click to Select a Line** is turned off, triple-click within the paragraph **C**.

or

If **Triple Click to Select a Line** is turned on, quadruple-click in the paragraph.

To select all the text in a frame or story:

If **Triple Click to Select a Line** is turned off, quadruple-click within any paragraph.

or

If **Triple Click to Select a Line** is turned on, quintuple-click in any paragraph.

She gave some to Toto. She then took a pail from the shelf. She carried it down to the little brook and filled it with clear, sparkling water.

A Double-click to select a single **word**, which is then highlighted.

She gave some to Toto. She then took a pail from the shelf. She carried it down to the little brook and filled it with clear, sparkling water.

B A **triple-click selects a single line** in a paragraph.

She gave some to Toto. She then took a pail from the shelf. She carried it down to the little brook and filled it with clear, sparkling water.

C An example of how a **triple-click or quadruple-click can select a paragraph**.

Keyboard, Mouse, or Menu?

One of the hot topics in working with software is the keyboard-versus-mouse debate. If you are a fast typist, you will work faster using keyboard shortcuts. There are times when you may consider using a mouse.

If my hands are already on the keyboard, I try to keep them there to select text or apply a formatting change.

But if my hands are on the mouse, I try to use it. So if I've just finished moving a text frame to a new position, I can easily highlight the text with the mouse.

Menu commands are another matter entirely. I try whenever possible to learn the keyboard shortcuts for menu commands.

That way I don't have to move the mouse all the way up to the top of the page to choose a command such as Cut, Copy, or Paste.

Quick Guide to the Shortcuts

Here are some easy ways to understand the selection shortcuts:

The up, down, left, and right arrow keys all jump around the text.

Add the Cmd/Ctrl keys to make the bigger jumps. Instead of a character, you jump a word. Instead of a line, you jump a paragraph. (Remember: you have more power when you take *Command* or *Control*!)

Adding the Shift key lets you select the text. The *S* in *Shift* stands for *Select*.

If you spend a lot of time typing and modifying text, you should learn the following techniques for selecting text.

To select text using keyboard shortcuts:

1. Use the following keyboard commands to select text using the keyboard:

Keystroke	Selects
Shift key and tap the left or right arrow key	Single character.
Shift key and tap the up or down arrow key	One line of text. Repeat to select additional lines.
Cmd/Ctrl+Shift keys and tap the left or right arrow key	One word and the space following it.
Cmd/Ctrl+Shift keys and tap the up or down arrow key	Paragraph.
Shift key and tap the Home or End key	All the text to the beginning or end of a line.
Cmd/Ctrl+Shift keys and tap the Home or End key	All the text to the beginning or end of a text frame or story.
Cmd/Ctrl+A	All the text within an entire text frame or story.

2. Repeat any of the above commands to select additional text.

TIP You can switch commands to first select a line and then the following word.

TIP You can quickly edit text by double-clicking a text frame with either selection tool. This switches to the Type tool and places an insertion point where you double-clicked.

TIP Press the Escape (esc) key to switch out of the text editing mode and then select the frame as an object.

Moving and Deleting Text

You can copy or move text from one place and then paste it into another. Text that is copied or cut is stored on the computer clipboard. *(See the sidebar on this page for an explanation of how the clipboard works.)*

To copy and paste text:

1. Select the text or text frame **A**.

2. Choose **Edit > Copy** or **Cut**.

TIP If you choose Cut, the highlighted text disappears and the remaining text reflows.

3. Position the insertion point where you want to put the copied or cut text **B**.

4. Choose **Edit > Paste.** The text is inserted into the new position **C**.

   or

   Choose **Edit > Paste Without Formatting** to paste the text so that its formatting (point size, typeface, style, etc.) matches the text it is being pasted into.

TIP The Paste Without Formatting command is very helpful if you want the text from one place to be pasted into a paragraph that has different formatting.

TIP You can select text before pasting to replace the selected text with the copied text.

Chapter 3

How Dorothy Saved the Scare-

A Select text in order to copy or cut it from one position to another.

How Dorothy Saved the Scare-crow

When Dorothy was left

B Click to put the insertion point where you want to insert the copied or cut text.

Chapter 3

When Dorothy was left alone she began to feel

C The **Paste command** inserts the copied or cut text at the insertion point.

What Is the Computer Clipboard?

The Copy command places the copied objects into an area of the computer memory called the clipboard. The contents of the clipboard stay within the memory until a new copy or cut command is executed or until the computer is turned off.

The clipboard can hold only one set of information at a time. So if you copy one sentence, you will lose it from the clipboard if you copy or cut something else later on.

She gave some to Toto.
She then took a pail from
the shelf. She carried it
down to the little brook
and filled it with clear,
sparkling water.

D Position the cursor inside the highlighted text to display the **Drag-and-Drop Text cursor.**

She gave some to Toto.
She then took a pail from
the shelf. She carried it
down to the little brook
and filled it with clear,
sparkling water.

E Drag to display the **destination insertion point** for drag-and-drop text.

She then took a pail from
the shelf. She carried it
down to the little brook
and filled it with clear,
sparkling water. She gave
some to Toto.

F Release the mouse button to drop the text into its new position.

You can also use the mouse to drag text from one place to another.

TIP Use the Preferences to set the options for drag-and-drop text to be active in the Story Editor and/or the Layout View.

To drag text from one place to another:

1. Select the text so that it is highlighted within the frame.

2. Position the cursor inside the highlighted text. The cursor changes to a curved arrow with the letter T next to it **D**.

3. Press with the mouse and drag to a new position. An insertion point appears at the new location **E**.

4. Release the mouse to move the text to the new position **F**.

TIP Hold the Opt/Alt key as you drag text to create a copy of the original text in the new location.

TIP Hold the Shift key as you drag text to force the text to inherit the formatting of the destination. This works for text dragged within InDesign as well as from external applications.

The Duplicate command copies and pastes a text frame all in one step.

To duplicate text:

1. Select the text or text frame.

2. Choose **Edit > Duplicate.** The copied text is duplicated as follows:

   • A text frame is created slightly offset from the original object.

   • Text inside a frame is pasted immediately following the original text.

TIP The Duplicate command does not replace the contents of the clipboard.

Using the Character Panel

Character formatting refers to attributes that can be applied to a single character or *glyph* in a paragraph without applying that formatting to the entire paragraph. The Character panel controls character attributes.

TIP As you work with text frames, the Control panel changes to display most of the controls found in the Character panel. This lets you style text using just the Control panel.

To work with the Character panel:

1. If the Character panel is not visible, choose **Window > Type & Tables > Character** or **Type > Character**. This opens the Character panel .

   or

   Click the Character panel tab to move it to the front of a set of nested panels.

2. Click the panel tab to reveal all the panel options.

   or

   Choose Show Options from the Character panel menu **B**.

TIP The Character panel menu also contains additional controls for formatting text.

A The **Character panel** lets you change the character attributes.

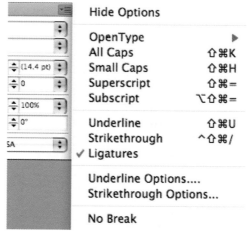

B The **Character panel menu** contains additional controls for formatting text.

Setting the Text Defaults

When you first open InDesign, text frames are set with the fonts that the Adobe folks thought you'd like to work with. You don't have to live with those settings.

Deselect all objects and change the text settings to whatever you like. Those settings will become the defaults for that document. You can also set the defaults for all new documents by changing the settings with no document open.

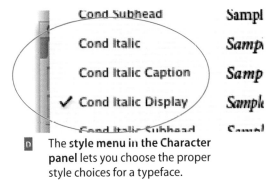

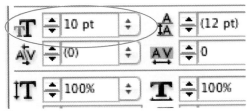

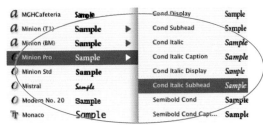

C The **font menu in the Character panel** lets you choose the typeface for text. The style menu next to each font name displays the style choices.

D The **style menu in the Character panel** lets you choose the proper style choices for a typeface.

E The **point size field in the Character panel** lets you choose common point sizes or enter a specific size in the field.

Setting the Typeface and Point Size

The design of type is called the *typeface*. The typeface you are reading now is called Myriad Pro SemiCondensed. The typeface of the subhead below is called Myriad Pro Bold Condensed.

To choose a font (typeface):

1. Choose **Type** > **Font** and then choose the typeface from the font menu. The font menu can be set to preview the typefaces.

   or

   In the Character panel, choose a typeface from the font menu C.

2. If necessary, choose the styling for the font from the style menu next to the name of the font.

   or

   Use the style list in the Character panel to choose the styling D.

TIP The style list changes depending on the typeface and the fonts you have installed. If you do not have the bold version of a font, for example, it will not be listed.

TIP You can use the keyboard commands to apply styling such as regular, bold, italic, and bold italic.

3. The size of type is measured using a system called *points*. There are 72 points per inch. The point size of this text is 10.25.

To change the point size:

Choose **Type** > **Size** and then choose a point size from the list.

or

Use the point size field controls to enter a custom point size E.

Styling Text

InDesign also lets you apply electronic styling such as All Caps, Small Caps, Subscript, and Superscript.

To apply electronic styles:

Choose one of the styles listed in the Character panel menu 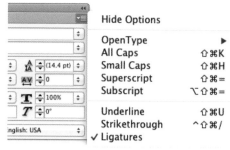. The text changes to the style chosen **B**.

- **All Caps** converts lowercase letters to all capital letters.
- **Small Caps** converts lowercase letters to reduced capitals.
- **Superscript** reduces and raises the text above the baseline.
- **Subscript** reduces and lowers the text below the baseline.
- **Underline** draws a line under the text.
- **Strikethrough** draws a line through the text.
- **Ligatures** automatically substitutes the combined letterforms for characters such as fi and fl **C**.

TIP The All Caps style has no effect on text typed with the Caps Lock or Shift key held down.

TIP The sizes of the Small Caps, Subscript, and Superscript are controlled in the text preferences.

A The **electronic style options** in the Character panel menu.

Dorothy and TOTO — All caps

L. FRANK BAUM — Small caps

Emerald City® — Superscript

H$_2$O — Subscript

Tin Woodman — Underline

~~Cowardly~~ Lion — Strikethrough

B Examples of the electronic styles applied to text.

first flower

first flower

C Applying the **Ligatures command** to the top text replaces specific pairs of letters with combination letterforms such as those on the bottom.

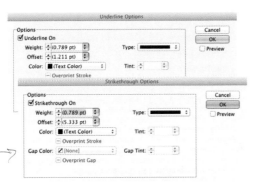

D The **Underline Options and Strikethrough Options dialog boxes** let you customize the appearance of the Underline and Strikethrough effects.

Underlines as Highlights!

One of the most exciting uses for the custom underlines and strikethrough effects is to use them as highlights for individual lines or words of text. This is something designers have wanted to do for years.

All you have to do is set the weight of the line to slightly thicker than the text point size. And use the offset to position the line around the text. You can then apply these custom underlines as highlights for text. You can also combine the underline and strikethrough lines above and below the text **E**.

The Wonderful

Wizard of OZ

E An example of how custom underlines and strikethrough settings can be used for highlights and other special effects.

As mentioned on the previous page, you can change the appearance of the Underline and Strikethrough effects.

To customize Underline and Strikethrough Options:

1. Select the text.

2. Choose Underline Options or Strike-through Options from the Character panel menu. The Underline Options or Strikethrough Options dialog box appears **D**.

3. Click Underline On or Strikethrough On to turn on the effect.

TIP The effect will already be on if it was applied in the Character panel menu.

4. Use the Weight controls to set the thickness of the line.

5. Use the Offset controls to move the line as follows:

   - **Positive underline numbers** move the line *below* the baseline.

   - **Positive strikethrough numbers** move the line *above* the baseline.

6. Choose one of the rules from the Type list.

7. Choose a color and tint from the Color and Tint lists.

8. If your line type has a gap, such as in a dashed line, use the Gap Color and Gap Tint lists to color the gap.

9. If desired, check the Overprint Stroke and Overprint Gap options. *(See Chapter 5, "Working in Color," for more information on overprinting colors.)*

Setting Line and Character Spacing

Leading is the space between lines of type within a paragraph **A**. (It is pronounced *led-ding*, because it refers to the lead metal formerly used to set type.) Leading is specified as an absolute point size or as auto leading. The leading of this paragraph is 12 points.

To set the leading:

1. Select the paragraph of text.

2. Use the leading controls in the Character panel to enter an amount of leading **B**.

   or

   Set the leading to Auto to have the leading automatically change to an amount based on the point size.

TIP The amount of the auto leading is set in the Paragraph panel's Justification menu.

Kerning is the space between two letters. It is applied so letters fit snugly together **C**.

To set kerning:

1. Select the text you want to kern, or place an insertion point between the letters.

2. To use the kerning pairs in the typeface, choose Metrics from the kerning list **D**.

   or

   Choose Optical to adjust the kerning using a visual representation of the text.

TIP Use optical kerning when there are no built-in font metrics (for instance, when you combine two different typefaces).

3. To apply a specific kerning amount, use the kerning controls or pop-up menu to apply a numerical amount.

TIP Positive numbers increase the space. Negative numbers decrease the space. Zero indicates no kerning is applied.

When Dorothy was left alone she began to feel hungry. So she went to the cupboard and cut herself some bread, which she spread with butter.

When Dorothy was left alone she began

to feel hungry. So she went to the cup-

board and cut herself some bread, which

she spread with butter.

A The 16-point leading (top) has less line space than the 24-point leading (bottom).

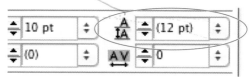

B The **leading controls in the Character panel** let you change the amount of space between lines.

Avoid
Avoid
Avoid

C A comparison of the different kerning settings: 0 (top), Metrics (middle), Optical (bottom).

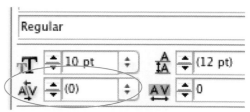

D The **kerning controls in the Character panel** change the space between characters.

Emerald City
Emerald City

E Tracking of 70 increases the space along all the letters.

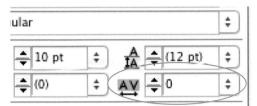

F The **tracking controls** in the Character panel change the space across a sequence of letters.

Wonderful Wizard

G A negative baseline shift lowers the capital letters from the rest of the characters.

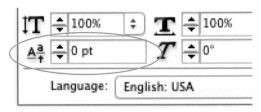

H The **baseline shift controls** in the Character panel move text above or below the line.

Tracking is similar to kerning; however, unlike kerning, which applies to letter pairs, tracking is applied to a range of letters **E**. Tracking is very useful, because as you increase the space between the letters, you don't lose the relative spacing that is applied by kerning.

To set tracking:

1. Select the text you want to track.

2. Use the tracking controls in the Character panel to set the amount of tracking **F**.

TIP Positive numbers increase the space between letters. Negative numbers decrease the space. Zero indicates no tracking is applied.

Baseline shift moves text up or down from the *baseline*, or the imaginary line that the letters sit on. Baseline shift is often applied to shift bullets or parentheses so they sit better next to text. It can also be used for special effects in display or headline text **G**.

To set the baseline shift:

1. Select the text that you want to reposition.

2. Use the baseline shift controls in the Character panel to move the text away from the baseline **H**.

TIP Positive numbers move the text up. Negative numbers move the text down.

Applying Text Distortions

InDesign also lets you apply horizontal or vertical scaling to text. This distorts the text to increase its height or width **A**. This changes the type from the original design of the characters. Typographic purists (such as this author) disdain distorting text.

To apply horizontal scaling:

1. Select the text that you want to distort.

2. Use the horizontal scale field controls in the Character panel to change the width of the text **B**.

To apply vertical scaling:

1. Select the text that you want to distort.

2. Use the vertical scale field controls in the Character panel **C**.

Skewing allows you to slant or tilt text **D**. This is also called *false italic* because it resembles the slant of italic text.

To skew text:

1. Select the text that you want to skew.

2. Enter an angle in the skew field in the Character panel to specify how much the text should be slanted **E**.

TIP Positive numbers to 180 degrees tilt the text to the left. Negative numbers to 180 degrees tilt the text to the right.

DOROTHY   Vertical scale

DOROTHY   Normal

DOROTHY   Horizontal scale

A The effects of applying either vertical scaling or horizontal scaling to text.

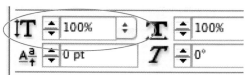

B Use the **horizontal scale controls in the Character panel** to distort the width of text.

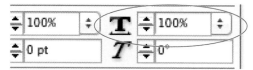

C The **vertical scale controls in the Character panel** let you distort text height.

CYCLONE!

D You can apply negative and positive skew to text to create a special effect.

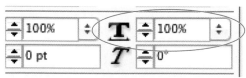

E The **skew controls in the Character panel** let you create fake oblique and slanted text.

```
⊢ CHARACTER

Times

Regular

T  ⇕ 12 pt          [No Language]
                    Bulgarian
A|V ⇕ Metrics       Catalan
                    Croatian
                    Czech
T  ⇕ 100%           Danish
                    Dutch: 2005 Reform
Aᵃ ⇕ 0 pt           Dutch: Old Rules
                    English: Canadian
                    English: UK
Language: ✓ English: USA
                    English: USA Legal
                    English: USA Medica
```

F The **Language menu** lets you set the language used for spelling checks as well as for typographer's quotes.

Setting the Language

You can also set the language. This ensures that foreign words as well as your native language are spell-checked and hyphenated using the proper dictionary. (Sorry, but changing the language doesn't translate the text.)

TIP If you have [No Language] selected, InDesign can't substitute typographer's quotes ("curly" quotes) for the ordinary typewriter quotes ("straight" quotes).

To set the language:

1. Select the text that you want to set the language for.
2. Choose the language from the pop-up menu in the Character panel **F**.

Electronic Styling: Myths and Realities

As you set type using programs such as InDesign, people may tell you *never* to style fonts electronically. So if you use the Roman version of a font (such as Minion), you should never press the keyboard shortcut for italic. You should only choose the actual typeface (Minion Italic) from the font menu.

This rule emerged because some typefaces do not have an italic or bold version. The styling shows on the screen, but it doesn't print. Techno or Zapf Dingbats are examples of fonts that shouldn't be styled electronically. When people see their printed samples, they're disappointed that there is no bold or italic appearance.

Fortunately, InDesign prevents you from making errors like that. If you apply the shortcut for italic, InDesign applies the actual italic version. If there is no version, InDesign does not change the font. So there is no harm styling electronically using InDesign.

I've also heard people advise to avoid all caps, subscript, small caps, and other electronic styles on type. In most cases, there is nothing wrong with applying those styles, and InDesign allows you to apply those electronic styles to text.

In some cases you'll have better results with a small-caps version of a font than with the electronic style for small caps. However, a special small-caps font offers a subtle effect that few people will recognize.

I personally hate the electronic styling for Vertical and Horizontal Scale. They distort the type horribly. The Skew command is even worse! However, I do accept that there might be times (grotesque Halloween cards?) where those distortions are acceptable.

Applying Paragraph Formatting

Paragraph formatting refers to the attributes that are applied to the paragraph as a whole. For instance, you cannot have half of the paragraph centered and the other half on the left size of the page. The alignment must be applied to the whole paragraph. InDesign paragraph formatting is applied using the Paragraph panel.

TIP As you work with text frames, the Control panel changes to display many of the text controls found in the Paragraph panel. This makes it possible to style text using just the Control panel.

To work with the Paragraph panel:

1. If the Paragraph panel is not visible, choose **Window > Type & Tables > Paragraph** or **Type > Paragraph.** This opens the Paragraph panel 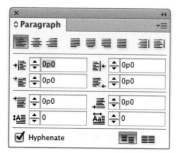.

   or

   Click the Paragraph panel tab to move it to the front of a set of tabbed panels.

2. To display all the paragraph formatting controls, choose Show Options from the Paragraph panel pop-up menu.

TIP The Paragraph panel menu also contains additional controls for formatting text **B**.

TIP The following techniques are useful when applying paragraph attributes:

- To apply attributes to a single paragraph, click to place an insertion point within the paragraph.

- To apply attributes to more than one paragraph, select a portion of the first and last paragraphs and the paragraphs in between.

A The **Paragraph panel** controls attributes that are applied to the whole paragraph.

B The **Paragraph panel menu** contains additional controls for paragraph attributes.

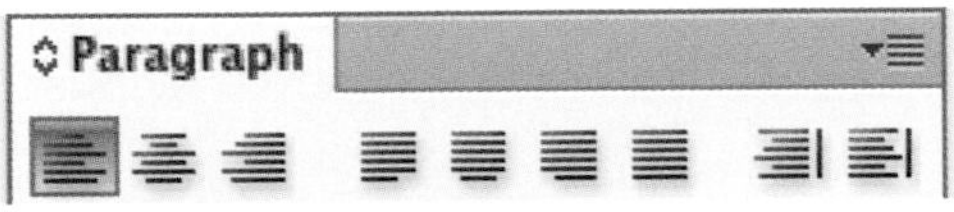

C The **Alignment buttons** on the Paragraph panel control how the type is aligned to the frame edges.

Setting Alignment and Indents

In addition to the common paragraph alignment controls found in page layout or word processing programs, InDesign offers some special controls for setting alignment.

To set paragraph alignment:

1. Select a paragraph.
2. Click one of the Alignment buttons **C** to set the alignment as follows:

Alignment	Icon	Example	Description
Flush Left		I have been wicked in my day but I never thought a little girl like you would be able to melt me.	Sets the text to align at the left margin.
Centered		I have been wicked in my day but I never thought a little girl like you would be able to melt me.	Sets the text to align at the center of the paragraph.
Flush Right		I have been wicked in my day but I never thought a little girl like you would be able to melt me.	Sets the text to align at the right margin.
Justified Last Left		I have been wicked in my day but I never thought a little girl like you would be able to melt me.	Sets the text to align at both the left and right margins, but aligns the last line flush left.
Justified Last Centered		I have been wicked in my day but I never thought a little girl like you would be able to melt me.	Sets the text to align at both the left and right margins, but centers the last line.
Justified Last Right		I have been wicked in my day but I never thought a little girl like you would be able to melt me.	Sets the text to align at both the left and right margins, but aligns the last line flush right.
Justified All		I have been wicked in my day but I never thought a little girl like you would be able to melt me.	Sets the text to align at both the left and right margins.
Align Towards Spine		I have been wicked in my day but I never thought a little girl like you would be able to melt me.	Sets the text to align along the spine of the document. This flips the alignment on recto and verso pages.
Align Away From Spine		I have been wicked in my day but I never thought a little girl like you would be able to melt me.	Sets the text to align toward the outside edge of the pages. This flips the alignment on recto and verso pages.

TIP **Look closely and you'll see that the lines in the alignment buttons resemble how the alignment changes the position of the text.**

You might want to indent a paragraph so that it stands from the rest of the text.

To set the margin indents:

1. Select a paragraph.

2. Use the margin indent controls **A** to move the text as follows **B**:

   - **Left Indent** moves the left side of the paragraph away from the left side of the text frame.

   - **First Line Left Indent** moves the first line of the paragraph away from the left edge of the rest of the paragraph.

   - **Right Indent** moves the right side of the paragraph away from the right side of the text frame.

   - **Last Line Right Indent** moves the last line of the paragraph away from the right side of the text frame.

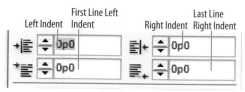

A The **margin indent fields** control the space around a paragraph and the first and last lines.

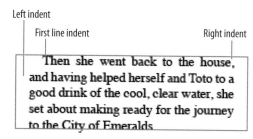

B The effect of applying margin indents to text inside a text frame.

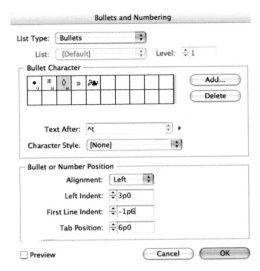

c   The **Bullets icon** in the Control panel quickly applies bulleted lists.

D   The **Bullets options** of the **Bullets and Numbering dialog box** let you select and format bullets automatically.

Bullets and Numbering

InDesign can also automatically add bullets and numbers in front of paragraphs. This makes it easier to create and format those paragraph lists.

To apply bullets to paragraphs:

Click the Bullets icon in the Control panel **c**. Choose **Type** > **Bulleted & Numbered Lists** > **Apply Bullets.**

TIP This applies the last-used setting of the bullet options.

You will most likely want to format your own custom bullets.

To format the bullets in a paragraph:

1. Choose Bullets and Numbering from the Paragraph panel menu. The Bullets and Numbering dialog box appears **D**.

2. Choose Bullets from the List Type menu. This displays the bullets options.

3. Choose a bullet from the Bullet Character glyph display.

TIP The letter U under the character indicates that the bullet can be styled with any font. Bullets without a U are confined to a single font.

4. Use the Text After field to type which characters you want to separate the bullet from the start of the text.

5. If desired, use the Character Style list to choose a character style to format the bullets. *(See Chapter 15, "Styles," for more information on character styles.)*

TIP The position settings described later in this section control how the bullets hang outside the text indent.

To add custom bullet characters:

1. Click the Add button in the Bullets and Numbering dialog box. The Add Bullets dialog box opens 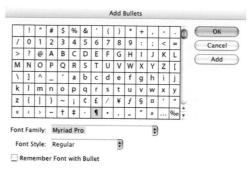.

2. Use the glyphs area to choose the character for the bullet.

3. If you want, choose the Font Family and Font Style for the bullet.

4. To set the bullet to a specific font, select Remember Font with Bullet.

5. Click Add or OK to add the character to the bullet list and choose new characters.

Bullets are just one type of character that can be added to paragraphs. You can also automatically create numbered lists with the Bullets and Numbering controls.

To apply numbers to paragraphs:

Click the Numbers icon in the Control panel **B**. Choose **Type** > **Bulleted & Numbered Lists** > **Apply Numbers**.

To format numbers in paragraphs:

1. In the Bullets and Numbering dialog box, choose Numbers from the List Type menu to display the numbers options **C**.

2. Use the Format list to choose Roman or Arabic numerals, or letters for the list.

3. Use the Number field to choose which characters should follow the number. You can also type your own character.

4. Use the Character Style list to choose a format for the numbers.

5. Use the Mode list to choose to start the list at a number or continue from a previous number.

A The **Add Bullets dialog box** lets you add new bullet characters.

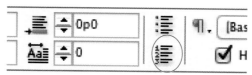

B The **Numbers icon** in the Control panel quickly applies numbered lists.

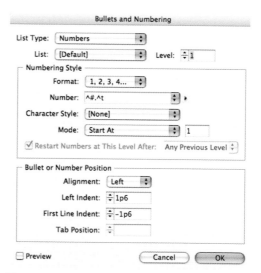

C The **Numbers options** of the **Bullets and Numbering dialog box** let you select and format numbers automatically.

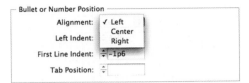

D The **Position controls** of the **Bullets and Numbering dialog box**.

Bullets and Numbers in This Book

You can see the results of using automatic bullets and numbered lists throughout this book.

All the numbered lists have been set with automatic numbering. This makes it possible to insert new items in a list without having to go back and renumber all the other steps.

It also has meant I can move list items around quickly and easily.

I also use automatic bullets for all the bulleted lists in the book.

One of the benefits of the automatic bullets and numbers is that you don't have to worry about inserting tab characters or setting the left and first line indents. The Bullet or Number Position area lets you control those positions.

To set the position of bullets or numbers:

1. Open the Bullets and Numbering dialog box.

2. Use the Alignment list to choose Left, Center, or Right alignment .

   TIP **Use the Right alignment for numbers so that double-digit numbers align correctly.**

3. Use the Left Indent field to set how the left margin of the text is indented.

4. Use the First Line Indent to set how the first line should be indented separately from the left indent.

5. Use the Tab Position field to set the position of the first character after the bullet or number.

There may come a time when you want the automatic bullets or numbers to become ordinary text and stop responding to the automatic controls.

To convert bullets or numbers to ordinary text:

1. Select the text.

2. Choose **Type > Bulleted & Numbered Lists > Convert [Bullets or Numbering] To Text**.

   TIP **Use this command if you are going to export the text or save the document to a previous version of InDesign.**

Setting Paragraph Effects

The paragraph effects are available when Show Options is chosen in the Paragraph panel menu. One of the paragraph effects is to add space above and below a paragraph **A**. For instance, the space between this paragraph and the one following is controlled by adding space below.

To add space between paragraphs:

1. Select the paragraphs that you want to add space above or below.

2. Use the Space Before field controls to add space before the paragraphs **B**.

3. Use the Space After field controls to add space after the paragraphs **B**.

TIP Never insert paragraph returns to add space between paragraphs. That can cause problems later if text reflows!

Drop caps increase the size of the first character or characters and positions them so that they drop down into the rest of the paragraph **C**. The opening page for each chapter of this book contains a paragraph that has a drop cap applied.

To create drop caps:

1. Select the paragraph you want to set with a drop cap.

2. Use the Drop Cap Number of Lines field to set the number of lines that the letter should occupy **D**.

3. Use the Drop Cap Number of Characters field to set how many characters of the text should have the drop cap applied **D**.

When Dorothy was left alone she began to feel hungry. So she went to the cupboard and cut herself some bread, which she spread with butter.

— Paragraph space

She then took a pail from the shelf. She carried it down to the little brook and filled it with clear, sparkling water. She gave some to Toto.

Toto ran over to the trees and began to bark at the birds sitting there. Dorothy went to get him, and saw such delicious fruit hanging from the branches that she gathered some of it, finding it just what she wanted to help out her breakfast.

A An example of **adding space between paragraphs**.

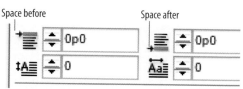

Space before   Space after

B Use the **Paragraph Space controls** to add space before or after a paragraph.

When Dorothy was left alone she began to feel hungry. So she went to the cupboard and cut herself some bread, which she spread with butter.

C An example of a **drop cap** set for one character and three lines.

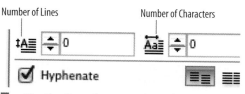

Number of Lines   Number of Characters

☑ Hyphenate

D Use the Drop Cap controls to change the appearance of a paragraph drop cap.

E The **Drop Caps and Nested Styles dialog box** allows you to refine the settings for drop caps.

By the time they stopped, she was very tired. "You should come with me.

By the time they stopped, she was very tired. "You should come with me.

F An example of how **Align Left Edge** forces the drop cap character to align to the left margin edge.

By the time they stopped, she was very tired. "You should come with me.

By the time they stopped, she was very tired. "You should come with me.

G An example of how **Scale for Descenders** changes the size of the drop cap so that descenders don't touch the other lines of text.

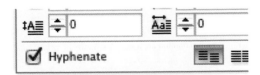

H Use the **Hyphenate checkbox** to hyphenate words at the ends of lines.

The Control panel contains only the basic options for drop caps. There are additional controls for refining the appearance of drop cap characters.

To set the additional drop cap attributes:

1. Choose Drop Caps and Nested Styles from the Control panel menu or the Paragraph panel menu. This opens the Drop Caps and Nested Styles dialog box **E**.

2. Check the Align Left Edge option to force the drop cap character to align flush to the left side of the paragraph **F**.

3. Check the Scale for Descenders option to reduce the size of the drop cap letters to keep character descenders from touching lines of text **G**.

4. Use the Character Style menu to apply a different typeface or other character attribute to the drop cap. (*See Chapter 15, "Styles" for information on how to create a character style.*)

You can also control whether the text within a paragraph is hyphenated or not.

To turn on hyphenation:

1. Select the paragraphs you want to set the hyphenation for.

2. To turn on hyphenation, click the Hyphenate checkbox in the Paragraph panel **H**. Depending on what words are hyphenated, the text may reflow. (*See Chapter 16, "Typography" for information on controlling the number of hyphens in a paragraph.*)

Working with Hidden Characters

Every time you tap the Spacebar, Tab key, Return key, or Enter key, you create a non-printing character in the text. These hidden characters can be turned on to let you see where the spaces, tab characters, and paragraph returns fall in the text.

To show or hide hidden characters:

Choose **Type** > **Show Hidden Characters**. This displays the characters in the same color as the highlight for the layer 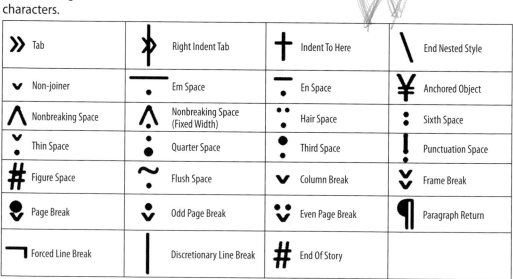.

or

Choose **Type** > **Hide Hidden Characters** to hide the hidden characters.

TIP Hidden characters are hidden when you turn on the Preview mode or Overprint Preview.

TIP You can change the color of the hidden characters by changing the color of the Layer in the Layers panel.

The following is a chart of the various hidden characters.

A An **assortment of the hidden characters** displayed within text.

	Tab		Right Indent Tab		Indent To Here		End Nested Style
	Non-joiner		Em Space		En Space		Anchored Object
	Nonbreaking Space		Nonbreaking Space (Fixed Width)		Hair Space		Sixth Space
	Thin Space		Quarter Space		Third Space		Punctuation Space
	Figure Space		Flush Space		Column Break		Frame Break
	Page Break		Odd Page Break		Even Page Break		Paragraph Return
	Forced Line Break		Discretionary Line Break		End Of Story		

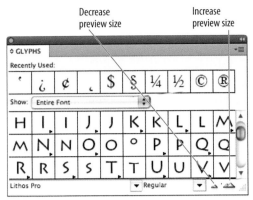

Decrease preview size

Increase preview size

B Use the **Glyphs panel** to insert characters from fonts.

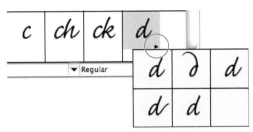

C Press the triangle under the glyph to display the alternatives for the glyph.

Using the Glyphs Panel

Quick — what's the keystroke for a trademark character? The Euro or Japanese Yen characters? The pointing hand in Zapf Dingbats? If you can't remember the keystrokes for all the characters you use, then you need to open the Glyphs panel. The Glyphs panel lets you easily see all the characters in a typeface. You can also use the panel to display the alternate letterforms in OpenType fonts.

To insert characters:

1. Place the insertion point where you would like the character to be inserted.

2. Choose **Type > Glyphs.** This opens the Glyphs panel **B**.

3. Choose the typeface and style of the character you want to insert.

4. Scroll through the Preview area to find the character you want to insert.

TIP Use the Preview Size controls to increase or decrease the size of the preview.

5. Double-click the character you want to insert.

6. Repeat step 5 to insert any additional characters.

TIP The Glyphs panel allows you to insert characters that are not usually available for certain operating systems. For instance, Macintosh users can insert fractions and Windows users can insert ligatures.

To access alternative characters:

1. Place your insertion point where you want to insert the alternative characters.

2. Press the small triangle next to the glyph in the Glyphs panel **C**. This opens the alternative letterforms for that character.

3. Choose the alternative character. This inserts the character into the text.

As you hunt through the Glyphs panel, you may find there are too many glyphs to look through. You can access the recently used glyphs or you can create your own custom glyph sets.

To access the recently used glyphs:

1. Make sure Show Options is chosen in the Glyphs panel menu.

2. Double-click one of the glyphs in the Recently Used area. This adds the glyph to your document.

To create a custom glyph set:

1. Choose New Glyph Set from the Glyphs panel menu.

2. Name the set in the New Glyph Set dialog box .

3. Choose where you want new additions to the set to appear.

4. Click OK to add the set.

TIP You can have many different glyph sets. Organize them however you want.

Once you have created a glyph set, you can add your favorite characters from any font into the glyph set.

To add characters to a glyph set:

1. Use the Glyphs panel to select the character you want to add to an existing glyph set.

2. Choose Add to Glyph Set > [Set Name] from the Glyphs panel menu. The character appears in the glyph set.

3. Choose what order you want the glyphs to appear in the set from the Insert Order list 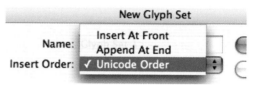.

4. Click OK to create the glyph set.

A The **New Glyph Set dialog box** lets you name the new glyph set.

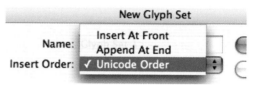

B The **Insert Order list** lets you control how glyphs are added to a set.

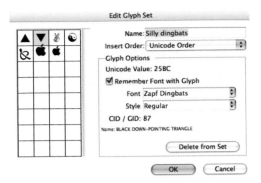

c The **Edit Glyph Set dialog box** lets you delete or modify the glyphs in a custom glyph set.

So What's a Glyph?

If you're like me, you're probably wondering about the word *glyph*. Why use that word? Why not call it the Character panel?

The answer has to do with being precise. You know what a letter is: a, b, c, X, Y, or Z. You wouldn't call things like 1, @, ? or $ letters, though. They're characters.

Well, glyphs are the proper name for everything including letters, characters, and alternative letterforms for things like ligatures and swashes.

So rather than call it the Insert Letters/Characters/Alternative Letterforms panel, Adobe calls it the Glyphs panel.

I could have sworn that the word glyph was some special Adobe typographic term; but then one of my students reminded me of Egyptian hieroglyphics. And then I remembered the Hawaiian petroglyphs.

So glyph really isn't as strange a word as I originally thought.

To insert characters in a glyph set:

1. Choose the glyph set from the Glyph Set menu in the Glyphs panel.

2. Double-click to insert the glyph.

Once you have created a glyph set, you can edit the items in the set.

To edit the characters in a glyph set:

1. Choose **Edit Glyph Set** > **[Set Name]** from the Glyphs panel menu. The Edit Glyph Set dialog box appears **c**.

2. Select the glyph item that you want to edit.

3. Use the Insert Order list to change where new glyphs are added.

4. Choose Remember Font with Glyph to set the glyph to a specific font. This means the glyph does not change to match the font in the text it's inserted into.

   or

   Deselect Remember Font with Glyph to use the Unicode value of the current font. This option lets you match a character such as the Euro symbol to the text it is inserted into.

5. If you have selected Remember Font with Glyph, you can change the typeface and style in the Edit Glyph dialog box.

6. Click the Delete from Set button to delete a glyph from a set.

7. Click OK to apply the changes to the set.

Working with Text Flow

As mentioned earlier in this chapter, if text is too long to fit in its text frame, you can link the text into another frame.

To link text between frames:

1. Click the overset text symbol. The cursor changes to the load text cursor **A**.

2. Move the cursor over to the frame you want to flow the text into. The cursor changes to the link text cursor **B**.

TIP Unlike with QuarkXPress, the second text frame does not have to be empty.

3. Click in the text frame. The link indicators show that the text in the frame flows to or from another frame **C**.

TIP You can use the same steps to link empty text frames. This makes it easy to flow text into the layout later.

To change the link between frames:

1. Click the link indicator in the frame where you want to break the link. The cursor turns into a link text cursor.

2. Click in a new text frame to flow the text into a new frame.

   or

   Click inside the text frame to keep all the text within that frame. (The overset text symbol appears.)

InDesign also displays *text threads*, which show you the links between text frames.

To show the links between frames:

1. Select the text frame that you want to see the links for.

2. Choose **View > Show Text Threads**. This displays lines that show which frames are linked together **D**.

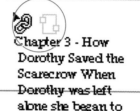

A The **load text cursor** indicates that you can continue the overset text in another frame.

B The **link text cursor** indicates you can click to fill the next frame with text.

C The **link indicators** show that the text flows into and out of the text frame.

D The **text threads** show the links between frames.

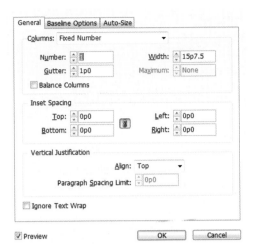

The **Text Frame Options dialog box** controls the flow of text within a frame.

The **Columns settings** for the Text Frame Options dialog box.

The **Columns settings** for the Text Frame Options dialog box.

Setting Text Frame General Controls

Once you create a text frame, you can still control the flow of text within the frame. This is similar to creating a mini-layout within the text frame.

To change text frame options:

1. Select the text frame.

2. Choose **Object > Text Frame Options.** This opens the Text Frame Options dialog box **E**.

3. Click the General tab.

4. Make whatever changes you want to the settings.

TIP As you modify the text frame options, click the Preview checkbox to see the effects of your changes.

You can create a fixed number of columns within a text frame.

To create a fixed number of text columns:

1. Choose Fixed Number from the Columns menu.

2. Set the following options in the Columns area **F**:

   - **Number** sets the number of columns.
   - **Width** sets the column width.
   - **Gutter** controls the space between the columns.

TIP When set to Fixed Number, the number of columns does not change if the width of the text frame changes. The width of the columns does change **G**.

InDesign helps you maintain a fixed column width when working with a text frame. This is very useful for magazine and newspaper layouts where all text should be the same column width.

To use Fixed Width:

1. Choose Fixed Width from the Columns menu in the Text Frame Options dialog box .

2. Set the options as described for the Fixed Number option.

3. Drag to resize the frame width. The text frame width automatically jumps to whatever size can accommodate an additional column **B**.

You can also control the maximum width that a column will be as you increase the width of the text frame. The is called a flexible width.

To use Flexible Width:

1. Choose Flexible Width from the Columns menu in the Text Frame Options dialog box.

2. Set the options as described for the Fixed Number option.

3. Set the maximum width for the column in the Maximum field.

4. Drag to resize the frame width. The width of the column increases until it reaches the maximum amount. Then a new column is created **C**.

A The **Columns menu** controls how the number of columns or column widths change.

B Applying **Fixed Width** ensures that the columns in a text frame are always the same size.

C Applying **Flexible Width** lets the column width increase to a specific amount and then change the number of columns.

| All this time Dorothy and her companions had been walk-ing through the thick woods. The road was still paved with yel- | low brick, from the trees, and the walking was not at all good. There were few birds in this part of the forest, for birds love the | open country close to Doro-thy's side, and did not even bark in return. | Off |

| All this time Dorothy and her companions had been walk-ing through the thick woods. The road was still | paved with yel-low brick, from the trees, and the walking was not at all good. There were few birds in this part | of the forest, for birds love the open country close to Doro-thy's side, and did not even bark in return. | On |

D The result of applying the **Balance Columns** command to a text frame.

E The Inset Spacing settings for the Text Frame Options dialog box.

"At the East, not far from here," said one, "there is a great desert, and none could live to cross it."
"It is the same at the South," said another, "for I have been there and seen it. The South is the country of the Quadlings."
"I am told," said the third man, "that it is the same at

F A **text frame with inset spacing** has space between the text frame and the text.

You may find that when you divide a text frame into columns the text creates an uneven number of lines. You can balance the number of lines in the columns so the text looks more evenly distributed.

To balance the text in columns:

Check Balance Columns in the Text Frame Options dialog box. InDesign moves lines from some columns into others to make the number of lines more evenly distributed **D**.

You can also add space between the text and the frame. This is called the *inset spacing*.

To control the frame inset:

1. Select the text frame and open the Text Frame Options dialog box.

2. Enter the values in the Inset Spacing fields to control the amount of space between the text and the top, bottom, left, and right edges of the frame **E**.

3. Click OK to apply the changes to the column **F**.

TIP If you have applied a stroke to a frame, you will most likely want to create an inset spacing so that the text does not touch the stroke.

The vertical justification of a text frame controls where the text is positioned from the top to the bottom of the frame.

To set the vertical justification:

1. Select the text frame and open the Text Frame Options dialog box.

2. Choose one of the four options in the Vertical Justification Align pop-up list :

   - **Top** positions the text so that the first line sits at the top of the frame .

   - **Center** positions the text so it is centered between the top and bottom of the frame .

   - **Bottom** positions the text so that the last line sits at the bottom of the frame .

   - **Justify** positions the text so that it fills the entire frame from top to bottom .

When you set the vertical alignment to Justify, you can set how the space between paragraphs is applied.

To set the paragraph spacing limit:

1. Set the Vertical Justification Align list to Justify.

2. Set an amount in the Paragraph Spacing Limit field 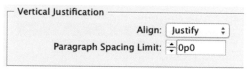. The higher the number, the more space between paragraphs and the less likely the leading between the lines will be affected by justifying the text vertically.

TIP Set an amount equal to the height of the text frame to add space only between the paragraphs, not between the lines .

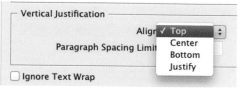

A The **Vertical Justification Align menu** lets you choose where text is positioned vertically.

B The four vertical alignment settings change the position of text within a frame.

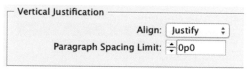

C The **Paragraph Spacing Limit** for justified vertical alignment controls how much space will exist between paragraphs before the leading is increased.

D A paragraph spacing limit of 0p causes the leading to increase. A limit of 1p only adds space between the paragraphs, not the leading.

BROADWAY GOES GREEN¶

Following·WICKED's·lead,··all··of·Broadway has·joined·us·in·creating·a·new·theatre-wide initiative,·BROADWAY·GOES·GREEN.·Back·in 2006,·producer·David·Stone·decided·to·"challenge·all·of·the·companies·of·WICKED·across North·America··to··take··a·stand··to·protect our·planet."·Since··then,··WICKED's··carbon footprint·has·been·reduced·by·taking·many small·steps,·including·washing·costumes·in

ergy-efficient·lighting·in·the·dressing·roc and·on·the·set.¶

To·help·announce·this·Broadway-wide·green tiative,·New·York·City·Mayor·Michael·R.·Blo berg·asked·our·very·own·green·girl,·Elphab: introduce·him·and·kick·off·the·press·confer on·November·25.·And·the·Ozmopolitan·New vites·you·to·join·our·efforts·by·taking·any·s

E An example of headline text that **spans across columns.**

Paragraph Layout	✓ Single Column
	Span Columns
Spar	Split Column

F The **Paragraph Layout choices** of the Span Columns dialog box.

Paragraph Layout: | Span Columns |

Span: ⇕ All | Columns

Space Before Span: ⇕ 0p0

Space After Span: ⇕ 0p0

G The controls to set text to span across columns.

WITCH·OF·THE·WEST·BREAKING· RECORDS·NATIONWIDE!¶

WICKED··defied·his= tory··in··Los·Angeles and·Chicago·by·shat= tering··major·theatre records.···Once··the Chicago····produc= tion··closes··on·Janu= ary·25th,·it··will·have played··1,500·perfor= mances··—the·longest running··Broadway musical··in··Chicago

history.·Over··on··the West·Coast,··the··Los Angeles··production closed···on···January 11th·as··one··of··the highest···grossing shows·in·L.A.·theatre history,·twice·break= ing·the·box·office·re= cord·in··its··final··two weeks¶

Oh,··what··a··celebration·San·Francisco have·when·WICKED·returns·to·the·city·wh the··show··premiered··before··following· Yellow·Brick·Road·to·Broadway!¶

When··the··open-ended··San··Francisco starts·on·January·27th,·it'll·feature·two·of favorite·witches.·Teal·Wicks·will·defy·gra\ as·Elphaba,·flying·in·on·her·broom·from L.A.·engagement.·And·it·will·be·good·to Kendra·Kassebaum·again·as·Glinda,·float in·on·her·bubble·from·the·Broadway·prod tion.·The·San·Francisco·cast·will·also·incl\ famous··faces··and··Broadway··alums··C: Kane·and·David·Garrison.¶

San·Francisco·Welcomes·Elphaba·and·Glinda Home¶

H An example of text that has been set to **split columns.**

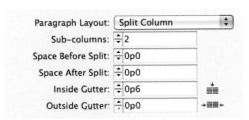

Paragraph Layout: | Split Column |

Sub-columns: ⇕ 2

Space Before Split: ⇕ 0p0

Space After Split: ⇕ 0p0

Inside Gutter: ⇕ 0p6

Outside Gutter: ⇕ 0p0

I The controls to set text to split within a column.

Spanning and Splitting Columns

Ordinarily, text stays within the boundaries of a column. However, you may want the headline for a story to stretch across (span) the columns in a text frame **E**.

To set text to span columns:

1. Select the text and choose Span Columns from the Paragraph panel menu. The Span Columns dialog box appears.

2. Choose Span Columns from the Paragraph Layout choices **F**.

3. Use the Span Columns field to control how many columns you want the text to span **G**.

4. Use the Space Before Span or Space After Span to add space above or below the text.

Another way to customize text within a column is to split the text into sub-columns. This is called a split column and is very popular for highlighting text in a story **H**.

To set text to split within a column:

1. Choose Split Columns from the Paragraph Layout choices.

2. Use the Sub-columns field to control how many columns you want to split the text into **I**.

3. Use the Space Before Split or Space After Split to add space above or below the split text **I**.

4. Use the Inside Gutter field to add space between the split columns. This is similar to the gutter space within text frames.

5. Use the Outside Gutter field to add space between the outside edge of the text and the column.

Using the Control Panel for Text

The Control panel changes its settings depending on the type of object selected. For example, when a text object is selected, the Control panel displays a combination of the Character and Paragraph panel controls.

To use the Control panel for character settings:

1. Use the Type tool to create an insertion point within a text frame. The Control panel displays the text options.

2. Click the Character icon to display the character attributes in the first position in the Control panel **A**. The paragraph attributes follow.

TIP Cmd-Opt-7 (Mac) or Ctrl-Alt-7 (Win) switches the focus between the Character and Paragraph settings in the Control panel.

To use the Control panel for paragraph settings:

1. Use the Type tool to create an insertion point within a text frame. The Control panel displays the text options.

2. Click the Paragraph icon to display the paragraph attributes in the first position in the Control panel **B**. The character attributes follow.

Character icon

A Click the **Character icon** to move the character attributes to the first position in the Control panel.

Paragraph icon

B Click the **Paragraph icon** to move the paragraph attributes to the first position in the Control panel.

Using Special Text Characters

Text does not consist of just alphanumeric characters. There are special characters and spaces that are used as part of professional typography. InDesign lets you insert those characters into your documents.

To insert special characters:

1. Place the insertion point where you want to insert the special character.

2. Choose **Type > Insert Special Character**.

   or

   Control-click (Mac) or right-mouse click (Win) and choose Insert Special Character from the contextual menu.

3. Choose a character from the submenu.

You can insert white space characters, which are fixed spaces such as *em* and *en* spaces. You can also insert a nonbreaking space that forces two words to stay together.

TIP See the sidebar on the left for descriptions of the size of the white spaces.

To insert special space characters:

1. Place the insertion point where you want to insert the special character.

TIP You can highlight a regular space to replace it with a white space character.

2. Choose **Type > Insert White Space**.

   or

   Control-click (Mac) or right-click (Win) and choose Insert White Space from the contextual menu.

3. Choose a white space character listing from the submenu.

Working with Objects 4

Back in the old days of board mechanicals, advertising agencies and design studios had a production area called the bullpen. It was the people in the bullpen — called bullpen artists — who actually created the mechanical. Most of them were kids just out of design school; the bullpen was usually their first step up the ladder in advertising or design.

The kids in the bullpen were amazing. Although not professional illustrators, they could create all sorts of artwork for the layout.

The same is true when working with InDesign. Although InDesign is not a full-fledged drawing program such as Adobe Illustrator, you can use InDesign's tools to create a wide variety of effects by distorting, moving, resizing, duplicating, and aligning objects. It's your electronic bullpen.

Types of Frames

Frames are the containers in which you place graphics or text. Frames can also be used as graphic shapes. There are three types of frames you can create: unassigned, graphic, and text.

Unassigned frames

Unassigned frames are created with the Rectangle, Ellipse, and Polygon tools 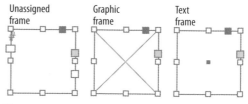. These frames are useful for adding color to your layout or a stroke around an area without inserting a graphic or text.

Graphic frames

Graphic frames are created with the Rectangle Frame, Ellipse Frame, and Polygon Frame tools. When you create a graphic frame, diagonal lines inside the frame indicate that you can insert a graphic inside the frame **A**.

TIP Although most people insert images inside graphic frames, there is nothing to prevent you from flowing text inside a graphic frame.

Text frames

Text frames are created using the Text tool or by converting frames. When you create a text frame, two link boxes appear on the sides of the frame in addition to the bounding box handles. Text frames also display a blinking insertion point when they are selected **A**.

A The **three different types of frames:** unassigned, graphic, and text.

Diagonal Lines in Graphic Frames?

The diagonal lines inside a graphic frame come from a convention that was used in traditional pasteboard mechanicals.

When pasteboard artists drew the lines on mechanicals, they would often block off an area with diagonal lines to indicate that a picture or graphic was to go there.

Electronic page-layout programs such as Adobe InDesign and QuarkXPress use the same convention. The diagonal lines indicate where photos or graphics need to be inserted.

However, there is absolutely no rule that says you can only place images in graphic frames. You can place text in graphic frames or images in unassigned frames. The choice is yours.

The **Rectangle Frame tool in the Tools panel** creates rectangular graphic frames.

The **Ellipse Frame tool in the Tools panel** creates elliptical graphic frames.

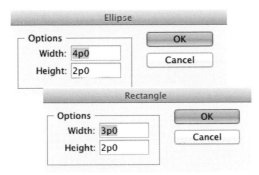

D The **Ellipse and Rectangle dialog boxes** let you create frames with precise width and height.

Using the Transformation Values?

You may notice that there is a label that appears when you drag or create objects that contains feedback as to the position, size, or angle of the object. This is the Transformation Values cursor.

Rather than clutter the illustrations in this chapter, I've turned off the Transformation Values.

But you should get in the habit of using those labels to work more precisely.

Creating Basic Shapes

You use the rectangle, ellipse, and polygon frame tools to create graphic frames into which you place images.

TIP If another tool is visible, press the corner triangle to reveal the toolset.

To create a rectangular graphic frame:

1. Click the Rectangle Frame tool in the Tools panel **B**.
2. Drag across the page to create the rectangle.

TIP Hold the Opt/Alt key to draw the object from the center.

3. Release the mouse button when the rectangle is the correct size.

TIP Hold the Shift key to constrain the rectangle into a square.

To create an elliptical graphic frame:

1. Click the Ellipse Frame tool in the Tools panel **C**.
2. Drag across the page to create the ellipse.

TIP Hold the Opt/Alt key to draw the object from the center.

3. Release the mouse button when the ellipse is the correct size.

TIP Hold the Shift key to constrain the ellipse into a circle.

You can also create rectangles and ellipses by specifying their size numerically.

To create objects numerically:

1. Click with either the Rectangle or Ellipse Frame tools. A dialog box appears **D**.
2. Enter the width and height amounts.
3. Click OK. The frame appears where the mouse was clicked.

To create a polygon graphic frame:

1. Choose the Polygon Frame tool in the Tools panel .

2. Click on the page. This opens the Polygon dialog box **B**.

3. Enter a number in the field for the Number of Sides to the polygon.

4. To create a star, change the amount in the Star Inset field from 0% to a higher number.

5. Click OK. The polygon is created.

TIP Hold the Opt/Alt key to draw the object from the center.

TIP Hold the Shift key to constrain the width and height of the object to the same amount.

TIP You can also drag across the page to create the polygon or star.

The Line tool lets you draw a straight line.

To create straight lines:

1. Click the Line tool in the Tools panel **C**.

2. Position the cursor where you want the line to start.

TIP Hold the Opt/Alt key to draw the line from its centerpoint.

3. Drag to create a line.

TIP Hold the Shift key to constrain the line to 45-degree angles.

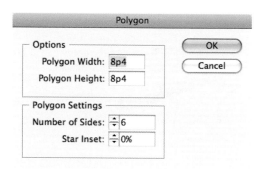

A Use the **Polygon Frame tool** to create polygon and star graphic frames.

B The **Polygon Settings dialog box** creates either polygons or stars.

C The **Line tool in the Tools panel** creates straight lines.

Converting Shapes

So what if you've created a circle and later on realize you need a rectangle? What do you do?

Simple, you can use the Pathfinder Convert Shape commands to change an object from one shape to another. *(See Chapter 7, "Points and Paths," for more information on the Pathfinder commands.)*

Selection tool   Direct Selection tool

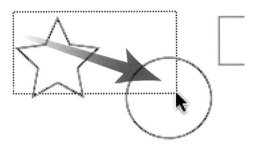

D   The **Selection tool in the Tools panel** selects entire objects. The **Direct Selection tool** selects a point on an object.

E   Drag to create a marquee to select objects.

What Are the Differences Between the Selection Tools?

Perhaps the most confusing part of InDesign is the difference between the Selection tool (black arrow) and the Direct Selection tool (white arrow) **D**.

The Selection tool will always select the object as a whole. Use this tool when you want to manipulate the entire object.

The Direct Selection tool will always select the points or segments that make up a frame. Use the Direct Selection tool to reshape a path.

Both tools can select placed images within a frame as covered in Chapter 8, "Imported Graphics."

If you've ever worked with Adobe Illustrator, you'll instantly recognize the two selection tools as identical to their Illustrator cousins.

Selecting Objects

Once you've created objects, you can use different techniques to select them.

To select by clicking:

1. Choose the Selection tool (black arrow) in the Tools panel **D**.

2. Click the object you want to select.

3. Hold the Shift key to select any additional objects.

TIP Hold the Shift key and click on a selected object to deselect that object.

TIP To select objects behind others, hold the Cmd/Ctrl key as you click the mouse button.

TIP Double-click on a graphic frame to toggle between the Selection and Direct Selection tools.

You can also select an object by dragging an area, or *marquee,* around the object.

To select by dragging a marquee:

1. Choose the Selection tool.

2. Drag along a diagonal angle to create a marquee around the objects you want to select **E**.

TIP You do not need to marquee the entire object to select it. Objects are selected if any portion is within the marquee.

TIP Hold the Shift key and drag around another area to add to a selection.

You can also use a menu command to select all the objects on a page.

To select all the objects on a page:

Choose Edit > Select All.

TIP This command works only if you do not have an insertion point blinking inside a text frame.

Moving Objects

The simplest way to position an object on a page is to drag it to a new position, but you can also move objects by using menu and keyboard commands, or by typing specific numerical locations into a dialog box, as you'll learn later in this chapter.

To move an object by dragging:

1. Choose the Selection tool in the Tools panel.

2. Click the object you want to move. A bounding box with eight handles appears around the object. This indicates the object is selected.

3. Position the Selection tool on the edges of the bounding box (but not on the handles of the bounding box).

TIP If an object has a fill color, gradient, or image inside it, you can drag with the Selection tool directly inside the object. Otherwise, you must drag by the stroke or bounding box.

4. Drag to move the object. If you drag quickly, you will see only a bounding box preview of the object being moved **A**.

   or

   Press and pause for a moment before you drag the object. The pause gives InDesign enough time to let you see a preview of the object as you move it **B**.

A Quickly drag to see the bounding box of the object being moved.

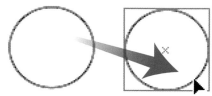

B Pause before you drag to see a preview of the object being moved.

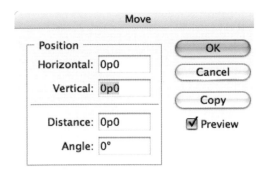

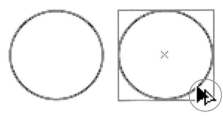

C The **Move dialog box** gives you numerical controls for moving objects.

D The **double-headed arrow** indicates that a copy is being created of the moved object.

You can also move an object more precisely. One way to do this is with the Move command in the Transform menu.

To use the Move command:

1. Select the object or objects.

2. Choose **Object > Transform > Move**. This opens the Move dialog box **C**.

TIP This command is also available in a contextual menu or by double-clicking the Selection or Direct Selection tools.

TIP Select the Preview checkbox to see the results of your actions as you enter numbers in the dialog box.

3. Use the Horizontal and Vertical fields to move the object along those axes.

4. Use the Distance field to move the object an absolute distance.

5. Use the Angle field to set the angle along which the object moves.

6. Click OK to move the original object.

   or

   Click Copy to create a duplicate of the object in the new position.

To copy an object as you drag:

1. Hold the Opt/Alt key before you start the move.

2. Move the object as described on the opposite page. A double-headed arrow indicates that a copy is being created **D**.

3. Release the mouse button. The copy appears in the new position.

Replicating Objects

There are several commands you can use to create duplicates of objects. Use the Copy command when you want to put the object on the clipboard so you can paste it somewhere else.

To copy objects:

1. Select an object to copy.

2. Choose **Edit > Copy**.

Use the Cut command to remove the object from the page so it can be pasted elsewhere.

To cut objects:

1. Select an object to cut.

2. Choose **Edit > Cut**.

Use the Paste command to see the contents of the clipboard.

To paste objects:

Choose **Edit > Paste**. The contents of the clipboard appear in the center of the window area 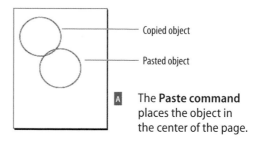.

or

Choose **Edit > Paste in Place**. The contents of the clipboard appear in the same location on the page as when they were originally selected.

The Duplicate command makes a copy without changing the contents of the clipboard.

To duplicate objects:

1. Choose the object to duplicate.

2. Choose **Edit > Duplicate**. The selected object appears on the page at the same distance that the last object was moved B.

Copied object

Pasted object

A The **Paste command** places the object in the center of the page.

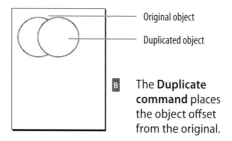

Original object

Duplicated object

B The **Duplicate command** places the object offset from the original.

Using Paste in Place

I always wondered just how useful the Paste in Place command is. After all, if you already have a copy of an object in one place, why would you need a second copy right over it?

That's not the point of Paste in Place. The power of the command is that you can paste an object in the same place on different pages. You can even paste in the same place in different documents. This is very helpful for creating documents that all look the same.

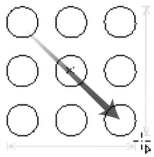

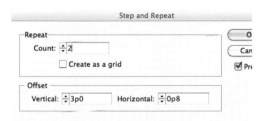

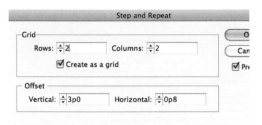

C Press the up/down or left/right arrows as you drag with a tool to **create a grid** of the objects.

D Use the **Step and Repeat dialog box** to make multiple copies of an object positioned at specific horizontal and vertical intervals.

E The **Step and Repeat dialog box** set to create a grid of repeated objects.

InDesign makes it easy to create a grid of an object as you drag to create it. This is known as the *gridify* feature.

To create a grid as you draw an object:

1. Select one of the drawing tools and start the drag to draw the object.

2. Without releasing the mouse button, press the up/down or left/right arrows. This creates rows and columns that duplicate the object as follows:

   - The up and down arrows increase and decrease the number of rows.

   - The left and right arrows increase and decrease the number of columns.

TIP Add the Cmd/Ctrl key and use the arrow keys to change the spaces between the rows or columns.

3. Release the mouse button when you have as many objects you you need **C**:

The gridify feature doesn't give you numerical control over the space between the rows and columns. That's when you want to use the Step and Repeat command.

To duplicate multiple objects:

1. With an object selected, choose **Edit > Step and Repeat**. The Step and Repeat dialog box appears **D**.

2. In the Repeat Count field, enter the number of duplicates you want to create.

3. If desired, check Create as a grid. This changes the Repeat Count to Rows and Columns **E**.

4. In the Horizontal Offset field, enter a distance for the horizontal space between duplicates.

5. In the Vertical Offset field, enter a distance for the vertical space between duplicates.

6. Click OK.

Resizing Objects

Very often things need to be made bigger or smaller. InDesign gives you several different ways to scale objects. You can also use the bounding box handles to change the dimensions of the object visually. This is the easiest way to quickly resize an object.

To resize using the bounding box handles:

1. Choose the Selection tool.

2. Choose which handle to drag based on the following options 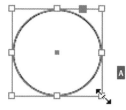:

   - Drag the corner handles to change both the width and height.

   - Drag the top or bottom handles to change the height only.

   - Drag the left or right handles to change the width only.

3. Drag the handle. If you drag quickly, you will see only the bounding box of the object **B**.

   or

   Press and hold for a moment and then drag the handle. This shows a preview of the object as you resize the bounding box **C**.

   TIP Hold down the Shift key as you drag a corner to keep the original proportions of the width and height.

   TIP Hold the Cmd/Ctrl key as you drag to scale the frame as well as any text and images inside the object.

4. Release the mouse button when the object is the correct size.

A Use the **bounding box handles** to resize an object.

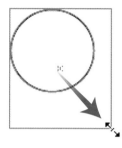

B If you **drag quickly**, you only see a box as you resize an object.

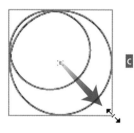

C If you **press and pause a moment**, you see an actual preview as you resize an object.

Resizing or Scaling?

Although you and I might feel the words are the same, InDesign treats them differently. When you *resize* an object, you change its width or height. The amount of scaling stays the same in the Control panel or the Transform panel. You have to resize the object again to get it back to its original size.

When you *scale* an object, the width and height change, and the amount of scaling applied to the object is shown in the Scale fields in the Control panel or Transform panel. You can convert the object back to its original size by setting the scaling to 100%.

Toto ran over to the
trees and began to
bark at the birds sitting
there #

D Objects selected with the Selection tool
have both the object and its content
transformed by the transform tools.

Toto ran over to the
trees and began to
bark at the birds sitting
there #

E Objects selected with the Group
Selection tool have only the object
transformed by the transform tools.

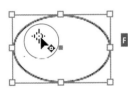

F The indicator that
the reference point
can be moved to
a new position.

Using the Transform Tools

The transform tools resize and distort objects.
You can transform the object itself (also called
the container) or the object as well as any
content. How you select objects changes the
effect of the transform tools.

To control the effect of the transform tools:

Select the object using the Selection
tool. This type of selection causes the
transform tools to affect both the
container and any text or images
inside it **D**.

or

Hold the Opt/Alt key as you click the
frame with the Group Selection tool
(Direct Selection tool). This causes
the transformation to affect only the
container, not any text or images
contained in the frame **E**.

TIP The plus (+) sign next to the Direct Selection
tool indicates that the tool is now the Group
Selection tool.

All the transformations take place in relation
to a reference point. Each object has a default
reference point, but you can change it if
necessary.

To control the reference point:

1. Select the object to be transformed.

2. Choose one of the transform tools. A
   reference point appears inside the object.

3. Move the cursor near the reference point.
   A small icon appears next to the cursor
   that indicates you can move the reference
   point **F**.

4. Drag the reference point to a new
   position.

   or

   Click to position the reference point in a
   new position.

The Scale tool lets you increase or decrease the size of objects.

To scale objects visually using the Scale tool:

1. Select the object or objects.

2. Choose the Scale tool in the Tools panel . The Scale tool is in the flyout menu under the Free Transform tool.

3. If necessary, change the position of the reference point.

4. Move the cursor away from the reference point, and drag to scale the object B.

TIP Hold down the Shift key to constrain the tool to horizontal, vertical, or proportional scaling.

TIP To see a preview of the image as you scale, press and hold the mouse button for a moment before you start to drag.

TIP Hold down the Opt/Alt key to copy the object as you scale it.

If you prefer, you can resize objects numerically using the Scale command.

To scale objects using the Scale command:

1. Select the object or objects.

2. Choose **Object > Transform > Scale**. This opens the Scale dialog box C.

3. Enter an amount for the Scale X (horizontal) field.

4. Enter an amount for the Scale Y (vertical) field.

TIP If the chain icon is selected, the X and Y fields scale the same amounts.

5. Select the Preview checkbox to see the effects of entering the amounts.

6. Click OK to scale the object or click Copy to create a scaled copy of the object.

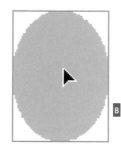

A The **Scale tool in the Tools panel** is used to change the size of objects.

B The arrowhead appears while scaling an object.

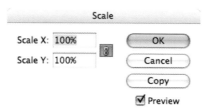

C The **Scale dialog box** lets you scale objects using numerical values.

Making Copies as You Scale, Rotate, and Shear

As you use the Scale, Rotate, and Shear tools, you can duplicate the object as you transform it.

Drag, as usual, to start the transformation, but then add the Opt/Alt key *after* you start the drag. You will see the double-headed arrow that indicates you are duplicating the object.

Release the mouse button first, and then the Opt/Alt key to finish the transformation and duplication.

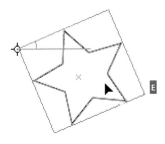

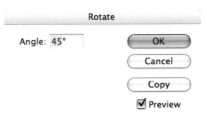

D The **Rotate tool in the Tools panel** is used to change the orientation of objects.

E Rotating an object around its reference point.

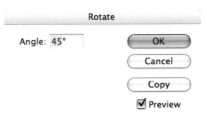

F The **Rotate dialog box** lets you rotate objects using numerical values.

To scale objects numerically using the Scale tool:

1. Select the object or objects.

2. Choose the Scale tool in the Tools panel.

3. Hold the Opt/Alt key and click to designate the position of the reference point. This opens the Scale dialog box C.

4. Set the dialog box controls as described in the previous exercise.

The Rotation tool changes the orientation, or angle, of the object on the page.

To rotate objects visually using the Rotate tool:

1. Select the object or objects.

2. Click the Rotate tool in the Tools panel D. The Rotate tool is in the flyout under the Free Transform tool.

3. If necessary, change the default reference point.

4. Move the cursor away from the reference point, and drag to rotate the object E.

TIP Hold down the Shift key to constrain the rotation to 45-degree increments.

To rotate objects using the Rotate command:

1. Select the object or objects.

2. Choose **Object > Transform > Rotate**. This opens the Rotate dialog box F.

3. Use the Angle field to set how much the object should rotate.

4. Select the Preview command to see the effects of entering the angle.

5. Click OK to rotate the object or click Copy to create a copy as you rotate the object.

To rotate objects numerically using the Rotate tool:

1. Select the object or objects.

2. Choose the Rotate tool in the Tools panel.

3. Hold the Opt/Alt key and click to set the position of the reference point. This opens the Rotate dialog box.

4. Set the dialog box controls as described in the previous exercise.

The Shear tool distorts the shape of objects.

To shear objects visually using the Shear tool:

1. Select the object or objects.

2. Click the Shear tool in the Tools panel . The Shear tool is in the flyout under the Free Transform tool.

3. If necessary, drag the reference point to a new position. The cursor indicates the reference point can be moved.

4. Move the cursor away from the reference point, and drag to shear the object **B**.

To shear objects using the Shear command:

1. Select the object or objects.

2. Choose **Object > Transform > Shear**. This opens the Shear dialog box **C**.

3. Use the Shear Angle field to set the amount of distortion.

4. Select one of the Axis options:

   • **Horizontal** shears along the horizontal axis.

   • **Vertical** shears along the vertical axis.

5. Select the Preview command to see the effects of entering the shear angle and choosing the axis.

6. Click OK to shear the object.

   or

   Click Copy to create a sheared copy of the object.

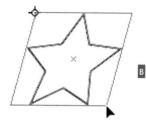

A Use the **Shear tool in the Tools panel** to distort objects.

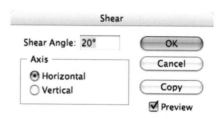

B Shearing an object around the reference point.

C The **Shear dialog box** lets you distort objects using numerical values.

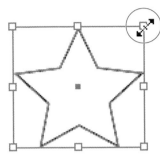

D Choose the **Free Transform tool in the Tools panel** to scale, rotate, and shear objects.

E The double-headed arrow indicates that the Free Transform tool is in the scale mode.

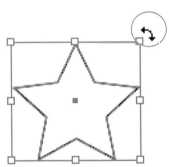

F The curved double-headed arrow indicates that the Free Transform tool is in the rotation mode.

To shear objects numerically using the Shear tool:

1. Select the object or objects.

2. Choose the Shear tool in the Tools panel.

3. Hold the Opt/Alt key and click to set the position of the reference point. This opens the Shear dialog box **C**.

4. Set the dialog box controls as described in the previous exercise.

Rather than switching between the Scale, Rotate, and Shear tools, you can use the Free Transform tool to scale, rotate, or shear an object.

To use the Free Transform tool:

1. Select the object or objects.

2. Click the Free Transform tool in the Tools panel **D**. A bounding box appears around the object.

3. To scale the object, place the cursor over one of the handles. The cursor changes to a double-headed arrow **E**.

   or

   Place the cursor outside one of the handles of the bounding box. The cursor changes to a curved double-headed arrow **F**.

   or

   Drag one of the handles and then hold the Cmd/Ctrl key *after* you have started the drag. The cursor does not change appearance, but the object will be sheared.

4. Release the mouse button to apply the transformation.

Using the Transform Panel

The Transform panel allows you to move, scale, rotate, and shear objects precisely, using numerical values.

TIP When you have objects selected, the Control panel displays many of the controls that are found in the Transform panel.

To open the Transform panel:

Choose **Window > Object & Layout > Transform** to open the panel 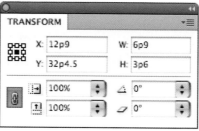.

or

If the Transform panel is behind other panels, click the Transform panel tab.

As you work with the Transform panel, it is important to know its reference point on the object. This is the same as the reference point used with the transform tools.

To set the Transform panel reference point:

1. Select the object or objects that you want to transform.

2. Click the reference point control on the Transform panel to choose the point around which the object moves **B**.

A The **Transform panel** is a command center for positioning and transforming objects.

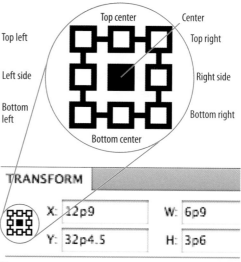

B The **reference point** controls where in the object the transformation occurs.

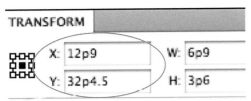

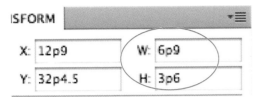

c The **X and Y fields in the Transform panel control** the position of an object.

D The **W and H fields in the Transform panel** control the width and height of objects.

You can use the Transform panel to move objects numerically.

To move an object with the Transform panel:

1. Select the object or objects that you want to move.

2. To move the object horizontally, enter an amount in the X field **c**.

TIP As you increase the numbers, the object moves to the right.

3. To move the object vertically, enter an amount in the Y field **c**.

TIP As you increase the numbers, the object moves down.

4. Press Enter or Return to apply the changes.

You can use the Transform panel to resize an object numerically.

To resize with the Transform panel:

1. Select the object or objects.

2. If necessary, change the reference point as explained on the preceding page.

3. To change the width of the object, enter an amount in the W field **D**.

4. To change the height of the object, enter an amount in the H field **D**.

5. Press Enter or Return to resize the object.

You can resize proportionally even if you know the size for only one side of the object.

To resize proportionally:

1. Select the object or objects.

2. Enter the new size in the W field or H field **D**.

3. Hold Cmd/Ctrl as you press Enter or Return. The amount in both the W and H fields changes proportionally.

You can also scale using the Transform panel.

To scale with the Transform panel:

1. Select the object or objects.

   TIP Use the Selection tool to scale the object and its contents. Use the Direct Selection tool to scale only the object.

2. If necessary, change the reference point.

3. To change the horizontal size, enter a percentage in the Scale X field 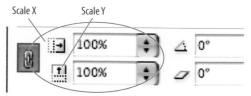.

4. To change the height of the object, enter a percentage in the Scale Y field.

   TIP The Scale X and Y fields also have pop-up lists from which to choose the amount of scaling.

5. Press Enter or Return to apply the changes.

   TIP You can also scale text within a text frame by dragging on the edge of the frame while holding the Cmd/Ctrl key. Hold Cmd/Ctrl-Shift and drag by a corner point to scale proportionally. This also applies to text frames in groups.

To scale proportionally with the Transform panel:

1. Select an object or objects.

2. If the Link icon is in the open state, click to close it **B**.

3. Enter an amount in either the Scale X or Scale Y fields. You do not have to enter an amount in both fields. The closed Link icon forces both fields to display the same amount.

4. Press Enter or Return to apply the changes.

   TIP Hold the Cmd/Ctrl key as you press the Enter or Return key to scale proportionally even if the Link icon is in the open state.

Scale X   Scale Y

A The **Scale X and Y fields in the Transform panel** let you apply percentage amounts to scale objects.

Closed state   Open state

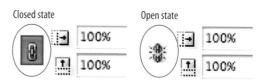

B The **Link icon in the closed state** forces both the Scale X and the Scale Y fields to the same amount. In the open state, you can enter different amounts for the Scale X and Scale Y fields.

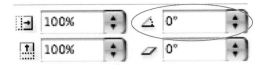

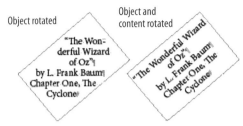

Object rotated

Object and content rotated

"The Wonderful Wizard of Oz" by L. Frank Baum Chapter One, The Cyclone

C The Rotation field in the Transform panel lets you change the angle of objects.

D The difference between rotating an object or rotating an object and its content.

E The Shear field in the Transform panel lets you distort the shape of objects.

Object sheared

The Cyclone

Object and content sheared

The Cyclone

F The difference between shearing an object or shearing an object and its content.

You can also rotate objects using the Transform panel.

To rotate with the Transform panel:

1. Select the object or objects.

   TIP Use the Selection tool to rotate the object and its contents. Use the Direct Selection tool to rotate only the object.

2. If necessary, change the reference point.

3. Enter the amount of rotation in the Rotation field **C**.

   TIP The Rotation field also has a pop-up list from which to choose the amount of rotation.

4. Press Enter or Return to apply the changes **D**.

You can also shear objects using the Transform panel.

To shear with the Transform panel:

1. Select the object or objects.

   TIP Use the Selection tool to shear the object and its contents. Use the Direct Selection tool to shear only the object.

2. If necessary, change the reference point.

3. Enter the amount of distortion in the Shear field **E**.

   TIP The Shear field also has a pop-up list from which to choose the amount of shearing.

4. Press Enter or Return to apply the changes **F**.

Using the Transform Commands

In addition to the transform tools and transform fields, there are a whole bunch of transform commands you can use on objects. These commands make it easy to perform commonly used transformations, such as rotating and flipping objects.

To rotate with the transform commands:

1. Select an object or objects.
2. Click to open the Transformation panel menu.

   or

   Choose **Object > Transform**.
3. Choose one of the rotation settings as follows 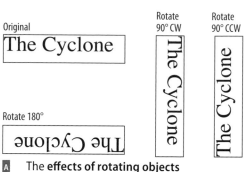:
   - Rotate 90° CW (clockwise).
   - Rotate 90° CCW (counter-clockwise).
   - Rotate 180°.

To flip objects using the transform commands:

1. Select an object or objects.
2. Click to open the Transform panel menu.

   or

   Choose **Object > Transform**.
3. Choose one of the flip settings as follows 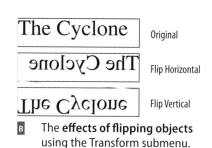:
   - Flip Horizontal.
   - Flip Vertical.

A The **effects of rotating objects** using the Transform submenu.

B The **effects of flipping objects** using the Transform submenu.

Circle moved to new position

Transform Again command applied to triangle

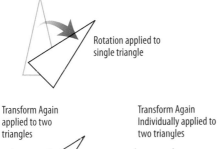

C The **Transform Again command** allows you to duplicate transformation commands applied to objects.

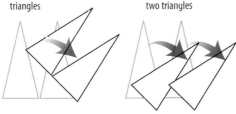

Rotation applied to single triangle

Transform Again applied to two triangles

Transform Again Individually applied to two triangles

D The differences between the Transform Again command and the Transform Again Individually command when applied to multiple objects.

When you perform a transformation on an object, that transformation is stored in InDesign's memory. You can then perform the same transformation again on another object — even in another document! This is similar to Illustrator's Transform Again command.

To repeat transformations:

1. Use any of the transform commands on a selection.

2. Select a different object or objects.

3. Choose one of the following from the **Object > Transform Again** submenu.

   - **Transform Again** applies the last single transform command to the selection as a whole C.

   - **Transform Again Individually** applies the last single transform command to each object in the selection D.

   - **Transform Sequence Again** applies the last set of transformation commands to the selection as a whole.

   - **Transform Sequence Again Individually** applies the last set of transformation commands to each object in the selection.

> TIP InDesign remembers all the transformation commands until you select a different object or perform a different task.

> TIP InDesign can even remember an Opt/Alt-drag transformation that duplicated an object.

Using the Arrange Commands

Objects in InDesign are layered on top of one another in the same order they were created. (This is sometimes called the *stacking order.*) The first object created is behind the second, the second behind the third, and so on. Though you may not see the layering when objects are side by side, it is apparent when they overlap .

A When two objects overlap, it is obvious which object is in front of the other.

> **TIP** The layering of objects is not the same as the layers of a document. *(See Chapter 11, "Layers," for more information on working with layers.)*

The Arrange commands allow you to move objects through the stacking order.

To move up or down one level in a stack:

1. Select the object you want to move.

2. Choose **Object > Arrange > Bring Forward** to move the object in front of the next object in the stacking order .

   or

   Choose **Object > Arrange > Send Backward** to move the object behind the next object in the stacking order .

To move up or down the entire stack:

1. Select an object you want to move.

2. Choose **Object > Arrange > Bring to Front** to move the object in front of all the others in its layer .

   or

   Choose **Object > Arrange > Send to Back** to move the object behind all the others in its layer .

Star in back   Bring Forward applied

B Effects of the Bring Forward command.

Star in front   Send Backward applied

C Effects of the Send Backward command.

Star in back   Bring to Front applied

D Effects of the Bring to Front command.

Star in front   Send to Back applied

E Effects of the Send to Back command.

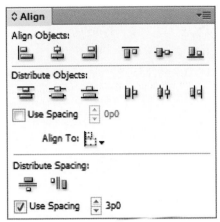

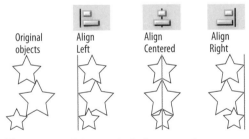

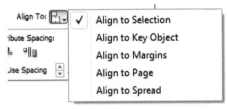

F   Use the **Align panel** to arrange objects in an orderly fashion.

G   The **Alignment menu** lets you choose how the objects should be aligned.

H   Effects of the **vertical alignment icons**.

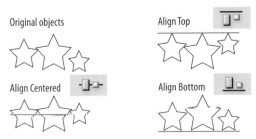

I   Effects of the **horizontal alignment icons**.

Aligning Objects

The Align panel provides commands that align objects or distribute them evenly along a horizontal or vertical axis.

To work with the Align panel:

1. Choose **Window** > **Object & Layout** > **Align**. This opens the Align panel F.

2. Choose Show Options from the Align panel menu to see all the commands in the panel.

To align objects:

1. Select two or more objects.

2. Use the Alignment menu to choose to what items the objects should align G.

   - **Align to Selection** uses the objects themselves for alignment.

   - **Align to Key Object** lets you designate a specific object to which the others align. *(See the next exercise for how to designate the key object.)*

   - **Align to Margins** uses the margins for alignment.

   - **Align to Page** uses the page trim for alignment.

   - **Align to Spread** uses the size of the spread for alignment.

3. Click an alignment icon as follows:

   - Click a vertical alignment icon to move the objects into left, centered, or right alignment H.

   - Click a horizontal alignment icon to move the objects into top, centered, or bottom alignment I.

TIP The align commands move objects based on the best representation of the controls. For instance, the Align Left command uses the leftmost object; Align Top uses the topmost object, and so on.

To align to a key object:

1. With the objects selected, choose Align to Key Object from the Alignment menu. A thick border appears around one of the selected objects 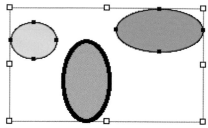.

2. Click another object. The thick border appears around that object. That is the new key object.

3. Click one of the alignment options in the Align panel. The objects align to the designated key object.

You can also move objects so the spaces between certain points of the objects are equal. This is called *distributing* objects.

To distribute objects:

1. Select three or more objects.

2. Click a distribute icon as follows:
   - Click a vertical distribute icon to move the objects so that their tops, centers, or bottoms are equally distributed **B**.
   - Click a horizontal distribute icon to move the objects so that their left edges, centers, or right edges are equally distributed **C**.

You can also distribute objects based on their size. This ensures that the space between the objects is equal.

To distribute the space between objects:

1. Select three or more objects.

2. Click a distribute space icon as follows:
   - Click the vertical space icon to move objects so the vertical spaces between them are equal **D**.
   - Click the horizontal space icon to move objects so the horizontal spaces between them are equal **E**.

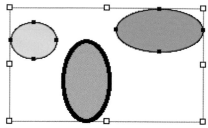

A The **designated key object** is indicated by a thick border.

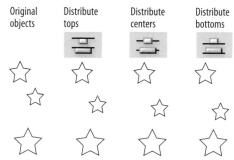

B Effects of the **vertical distribute icons**. Notice that the middle object changes position to create an even distribution.

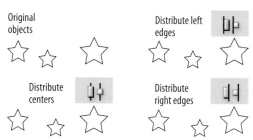

C Effects of the **horizontal distribute icons**. Notice that the middle object changes position to create an even distribution.

Original objects — Distribute vertical space

D Effect of the **vertical distribute space icon**.

Original objects — Distribute horizontal space

E The effect of the **horizontal distribute space command**.

Distribute Objects:

☑ Use Spacing 0p0

F The **Use Spacing option for Distribute Objects** lets you set a specific distance between the tops, centers, bottoms, or sides of objects.

Distribute Spacing:

☑ Use Spacing 0p0

G The **Use Spacing option for Distribute Spacing** lets you set a specific distance between objects.

The Align panel also has controls to space objects numerically. You can apply a numerical distance between the tops, centers, bottoms, or sides of objects.

To use spacing to distribute objects:

1. Select two or more objects.

2. Select Use Spacing in the Distribute Objects section of the Align panel **F**.

3. Enter the numerical distance in the Use Spacing field.

4. Click one of the Distribute Objects icons. Now the objects are separated by a specific space inserted between the tops, centers, bottoms, or sides of the objects.

TIP If a positive number moves the objects in the wrong direction, use a negative number.

You can also set a specific numerical distance between the objects themselves. This is very useful when you want the same amount of space between objects, but the objects themselves have different sizes.

To set the spacing between objects:

1. Select two or more objects.

2. Select Use Spacing in the Distribute Spacing section of the Align panel **G**.

3. Enter the numerical distance in the Use Spacing field.

4. Click one of the Distribute Spacing icons. Now a specific amount of space is added between the objects horizontally or vertically.

TIP If a positive number moves the objects in the wrong direction, use a negative number.

Smart Dimensions; Smart Spacing

Just as Smart Guides can align to margins and objects, they also give you feedback that can help you create an object that is the same size as another object on the page.

To show or hide Smart Guides:

Choose **Window > Grids & Guides > Smart Guides**. This turns the Smart Guides on or off.

One of the options for Smart Guides is the Smart Dimensions feature. This helps you create objects that have the same width or height.

To create objects with the same dimensions:

1. Create one object that has a certain width or height.
2. Drag to create a new object. As you drag, watch for a dimension arrow that appears next to the width or height 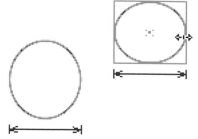. This is the Smart Dimension indicator that says the two objects have the same dimension.

Onother option for Smart Guides is the Smart Spacing feature. This make it easy to evenly distribute objects so that the spaces between them are equal.

To position objects with the same spacing:

1. Create two objects that have a certain space between them.
2. Position a third object on the page. As you drag, watch for the Smart Spacing indicators that appear between the objects . This indicates that the three objects are spaced evenly.

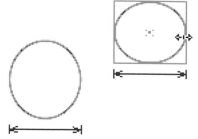

A The **Smart Dimension indicators** appear when an object is the same width or height as another.

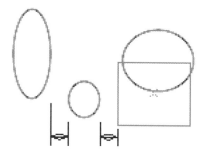

B The **Smart Spacing indicators** appear when an object is the same distance away from one object as it is from another.

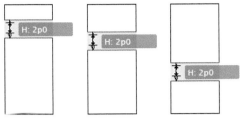

The **Gap tool in the Tools panel** changes the size of objects without affecting the size of the space between the objects.

As the Gap tool drags between two objects, the **size of the objects changes while the size of the gap remains constant.**

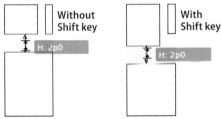

When the Shift key is pressed, the Gap tool effect is applied only to the **two objects closest to the cursor.**

Using the Gap Tool

Gaps are the spaces between objects. There may be times when you want to change the size of two objects, but keep the same amount of space (gap) between them. The Gap tool makes it very easy to change the width or height of the objects without affecting the size of the gap between them.

TIP The Gap tool can work on either horizontal or vertical gaps.

To use the Gap tool to resize objects:

1. Select the Gap tool in the Tools panel **C**.

2. Move the cursor inside the space between two objects. A gray highlight and double-headed gap cursor appear. This indicates that the gap space has been selected.

3. Drag the cursor up and down for horizontal gaps or left and right for vertical gaps. The gap remains constant while the sizes of the objects change **D**.

4. Use the following modifiers to change how the Gap tool works:

   - Hold the Shift key to apply the effects of the Gap tool to only the two objects closest to the cursor **E**.

   - Hold the Cmd/Ctrl key to resize the gap instead of moving it.

   - Hold the Opt/Alt key to move the objects and the gap without changing their sizes.

   - Hold the Cmd+Opt/Ctrl+Alt keys to resize the gap and move the objects.

TIP The Gap tool can be applied even if there is no space between two objects. The Gap tool then modifies the size of the objects without opening any space between them.

Grouping and Pasting Into Objects

You can group objects so you can easily select and modify them as a unit.

To group objects:

1. Select the objects you want to group.
2. Choose **Object** > **Group**. A dotted-line bounding box encloses all the objects .

You can also create groups within groups. This is called *nesting*.

To nest groups:

1. Select the grouped objects.
2. Hold the Shift key and select another object or group.
3. Choose **Object** > **Group**.

Once you have grouped objects, you can select individual objects within the group.

To select groups or objects within groups:

Click once on any item in the group. The group is selected as a whole.

or

Double-click to select a specific item in the group 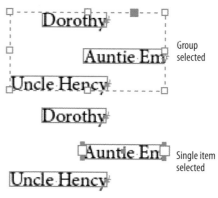.

TIP The first double-click may act like the Direct Selection tool and select just part of the object. If this happens, double-click again to select the entire item.

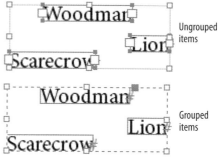

Ungrouped items

Grouped items

A When selected with the Selection tool, **grouped items display a dashed line around the group.**

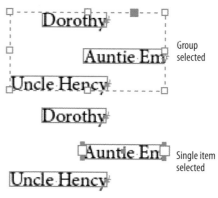

Group selected

Single item selected

B When selected with the Direct Selection tool, **a single item in a group is displayed on its own.**

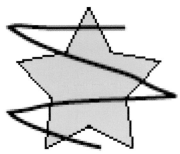

An object to be pasted into another should be positioned over the other.

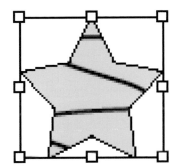

The **Paste Into command** displays the content only within the borders of the container.

To use commands to select objects within groups:

1. Use the Selection tool to select the group.

2. Choose **Object > Select > Content**. This selects the topmost object in the group.

3. Choose **Object > Select > Previous Object**. This selects the object that is layered below the selected object.

   or

   Choose **Object > Select > Next Object**. This selects the object that is directly above the selected object.

To ungroup objects:

1. Select the group.

2. Choose **Object > Ungroup**.

3. If you have nested groups, continue to ungroup the objects as necessary.

You can also paste an object into a frame. InDesign refers to the object that is pasted as the *content*. It refers to the frame that holds the object as the *container*.

To paste an object into another:

1. Select the first object and position it over the second object C.

2. Choose **Edit > Cut** to place the first object on the computer clipboard.

3. Select the second object and choose **Edit > Paste Into**. The content appears within the borders of the container D.

TIP To paste multiple objects, group the objects together.

To remove pasted-in content:

1. Use the Direct Selection tool to select the pasted-in content.

2. Choose **Edit > Cut**.

TIP The pasted-in content can be placed back on the page by choosing Edit > Paste.

Using the Measure Tool

There are many places where you can find the numerical sizes of items. But what if you want to measure the distance to another item? That's where the Measure tool is so helpful.

To measure distances using the Measure tool:

1. Choose **Window > Info** to open the Info panel.

TIP All amounts measured by the Measure tool are displayed in the Info panel.

2. Click the Measure tool in the Tools panel . The Measure tool is in the flyout menu under the Eyedropper tool.

3. Place the Measure tool on the start point and drag to the end point. A measuring line appears on the page **B**. The Info panel displays the following attributes **C**:

   - **Horizontal position** displays the X coordinate of the first point in the line or whichever point is then moved.

   - **Vertical position** displays the Y coordinate of the first point in the line or whichever point is then moved.

   - **Distance** shows the length of the line.

   - **Width** shows the width of the bounding box that would enclose the line.

   - **Height** shows the height of the bounding box that would enclose the line.

   - **Angle** shows the angle on which the line was drawn.

A The **Measure tool in the Tools panel**.

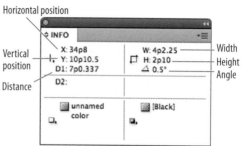

B **Drag the Measure tool** to measure the distance between two points.

C The **measurements displayed in the Info panel** for the measuring line drawn with the Measure tool.

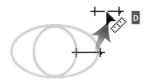

D Drag the line segment of the measuring line to move it to a new position.

E The **angle cursor** indicates that you are about to create a second measuring line.

F Two measuring lines let you measure angles with the Measure tool.

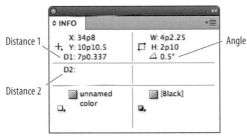

Distance 1

Distance 2

Angle

G The **Info panel display for two measuring lines**.

Once you have drawn a measuring line, you can move it to other areas of the page.

To move a measuring line:

1. With the Measure tool still selected, position the cursor over the measuring line.

2. Drag the line to a new position **D**.

TIP Do not position the cursor over the start or end points of the measuring line.

You can also change the start or end points of the measuring line.

To reposition the points of the measuring line:

1. With the Measure tool still selected, position the cursor over either point in the measuring line.

2. Drag the point to a new position.

You can also extend a second line out from the origin of the measuring line to create an electronic protractor to measure angles.

To measure angles:

1. Drag the first line with the Measure tool.

2. Hold the Opt/Alt key and move the Measure tool back to the origin of the first line. An angle cursor appears **E**.

3. Drag to create a second line extending out from the origin point **F**. The Info panel displays the distance of the second line, as well as the angle between the measuring lines **G**.

TIP No bounding box is displayed when two measuring lines are created.

Using the Info Panel with Objects

The Info panel also gives you information about the document, text, and placed images.

To see the document information:

Deselect any objects on the page. The Info panel displays the following 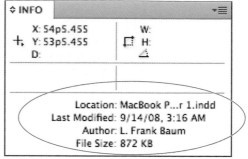:

- **Location** of the file on the computer.
- **Last Modification** date and time.
- **Author** as entered in the File Info (**File > File Info**) dialog box.
- **File size**.

To see the text information:

Place your insertion point inside a text frame or highlight the text in the frame. The Info panel displays the following **B**:

- **Characters** in the frame or selection.
- **Words** in the frame or selection.
- **Lines** in the frame or selection.
- **Paragraphs** in the frame or selection.

TIP If there is any overset text, it is displayed as a number with a plus sign.

To see the placed object information:

Select a frame that contains a placed image, or the placed image itself. The Info panel displays the following **C**:

- **Type** of placed image.
- **Actual ppi (points per inch)** resolution of the image.
- **Effective ppi** resolution of the image if you have scaled it in InDesign.
- **Color Space** of the image.
- **ICC Profile** (if applicable) may also be shown.

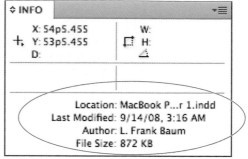

A With no objects selected, the Info panel displays **document information**.

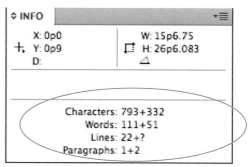

B With text selected, the Info panel displays **text information**.

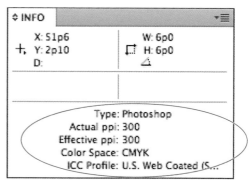

C With a placed image selected, the Info panel displays **placed image information**.

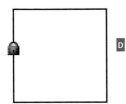

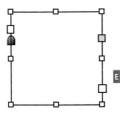

D The **Padlock cursor** indicates that the Lock Position command has been applied.

E An object that is locked and that has also been selected.

Object Editing ─────────────

☑ Prevent Selection of Locked Objects

F Deselect the preference **Prevent Selection of Locked Objects** to be able to select locked objects.

Locking Objects

You can also lock objects so they cannot be moved or modified. This prevents people from inadvertently destroying your layout.

To lock the position of an object:

With the object you want to lock selected, choose **Object > Lock Position**. A small padlock appears if you try to move or modify the object D.

To unlock objects:

Choose **Object > Unlock All on Spread**. This unlocks the objects and leaves them selected on the page.

TIP In previous versions of InDesign, locked objects were locked only for position. You could still select and change the colors and contents of locked objects E. If you want InDesign to work this older way, choose Preferences > General and deselect the option Prevent Selection of Locked Objects F.

Selecting Frames

Use this chart as a guide to let you know what type of object you have selected and which parts of the object can be selected using the Selection tool or the Direct Selection tool.

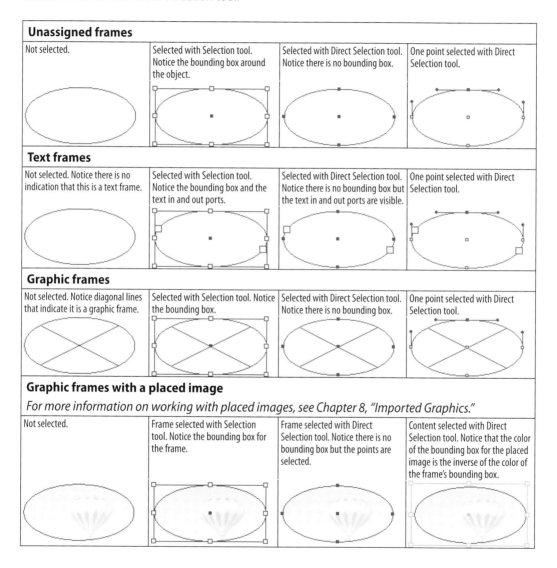

Unassigned frames

| Not selected. | Selected with Selection tool. Notice the bounding box around the object. | Selected with Direct Selection tool. Notice there is no bounding box. | One point selected with Direct Selection tool. |

Text frames

| Not selected. Notice there is no indication that this is a text frame. | Selected with Selection tool. Notice the bounding box and the text in and out ports. | Selected with Direct Selection tool. Notice there is no bounding box but the text in and out ports are visible. | One point selected with Direct Selection tool. |

Graphic frames

| Not selected. Notice diagonal lines that indicate it is a graphic frame. | Selected with Selection tool. Notice the bounding box. | Selected with Direct Selection tool. Notice there is no bounding box. | One point selected with Direct Selection tool. |

Graphic frames with a placed image

For more information on working with placed images, see Chapter 8, "Imported Graphics."

| Not selected. | Frame selected with Selection tool. Notice the bounding box for the frame. | Frame selected with Direct Selection tool. Notice there is no bounding box but the points are selected. | Content selected with Direct Selection tool. Notice that the color of the bounding box for the placed image is the inverse of the color of the frame's bounding box. |

Working in Color 5

When I first started in advertising, only the senior creative teams could work in color. The junior teams were assigned only black-and-white ads. Later on they might be able to work on a two-color job, but the four-color work was handled by senior art directors.

Fortunately, you're not limited by such constraints. InDesign gives you, right from the first day you use it, all the color controls you could ever wish for. However, with that power comes some responsibility.

When you define colors and use them on your pages, you are wearing two hats. Your first hat is that of a designer who looks at the aesthetics of the page and then applies colors. This is where you have fun with your creativity.

Your second hat is that of production manager. Wearing that hat you need to understand some of the principles of color and printing color documents. You also need to make sure your colors are defined so they print correctly.

The Basics of Color

Here's a quick primer to help you understand what happens when you define and apply colors in your InDesign layout, as well as other programs.

Type of color	How it is used	How it is created	Comments
CMYK	CMYK stands for the cyan, magenta, yellow, and black inks that are combined to create other colors. Also called process color, this is the primary type of color used in color printing. Most magazines and brochures are printed using the four process color inks.	Use the Color panel set to CMYK or the New Color Swatch dialog box set to CMYK or the Color Picker in the CMYK mode.	Color images are saved in the CMYK mode before they are imported into InDesign.
RGB	RGB stands for the red, green, and blue lights that are used in computer monitors to display colors. Because RGB colors are based on light waves, not inks, there will always be a slight difference between colors defined as RGB and those defined as CMYK. RGB colors can be used to define colors for documents that will be displayed onscreen. But you should not use them for print work.	Use the Color panel set to RGB or the New Color Swatch dialog box set to RGB or the Color Picker in the RGB mode.	Most digital cameras and scanners save images as RGB files. You must use a program such as Adobe Photoshop to convert those images to CMYK.
Lab	The Lab is another light-based color model that uses luminance (L) combined with the green to red (A) plus yellow to blue (B). As with RGB, you should not define print colors using this system.	Use the Color panel set to Lab or the New Color Swatch dialog box set to Lab or the Color Picker in the Lab mode.	

Type of color	How it is used	How it is created	Comments
Spot colors	Spot colors are specialty colors that are printed without using the four process color inks. For instance, a metallic gold in a brochure is printed using metallic gold ink, not a combination of CMYK colors. Spot colors can be mixed to display colors that could not be created using simple CMYK colors.	Use the New Color Swatch dialog box set to Spot.	Spot colors can be defined by the user or you can use the commercial spot color libraries produced by companies such as Pantone and Dicolor and Toyo. Other names for spot colors are specialty, second color, fifth or sixth color, or flat colors.
Tints	Tints are colors that have been screened so that only a percentage of their color appears on the page.	Tints can be created from named colors using the New Tint dialog box.	
Mixed inks	Mixed inks are combinations of at least one spot color and another spot or process color.	Mixed inks can be created using the Swatches panel menu. One spot color must also have been previously defined.	Mixed Ink Groups are combinations of different percentages for Mixed ink colors.

Using the Color Panel

There are three different models for defining colors: CMYK, RGB, and Lab. Each model is used for different purposes. You choose the color mode and mix colors in the Color panel. *(See Chapter 6, "Fills, Strokes, and Effects," for how to apply colors to objects and text.)*

To choose the options in the Color panel:

1. If the Color panel is not visible, choose **Window** > **Color** > **Color** to open the panel 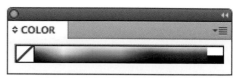.

2. If the color sliders are not visible, click the panel tab or choose Show Options from the Color panel menu **B**.

TIP Hold the Shift key as you drag one slider to have the others move along with it.

The CMYK color model is used primarily for print work. CMYK colors are mixed using percentages of the four inks used in process printing: cyan, magenta, yellow, and black.

To define CMYK colors:

1. Choose CMYK from the Color panel menu. This opens the panel in the CMYK mode **C**.

2. Choose one of the following methods to define the amount of cyan, magenta, yellow, or black ink in the color:

   • Type a value from 0 to 100 in each of the four color fields.

   • Drag the sliders for each of the four color fields.

   • Click a color in the CMYK spectrum area.

TIP Click the solid white or black rectangles to the right end of the spectrum to quickly get 100 percent black or white.

A The **Color panel** with the options hidden shows only the spectrum or ramp for choosing colors.

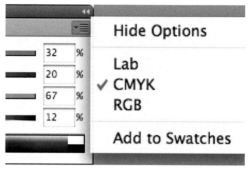

B The **Color panel menu** lets you choose among the three color models.

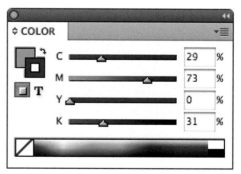

C The **Color panel with the CMYK** (cyan, magenta, yellow, and black) color controls.

The Black Color Panel

If your Color panel displays a single slider for Black, it is because the Black color in the Swatches panel is your default color. Simply change it to CMYK to get the full set of CMYK color sliders.

Understanding CMYK Color

Each of the colors in CMYK corresponds to one of the inks used in typical four-color printing. Cyan is a shade of blue. Magenta is a shade of red. Yellow is … well, yellow. And black is black — I want my baby back.

If you are creating print documents, you will want to define your colors using CMYK colors. Not only is the CMYK system overwhelmingly used for print work, it is the system you are most familiar with, whether you're aware of it or not. Yellow and cyan make green; magenta and yellow make orange, and so on.

In theory, you shouldn't need more than three colors for printing. If you mix cyan, magenta, and yellow together, you should get a solid black color. In reality, however, those inks are not pure enough to create solid black; instead they create a dark brown.

That's why process printing uses four colors. In addition to cyan, magenta, and yellow, a fourth key color — black, indicated by the letter K — is added to create the really black areas. That's where the term CMYK comes from.

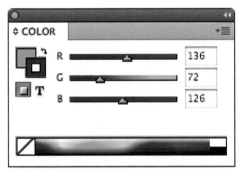

D The **Color panel set for mixing RGB** (red, green, blue) color controls for onscreen display such as Web sites.

Mixing Colors in RGB

Maybe some Web designers and video engineers can think in RGB, but I confess, I can't. With the RGB sliders, red plus green creates yellow; green plus blue creates a shade of cyan, and all three colors together create white. To create black, you set all three colors to zero. It's the exact opposite of CMYK where the four colors combine to create black.

The RGB color model is used primarily for onscreen work such as presentations and Web sites. The RGB colors — red, green, and blue — are mixed using representations of the three colors of light. This is what you see on television screens and computer monitors. RGB colors have a wider range of colors than CMYK colors.

To mix RGB colors:

1. Choose RGB from the Color panel menu. This opens the panel in the RGB mode **D**.

2. Choose one of the following methods to define the amount of red, green, or blue in the color:

   • Type the value from 0 to 255 in each of the three color fields.

   • Drag the sliders for each of the three color fields.

   • Click a color in the RGB spectrum area.

The Lab color model defines colors according to a *luminance* (lightness) component, and two color components, a and b. The a component defines green to red values. The b component defines blue to yellow values. Lab colors are device-independent so that colors don't change from one source to another.

TIP The proper name for Lab is L*A*B and is pronounced by spelling out the name (*el-ay-bee*), not by saying the word "Lab."

To mix Lab colors:

1. Choose Lab from the Color panel menu. This opens the panel in the Lab mode 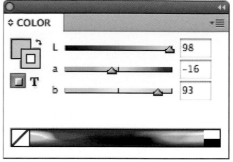.

2. Choose one of the following methods to define the three components of the color:
   - Type the value from 0 to 100 in the L field or type the value from -128 to 127 in the a or b field.
   - Drag the sliders for each of the fields.
   - Click a color in the Lab spectrum area.

The out-of-gamut symbol appears if you choose an RGB or Lab color that cannot be printed using process inks **B**.

To convert out-of-gamut colors:

Click the small square next to the out-of-gamut symbol. This converts the color to the closest process-color equivalent.

You can use the Color panel to apply colors to selected objects.

TIP This technique, although convenient to use, creates unnamed colors or colors that are not listed in the Swatches panel. *(See the sidebar "Avoiding Unnamed Colors" for why creating unnamed colors can be a problem.)*

A The **Lab Color panel** mixes colors that look consistent no matter whether you print them or display them onscreen.

Out-of-gamut symbol

Color conversion square

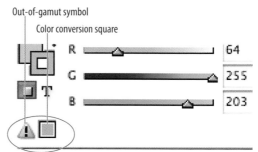

B The **out-of-gamut symbol** for RGB or Lab colors indicates that the color shown on screen will not print as seen using process color inks.

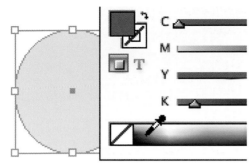

C With an object selected, **click the color ramp in the Color panel** to apply a color to an object.

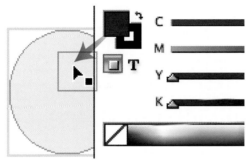

D **Drag a color from the Color panel** to apply a color to an object.

To apply colors to a fill or stroke:

With an object or text selected, use the Color panel to define a fill color. This applies the unnamed color to the fill of the object or text.

or

With an object or text selected, use the Color panel to define a stroke color. This applies the unnamed color to the stroke of the object or text.

TIP You can choose colors by clicking the ramp section of the Color panel **C**.

TIP You can also drag a color directly from the Color panel onto objects **D**. This also creates unnamed colors.

TIP A square dot appears next to the cursor when you drag a swatch color onto objects. This indicates you are dragging a fill color onto the object.

You can add colors from the Color panel to the Swatches panel so you can easily reuse them.

To transfer colors from the Color panel:

1. Define the color in the Color panel.
2. Choose Add to Swatches from the Color panel menu. The color appears as a new color swatch in the Swatches panel.

Defining and Storing Swatches

Although it is very quick to create a color using the Color panel, you will find it more efficient to create color *swatches*. A swatch is a color that has been defined and is stored in the Swatches panel.

TIP Unnamed colors are not available for all places where you use colors. For instance, only named color swatches can be used as part of text styles. So it is helpful to define colors as swatches before you do too much work later.

To work with the Swatches panel:

1. If the Swatches panel is not visible, choose **Window** > **Color** > **Swatches** to open the panel 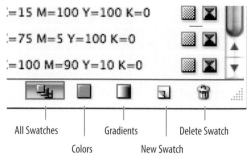.

2. To see the different types of swatches, click the icons at the bottom of the panel as follows:

   - **Show All Swatches** displays both the color and the gradient swatches.
   - **Show Color Swatches** displays only the color swatches.
   - **Show Gradient Swatches** displays only the gradient swatches.

3. To change the display of the swatches in the panel, choose the following from the Swatches panel menu:

   - **Name** displays a list of the swatch names in a large typeface.
   - **Small Name** uses a more compact typeface to display the swatch names.
   - **Small Swatch** displays only the square of the swatch color or gradient.
   - **Large Swatch** displays a larger square of the swatch color or gradient.

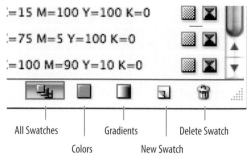

All Swatches   Gradients   Delete Swatch
Colors   New Swatch

A The **controls for the Swatches panel**.

The Color "Paper"

The swatch labeled [Paper] in the Swatches panel allows you to change the background color of the pages in your document. This can be helpful if your document will be printed on colored paper, specialty paper, or even newsprint that is not completely white. You can modify the paper color to help judge how your images will look when printed.

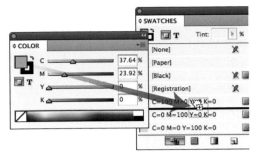

B You can **drag colors from the Color panel** into the Swatches panel.

The Registration Color

"Registration" is a color that is set to print on all plates of a document. For instance, if your document will be printed using process colors, you might want to create a note or mark that should be seen on all four plates. Rather than make the note in a combination of cyan, magenta, yellow, and black, you can apply the color Registration to the text for the note. This prints the note as a combination of all four inks.

Although you can apply colors to objects and text directly from the Color panel, this is not considered a good production workflow. Instead, use the Swatches panel to add the color currently defined in the Color panel.

TIP If you apply colors from the Color panel, they are called unnamed colors. Unnamed colors can cause production problems later on and should be avoided.

To add a color to the Swatches panel:

1. Use the Color panel to define a color.

2. Click the New Swatch icon at the bottom of the panel. The new color, named with the color values, is automatically added to the Swatches panel.

TIP You can also add colors to the Swatches panel using the Color Picker.

InDesign also lets you drag colors from the Color panel into the Swatches panel.

To drag colors into the Swatches panel:

1. Create the color in the Color panel.

2. Drag the color from the Color panel fill or stroke box to the bottom of or between two colors in the Swatches panel.

3. Release the mouse button when a black line appears in the Swatches panel **B**. The new color is added and automatically takes its name from the color values.

TIP The cursor displays a plus sign as you drag the color into the Swatches panel. On the Mac the cursor is the image of a fist. On Windows the cursor is an arrow.

You can define and add new colors to your document using only the Swatches panel.

To define a new color swatch:

1. Choose New Color Swatch from the Swatches panel menu. This opens the New Color Swatch dialog box 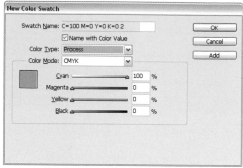.

   or

   Opt/Alt-click the New Swatch icon at the bottom of the Swatches panel.

2. To name the color swatch yourself, deselect the checkbox for Name with Color Value and then type a name in the Swatch Name field.

   or

   Leave the setting selected to name the color swatch using the values that define the color. This option is not available for spot colors.

3. Choose Process or Spot from the Color Type pop-up list **B**.

4. Choose Lab, CMYK, or RGB from the Color Mode menu **C**.

   or

   Choose one of the Swatch Libraries at the bottom of the Color Mode menu **C**.

5. If you have chosen Lab, CMYK, or RGB, use the sliders to change the values from the ones originally defined.

6. Click OK. This adds the swatch and closes the dialog box.

   or

   Click Add to add the swatch without closing the dialog box. This allows you to define additional colors.

A Use the **New Color Swatch dialog box** to define colors to be added to the Swatches panel.

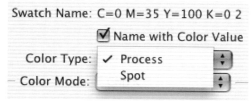

B Use the **Color Type menu** to choose either process or spot colors.

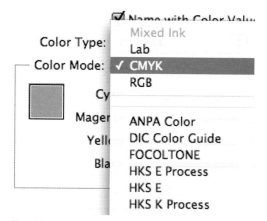

C The **Color Mode menu** in the New Swatch dialog box.

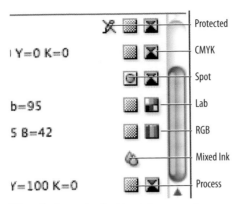

Protected
CMYK
Spot
Lab
RGB
Mixed Ink
Process

Y=0 K=0

b=95

S B=42

Y=100 K=0

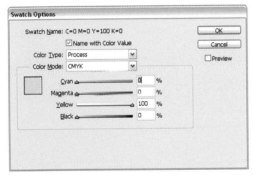

D The **icons in the Swatches panel** identify the different types of colors and color modes.

E Once you define a swatch, you modify it in the **Swatch Options dialog box**.

The colors that appear in the Swatches panel are displayed with icons that give you information about the type of color, the color mode, and other attributes **D**. Of course, once you have defined a color swatch, you can modify its color definition. This changes the appearance of all text and objects that use that color, even if they are not selected.

TIP The color Black is protected and cannot be modified. If you need a variation of Black, create a new color swatch.

To modify a color swatch:

1. Select the swatch and choose Swatch Options from the Swatches panel menu. This opens the Swatch Options dialog box **E**. These are the same controls as in the New Color Swatch dialog box.

   or

   Double-click the swatch in the panel.

2. Make changes to the color.

TIP Select the Preview checkbox to see how the changes affect the colors applied to objects in the document.

3. Click OK to apply the changes.

TIP The Swatch Options dialog box does not have an Add button. This is because you use this dialog box only to modify existing colors — not to add new ones.

Process or Spot?

Process colors are those printed using small dots of the four process inks: cyan, magenta, yellow, and black. Spot colors are printed using special inks. For example, if you look at the process-color green printed in a magazine, that color is actually a combination of cyan and yellow printed together in a series of dots. However, a spot-color green is printed by using actual green ink.

One benefit of spot colors is that you can exactly match a special color or use specialty colors such as fluorescents or metallics that could never be created using process inks. You can also use a spot color together with black as a two-color job. This is cheaper than printing four-color process colors. The benefit of process colors is that you use just four inks to create thousands of different color combinations.

Once you create color swatches, you can apply them via the Fill and Stroke controls.

To apply a swatch color:

1. Create the object or text that you want to color.

2. Select either the Fill or Stroke icons in the Color panel, Tools panel, or Control panel. *(See Chapter 6, "Fills, Strokes, and Effects," for more information on using the Fill and Stroke icons.)*

3. Click the color in the Swatches panel. This applies the swatch to the object.

To delete swatches:

1. Select the color you want to delete.

TIP To select a series of adjacent swatches, select the first swatch and then hold the Shift key and select the last swatch in the series. This highlights the first and last swatch and all the swatches in between.

TIP Hold the Cmd/Ctrl key to select nonadjacent swatches.

2. Click the Delete Swatch icon **A** or choose Delete Swatch from the Swatches menu.

3. If the swatch is used within the document, the Delete Swatch dialog box appears, asking how you want to replace the deleted swatch **B**:

   • To swap the color with one from the Swatches panel, choose Defined Swatch and then pick a swatch from the pop-up list.

   • To leave the color as an unnamed color applied to the object, choose Unnamed Swatch.

TIP The default swatches None, Paper, Black, and Registration cannot be deleted.

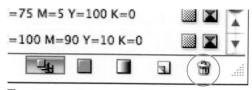

A Click the **Delete Swatch icon** to delete the selected swatches.

B The **Delete Swatch dialog box controls** what happens to colors when they are deleted from a document.

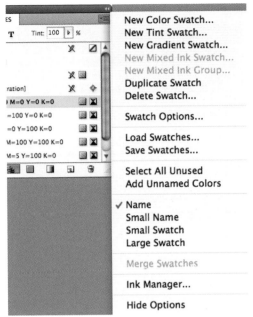

The **Swatches panel menu** contains the commands for working with color swatches.

If you have many colors in your document that you are not using, you may want to delete them to avoid confusion when the file is sent to a print shop.

To delete all unused swatches:

1. Choose Select All Unused in the Swatches panel menu **C**.

2. Click the Delete Swatch icon or use the Delete Swatch command in the Swatches panel menu.

You can also select several swatches and merge them into one color.

TIP The Merge Swatches command makes it easy to globally replace all instances of one defined color with another.

To merge swatches:

1. Click to select the first color. This is the final color that you want the other colors to change to.

2. Hold the Cmd/Ctrl key and click to select another swatch. This is the color that you want to delete.

    or

    Hold the Shift key and click to select a range of swatches. These are the swatches you want to delete.

3. Choose Merge Swatches from the Swatches panel menu **C**. This deletes all the swatches except the swatch that was first selected. That swatch is applied to all text and objects that used the deleted swatches.

The position that swatches occupy in the panel comes from the order in which they were created. You can easily change the order of the swatches.

To move swatches to new positions:

1. Select a swatch in the panel.

2. Drag the swatch to a new position. A black line indicates where the swatch will be located 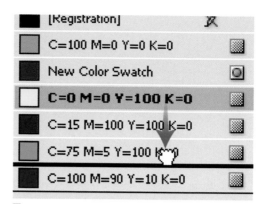.

3. Release the mouse button.

You may find it easier to duplicate a swatch and modify it than to start from scratch.

To duplicate a swatch:

Select the swatch and choose Duplicate Swatch from the Swatches panel menu.

or

Select the swatch and click the New Swatch icon.

or

Drag the swatch onto the New Swatch icon.

You can save a selection of swatches for use in other InDesign documents, or in Adobe Illustrator or Adobe Photoshop documents.

To save selected swatches:

1. Select the swatches in the Swatches panel that you want to save.

2. Choose Save Swatches from the Swatches panel menu.

3. Use the operating system dialog box to save the swatches as an Adobe Swatch Exchange (.ase) file.

A   **Drag a swatch** to move it from one position to another.

The Cost of Unused Colors

Why is it important to delete unused colors?

One reason is if you are going to send your documents to a service bureau or print shop for final output. It can be confusing to the people who are going to open your file if they see many colors in a document that's supposed to be printed in black and white.

At the very least, they're going to wonder if they've received the right instructions. At the worst, they'll delay printing the file until they talk to someone to make sure.

Also, it may seem like a little thing, but every color adds to the size of the file. Even in these days of huge hard drives, it's always better to keep your files as lean as possible.

You can import the swatches from one InDesign document into another. You can also import the swatches from an Adobe Swatch Exchange file.

To import swatches from other documents:

1. Choose Load Swatches from the Swatches panel menu. The operating system dialog box appears.

2. Navigate to find the document or Adobe Swatch Exchange file you want to import swatches from.

3. Click Open. The swatches are imported into the current document.

Unnamed colors are colors that are applied to objects directly from the Color panel or the Color Picker instead of through the Swatches panel. It is a good idea not to have unnamed colors floating around your document. Fortunately, you can easily convert unnamed colors into named colors.

To name unnamed colors:

Choose Add Unnamed Colors from the Swatches panel menu. All unnamed colors are added to the panel named with their percentage values.

You can create colors that are available as the default colors for all new documents.

To create default colors:

1. Close all documents but leave InDesign running.

2. Use any of the methods in this section, "Defining and Storing Swatches," to define and store a color in the Swatches panel. The color will appear in the Swatches panel of all new InDesign documents.

Using Swatch Libraries

Rather than defining your own color mixtures, you can use the swatch libraries for professional color systems from companies such as Pantone or Trumatch. These color libraries usually have printed samples that you can refer to in order to see how the color will appear when printed.

To add colors from swatch libraries:

1. Open the New Color Swatch dialog box or the Swatch Options dialog box.

2. Choose one of the swatch libraries listed in the Color Mode list 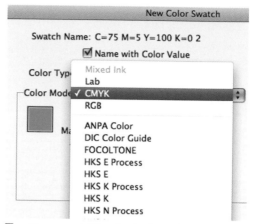. This displays the colors in the library 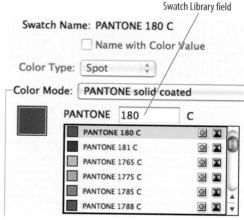.

3. Scroll through the library to select the color you want to add to your document.

   or

   Instead of scrolling through a long list, type the name or number associated with the color in the Swatch Library field. You can use the swatch libraries to open color panels from other InDesign documents and Adobe Illustrator documents.

Every InDesign document acts like its own color library. You can then open the colors in an InDesign document just as you do when opening a commercial color library.

To import swatches from other documents:

1. Choose Other Library from the Color Mode list **A**.

2. Navigate to select the InDesign document that contains the colors you want to use.

A The **swatch libraries** in the Color Mode list.

B An example of the window that displays **a swatch library**, such as the Pantone Solid Coated colors.

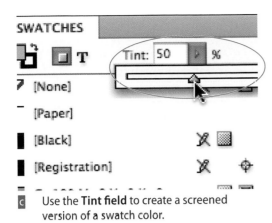

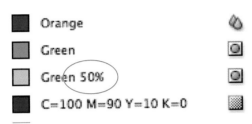

C Use the **Tint field** to create a screened version of a swatch color.

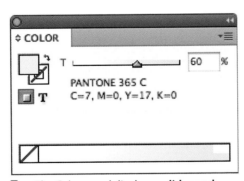

D A **tint swatch** is listed with the same name as the base color and the tint percentage.

E The Color panel displays **a slider and tint ramp** when a base color is chosen.

Creating Tints

To create a tint swatch:

1. Select the *base color*, that is, the swatch color that you want to tint.

2. Use the Tint field in the Swatches panel to create a screen of the swatch color C.

3. Click the New Swatch icon to store the tint percentage as a swatch in the Swatches panel.

TIP The tint swatch appears in the Swatches panel with the same name as the base color but with the tint percentage listed D.

TIP The tint field percentage continues to tint other swatches in the panel until you reset the field to 100%.

As you select a color swatch as a base color, the Color panel displays a slider and a ramp of the color.

To tint a swatch using the Color panel:

1. Select the swatch color that you want to tint.

2. In the Color panel, use the slider or click in the ramp to create a percentage of the base color E.

3. Click the New Swatch icon to create a tint swatch of the percentage you defined.

You can also create a tint swatch using the Swatches panel menu.

To store a tint swatch of a color:

1. In the Swatches panel, select the base color, that is, the color you want to tint.

2. Choose New Tint Swatch from the Swatches panel menu. The New Tint Swatch dialog box appears 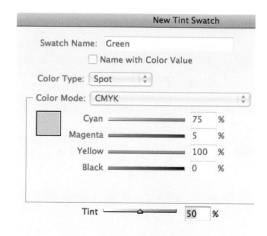.

3. Adjust the tint slider to a percentage.

4. Click OK. The tint swatch appears in the Swatches panel with the same name as the base color but with the tint percentage listed.

   or

   Click Add to add the tint to the Swatches panel and then create additional tints.

Once you store a tint swatch, you can modify the tint percentage. This updates all the objects that use that tint swatch.

To modify tint swatches:

1. Double-click the name of the tint swatch in the Swatches panel. This opens the Swatch Options dialog box for tints.

2. To change the tint value, adjust the Tint slider at the bottom of the dialog box.

3. Click OK to apply the changes.

TIP Anytime you modify the swatch used as a base color, all tints of that color update automatically.

A The **New Tint Swatch dialog box** lets you set the percentage of a tint.

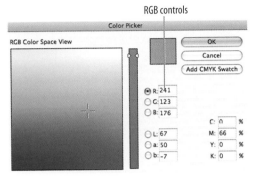

The **Fill and Stroke icons** let you open the Color Picker.

RGB controls

The **Color Picker in the RGB mode** lets you define and store RGB colors.

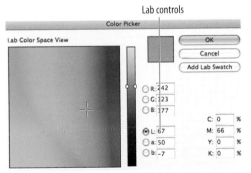

Lab controls

The **Color Picker in the Lab mode** lets you define and store Lab colors.

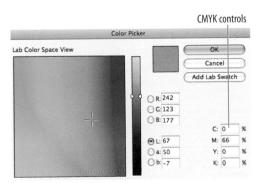

CMYK controls

The **CMYK controls** let you define and store CMYK colors.

Using the Color Picker

If you have used Photoshop, you are probably familiar with Photoshop's Color Picker, which is accessed through the foreground or background color icons in the Tools panel. InDesign also has a Color Picker, which is opened through the Tools panel.

To define a color using the Color Picker:

1. Double-click either the Fill icon or the Stroke icon in the Tools panel. This opens the Color Picker.

2. Use the RGB, Lab, or CMYK fields and to define the color.

3. Click OK to apply the color to the current fill or stroke.

TIP When you click the RGB or Lab controls, the Color Space area at the left of the dialog displays one of those color controls. When you click the CMYK controls, however, the Color Space area does not display the CMYK color controls.

To define a color swatch using the Color Picker:

1. Double-click either the Fill icon or the Stroke icon in the Tools panel to open the Color Picker.

2. Use the RGB, Lab, or CMYK fields to define the color.

3. Click the Add [RGB, Lab, or CMYK] Swatch button to add the color to the Swatches panel.

4. Click OK to close the Color Picker.

Creating Gradient Swatches

Gradients are blends that change from one color into another. InDesign creates gradients as swatches that can then be applied to objects. *(See Chapter 6, "Fills, Strokes, and Effects," for information on applying gradients.)*

To define a gradient:

1. Choose New Gradient Swatch from the Swatches panel menu. The New Gradient Swatch dialog box appears **A**.

2. Enter a name for the gradient in the Swatch Name field.

3. Choose Linear or Radial in the Type field **B**.

4. Click a color stop on the gradient ramp to define a color in the gradient **C**.

5. Choose the type of color for the selected stop from the Stop Color list **D**:

   - Swatches shows you the list of colors in the Swatches panel.

   - Lab, CMYK, or RGB displays the sliders that let you define the color using the Lab, CMYK, or RGB values.

6. Click the other gradient stop to define a color for it.

7. Adjust the midpoint control to change the position where the two colors blend equally.

8. Click OK to add the gradient to the Swatches panel **E**.

   or

   Click the Add button to add the current gradient to the Swatches panel and continue defining additional gradients.

TIP If you don't see the gradient listed in the Swatches panel, click either the Show All Swatches or Show Gradient Swatches icon at the bottom of the Swatches panel.

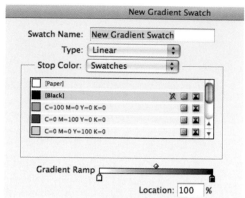

A Use the **New Gradient Swatch dialog box** to define a gradient of blended colors.

B A linear gradient changes colors along a line. A radial gradient changes colors in a circular pattern.

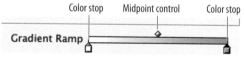

C Use the color stops and midpoint controls along the gradient ramp to modify a gradient.

D Use the **Stop Color menu** to choose the format for the colors used for the color stops.

White to blue

White to blue radial

Yellow to Magenta

E Gradients are stored in the **Swatches panel**.

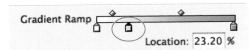

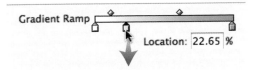

F Click under the gradient ramp to add a color stop to the gradient.

G Drag a color stop off the gradient ramp to delete that color from the gradient.

All gradients must have at least two colors. However, you can easily add more colors to a gradient by using the color stops.

To add gradient color stops:

1. Open the New Gradient Swatch dialog box.

   or

   Select a gradient and choose Swatch Options from the Swatches panel menu.

2. Click the area below the gradient ramp. This adds a color stop to the ramp area **F**.

3. Make whatever changes you want to the color stop.

4. If necessary, move the color stop to a new position.

5. Click OK to apply the changes to the gradient swatch.

To delete a gradient color stop:

Drag the color stop away from the ramp area and release the mouse button **G**. The gradient reblends according to the colors that remain.

To modify a gradient swatch:

1. Select the gradient swatch and choose Swatch Options from the Swatches panel menu. This opens the Gradient Options dialog box.

   or

   Double-click the gradient in the panel.

   TIP Use the Preview checkbox to see how the changes affect the gradients in the document.

2. Adjust the midpoint, color stops, or gradient type.

3. Click OK to apply the changes.

Just as you can create colors on the fly, you can also create gradients without using the Swatches panel. These gradients are created only within the Gradient panel and are not stored in the Swatches panel.

To work with the Gradient panel:

1. Choose **Window > Gradient** to open the Gradient panel 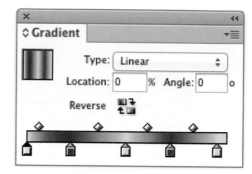.

2. Choose Show Options from the Gradient panel menu to see all the controls.

To create gradients from the Gradient panel:

1. Use the Type pop-up list to choose between Linear and Radial.

2. Select a color stop and adjust the sliders in the Color panel to define the color at that position.

   or

   Hold the Opt/Alt key and click the name of a swatch in the Swatches panel.

3. Select another color stop and use the sliders in the Color panel to define the color at that position.

4. Set the angle of the gradient in the Angle field.

5. Click the Reverse icon to reverse the positions of the color stops.

Once you have defined a gradient in the Gradient panel, you can store it as a swatch.

To store an unnamed gradient:

1. Create the gradient in the Gradient panel.

2. Click the New Swatch icon in the Swatches panel.

   or

   Drag the preview of the gradient from the Gradient panel into the Swatches panel.

3. Double-click the name of the gradient in the Swatches panel to rename it.

A Use the **Gradient panel** to create on-the-fly gradients.

Process and Spot Colors in Gradients

A gradient that's defined using process colors is separated onto CMYK plates.

A gradient that contains two tints of the same spot color will be separated onto the single spot color plate. If you want the gradient to fade to white, create a gradient between the spot color and a 0% tint of the spot color.

You can create a gradient between two spot colors. However, to avoid moiré patterns in the gradient, you must assign different screen angles to those spot colors in the Inks dialog box.

For instance, if you had a gradient of spot red to spot yellow, you would want to make sure each color had a screen angle that was 45 degrees different from the other. Ask your print shop for details on setting the screen angles for spot colors.

A gradient that contains both spot and process colors will be separated onto both the spot and process color plates.

B The **Eyedropper tool** lets you sample colors from placed images.

C Click with the **Eyedropper tool** over an area of an image that you want to sample.

Using the Eyedropper

The Eyedropper tool lets you sample colors from graphics that are placed in your document. *(See Chapter 8, "Imported Graphics," for more information on placing graphics.)*

To sample and store colors from placed graphics:

1. Click the Eyedropper tool in the Tools panel **B**.
2. Move the Eyedropper cursor over the color of a placed graphic.
3. Click to sample the color **C**.

TIP If you have already used the Eyedropper to sample a color, hold the Opt/Alt key to sample a new color.

4. Click the New Swatch icon in the Swatches panel. The sampled color is stored as a color swatch.

TIP The Eyedropper samples the color in the same color mode as the placed graphic. So RGB images yield RGB colors, and CMYK images yield CMYK colors.

TIP The Eyedropper can also sample and apply fills, strokes, and transparency attributes of objects and text formatting. *(See Chapter 6, "Fills, Strokes, and Effects," and Chapter 14, "Automating Your Work.")*

Overprinting Colors

Overprinting is a technique that allows you to set the color of one object to mix with any colors underneath. For instance, without overprinting, a yellow object placed over a blue background knocks out the blue and prints as yellow. But with overprinting turned on, the yellow object mixes with the blue background to create green.

To set a fill or stroke to overprint:

1. Select the object.
2. If the Attributes panel is not visible, choose **Window > Output > Attributes** to open the panel 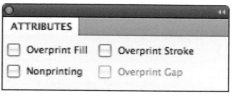.
3. Select Overprint Fill to set the object's fill color to overprint.
4. Select Overprint Stroke to set the object's stroke color to overprint.
5. Select Overprint Gap to set the color of the gap applied to stroke effects to overprint.

TIP Select Nonprinting in the Attributes panel to set an object not to print. This is helpful if you want to add comments for production use that aren't meant to be seen in the finished piece.

InDesign lets you see a simulation of over-printing onscreen.

To turn on the overprint preview:

Choose **View > Overprint Preview.** InDesign shows the effects of those colors set to overprint 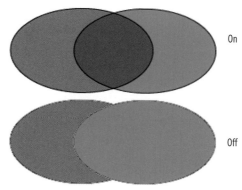.

A Use the **Attributes panel** to set the colors of an object to overprint.

B Turn on the **Overprint Preview command** to see the effects of overprinting onscreen.

Fills, Strokes, and Effects 6

Here's where you get a chance to express your creativity. Styling refers to applying fills, strokes, gradients, and effects to frames, lines, and text. If you're bored with plain black text on a white background, InDesign lets you change the text and background colors to almost anything you can imagine.

Most other graphics programs let you style objects and text with fills, strokes, and gradients. InDesign certainly does that also.

However, InDesign offers a plethora of amazing effects such as transparency, drop shadows, and glows. Although it has always been possible to create these effects in programs like Adobe Photoshop, having them in a page layout program makes it very convenient to apply those effects on the fly.

Meanwhile, it is *not* true that the Adobe End User Licensing Agreement (EULA) requires you to apply a drop shadow to every job you do in InDesign.

Applying Fills

Fills are the effects applied to objects, which can be the interior of frames or text within a frame. So you can apply one color fill to the text inside a frame and another color fill to the frame itself. A fill can be a solid color or a gradient.

To apply a fill to an object:

1. Select an object.

2. Make sure the Container icon is chosen in the Tools panel or the Swatches or Color panel **A**. This indicates that the object will be modified.

3. Click the Fill icon in the Tools panel or in the Swatches or Color panel **B**.

4. Choose a color or gradient in the Color, Gradient, or Swatches panel.

You don't have to select an object to apply a fill. You can just drag a swatch onto any object to apply a color or a gradient.

To drag fill effects onto objects:

1. Drag a gradient or color swatch from the Tools panel or the Color, Gradient, or Swatches panel onto the object **C**.

2. Release the mouse button when the swatch is inside the object. A square dot appears to indicate you are inside the object.

TIP If you release the mouse button when the swatch is on the edge of the object, you will apply the effect to the object's stroke instead of the fill.

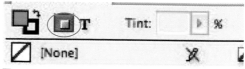

A The **Container icon** indicates an effect will be applied to an object, not text.

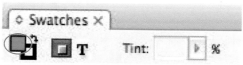

B The **Fill icon** indicates an effect will be applied inside an object.

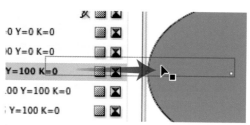

C You can drag a swatch inside an object to apply a fill.

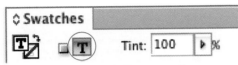

D Choose a swatch to apply the color or gradient to selected text.

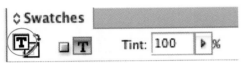

E The **Text icon** (circled) sets an effect to be applied to all the text within a frame.

F The **T inside the Fill icon** (circled) indicates that text is going to be styled.

G The **Gradient icon in the Tools panel** indicates that a color or gradient will be applied.

H The **gradient in the Fill box** indicates that the gradient will be applied as a fill.

You can also apply fill colors to selected text in a text frame.

To apply a fill to selected text:

1. Use the Text tool to highlight the text.
2. Click the Fill icon in the Tools panel or the Swatches or Color panel.
3. Choose a swatch in the Color, Gradient, or Swatches panel **D**.

TIP When text is highlighted, the color of the text is inverted. Deselect to see the actual text color.

You can also apply a fill to all the text in a frame with just the frame selected.

To apply a fill to all the text in a frame:

1. Select the text frame that contains the text to which you want to apply the fill.
2. Click the Fill icon in the Tools panel or the Swatches or Color panel.
3. Click the Text icon in the Tools panel or the Swatches or Color panel **E**.

TIP The *T* inside the Fill icon indicates the text will be affected, not the frame **F**.

4. Choose a swatch in the Color, Gradient, or Swatches panel.

You can also apply a gradient to text or objects.

To apply a gradient fill:

1. Click the Fill icon in the Tools panel or the Swatches or Color panel with the container or text icons selected.
2. Click the Gradient icon in the Tools panel **G**.

   or

   Click a gradient in the Swatches or Gradient panel. The gradient is displayed in the Fill box **H**.

Once you have applied a gradient to an object or text, you can modify how it is applied using the Gradient tool.

To adjust a gradient fill:

1. Select the object that contains the gradient you want to modify.

2. Choose the Gradient tool in the Tools panel .

3. Drag the Gradient tool along the angle that the linear gradient should follow 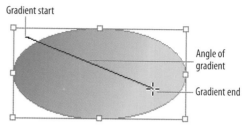.

   or

   Drag the Gradient tool to define the start and end points of a radial gradient .

TIP The start of the drag positions the first color. The end of the drag positions the final color.

A The **Gradient tool in the Tools panel** lets you modify the appearance of gradients.

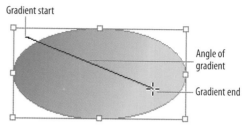

Gradient start

Angle of gradient

Gradient end

B Drag the Gradient tool to set the start and end points and the angle of a **linear gradient**.

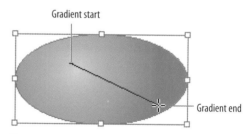

Gradient start

Gradient end

C Drag with the Gradient tool to set the start and end points of a **radial gradient**.

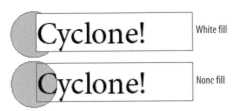
White fill

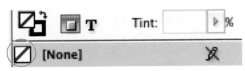
None fill

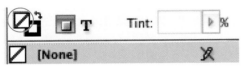

D The difference between a text frame with a white fill and a none fill.

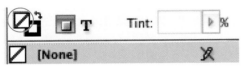

E The **None icon** (circled) removes the color applied to an object.

F The **None symbol in the Fill icon** (circled) indicates there is no color for the fill applied to the object.

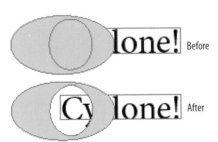
Before

After

G An example of how a compound path creates a hole in an object.

You can also apply a fill of None to an object. This makes the background of the object transparent **D**.

To apply a fill of None:

1. Select the object.

2. Click the None icon in the Tools panel or the Swatches or Color panel **E**.

TIP If the object is not in front of others, you may not see a difference between a white and a none fill. Check the icon to be sure **F**.

Another way to style objects is to create a compound path. A compound path allows one path to punch a hole in another. This makes the inside path transparent while the outside path is solid **G**.

To create a compound path:

1. Select two paths that overlap.

2. Choose **Object > Paths > Make Compound Path.**

TIP If the second object is not completely contained inside the first, the hole appears only where the objects overlap.

TIP Compound paths must contain the same fill and stroke effects.

You can release a compound path back to separate objects to restore the inside path to a solid color.

To release a compound path:

1. Select the compound path.

2. Choose **Object > Paths > Release Compound Paths.**

Applying Stroke Effects

Strokes are the effects applied to the edge of objects and text, or along lines.

To apply a stroke to an object:

1. Select the object.

2. Make sure the Container icon is chosen in the Tools panel or the Swatches or Color panel. This indicates that the object will be modified.

3. Click the Stroke icon in the Tools panel or the Swatches or Color panel .

4. Choose a swatch in the Color, Gradient, or Swatches panel.

You can also apply a stroke color by dragging a swatch onto the edge of any object on the page.

To drag stroke effects onto objects:

1. Drag a gradient or color swatch from the Tools panel or the Color, Gradient, or Swatches panel onto the edge of the object.

2. Release the mouse button when you see a small line appear next to the mouse cursor **B**. This applies the color or gradient to the stroke.

TIP If you release the mouse button when the swatch is inside the object, you apply the effect to the object's fill instead of the stroke.

InDesign makes it easy to swap the fill and stroke colors applied to an object.

To swap the fill and stroke settings:

Click the double-headed arrow in the Tools panel **C**. This switches the colors of the fill and stroke applied to the object.

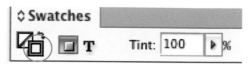

A The **Stroke icons** (circled) set an effect to be applied to the outside of an object or text.

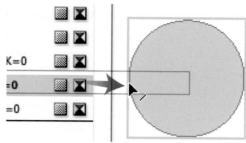

B Drag a swatch onto the edge to apply a stroke effect to an object.

C Click the Swap Fill and Stroke icon in the Tools panel to switch the settings.

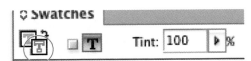

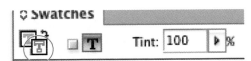

D A stroke effect applied to text.

E The outlined T in the Stroke icon (circled) indicates that a stroke has been applied to text.

Stroke Text Gently

If you have worked with desktop publishing programs, you may have seen that strokes on text deform the shape of the characters. This happens because the stroke is applied on both the outside and the inside of the text. As a result, most teachers like me warned our students never to add a stroke to text — not in headlines and never in body copy.

Although InDesign does put its strokes only on the outside of text, it does stroke the inside of bowls such as the holes in a lower case p. This results in a slight deformity in the text.

So, try to avoid adding a stroke to text. And if you absolutely must, keep the size of the stroke to a minimum.

You can also add a color or gradient stroke to the outside edges of text **D**.

To apply a stroke to selected text:

1. Use the Text tool to highlight the text.
2. Click the Stroke icon in the Tools panel or Color panel **E**.
3. Choose a swatch in the Color, Gradient, or Swatches panel.

To apply a stroke to all the text in a frame:

1. Select the text frame that contains the text to which you want to apply the stroke.
2. Click the Text button in the Tools panel or Color panel.
3. Click the Stroke icon in the Tools panel or Color panel.
4. Choose a swatch in the Color, Gradient, or Swatches panel.

You can also apply a gradient as a stroke to text or objects.

To apply a gradient stroke:

1. Click the Stroke icon in the Tools panel or the Swatches or Color panel.
2. Click the Gradient icon in the Tools panel or the Swatches or Gradient panel.
3. Use the Gradient tool to modify the angle or length of the gradient applied to a stroke.

TIP A linear gradient applied as a stroke creates a beveled effect. This may be combined with a solid or gradient fill for a three-dimensional effect.

Color is only one aspect of a stroke effect. The Stroke panel controls the rest of the stroke attributes.

To work with the Stroke panel:

If the Stroke panel is not visible, choose **Window > Stroke** to view it 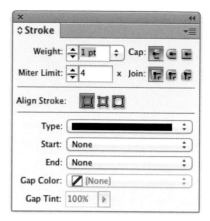.

or

If the Stroke panel is behind other panels, click the Stroke panel tab.

One of the most important attributes of a stroke is its thickness. This is controlled by changing the stroke weight 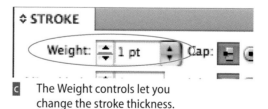.

To set the stroke weight (thickness):

1. Select the object.

2. Use the Weight field controls to set the thickness of the stroke .

TIP The stroke can be positioned on the outside, in the center, or inside the path using the Align Stroke controls.

A The Stroke panel with all its options displayed.

B Different stroke weights.

C The Weight controls let you change the stroke thickness.

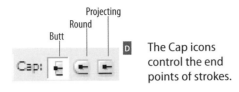

The Cap icons control the end points of strokes.

 D

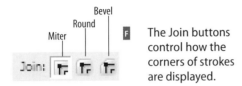

Butt

Round

Projecting

 E The three Cap settings applied to strokes.

The Join buttons control how the corners of strokes are displayed.

F

Bevel

Round

Miter

Join:

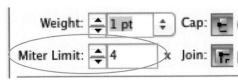

Miter   Round   Bevel

G The three Join settings applied to strokes.

Weight: 1 pt   Cap:

Miter Limit: 4   x Join:

H The Miter Limit field controls how long a miter point may extend.

A stroke's style is also controlled by the end caps and joins, which form points and corners.

To set the caps and joins:

1. Select an object that has a stroke applied to it.

2. In the Stroke panel, use the Cap icons **D** to change the way the ends of open paths are treated **E**:

   - **Butt** ends the stroke in a square. This is the default setting for a plain stroke.

   - **Round** ends the stroke in a semi-circle.

   - **Projecting** ends the stroke in a square that extends out from the end point.

TIP The Cap settings have no effect on closed paths such as rectangles, ellipses, and polygons.

3. Use the Join buttons **F** to change the way two segments of a path meet at corners **G**:

   - **Miter** joins the segments at an angle.

   - **Round** joins the segments with a curve.

   - **Bevel** joins the segments with a line between the segments.

Sometimes a mitered join becomes too long and pointed. Fortunately, you can stop the point from becoming too long by setting the miter limit.

To set the miter limit:

1. Select an object with a mitered join.

2. In the Stroke panel, increase the amount in the Miter Limit field to control the size of the angle between the segments **H**.

TIP If the size of the angle exceeds the miter limit, a bevel is substituted **G**. It does not mean a shorter point is substituted.

In traditional drawing programs, a stroke is distributed evenly on the outside and inside of its path. InDesign lets you choose the alignment of the stroke on the path 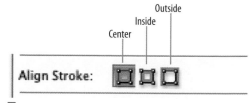.

TIP This is different from the position of a stroke applied to text.

To set the alignment of a stroke:

1. Apply a stroke to an object.

2. Choose one of the three alignment options for the stroke as follows **B**:

   • **Center** aligns the stroke so that half the stroke weight is inside the path and half is outside the path.

   • **Inside** aligns the stroke so that the entire thickness of the stroke weight is inside the path.

   • **Outside** aligns the stroke so that the entire thickness of the stroke weight is outside the path.

A Set the Align Stroke controls to set the position of the stroke along the path.

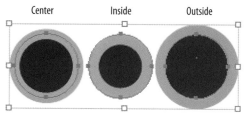

B Examples of how the Align Stroke controls change the position of the stroke on the path.

Uses for the Stroke Alignment

Most people will find they don't ever need to change the alignment options for a stroke. They use the traditional Center alignment all the time. However, for many others, the ability to specify where the stroke aligns on the path is a real benefit.

Say you have a placed image inside a frame. After you import the graphic, you may want to add a stroke to its frame, but you don't want the stroke to cover any part of the placed image.

If you applied a stroke with the traditional Center alignment, you would then have to enlarge the size of the frame by half the size of the stroke. By setting the stroke alignment to Outside, you ensure that the stroke does not cover any part of the image.

Or say you want to apply a stroke to an object without increasing its size. With the Center alignment, every time you change the stroke weight, the size of the object would increase or decrease. By setting the stroke alignment to Inside, the stroke only appears inside the object and doesn't add to the size of the object.

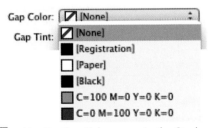

The 18 default strokes in the Stroke Type menu in the Stroke panel.

Use the Gap Color menu in the Stroke panel to set the color of the clear areas of a stroke.

Use the Gap Tint controls to set a screen for the gap color.

The default setting for strokes is a solid line. However, you can choose one of the specialty strokes such as stripes, dashes, hashes, dots, or diamonds. You can even pick a stroke that curves up and down along the path.

To apply stroke styles to strokes:

1. Apply a stroke to an object.

2. Choose one of the styles from the Stroke Type menu **C**.

The color of a stroke comes from choosing the Stroke icon and then picking a color. This method only colors the solid portion of a stroke. For strokes such as stripes and dashes, you can also color the gap, or the clear area between the solid colors of the stroke.

TIP This is the same technique used to set the gap color for the underline and strikethrough effects.

To set a stroke gap color:

1. Choose one of the specialty strokes that have both solid and clear areas.

2. Use the Gap Color menu to choose the color for the clear areas of the stroke **D**.

TIP This list contains the same colors and gradients as the Swatches panel.

3. If necessary, use the Gap Tint controls to set a screen for the gap color **E**.

The stroke list contains a dashed stroke that you can customize to set the size of the dashes and the gaps between them.

To create custom dashed strokes:

1. Apply a stroke to an object.

2. Choose Dashed from the Stroke Type pop-up menu. The dashed settings appear at the bottom of the Stroke panel .

TIP The dashed settings only appear when you select the stroke style named Dashed and not the ones labeled Dashed (3 and 2) or Dashed (4 and 4).

3. Enter an amount in the first dash field for the length of all of the dashes in the line.

4. Enter an amount in the first gap field for the size of the space between all of the dashes.

5. To create a series of dashes and gaps with irregular lengths, enter other values in the rest of the dash and gap fields.

6. If necessary, use the Corners list B to adjust the dashes and gaps C:

   • **None** leaves the dashes and gaps as they are. This can cause unequal dashes at the corners.

   • **Adjust dashes** changes the stroke so that the corner dashes are equal.

   • **Adjust gaps** changes the stroke so that the gap lengths are equal.

   • **Adjust dashes and gaps** changes the stroke to make the best fit so that both the corner dashes and gaps are equal.

   • **Dash (3 and 2)** creates a dash that is 3 times the stroke weight with a gap that is 2 times the stroke weight D.

   • **Dash (4 and 4)** creates dashes and gaps that are 4 times the stroke weight D.

A The Dashed settings at the bottom of the Stroke panel. These only appear when the Dashed stroke type is chosen.

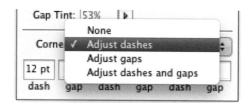

B Use the Corners menu to adjust how dashes and gaps are distributed on a stroke.

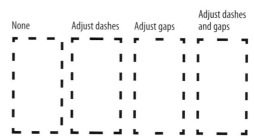

C Examples of how the Corners settings affect the appearance of a dashed stroke.

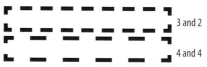

D The effects of the two preset dash styles on 3-point strokes.

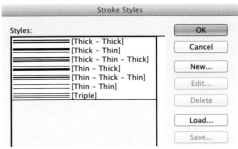

E The Stroke Styles dialog box lets you create, edit, and manage custom stroke styles.

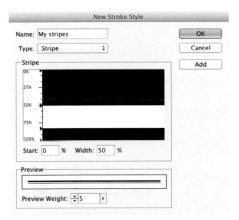

F The New Stroke Style dialog box is where you define the pattern for a custom stroke.

G Use the Type menu to choose the type of custom stroke style.

Creating Custom Stroke Styles

Stroke styles allow you to create custom stripes, dashes, and dots that you can add to your Strokes panel for reuse.

To create custom styles for strokes:

1. Choose Stroke Styles from the Stroke panel menu. The Stroke Styles dialog box appears **E**.

   TIP This dialog box contains the seven default stripe styles. You can't edit these default stripes, but you can use them as the basis for new stripe styles.

2. Click the New button to open the New Stroke Style dialog box **F**.

   or

   Choose one of the default stripes and then click the New button. This opens the New Stroke Style dialog box with the stripe style already set as the starting pattern.

3. Use the Name field to enter a name for the custom stroke style.

4. Choose the type of stroke style from the Type menu as follows **G**:

   - **Stripe** allows you to create multiple lines that run parallel to each other along the stroked path.
   - **Dotted** creates a series of dots repeated along the path.
   - **Dash** creates a single line that is broken into a series of individual elements.

5. The dialog box changes its controls according to the stroke style chosen in the Type menu.

6. When you have finished setting the stroke style, click OK to create the style.

   or

   Click the Add button to create the style and then define additional styles.

To create a custom stripe stroke style:

1. Choose Stripe from the Type menu of the New Stroke Style dialog box. The stripe controls appear 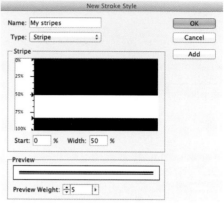.

2. Click inside the Stripe area to add a stripe to the stroke.

TIP New stripes appear in the Stripe area with no width and need to be adjusted in order to appear as part of the finished stroke.

3. Drag the Start control triangle on the percentage ruler or enter an amount in the Start field to set the initial position for the stripe on the stroke **B**.

TIP A setting of 0% positions the stripe to start at the very top of the stroke width.

4. Drag the Width control triangle on the percentage ruler or enter an amount in the Width field to set the width of the stripe **B**.

TIP The width of the stripe is a percentage of the final stroke weight of the stroke. For example, a stripe width of 50% applied to a 4-point stroke creates a 2-point stripe.

5. Drag the stripe itself up or down in the Stripe area to position it without changing its width.

6. If you need to delete a stripe, drag it up or down so that it is off the Stripe area.

7. Use the Preview control to increase or decrease the size of the preview for the stroke style **C**.

TIP A larger preview helps you see small elements added to the custom stroke style. However, it does not change the appearance of the stroke used in the document.

A The New Stroke Style dialog box set for the Stripe controls.

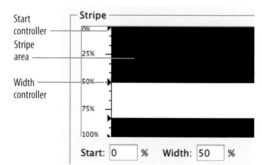

B The stripe controls in the New Stroke Style dialog box.

C Use the Preview display and Preview Weight to see what the stripe style will look like.

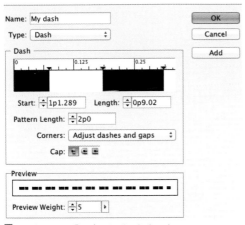

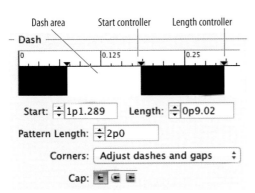

D The New Stroke Style dialog box set for the Dash controls.

E The Dash controls in the New Stroke Style dialog box.

F Use the Corners list to choose how dashes are distributed along a stroke.

To create a custom dashed stroke style:

1. Choose Dash from the Type menu of the New Stroke Style dialog box. The dash controls appear **D**.

2. Click inside the Dash area to add a dash to the stroke **E**.

TIP New dashes appear in the Dash area with no length and need to be adjusted in order to appear as part of the finished stroke.

3. Drag the Start control triangle on the percentage ruler or enter an amount in the Start field to set the initial position for the dash **E**.

TIP Unlike the Stripe controls, the length of a dash is set as an absolute amount, not a percentage of the stroke width.

4. Drag the dash itself to move it without changing its width.

5. Use the Pattern Length field to increase the length of the space that the dashes repeat within **E**.

6. If you need to delete a dash, drag it up or down so that it is off the Dash area.

7. Use the Corners list to choose how the dashes should be arranged around corners **F**.

8. Choose a Cap style to set how the dashes appear on the stroke.

9. Use the Preview control to increase or decrease the size of the preview for the stroke style.

To create a custom dotted stroke style:

1. Choose Dotted from the Type menu of the New Stroke Style dialog box. The dotted controls appear 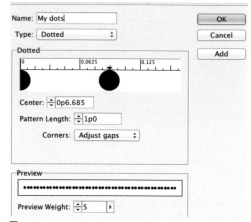.

2. Click inside the Dotted area to add a dot to the stroke B.

3. Drag the Center control triangle on the ruler or enter an amount in the Center field to set the initial position for the dot B.

4. Use the Pattern Length field to increase the length of the space that the dots repeat within B.

5. If you need to delete a dot, drag it up or down so that it is off the Dotted area.

6. Use the Corners list to choose how the dots should be arranged around corners C.

TIP Unlike the choices for dashes, the Corners list for dots only allows you to adjust gaps, as the dots themselves cannot change their length.

7. Use the Preview control to increase or decrease the size of the preview for the stroke style D.

To edit a stroke style:

1. Select the custom stroke style in the Stroke Styles dialog box and choose Edit. The Edit Stroke Style dialog box appears.

2. Click OK to apply the changes.

TIP The Edit Stroke Style dialog box is the same as the New Stroke Style dialog box, except that there is a Preview checkbox to help you see what your changes do to the stroke E. Also, the Edit Stroke Style dialog box does not have an Add button.

A The New Stroke Style dialog box set for the Dotted controls.

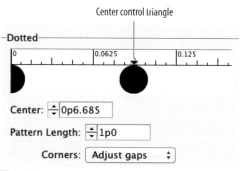

B The Dotted controls in the New Stroke Style dialog box.

C Use the Corners menu to control how dotted styles are applied to corners.

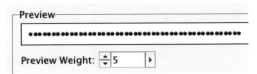

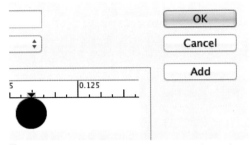

D Use the Preview display and Preview Weight to see what a dotted style will look like.

E Click the Preview checkbox to see how the stroke edits appear when applied to objects.

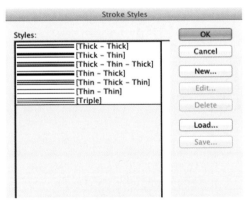

F The Stroke Styles dialog box lets you create, edit, and manage custom stroke styles.

Once you have defined a stroke style, it appears in the Type menu of the Stroke panel for that document. You may want to transfer strokes from one document to another. You do so using the Stroke Styles dialog box **F**.

To save strokes for use in another document:

1. Choose Stroke Styles from the Stroke panel menu.

2. Select the custom strokes that you want to transfer to another document.

TIP Hold the Shift key to select a range of strokes.

TIP Hold the Cmd/Ctrl key and click to select noncontiguous strokes.

3. Click the Save button. A dialog box appears where you can save the strokes as an .inst file, which contains the custom stroke definitions.

To transfer strokes from another document:

1. Choose Stroke Styles from the Stroke panel menu.

2. Click Load from the Stroke Styles dialog box.

3. Navigate to find the .inst file that contains the custom stroke definitions.

4. Click the Open button to add the strokes to the document.

TIP You can also add custom strokes by copying and pasting objects from one document to another.

To delete a stroke from a document:

1. Choose Stroke Styles from the Stroke panel menu.

2. Select the stroke or strokes you want to delete.

3. Click the Delete button.

TIP You can't delete the seven default strokes.

Adding Arrows

You can add arrowheads and other shapes to the open-ended objects that have strokes applied to them 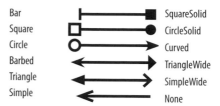.

To add arrowheads and end shapes:

1. Select an object with open ends.

2. Add a graphic to the beginning of the object by choosing a shape from the Start menu in the Stroke panel **B**.

3. Add a graphic to the end of the object by choosing a shape from the End menu.

Corner Options

You can modify the corners of objects so that they have special shapes. These effects are called corner options.

To apply corner options to objects:

1. Select an object with at least one corner point.

2. Choose Corner Options from the Object menu. The Corner Options dialog box appears **C**.

3. Choose one of the corner shapes from the menu list **D**.

4. Use the size fields to set the size of the corner option.

5. Click OK to apply the settings **D**.

TIP If the link icon is in the locked position, all the corners will have the same size and shape. In the unlocked position, you can assign individual shapes and sizes to each corner.

TIP Corner options can be applied to any type of object. For instance, you can change a star's points to curves by applying a rounded corner effect. Or you can convert an L-shaped line into a soft curve.

A The 12 different types of arrowhead styles for paths.

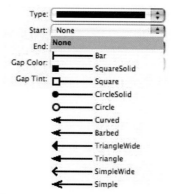

B Choose an arrowhead style from the Start or End menu in the Stroke panel.

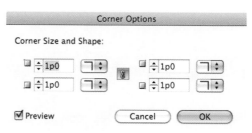

C The Corner Options dialog box lets you apply different corners to objects.

D The Corner options dialog box lets you apply different corners to objects.

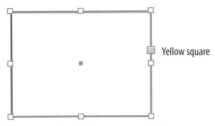

Yellow square

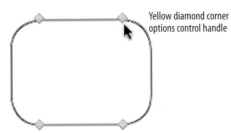

E Click the **yellow corner options square** to open the corner options controls.

Yellow diamond corner options control handle

F Drag one of the **yellow diamond control handles** to change the size of the corner options.

G Hold the Shift key to adjust the size of the individual corner options.

You can also set the size and shape of corner options directly to an object without opening the Corner Options dialog box using the Live Corner Options controls.

To use the Live Corner Options controls:

1. Use the Selection tool to select an object with corner points.

2. Click the yellow square to display the diamond corner option control handles **E**.

3. Drag the diamond handles to increase or decrease the size of the corner option **F**.

TIP As you drag the diamond handles, you are also changing the size of the numbers in the corner option fields.

4. If you want to modify the size of a single corner, hold the Shift key as you drag one of the diamond control handles **G**.

5. If you want to change the shape of the corners, hold the Opt/Alt key as you click one of the diamond control handles.

6. If you want to change the shape of just one of the corners, hold the Opt/Alt+Shift key as you click one of the diamond control handles.

Opacity and Blend Mode Effects

What I call *transparency* (the ability to see through objects, images, or text), InDesign calls *opacity*.

To apply opacity effects to an object:

1. Choose **Window > Effects** to open the Effects panel 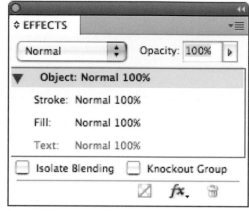.

   or

   Click the Opacity slider in the Control panel.

   or

   Choose **Objects > Effects > Transparency** to open the Effects dialog box set to the Transparency option 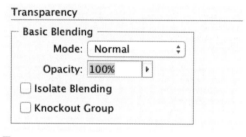.

   or

   Choose Transparency from the Effects panel menu.

2. Drag the Opacity slider or enter an amount in the Opacity field 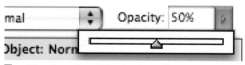. The lower the opacity percentage, the more you can see through the object.

TIP Once you have activated the Opacity field or slider, you can use the up and down arrow keys on the keyboard to increase or decrease the amount of opacity.

TIP Place a text frame filled with the color Paper at a reduced opacity over an image to "ghost" that area in the image .

A The **Effects panel**.

B The **Transparency controls** in the Effects dialog box.

C The **Opacity slider in the Effects panel** lowers the visibility of objects.

D An example of how a white text frame with the fill set to 70% opacity creates a **ghost area in the image**.

Use the **Settings for** list to choose to which parts of the object the opacity or blend mode is applied.

Object: Normal 100%

Stroke: Multiply 80%

Fill: Normal 70%

Select the **object attribute in the Effects panel** to apply the opacity or blend mode to just one part of the object.

You can also specify where the opacity or blend mode is applied.

To specify to which attributes the effect is applied:

Use the Settings for menu in the Effects dialog box E to choose one of the following:

- **Object** sets the effect to the entire object.
- **Stroke** sets the effect to just the stroke.
- **Fill** sets the effect to just the fill.
- **Text** sets the effect to just the text.

or

Click to target the object attribute in the Effects panel F.

TIP Use this technique when working with the other effects such as shadows, glows, bevel and emboss effects, satin, and feathers covered in the next sections.

Working with Effects

In addition to opacity and blend modes, you can also apply special effects such as shadows, glows, and feathers to objects. All these effects are controlled from the Effects dialog box 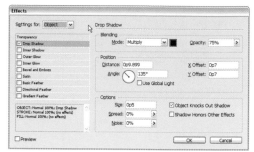.

To open the Effects dialog box:

Click the *fx* icon in the Effects panel or the Control panel to choose an effect from the menu **B**.

or

Choose **Object > Effects** and then one of the effects in the submenu.

or

Choose one of the effects in the Effects panel menu.

To remove effects:

Deselect the effect in the Effects dialog box.

or

Select the effect in the Effects panel and then click the Delete Effect icon in the Effects panel **C**.

or

Click the Clear All Transparency icon in the Effects panel to remove all effects as well as any opacity and blend mode settings **D**.

or

Choose Clear Effects from the Effect panel menu or **Object > Effects** submenu.

or

Choose Clear All Transparency from the Effects panel menu or **Object > Effects** submenu. This removes all effects as well as any opacity and blend mode settings.

A The **Effects dialog box** lets you choose effects as well as change their appearance.

B The *fx* icon in the Effects panel lets you apply special effects.

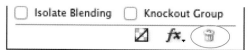

C The **Delete Effect icon** in the Effects panel removes effects from selections.

D The **Clear All Transparency icon** in the Effects panel removes all effects and makes the object opaque.

EFFECTIVE EFFECTS

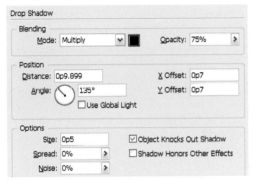

E A **drop shadow** applied to text.

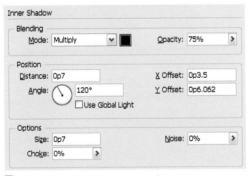

F The **Drop Shadow controls** in the Effects dialog box.

EFFECTIVE EFFECTS

G An **inner shadow** applied to text.

H The **Inner Shadow controls** in the Effects dialog box.

Shadow Effects

One of the most popular effects is a drop shadow set behind objects, text, or images **E**.

To add a drop shadow:

1. Select the object.
2. Open the Effects dialog box as described previously.
3. Select the Drop Shadow checkbox.
4. Set the Drop Shadow controls as follows **F**:
   - The **Blending area** controls the color and opacity of the shadow and how it interacts with other objects.
   - The **Position area** controls the placement of the shadow in relationship to the object.
   - The **Options area** controls the size and other attributes of the shadow.
5. Click OK to apply the shadow.

An inner shadow creates the appearance that the object is cut out of the page it is on **G**.

To add an inner shadow:

1. Select the object.
2. Open the Effects dialog box as described previously.
3. Select the Inner Shadow checkbox.
4. Set the Inner Shadow controls as follows **H**:
   - The **Blending area** controls the color and opacity of the shadow as well as how the shadow interacts with other objects.
   - The **Position area** controls the placement of the shadow in relationship to the object.
   - The **Options area** controls the size and other attributes of the shadow.
5. Click OK to apply the shadow.

Glow Effects

You can also add an outer glow around objects or an inner glow inside an object A – D.

To add an outer glow:

1. Select the object.

2. Open the Effects dialog box as described previously.

3. Select the Outer Glow checkbox.

4. Set the Outer Glow controls as follows B:

   • The **Blending area** controls the color and opacity of the glow as well as how the glow interacts with other objects.

   • The **Options area** controls the size and other attributes of the glow.

5. Click OK to apply the glow.

To add an inner glow:

1. Select the object.

2. Open the Effects dialog box as described previously.

3. Select the Inner Glow checkbox.

4. Set the Inner Glow controls as follows D:

   • The **Blending area** controls the color and opacity of the glow as well as how the glow interacts with the inside of the object.

   • The **Options area** controls the size and other attributes of the glow.

5. Click OK to apply the glow.

A An **outer glow** applied to text.

B The **Outer Glow controls** in the Effects dialog box.

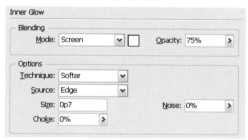

C An **inner glow** applied to text.

D The **Inner Glow controls** in the Effects dialog box.

EFFECTIVE EFFECTS

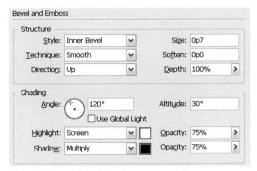

E   A **bevel effect** applied to text.

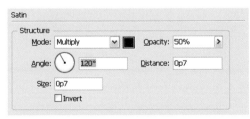

F   The **Bevel and Emboss controls** in the Effects dialog box.

EFFECTIVE EFFECTS

G   A **satin effect** applied to text.

H   The **Satin controls** in the Effects dialog box.

Bevel and Emboss Effects

A great way to add dimension to objects is with the bevel and emboss effects **E**.

TIP Bevel and emboss effects are simply variations in the style of one effect.

To add a bevel or emboss:

1. Select the object.
2. Open the Effects dialog box as described previously.
3. Select the Bevel and Emboss checkbox.
4. Set the controls as follows **F**:
   - The **Structure area** controls the style of the bevel or emboss as well as the size and other attributes.
   - The **Shading area** controls what colors are used for the highlights and shadows of the effect as well as the direction of the light that creates the effect.
5. Click OK to apply the bevel or emboss.

Satin Effect

The satin effect gives the appearance of a fabric texture applied to the object **G**.

To add a satin effect:

1. Select the object.
2. Open the Effects dialog box as described previously.
3. Select the Satin checkbox.
4. Set the Satin controls as follows **H**:
   - The **Structure area** controls how the satin texture is applied as well as the size, angle, and other attributes.
   - Choose **Invert** to reverse the appearance of the satin effect with the object's color.
5. Click OK to apply the satin effect.

Feather Effects

Feather refers to softening the edge of an object so that it fades to transparent. InDesign gives you three different types of feather effects. The Basic Feather creates a soft edge around the outside of objects .

To add a basic feather effect:

1. Select the object.

2. Open the Effects dialog box as described previously.

3. Select the Basic Feather checkbox.

4. Use the Options area to control the size and other attributes of the feather **B**.

5. Click OK to apply the feather.

A Directional Feather allows you to specify different amounts of softening for the top, bottom, left, and right sides of the object **C**.

To add a directional feather:

1. Select the object.

2. Open the Effects dialog box as described previously.

3. Select the Directional Feather checkbox.

4. Set the Directional Feather controls as follows **D**:

   • The **Feather widths area** controls the size of the feather for the four sides of the object.

   • The **Options area** controls the size and other attributes of the feather.

5. Click OK to apply the feather.

A   A **basic feather** applied to text.

B   The **Basic Feather controls** in the Effects dialog box.

C   A **directional feather** applied to text.

D   The **Directional Feather controls** in the Effects dialog box.

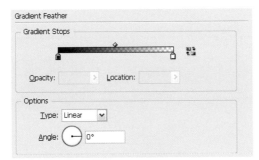

EFFECTIVE EFFECTS

F The **Gradient Feather controls** in the Effects dialog box.

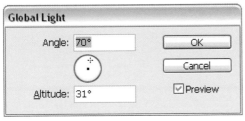

G The **Gradient Feather tool** allows you to drag across objects to apply a gradient feather.

H The **Global Light dialog box**.

Instead of a gradient that changes color, the Gradient Feather effect allows you to create a color that fades in and out of opacity **E**.

To add a gradient feather:

1. Select the object.

2. Open the Effects dialog box as described previously.

3. Select the Gradient Feather checkbox.

4. Set the Gradient Feather controls as follows **F**:

   • The **Gradient Stops area** allows you to set the opacity and location for each of the gradient transition points.

   • The **Options area** controls the type of gradient (linear or radial) and the angle of the gradient.

5. Click OK to apply the feather.

TIP You can also apply a gradient feather effect by dragging across the object with the gradient feather tool **G**.

Setting the Global Light

The Global Light setting allows you to set an angle and position of the electronic "light" that creates shadows and other dimensional effects.

To set the Global Light:

1. Choose Global Light from the Effects panel menu or the **Object** > **Effects** submenu.

2. Use the Global Light dialog box to set the angle and altitude of the global light **H**.

Using the Pathfinder Commands

I can't draw. So rather than struggle to create certain shapes, I use the Pathfinder commands to use multiple objects to create different shapes.

To use the Pathfinder commands:

1. Select the objects that you want to have interact with each other. You must select at least two objects.

2. Click one of the Pathfinder icons in the Pathfinder panel 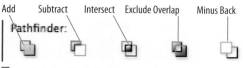 (**Window > Object & Layout > Pathfinder**) or choose one of the following from the **Object > Pathfinder** submenu:

   - **Add** combines the outer edges of the objects in a single shape **B**.

   - **Subtract** uses the frontmost object as a cookie cutter that changes the shape of the backmost object **B**.

   - **Intersect** creates a new shape based on the area intersected by the objects **B**.

   - **Exclude Overlap** creates a hole where the objects overlap **B**.

   - **Minus Back** uses the backmost objects as cookie cutters that change the shape of the frontmost object **B**.

The pathfinder commands may create a compound path. To separate the objects, you need to release the compound path:

To separate the results of the Pathfinder commands:

1. Select the objects created by the Pathfinder command.

2. Choose **Object > Paths > Release Compound Paths**.

3. Deselect the objects and then move each one to new positions **C**.

A   Click the **Pathfinder icons** in the Pathfinder panel.

Command	Objects before	Objects after
Add		
Subtract		
Intersect		
Exclude Overlap		
Minus Back		

B   Examples of how the **Pathfinder commands** change selected objects.

C   An example of how the **Exclude Overlap command** creates separate objects when the Compound Path is released.

Convert Shape:

D The **Convert Shape icons** in the Pathfinder panel allow you to change the shape of objects.

Icon	Function
☐	Rectangle
▢	Rounded Rectangle
◖	Beveled Rectangle
✛	Inverse Rounded Rectangle
○	Ellipse
△	Triangle
⬡	Polygon
╱	Line
✛	Orthogonal Line

E The **Convert Shape icons** and their functions.

You can use the Convert Shape commands to change objects from one shape to another.

To change the shape of objects:

1. Select the object that you want to convert.

2. Click one of the Convert Shape icons in the Pathfinder panel **D**.

   or

   Choose one of the following from the **Object > Convert Shape** menu:

   - **Rectangle** converts to a rectangle **E**.
   - **Rounded Rectangle** converts to a rectangle with rounded corners **E**.
   - **Beveled Rectangle** converts to a rectangle with flat, angled corners **E**.
   - **Inverse Rounded Rectangle** converts to a rectangle with inverted rounded corners **E**.
   - **Ellipse** converts the object to an ellipse **E**.
   - **Triangle** converts to a triangle **E**.
   - **Polygon** converts to a polygon using the current settings for the Polygon tool **E**.
   - **Line** converts the object to a line. The length is the diagonal of the bounding box of the object **E**.
   - **Orthogonal Line** converts the object to a line. The length is the width or height of the bounding box, whichever is greater **E**.

TIP The size of the corner options comes from the current corner radius setting in the Corner options.

The Pathfinder panel also contains the path modification commands.

To modify paths:

1. Select the object that you want to modify.

2. Click one of the Path icons in the Pathfinder panel .

   or

   Choose one of the following from the **Object > Paths** submenu:

   - **Join Path** joins the selected endpoints of two open paths or the selected endpoints of a single path ▣.

   - **Open Path** opens a closed path at a point ▣.

   - **Close Path** creates a segment between the end points of a path ▣.

   - **Reverse Path Direction** changes the direction of a path ▣.

TIP Apply the Close Path command to expand the electronic corner options into actual points on the path. This is similar to applying Illustrator's **Object > Expand** command.

Paths:

Ⓐ The **Paths icons** in the Pathfinder panel allow you to modify individual paths.

Icon	Function
	Join Path
	Open Path
	Close Path
	Reverse Path Direction

Ⓑ The **Paths icons** and their functions.

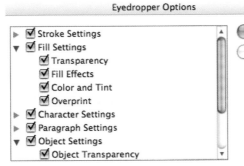

C The **Eyedropper tool** in the Tools panel lets you sample object attributes.

Eyedropper Options

☑ Stroke Settings
▼ ☑ Fill Settings
    ☑ Transparency
    ☑ Fill Effects
    ☑ Color and Tint
    ☑ Overprint
▶ ☑ Character Settings
▶ ☑ Paragraph Settings
▼ ☑ Object Settings
    ☑ Object Transparency

D Use the **Eyedropper Options dialog box** to set which attributes the Eyedropper will sample and apply.

E The **white eyedropper** lets you sample the object attributes.

F The **black eyedropper** applies object attributes from one object to another.

Using the Eyedropper

Imagine you've finished styling an object with exactly the right combination of fill, stroke, and effects. And now you'd like to apply those same settings to a different object. That's where the Eyedropper tool comes to the rescue.

To set the eyedropper options:

1. Double-click the Eyedropper tool in the Tools panel **C**. This opens the Eyedropper Options dialog box **D**.

2. Click the triangles to open each of the attribute categories.

TIP The object settings categories are Fill, Stroke, and Transparency.

3. Use the checkboxes to choose which attributes you want the Eyedropper tool to sample.

4. Click OK to set the options.

Once you set the eyedropper options, you can sample and apply object attributes.

To sample and apply object attributes:

1. Choose the Eyedropper tool.

2. Click with the white eyedropper cursor inside the object that you want to sample **E**. The cursor changes from white to black.

TIP If an object has a stroke, but no fill, click the object's outline to sample its stroke.

3. Click the black eyedropper cursor inside the object that you want to change **F**. This applies the first object's attributes to the second.

4. Click the eyedropper inside any other objects that you want to change.

As you work with the Eyedropper tool, you may change your mind and want to unload one set of attributes to sample new ones.

To sample new attributes:

1. Hold the Opt/Alt key. The eyedropper cursor changes to the white sample mode.

2. Click the cursor inside a new object that you want to sample.

3. Release the Opt/Alt key to apply the new attributes to objects.

You may not want to sample all the attributes in an object — just the fill or stroke. That's when you can use the Eyedropper tool in its precision mode. The precision mode allows you to sample and apply just the color to either a fill or a stroke.

To use the precision eyedropper:

1. Choose the Eyedropper tool. Hold the Shift key. A plus sign appears next to the white eyedropper cursor A. This indicates that the Eyedropper tool is in the precision mode.

2. Click the precision white eyedropper cursor on the fill or stroke color you wish to sample. The cursor turns into the precision black eyedropper B.

3. Click the precision eyedropper on either a fill or a stroke of the object that you want to change. Only the fill or stroke is changed.

TIP Only the color of the fill or stroke is changed. Point size, stroke styles, or effects are not applied or changed.

TIP As handy as the Eyedropper tool is, it doesn't come close to the power of object styles *(covered in Chapter 15, "Styles")*.

A The **white precision eyedropper** allows you to sample a specific color.

B The **black precision eyedropper** lets you apply a specific color to either the fill or a stroke.

c Click the **Default Fill and Stroke icon** in the Tools panel to set the fill to none and stroke to black.

Setting Object Defaults

You can make any of the object settings the default for any new objects you create. You can set the object defaults for the current document or globally for all new documents.

To set current document defaults:

1. With a document open, deselect any objects.

2. Make whatever changes you want in the Stroke panel or other panels. This sets the defaults for the open document.

3. Set whatever amounts you want for the Effects or Corner options dialog boxes.

To set global defaults:

With no document open, make whatever changes you want in the Stroke or other panels. This sets the global defaults for all new documents.

InDesign also has its own default fill and stroke setting of a black stroke and no fill. These are separate from the defaults you set yourself. This can be easily applied to objects.

To apply the InDesign fill and stroke defaults:

Click the Default Fill and Stroke icon in the Tools panel **c**.

Points and Paths 7

I remember the first time I tried to use the Pen tool in a computer graphics program. I clicked the tool and dragged across the screen in the way I thought would create a simple curve. Instead, I got a wild series of lines that shot out in different directions. When I tried to change the shape of the curves, things got even worse. I was so startled I immediately closed up the program and didn't use the Pen tool for a long, long time.

However, I really wanted to use the Pen tool, as I knew it was the best way to create curved shapes. So I forced myself to try the tool again. It took a lot of trial and error but eventually I was able to understand the Pen and Bezier controls. Later on, working with tools such as the Pencil and Eraser made it even easier to work with Bezier curves.

Once I got it, I realized the principles are simple. Even better, if you have used the Pen tool in Adobe Illustrator or Adobe Photoshop, you will find InDesign's Pen tool almost the same.

I wish someone had written out easy-to-understand, step-by-step instructions on how to use the Pen tool. So think of this chapter as the instructions for the Pen tool that I wish I had had back then.

Pen Points

One of the most important tools in any graphics program is the Pen tool. Fortunately InDesign has a Pen tool that lets you create much more sophisticated shapes in your layout than can be created with the basic shape tools. *(See Chapter 4, "Working with Objects," for more information on creating basic shapes.)*

TIP If you are familiar with the Pen tool in Adobe Illustrator, Adobe Photoshop, or Adobe Flash, you will find it very easy to master the Pen in InDesign.

If you've never used a Pen tool in any graphics program, you will understand more if you first become familiar with the elements of paths.

Elements of Paths

Paths are defined by points and line segments. When you draw with the Pen tool you create the following:

- **Anchor points,** which define a path at points where the path changes 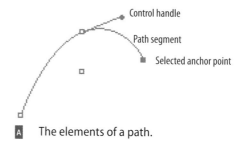. These can be plain corner points, smooth curve points, and corner curve points, as explained on the following pages.
- **Segments,** which are the paths that connect anchor points 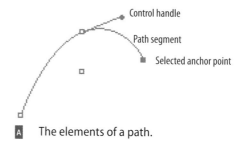.
- **Control handles** that extend out from anchor points; their length and direction control the shape of the segment's curves 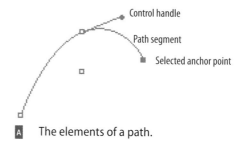.

Control handle

Path segment

Selected anchor point

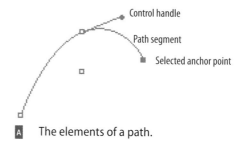 The elements of a path.

The Father of Bezier Curves

Some people call the curves created by the Pen tool *Bezier curves*. This is in honor of Pierre Bézier (*Bay-zee-ay*), the French mathematician.

Monsieur Bézier created the system of mathematics that is used to define the relationship of the control handles to the shape of the curve.

Adobe Systems, Inc., adopted this mathematical system when it created the PostScript language, which is used as the basis of graphics programs. InDesign, along with many other programs, uses Bezier curves as the mathematics behind each curve.

Drawing in a Page Layout Program?

I limit using InDesign's Pen tool to simple things. If I need some sort of curved or wavy line, I use InDesign's Pen tool. For instance, all the curved arrows in this book were created with the Pen tool. However, if I want a perfect spiral, I use Illustrator's Spiral tool. *(See Chapter 8, "Imported Graphics," for how to bring Illustrator paths into InDesign.)*

If I need to jazz up some text, I stay within InDesign. But if I need a complete map of New York State with highways, rivers, and scenic attractions, I work in Illustrator.

B Click the **Pen tool in the Tools panel** to create lines.

 C The **start icon** for the Pen tool.

 D Click with the Pen tool to create **a corner point**, shown as a small square.

E The **hollow arrow** indicates the Pen is aligned with a Smart Guide.

F Straight lines extend between the plain corner points.

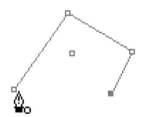

G The **small circle next to the Pen** cursor indicates that you will close the path.

Drawing Lines

Different types of anchor points create different line shapes. Straight lines are formed by creating *plain corner points*.

To create straight lines:

1. Click the Pen tool in the Tools panel **B**.

2. Position the cursor where the path should start. A small X appears next to the Pen, which indicates that you are starting the path **C**.

3. Click. A plain corner point appears as a colored square. The Pen cursor is displayed without any symbol next to it **D**.

TIP A small arrow next to the Pen **E** indicates it is aligned with a guide.

4. Position the cursor for the next point and click. This creates another plain corner point with a straight line that connects the first point to the second.

TIP Hold the Shift key to constrain the straight lines to 45-degree angles.

5. Continue clicking until you have created all the straight-line sides of the object **F**.

TIP If you have not closed the path (see the next exercise), hold the Cmd/Ctrl key and click with the Selection tool. This deselects the path and allows you to start a new one.

To close a path with a straight line:

1. Move the Pen over the first point. A small circle appears next to the Pen **G**. This indicates that you can close the path.

2. Click. This closes the path with a plain corner point and allows you to start a new path.

Drawing Curves

Smooth curve points create curves like the track a roller coaster follows. There are no abrupt changes from one curve to another.

To create smooth curves:

1. Drag the Pen tool where you want to start the curve. Handles extend out from the point.

   TIP The length and angle of the handle control the curve's height and direction.

2. Release the mouse button.

   TIP You do not see a curve until you create the next point of the path.

3. Move the cursor to where you want the next part of the curve. Drag to create the curved segment between the two smooth curve points .

4. Continue to create curved segments by repeating steps 2 and 3 B.

To close a path with a smooth curve:

1. Move the Pen over the first point. A small circle appears, indicating that you can close the path.

2. Drag backwards to close the path C.

A *corner curve point* creates curves with an abrupt change in direction. The path of a bouncing ball illustrates a corner curve.

To create a corner curve:

1. With the Pen tool active, drag to create an anchor point with control handles.

2. Without releasing the mouse button, hold the Opt/Alt key and then drag to pivot the second handle D.

3. Release the mouse button when the second handle is the correct length and direction.

A Drag with the Pen tool to create **smooth curves**.

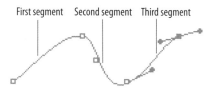

First segment   Second segment   Third segment

B A path with a series of curved segments.

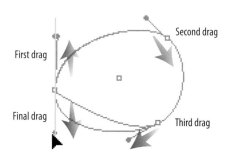

Second drag

First drag

Final drag

Third drag

C Dragging backwards closes a path with a smooth curve.

D Hold the Opt/Alt key to pivot the handles, which creates a **corner curve**.

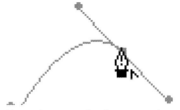

E Move the cursor back over a point and click to **retract a handle along a curve**.

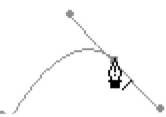

F Drag with the Pen tool over an existing anchor point to **extend a handle out from the point**.

General Pen Rules

As you work with the Pen tool, there are some rules you should follow:

Use the fewest number of points to define a path. Too many points add to the size of the file and make it difficult to edit the path later.

Try to limit the length of the control handles to one-third the length of the curve. This is sometimes called the *One-Third Rule*. The One-Third Rule makes it easier to edit and control the shape of curves.

Changing Curves and Corner Points

If you retract the handle that extends out from a curve point, the next segment becomes a straight line.

To retract a handle:

1. Drag to create a smooth curve point.

2. Move the Pen cursor back over the anchor point. A small angle symbol appears next to the cursor.

3. Click. The handle retracts back into the anchor point. The point is now a corner point with only one handle E.

4. Continue the path with either a straight line or a curved line.

TIP Click to make the next path segment straight. Drag to make the next path segment curved.

If you create a corner point with no control handles, you can extend a single handle out from that anchor point.

To extend a handle from a point:

1. Click to create a corner point with no handles.

2. Move the Pen cursor back over the anchor point you just created. A small angle symbol appears next to the cursor.

3. Drag to pull a single handle out from the anchor point F.

4. Continue the path with a curved line.

Modifying Paths

Once you create a path, you can still change its shape and the position of the points. You can also split a path into two separate segments or join two segments together. When you move points, you use the Direct Selection tool.

To move individual points:

1. Click the Direct Selection tool in the Tools panel .

2. Position the tool over the point you want to move.

3. Drag the point to the new position.

To select and move multiple points:

1. Click the Direct Selection tool in the Tools panel.

2. Drag to create a rectangular marquee around the points you want to select 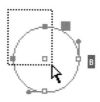. The selected points appear solid. The unselected points appear hollow.

   or

   Hold the Shift key as you click to select the points.

   TIP **You can select points in one path or multiple paths.**

3. Drag the points to the new position.

The Direct Selection tool also lets you change the length and direction of the control handles.

To move control handles:

1. Click the Direct Selection tool in the Tools panel.

2. Click a point on the path. This displays the control handles for that point.

3. Position the Direct Selection tool over the end point of the handle.

4. Drag the handle to the new position .

A The **Direct Selection tool** in the Tools panel; use it to move points.

B **Drag a marquee to select multiple points.** The center point does not turn solid.

C The Direct Selection tool changes the length and position of a control handle.

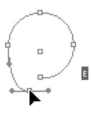

D The **Scissors tool** in the Tools panel allows you to snip paths in two.

E The Scissors tool splits a path into two points, one on top of the other.

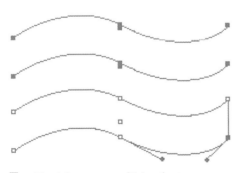

F The **Close Path command** joins the two end points of a path.

G The **Join command** joins the two end points of separate paths.

H The results of applying the **Reverse Path command** to a path with an arrowhead.

You may want to separate one path into two parts. The Scissors tool makes it easy to split or break a path into segments.

To split paths:

1. With the path selected, click the Scissors tool in the Tools panel **D**.

2. Position the cursor where you want to split the path.

3. Click to split the path at that point.

TIP The Scissors tool creates two points, one on top of the other. Use the Direct Selection tool to move one point away from the other **E**.

To open paths using a command:

Choose **Object > Path > Open Path**. This opens the path by creating two points, one on top of the other.

To close a path using a command:

Choose **Object > Path > Close Path**. This closes the path by creating a line segment between the end points of the path **F**.

To join two paths together:

1. Use the Direct Selection tool to select two endpoints on separate paths.

2. Choose **Object > Path > Join**. This creates a line segment that joins the end points of the two paths **G**.

The path direction comes from the order in which you draw the path. You can change the path direction.

To change the path direction:

1. Use the Direct Selection tool to select the path.

2. Choose **Object > Path > Reverse Path**. This switches the start and end points of the path **H**.

Modifying Points

So what happens if you create the wrong point with the Pen tool? Are you stuck? Does it mean you have to redraw the entire path? Thankfully, no—there are many ways to change the paths made with the Pen tool, as well as paths made with other tools. *(See Chapter 4, "Working with Objects," for more information on working with the basic shapes.)*

A simple way to change a path is to add a point. This helps you turn one shape into another.

To add points to a path:

1. With the path selected, choose the Add Anchor Point tool in the Tools panel .

2. Click the path where you want to add the point.

TIP The Pen tool automatically changes to the Add Anchor Point tool when positioned over a selected path segment .

You can delete points from a path without causing a break in the path.

To delete points from a path:

1. With the path selected, choose the Delete Anchor Point tool in the Tools panel .

2. Click to delete the point from the path.

TIP The Pen tool changes to the Delete Anchor Point tool when positioned over a point on a selected path .

 A The **Add Anchor Point tool** in the Tools panel.

 B The Add Anchor Point tool displays **a plus sign over a path segment**.

 C The Delete Anchor Point tool in the Tools panel.

 D The Delete Anchor Point tool displays **a minus sign over a point**.

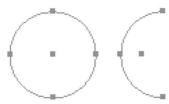

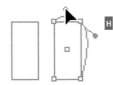

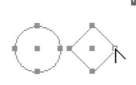

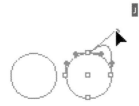

E When you select and delete a segment, you keep the points on either side of the segment.

F When you select and delete a point, you delete both segments that were attached to the point.

G The Convert Direction Point tool in the Tools panel.

H **Drag the Convert Direction Point tool** to change a corner point into a smooth curve point.

I **Click with the Convert Direction Point tool** to change a smooth curve point into a corner point.

J **Drag a handle with the Convert Direction Point tool** to change a smooth curve point into a corner curve point.

You can also create an open path by deleting a segment or the point between two segments.

To delete a segment in a path:

1. Use the Direct Selection tool to select the segment that you want to delete.

2. Press the Delete key or choose **Edit > Clear** to delete the segment **E**.

TIP If you select a point with the Direct Selection tool, the two segments on either side of the point can be deleted **F**.

You can also change the shape of segments by changing the type of anchor point.

To modify an anchor point:

1. Select the path.

2. Choose the Convert Direction Point tool in the Tools panel **G**.

3. Use the tool as follows to change the anchor points:

   - Press and drag a corner point to create a smooth curve point with two handles **H**.

   - Click a smooth curve point to create a corner point with no handles **I**.

   - Drag a handle of a smooth curve point to create a corner curve point **J**.

You can also use commands to change the control handles around a point.

To modify an anchor point:

Select the path and choose one of the following from the **Object > Paths > Convert Point** submenu:

- Plain
- Corner
- Smooth
- Smooth Symmetrical

Using the Pencil Tool

Unlike the Pen tool, which uses mathematical principles to draw paths, InDesign's Pencil tool works more like a traditional pencil. However, the Pen tool is a little more precise than the Pencil.

TIP If you are familiar with the Pencil tool in Adobe Illustrator, you will find you already know how to work with InDesign's Pencil tool.

To draw with the Pencil tool:

1. Click the Pencil tool in the Tools panel . A small cross next to the Pencil cursor indicates that you are about to start the path .

2. Press and drag with the Pencil **C**.

3. To close the path, even if you are far away from the start point, hold the Opt/Alt key. A small circle next to the cursor indicates that the path will be closed **D**.

4. Release the mouse button to create the path.

The Pencil tool can also be used to edit existing paths and reshape paths.

To edit paths with the Pencil tool:

1. Select the path that you want to reshape.

TIP The Pencil tool can edit paths created by tools such as the Pen or the frame tools.

2. Move the Pencil tool near the selected path. The cross next to the cursor disappears. This indicates that you are about to edit the path.

3. Drag along the path. When you release the mouse button, the path is reshaped **E**.

TIP If you don't get the results you expect, drag the Pencil tool in the opposite direction.

A The **Pencil tool** in the Tools panel.

B The **cross next to the Pencil cursor** indicates that you are about to start a new path.

C Press and drag to create a path with the Pencil tool.

D The **circle next to the Pencil cursor** indicates that the Opt/Alt key will close the path.

E Drag the Pencil tool next to a selected path to reshape the path.

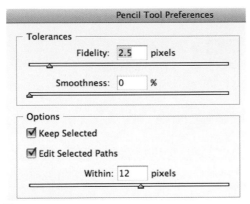

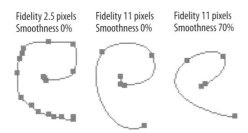

F The **Pencil Tool Preferences dialog box** allows you to control the appearance of the path.

Fidelity 2.5 pixels
Smoothness 0%

Fidelity 11 pixels
Smoothness 0%

Fidelity 11 pixels
Smoothness 70%

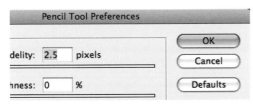

G The **Pencil tool Fidelity and Smoothness settings** change the appearance of the path.

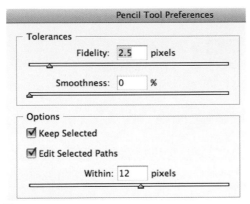

H Click the **Defaults button** in the Pencil Tool Preferences dialog box to reset the settings to their original amounts.

You can change how the Pencil tool responds to the movements of the mouse as you drag. The preferences also control how the Pencil tool edits paths.

To set the preferences for the Pencil tool:

1. Double-click the Pencil tool in the Tools panel. This opens the Pencil Tool Preferences dialog box **F**.

2. Set the amount of Fidelity using the slider or field. The lower the amount of Fidelity, the more the path will follow the motions of the mouse **G**.

3. Set the amount of Smoothness using the slider or field. The higher the setting for Smoothness, the more the path will follow curved shapes **G**.

4. Select Keep Selected to keep the path selected after you have drawn it. This makes it easier to reshape the path.

5. Select Edit Selected Paths to turn on the reshape option.

6. If the Edit Selected Paths option is turned on, use the slider or field to set how close the Pencil tool must come, in pixels, to the path you want to reshape.

TIP If you want to restore the Pencil tool to its original settings, click the Defaults button **H**.

Using the Smooth Tool

Once you have created a path, you may want to delete extra points so that the path is smoother.

TIP If you are familiar with Illustrator's Smooth tool, you will find it easy to use the Smooth tool in InDesign.

To smooth paths with the Smooth tool:

1. Select the path that you want to smooth.

2. Click the Smooth tool in the Tools panel .

3. Press and drag the Smooth tool along the path.

4. Release the mouse button. The path is redrawn with fewer points **B**.

You can change how the Smooth tool responds to the movements of the mouse as you drag.

To set the preferences for the Smooth tool:

1. Double-click the Smooth tool in the Tools panel to open the Smooth Tool Preferences dialog box **C**.

2. Use the slider or field to set the Fidelity amount. The lower the amount, the more the new path will follow the original path.

3. Use the slider or field to set the Smoothness amount. The higher the setting, the more curved the path.

4. Select Keep Selected to keep the path selected after you have smoothed it. This makes it easier to increase the smoothness of the path.

TIP If you want to restore the Smooth tool to its original settings, click the Defaults button.

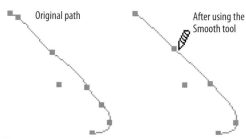

A The **Smooth tool** in the Tools panel.

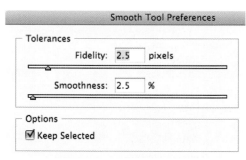

B Drag the Smooth tool along a path to **remove points and eliminate small bumps and curves**.

C The **Smooth Tool Preferences** allow you to control how much the Smooth tool affects the appearance of paths.

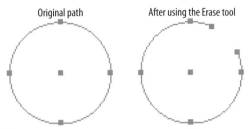

Original path   After using the Erase tool

D The **Erase tool** in the Tools panel.

E The Erase tool deletes portions of the segments as you drag it along a path.

Deleting or Removing Points: Which Tools or Commands Do What?

You may find yourself confused by all the different tools and commands for deleting or removing points and segments.

When does the action cause a break in a path? When does an action remove points without opening the path?

See the table on the next page for a review of how points are removed from paths, and the result.

Using the Erase Tool

You may want to delete parts of paths. Rather than selecting and deleting individual points, you can use the Erase tool to drag to delete parts of a path.

TIP If you are familiar with the Erase tool in Adobe Illustrator, you will find it easy to use the Erase tool in InDesign.

To delete paths with the Erase tool:

1. Select the path that you want to delete parts of.

2. Choose the Erase tool in the Tools panel **D**.

3. Press and drag the Erase tool along the path.

4. Release the mouse button to display the new path **E**.

TIP The Erase tool will always open a closed path.

TIP If you drag the Erase tool over the middle of an open path, you create two separate open paths. Both open paths will be selected.

Adding or Deleting Points on Paths

The following table compares the different tools and commands as to their effect when adding or deleting points on a path.

Tool or Command	Action	Result
Add Anchor Point tool	Click a segment on the path	Always adds a point to the path.
Delete Anchor Point tool	Click an existing point on the path	Deletes the point. The path reshapes without any break.
Erase tool	Drag along a path	Creates a break in the path, which can be a portion of a segment.
Scissors tool	Click a point or a segment	Creates two end points at that position. The points can then be separated to create a break in the path.
Open Path command	Applied to a path	Creates two end points at the origin of the path. The points are indicated by selection. The points can then be separated to create a break in the path.
Close Path command	Applied to a path	Creates a segment that joins two end points of a path.
Join command	Applied to two endpoints of two separate paths selected with the Direct Selection tool	Creates a segment that joins the two separate paths into a single path.
Delete command	Applied to points or segments selected with the Direct Selection tool	If applied to a selection in the middle of a path, the command breaks the path into two segments. If applied to a selection at the end of a path, the command shortens the path.

Imported Graphics 8

One reason desktop publishing became so popular is how easy it made combining graphics such as photographs and illustrations with type for layouts.

In the years before designers began using personal computers, specialized workers, toiling under the exotic name of *strippers*, manually trimmed away the blank areas around graphics so that text could be placed around the image. (The name stripper is derived from combining strips of film together.)

Even more complicated was placing text over an illustration. The image and text had to be combined by photography and then stripped into the layout.

Certainly you expect InDesign to import images in the formats that are used by other page-layout programs. But because this is *Adobe* InDesign, you also get some special benefits when working with other Adobe products.

Here's where you learn how to add imported artwork to your page layouts. It only takes a few clicks of a mouse to combine type and artwork together. It's enough to make old-time strippers hang up their tassels!

Placing Artwork

Most artwork that's used in InDesign comes from other sources such as Adobe Photoshop, Adobe Illustrator, or Adobe Acrobat. You can even place the contents of one InDesign file as a graphic into another. In all of these instances you use the Place command to add the artwork to your file.

To import artwork into InDesign:

1. Choose **File** > **Place**. This opens the Place dialog box .

2. Navigate to find the file you want to import.

3. Select the Show Import Options checkbox to open the Import Options dialog box before you place the file.

4. Click Open to load the graphic into an image cursor **B**.

TIP Hold the Shift key as you click Open to open the Import Options dialog box, even if the option is not selected.

Once you have imported the artwork into an image cursor, there are choices as to how to add the graphic to the file.

To place the graphic at its actual size:

Click the cursor to place the graphic in a rectangular frame the same size as the artwork.

To place the graphic into an existing frame:

Position the cursor over an empty frame and click. Curves appear around the cursor indicating you are about to place the image within the frame **C**.

TIP Hold the Opt/Alt key to place the image into a frame that already contains an image.

A Use the **Place dialog box** to open a file you wish to place. Select Show Import Options to make refinements to the imported file.

B The **loaded image cursor** appears when you prepare to place artwork.

C The **curved loaded image cursor** appears when you position the loaded cursor over an existing frame.

 **Drag to create a custom-sized frame** that contains a placed image.

File Formats

A wide variety of graphic formats can be added to InDesign documents. These formats are recommended for professional printing:

- Adobe Illustrator (AI)
- Adobe Photoshop (PSD)
- Adobe InDesign (ID)
- Encapsulated PostScript (EPS)
- Desktop Color Separation (DCS)
- Joint Photographic Experts Group (JPEG)
- Portable Document Format (PDF)
- Portable Network Graphics (PNG)
- PostScript (PS)
- Scitex Continuous Tone (SCT)
- Tagged Image File Format (TIFF)

These formats should be used only for onscreen PDF review, or for printing to non-PostScript printers:

- Enhanced Metafiles (EMF)
- Macintosh Picture (PICT)
- Graphics Interchange Format (GIF)
- PC Paintbrush (PCX)
- Windows Bitmap (BMP)
- Windows Metafile (WMF)

To place artwork into a custom-sized frame:

Drag the image cursor to define the size of the rectangular frame. The frame size is constrained to the correct proportion to hold the image **D**.

TIP Hold the Shift key as you drag to create the frame in any other proportion.

You can also place artwork directly into a selected frame. This is handy if you have set up empty frames as placeholders for graphics.

To place artwork into an existing frame:

1. Use one of the tools to create a rectangular, elliptical, or polygonal frame.

TIP You can use either the frame tools that create graphic frames or the tools that create unassigned frames.

2. Use either the Selection or Direct Selection tool to select the frame.

3. Choose **File > Place** and navigate to find the image you wish to place in the frame.

4. Click Open in the Place dialog box. The file automatically is inserted within the frame.

TIP You can also use the Pen tool to create frame shapes.

To replace the artwork in an existing frame:

1. Use either Selection tool to select the frame that contains the artwork you want to replace.

2. Choose **File > Place** and navigate to find the image you wish to place.

3. Click Replace Selected Item in the Place dialog box.

4. Click Open in the Place dialog box. The new image automatically replaces the contents of the frame.

To move or copy artwork between frames:

1. Use the Direct Selection tool to select the artwork you want to replace.

2. Choose **Edit** > **Cut** or **Edit** > **Copy**. This places the artwork on the clipboard.

3. Select the frame that you want to move the artwork into.

4. Choose **Edit** > **Paste Into**. The contents of the clipboard are pasted into the frame.

You can also select multiple items in the Place dialog box and then add all the items to your document. This way you don't have to keep going back to the Place dialog box.

To place multiple items at once:

1. Choose **File** > **Place** to open the Place dialog box.

2. Use the Cmd/Ctrl key to select the items you want to place.

    or

    Use the Shift key to select a range of items.

3. Click the Open button. The cursor displays a preview of the placed file. A number next to the preview indicates there are multiple files .

4. Click or drag to place each item. The number reduces as you place each item.

TIP Use the up/down or left/right arrow keys to cycle through the placed items.

TIP Use the ESC key to delete an item from the loaded cursor.

TIP Use the Opt/Alt key to swap the item in a frame with the item in the loaded cursor.

TIP You don't have to limit yourself to one kind of item. You can load the cursor with Photoshop, PDF, or other types of files. You can even mix text files with image files!

A The **numbered loaded cursor** indicates you have more than one placed item.

What can you do with a loaded cursor?

Be careful when you've got a loaded cursor in your hand. Never point it at anyone unless you intend to use it.

Once you have the loaded cursor, what can you do without losing the placed items? Surprisingly, there's a lot you can do.

You can go to any menu, open panels, or even go to another document. Your cursor remains loaded when you come back to your document.

However, you will lose the items in a loaded cursor if you choose any tool in the Tools panel or press a key that chooses a tool.

Placing ID files into another ID file

There's something very existential about it, but you can place an InDesign file as a graphic into another InDesign file.

The placed file behaves exactly like a placed PDF document. When you modify the placed graphic, it updates in the InDesign layout. You can turn the layers on or off just like you can with PDF documents.

B The **grid icon** indicates you will place graphics in a grid on the page.

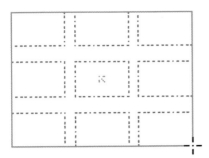

C Drag to create a **grid of frames** for multiple-placed images.

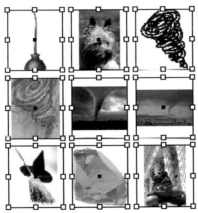

D A **grid of frames** for multiple images.

This is fun! Once you have loaded multiple images, you can place them all at once on the page in a grid of frames.

To place imported graphics into a grid of frames:

1. Use steps 1–3 in the previous exercise to load the cursor with multiple items.

2. Hold the Cmd/Ctrl-Shift keys. The cursor changes to the grid icon **B**.

3. Drag the mouse to create an area for the grid **C**. As you drag you can release the Cmd/Ctrl-Shift keys.

4. Continue to drag the mouse and press the following modifier keys to adjust the number of frames inside the grid:
   - **Left arrow** decreases the number of columns.
   - **Right arrow** increases the number of columns.
   - **Down arrow** decreases the number of rows.
   - **Up arrow** increases the number of rows.

5. Without releasing the mouse button, press the Cmd/Ctrl key and use the following modifier keys to adjust the spaces between the frame grid:
   - **Left arrow** decreases the space between the columns.
   - **Right arrow** increases the space between the columns.
   - **Down arrow** decreases the space between the rows.
   - **Up arrow** increases the space between the rows.

6. Release the mouse button when you have the correct size and number of frames in the grid **D**.

TIP Click to place the grid at the same size as the page.

Using Bridge and Mini Bridge

Adobe Bridge is a separate application that is installed automatically when you install InDesign. Bridge is a file browser that lets you organize, sort, and view artwork. It also lets you drag graphics directly onto InDesign pages.

To open Bridge:

Choose **File > Browse in Bridge**. The Bridge window appears. You can also click the Bridge icon in the Application panel **A**.

To place artwork from Bridge:

1. Position the Bridge and InDesign windows so that both are visible.

2. Select one or more files in the Bridge window.

3. Drag the file or files from Bridge onto the InDesign page **B**. Release the mouse button to place the item.

4. If you have dragged multiple files, click or drag to place the additional images on the InDesign pages.

Bridge takes up a lot of screen space. Mini Bridge is a smaller version of the full Bridge that lets you preview and drag files into InDesign files.

TIP Mini Bridge is also convenient to use as it always stays in front of the InDesign application window.

To open and use Mini Bridge:

1. Choose **Window > Mini Bridge** to open the Mini Bridge panel **C**.

2. Drag images from the panel onto the InDesign pages.

A **Click the Bridge icon** in the Application panel to open Adobe Bridge.

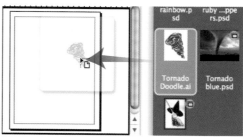

B **Drag an image from Adobe Bridge** to place it onto an InDesign page.

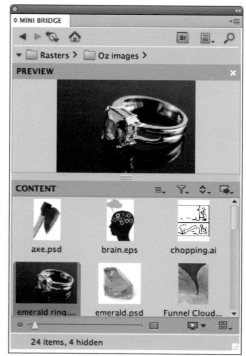

C **Mini Bridge** is a smaller version of the full Adobe Bridge.

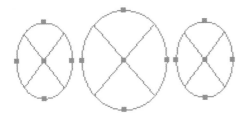

D Individual frames that act independently display diagonal lines within each object.

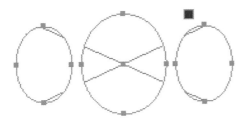

E A **compound shape displays the diagonal lines** across the entire set of frames.

F A **placed image is seen across all the items** in a compound shape.

Specialty Frames

Frames don't have to be single items drawn from scratch. You can join frames into one compound shape or you can convert text into frames that can hold images. You can also bring paths from other programs into InDesign to act as frames.

You can make multiple frames act as a single item by converting them to a compound shape. Frames combined into a compound shape display a single image across all the items in the compound.

To create a compound shape:

1. Select the frames you want to combine into a compound shape.

TIP If the frames overlap, InDesign displays a transparent hole where they overlap.

2. Choose **Object > Paths >Make Compound Path**. If the frame is a graphic frame, the diagonal lines cross through all the frames in the compound **D** and **E**.

To add an image to a compound shape:

1. Use either Selection tool to select the compound shape.

2. Use any of the techniques described on the previous pages to place the image in the selected frame. The image tiles across the spaces between the elements of the compound shape **F**.

To split a compound shape:

1. Select the compound shape.

2. Choose **Object > Paths > Release Compound Path**. The image is shown only through the first frame; the rest of the compound frames are available to hold other images.

You can also create unique frame shapes by converting text to frames so graphics assume the shapes of letters.

TIP If you can't draw for beans, you can convert the characters in dingbat or symbol fonts into graphic shapes such as hearts, arrows, snowflakes, and so on.

To convert text to frames:

1. Use the Selection tool to select the frame that contains the text.

   or

   Highlight the selected text within the frame.

2. Choose **Type** > **Create Outlines**. Each character of text is converted to paths that can be modified .

TIP You can also place images into the converted text paths just like you can with compound shapes .

TIP The converted paths are created as compound paths. If you want to place different images or colors in each of the frames, release the compound shape first.

TIP If you select only a portion of the text within the frame, the highlighted text is converted to inline graphics within the frame.

A The **Create Outlines command** converts text into paths that can then be modified.

B Text converted to paths can also hold imported graphics.

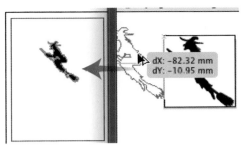

C Artwork can be dragged from a vector program and converted into InDesign frames.

D Graphics converted to frames can hold images or text.

Dragging from Illustrator

If you want to import paths from Adobe Illustrator, you need to make sure that Illustrator's preferences are set correctly.

Choose File Handling And Clipboard in Illustrator's Preferences dialog box. Under the Clipboard section, select the AICB (no transparency setting) option. Then click the Preserve Paths button.

If this is not done, the Illustrator paths will not be converted to frames.

If you work with a vector-drawing program such as Adobe Illustrator or FreeHand, you can also convert the paths in those programs to InDesign frames.

TIP In addition to Illustrator and FreeHand, this technique can be used with any other program that copies paths using the AICB (Adobe Illustrator Clipboard). Check your vector-drawing program manual for more information.

To import paths as frames:

1. Position the windows of the vector-drawing program and InDesign so they are both visible onscreen.

2. Select the paths in the vector-drawing program with the appropriate tool in that application.

3. Drag the paths from the vector-drawing program onto the window of the InDesign document.

4. When a black line appears around the perimeter of the InDesign window, release the mouse button. The paths are converted to InDesign unassigned frames **C**.

TIP If you don't have the screen space to see both windows at once, you can also use the clipboard to copy the paths from the vector program and paste them into InDesign.

TIP Once the vector path has been converted to an InDesign frame, it can be used to hold an image or text **D**.

Setting the Image Import Options

When you import a graphic, you can use the Image Import Options dialog box to control how that image is placed.

TIP The following chart shows which types of import options are applied to pixel images.

Import Options for Placed Images	
TIFF	Image Import Options with controls for Image and Color
JPEG	Image Import Options with controls for Image and Color
PSD	Image Import Options with controls for Image, Color, and Layers
EPS	**EPS** Import Options
Illustrator	**PDF** Import Options with controls for Layers
PDF	**PDF** Import Options with controls for Layers
InDesign	**PDF** Import Options with controls for Layers

To set the options for TIFF and JPEG images:

1. In the Place dialog box, select the Import Options checkbox.

2. Choose a TIFF or JPEG image and click Open. This opens the Image Import Options dialog box for TIFF or JPEG images .

3. Select the Image tab. If the image has a clipping path, you can choose Apply Photoshop Clipping path.

4. Select the Color tab. Use the controls to set the Color Management settings.

5. Click OK to place the image.

A The **Image Import Options** dialog box for TIFF and JPEG images.

Best File Format from Adobe Illustrator?

If you work in Adobe Illustrator, you will notice that there are several file formats you can choose from when you save your work: native Illustrator, EPS, or Adobe PDF. Which one works best with InDesign?

All three file formats can be placed into InDesign documents. However, native Illustrator files have the best preview.

You may have old Illustrator documents that were saved as EPS files. There's no need to resave them. You can place them into InDesign too.

However, you may see a white background behind artwork that has been saved on a Macintosh as an EPS. If that is a problem, use the Rasterize the PostScript option during import to eliminate the white background.

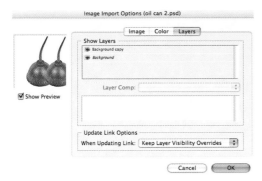

B The **Image Import Options for Photoshop files.**

C The **EPS Import Options dialog box** lets you control imported EPS files.

Working with Photoshop Layer Comps

A layer comp is a snapshot of a state of the Layers panel. Layer comps record the visibility, position and appearance of the layers in a Photoshop file.

You create layer comps in Photoshop. The names of the layer comps are then available within InDesign.

Using layer comps makes it possible to have several variations of the same file within InDesign.

To set the options for PSD images:

1. In the Place dialog box, select the Show Import Options checkbox.

2. Choose a Photoshop image and click Open. This opens the Image Import Options dialog box for Photoshop files **B**.

3. Choose Show Preview to see a preview of the file.

4. Select the Image tab. If the image has a clipping path, you can choose Apply Photoshop Clipping path.

5. Select the Color tab. Use the controls to set the Color Management settings.

6. Select the Layers tab. If the image has layers or layer comps, you can choose which layers are visible in the InDesign layout.

7. Click OK to place the image.

To set the import options for EPS images:

1. In the Place dialog box, select the Show Import Options checkbox.

2. Choose an EPS file. This opens the EPS Import Options dialog box **C**.

3. Don't select Read Embedded OPI Image Links unless your service bureau has instructed you to have InDesign perform the image swapping.

4. If the image has a clipping path, you can choose Apply Photoshop Clipping Path.

5. Set the options in the Proxy Generation to control the preview of the image:

    • **Use** TIFF **or** PICT **Preview** uses the preview that was created with the file.

    • **Rasterize the PostScript** displays the actual PostScript data as a preview. This lets you see custom PostScript code such as is found in FreeHand.

6. Click OK to place the image.

InDesign also lets you place PDF files or other InDesign files as graphics.

To set the options for placed PDF files:

1. In the Place dialog box, select the Show Import Options checkbox.

2. Choose a PDF file. This opens the Place PDF dialog box .

3. Choose Show Preview to see a preview of each page of the placed document.

4. Use the page selectors to select the page you want to place **B**.

5. Click the General tab to see those options.

6. Use the Crop To list to determine how the image should be cropped **C**.

   • **Bounding Box** crops to the active page elements, which includes printer marks. You can choose to limit to the visible layers or all layers.

   • **Art** crops to the area defined as placeable art.

   • **Crop** crops to only the printable area, not to the printer marks.

   • **Trim** crops to the area that is the final trim size.

   • **Bleed** crops to the area that is the total size of the image if a bleed area has been specified.

   • **Media** crops to the page size of the original document.

7. Choose Transparent Background to show only the elements of the page, without the opaque background **D**.

   TIP If you choose Transparent Background, you can make it opaque by adding a fill color to the frame that contains the PDF.

8. Click the Layers tab to set the layers for the PDF.

9. Click OK to place the image.

A The **Place PDF dialog box** lets you preview and control the options for PDF files.

B The **page selectors** let you preview the pages of a multipage PDF.

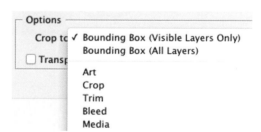

C The **Crop To Menu** in the Place PDF dialog box controls the size of the placed artwork.

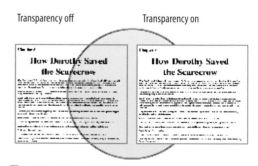

D The effect of the **Transparent Background** on a placed PDF image.

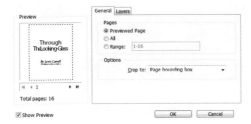

The **Place InDesign Document dialog box** lets you preview and control the options for placed InDesign files.

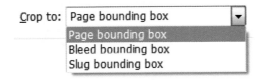

The **Crop To Menu** in the Place InDesign Document dialog box controls the size of the placed artwork.

To set the options for placed InDesign files:

1. In the Place dialog box, select the Show Import Options checkbox.

2. Choose a PDF file. This opens the Place InDesign Document dialog box **E**.

3. Choose Show Preview to see a preview of each page of the placed document.

4. Use the page selectors to select the page you want to place.

5. Click the General tab to see those options.

6. Use the Crop To list to determine how the image should be cropped **F**.

   - **Page bounding box** crops to the trim of the page.

   - **Bleed bounding box** crops to the bleed boundary of the page.

   - **Slug bounding box** crops to the page and slug area of the page.

7. Click the Layers tab to set the layers for the InDesign document.

8. Click OK to place the image.

PDF and InDesign documents can contain more than one page. If you want, you can place those multiple pages all at once, without having to go back to the Place dialog boxes.

TIP Illustrator CS5 and above allows you to save multiple artboards with a file. These import with the same controls as the multiple pages in PDF or InDesign files .

To place multiple pages:

1. In the Place dialog box, choose one of the following:

   - **Previewed Page** selects whatever page is selected in the Preview area.

   - **All** selects all the pages in the document.

   - **Range** allows you to specify individual pages or a range of pages. Use commas to separate individual pages; use a hyphen to specify a range of pages.

2. Click OK to load the cursor.

TIP The cursor for a multiple page document displays a plus (+) sign when it is loaded with multiple pages .

3. Click as many times as necessary to load all the pages. When the plus sign disappears from the cursor, you have reached the last page to be placed.

A The **plus sign (+) in the place cursor** indicates that you can place multiple pages.

Placing Multiple PDF Pages from Bridge

Part of my job is not only to tell you what you *can* do in InDesign, but also to tell you what you *can't* do. Sadly, this sidebar is to tell you what you can't do when placing a PDF file from Adobe Bridge into InDesign.

When you select a PDF in Bridge, the Preview pane adds page controls that allow you to view the various pages in the PDF.

I would have sworn that the Adobe engineers would have designed the program so that whatever page was displayed in the Bridge Preview would automatically be the page placed when you dragged from Bridge onto an InDesign page.

Nope, it doesn't work that way. Even if you set the PDF import option to place a specific page, dragging from Bridge places only the first page of the PDF.

As much as I am a big fan of using Bridge in my workflow, this is an example of where Bridge is not as useful as working with the ordinary Place dialog box.

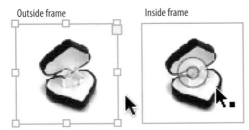

Outside frame   Inside frame

B The Selection tool **displays the content grabber (the donut)** when it comes into the area of the frame.

C **Click on the selection content grabber** to select the image inside a frame.

D **Press and drag on the content grabber** to move the image inside a frame.

Working with Images Inside Frames

After you place an image, you may want to move or modify it. Which tool you use and where you click affects what will be selected.

To select and move both the frame and the image:

1. Use the Selection tool and click the frame holding the image. A bounding box appears that indicates that the frame and its content are selected **B**.

2. Move the Selection tool inside the bounding box and drag to move both the frame and the image **B**.

TIP Do not drag the content grabber (the donut) or you will select and move the image inside the frame.

You can also use the Selection tool to move an image within a frame. This requires viewing and dragging the content grabber (the donut) within the frame. (Honest! Adobe calls this the donut.)

To select the image inside the frame:

1. Move the Selection tool inside the frame and position it over the content grabber. The grabber hand appears.

2. Click with the grabber hand. This selects the image within the frame **C**.

To select and move the image inside the frame:

1. Move the Selection tool inside the frame and position it over the content grabber. The grabber hand appears.

2. Press and drag to move the image within the frame **D**.

TIP You can also use the Direct Selection tool to select an image within a frame.

You can use the Selection tool to resize both the frame and the image as you drag.

To resize a frame and image by dragging:

1. Select the image to be resized.

2. Click the Auto-Fit command in the Control panel.

3. Drag the one of the handles for the frame. The image and frame resize together.

TIP You can also hold the Cmd/Ctrl key as you drag the frame to resize the image inside the frame.

When you apply transformations to frames that contain placed images, you have a choice as to which objects — the frame, the image, or both — are transformed. Here are some helpful guides.

TIP If you pause before you drag with any of the transform tools, you will see a preview of the image as you transform it.

To transform both the frame and the placed image:

1. Use the Selection tool to select both the frame and the placed image.

2. Use any of the Transform panel fields or transform tools .

To modify the content only:

1. Click the image grabber within a frame to select the artwork.

2. Use any of the Transform panel fields or transform tools to modify only the selected image .

To modify the container frame only:

1. Use the Direct Selection tool to select the frame that contains the image.

2. Use any of the Transform panel fields or transform tools to modify only the selected frame .

A An example of **a frame and image that have been transformed**.

B An example of **an image that has been transformed** without changing the frame that holds the image.

C An example of **a frame that has been transformed** without changing the image within the frame.

D The effect of the **Fit Content Proportionally command**.

E The **Fit Content Proportionally command** may leave a gap between the frame and the image. The **Fill Frame Proportionally command** always fills the frame.

F The effect of the **Fit Frame to Content command**.

"Why Does the Frame Say 100% Even Though I Resized the Image?"

Try this: import an image into a frame, and then shrink the image.

When you look at the Control panel the frame size is listed at 100%. How can the image which has just been shrunk down still be listed as 100%? The answer is that the *frame* may be listed as 100%, but if you select the *image* with the Direct Selection tool, you'll see the percentage that the image was scaled.

Fitting Graphics in Frames

Placed images don't always fit perfectly into preexisting frames. InDesign gives you several commands that let you quickly position and resize artwork in frames.

To proportionally resize to the frame size:

1. Use either selection tool to select the frame or the graphic inside the frame.

2. Choose **Object > Fitting > Fit Content Proportionally**. This changes the size of the graphic to fit completely, and without distortion, within the frame **D**.

TIP Use the Fit Frame to Content command to resize the frame to the size of the graphic.

The Fit Content Proportionally command usually leaves some empty space between the graphic and the frame. What if you want to resize the image so that it fills the entire frame? That's where the Fill Frame Proportionally command comes to the rescue.

To resize the graphic to fill the frame:

1. Use either selection tool to select the frame or the graphic inside the frame.

2. Choose **Object > Fitting > Fill Frame Proportionally**. This changes the size of the graphic to fit completely, and without distortion, within the frame **E**.

To resize the frame to the graphic size:

1. Use either selection tool to select the frame or the graphic inside the frame.

2. Choose **Object > Fitting > Fit Frame to Content**. This changes the size of the frame so that the artwork fits completely within the area of the frame **F**.

If a frame is larger than the content, you can resize the frame to the size of the graphic by clicking the frame handles.

To resize the frame by clicking the handles:

1. Use the Selection tool to select the frame.
2. Click the frame handles as follows:
   - Double-click a corner handle to resize both horizontally and vertically.
   - Double-click the left or right handles to resize either horizontally.
   - Double-click the top or bottom handles to resize vertically.

TIP This works on both images and text.

Sometimes you need to put a graphic in the center of a frame. This is especially helpful if an image has been transformed so it is no longer visible within the frame.

To center the graphic within the frame:

1. Use either selection tool to select the frame or the graphic inside the frame.
2. Choose **Object > Fitting > Center Content**. This centers the graphic within the frame without changing the size of either the graphic or the frame 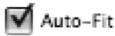.

TIP The Fitting commands are also available on the Control panel .

Before   After

 The effect of the **Center Content command**.

Fill Frame   Fit Content   Fit Content   Fit Frame   Center
Proportionally Proportionally   to Frame   to Content   Content

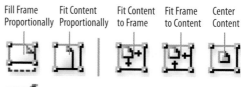

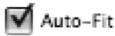 Use the **Fit icons in the Control panel** to modify placed images and frames.

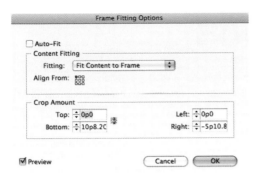

A Use the **Frame Fitting Options dialog box** to set how images appear when placed into a frame.

B The **Fitting controls list** lets you choose the Fitting options for how an image is scaled when placed in an empty frame.

Many designers work with frames already in the layout to which they add images. What they want is their image to automatically be placed at the correct size — filling the frame, or scaled proportionally. InDesign lets you apply that setting to empty frames.

To apply the fitting commands to empty frames:

1. Select the frame.

2. Choose **Object > Fitting > Frame Fitting Options** to open the Frame Fitting Options dialog box **A**.

3. Use the Crop Amount to specify how much area of the image should be outside the frame.

4. Set the Alignment Reference Point to choose how the image should be positioned when cropped or scaled.

5. Use the Fitting list to set how the image will be scaled when placed into an empty frame **B**.

   or

   Choose None to leave the image unscaled when placed.

6. Check Auto-Fit to have the image resize automatically when you resize the frame.

TIP The Auto-Fit setting is also found in the Control panel under the Fit icons.

Linking Graphics

When you place an image, you don't actually place the image into the document. You place a screen preview of the image that links to the original graphic. In order to print the file, InDesign needs to follow that *link* to the original graphic.

TIP It is possible to link text files as well as graphics, but those are primarily used together with InCopy.

To examine the links in a document:

1. Choose **Window > Links**. This opens the Links panel **A**. The Links panel shows all the linked images in the document with their page numbers. Special icons indicate the status of the image **B**.

   - **Missing Link** indicates that InDesign can't find the original graphic.

   - **Modified Link** indicates that the graphic has changed and has a different modification date from when it was originally placed.

2. Click the page numbers to go to that instance of the link.

TIP When there is more than one instance of a link, the link name appears with an arrow that groups all instances of that link. Click the arrow to display all the instances.

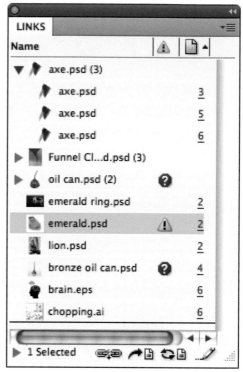

A The **Links panel** displays the names of the placed images in the document.

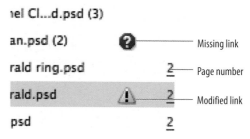

Missing link

Page number

Modified link

B The **icons and page numbers next to a listing in the Links panel** tell you the status of a placed image.

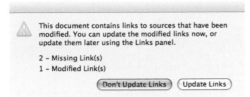

The Missing or Modified Links notice appears when you open a file whose link is missing or has been changed **c**.

To relink graphics when you open a document:

1. Click the Update Links button in the Missing or Modified Links notice. All modified graphics are automatically updated.

2. If there are missing links, the operating system navigation dialog box opens. Use it to find each missing graphic.

You can use the Links panel to relink missing graphics to the screen preview.

To relink a missing graphic:

1. Select the missing link in the Links panel.

TIP **You can also select multiple links. Shift-click to select a range of links. Cmd/Ctrl-click to select noncontiguous links.**

2. Click the Relink button. This opens the navigation dialog box, which you can use to find the missing file.

   or

   Choose Relink from the Links panel menu.

3. Navigate to find the missing file.

4. Select the Search for Missing Links in This Folder checkbox to relink all missing graphics that are in that folder **d**.

5. Select the Show Import Options checkbox to open the Import Options dialog box before you relink the graphic.

6. Click Open to relink the graphic.

c The **Missing or Modified Links notice** appears when you open an InDesign document that has a link to a graphics file that is missing or modified.

d Select the **Search for Missing Links in This Folder option** to update all missing images in that folder.

Working With Missing Images

I often transfer an InDesign file from a storage CD onto my hard drive. When I do, InDesign notifies me that the links for the file are missing.

I don't often update those links because I know that as soon as I eject the CD, I'm going to get the notice that the images are missing.

I just work on the InDesign file and then update the links when I'm ready to send the finished file to my publisher. It doesn't really matter to work on a file with missing links.

I just click the Don't Update Links notice.

If a graphic has been modified, you can use the controls at the bottom of the Links panel to update the link.

To update modified links:

1. Select the modified link in the Links panel.

2. Click the Update Link button  or choose Update Link from the Links panel menu.

TIP Shift-click to select a range of links. Cmd/Ctrl-click to select noncontiguous links.

The Links panel also lets you move quickly to a specific graphic.

To jump to a linked graphic in the document:

1. Select the link in the Links panel.

2. Click the Go to Link button A or choose Go to Link from the Links panel menu.

The Links panel can also be used to open and edit a graphic.

To edit a linked graphic:

1. Select the graphic you want to edit.

2. Choose Edit Original from the Links panel menu. The graphic opens in the program that created it.

   or

   Click the Edit Original icon in the Links panel A.

TIP To force a graphic to open in a certain program, choose Edit With and then choose a program from the Links panel menu.

TIP Hold the Opt/Alt key and double-click the graphic to edit the original.

A The **icon commands in the Links panel** allow you to access frequently used commands.

Linking Objects, Text, and Images

You can also select objects, text, and images and place and link them elsewhere in the document or other documents. Place and link means that if you modify the original items, the linked items can be updated.

For more information on placing and linking items see Chapter 18, "Working with Layouts."

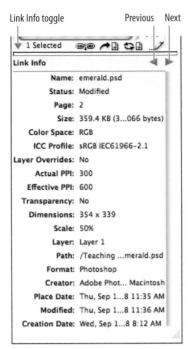

Link Info toggle   Previous   Next

B   The **Link Info area** in the Links panel gives you information about a placed graphic.

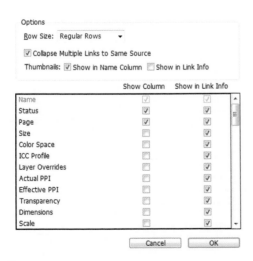

C   The **Panel Options** for the Links panel.

You may want to find a placed image in the Macintosh Finder, Windows Explorer, or Bridge window.

To find the linked file:

1. Select the graphic in the Links panel.

2. Choose one of the following in the Links panel menu:

   • **Reveal in Finder** (Mac) or **Reveal in Explorer** (Win) to select the file in the operating system directory.

   • **Reveal in Bridge** to select the file in the Bridge window.

The Link Information dialog box gives you information about an imported graphic.

To see the link information:

1. Select the graphic in the Links panel.

2. If the Link Info is not visible, click the Link Info toggle in the Links panel. This reveals the link information area B.

3. Use the Next or Previous buttons to move to other graphics in the Links panel.

If all the information in the Link Info area is too much to handle, you can customize what items are displayed.

To customize the Link Info items:

1. Choose Panel Options from the Links panel.

2. Use the Row Size menu to make the list of linked items larger or smaller C.

3. Click the options for Thumbnails to Show in the Column and/or Show in Link Info.

4. Use the Show Column checkboxes to show information in the top of the Links panel.

5. Use the Show in Link Info checkboxes to show information in the Link Info area.

Setting Layer Visibility

When you import Photoshop, Illustrator, InDesign, and PDF files, you have the chance to set the visibility of the layers in those files.

To set the layer options as you import files:

1. Choose Show Import Options when you place a layered Photoshop, Illustrator, InDesign, or PDF file.
2. Click the Layers option in the Show Import Options dialog box A.
3. Click the visibility icon for each layer to show or hide that layer.
4. If you have chosen a Photoshop file with layer comps, use the Layer Comp list to choose the layer comp that you want to apply to the image B.

TIP The layer comp description appears in the field under the Layer Comp list.

5. Select one of the following from the When Updating Link list:
   - **Use Photoshop's/PDF's Layer Visibility** resets any overrides you have made in InDesign to the settings of the original.
   - **Keep Layer Visibility Overrides** maintains any layer settings you have made in InDesign.

TIP The Layer Overrides information in the Links panel indicates if you have set the layers differently from the saved state of the file C.

Once you have imported a layered file, you can also change the visibility of the layers.

To edit the layer options of a placed file:

1. Select the placed image.
2. Choose **Object > Object Layer Options**.
3. Use the steps in the previous exercise to make any changes.

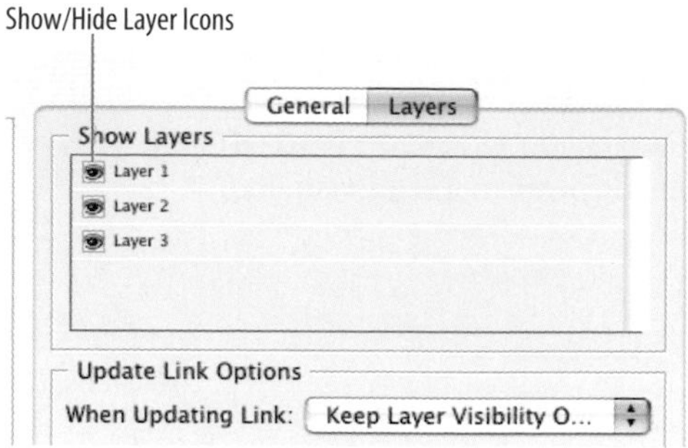

A The **Layer controls** of the Place PDF dialog box.

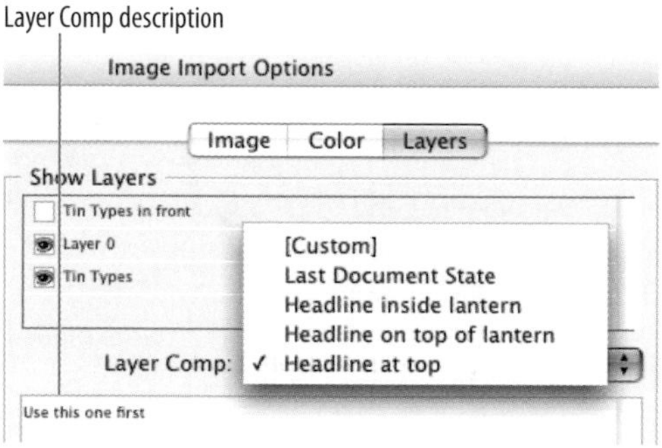

B The **Layer Comp list of the Image Import Options** for a Photoshop file.

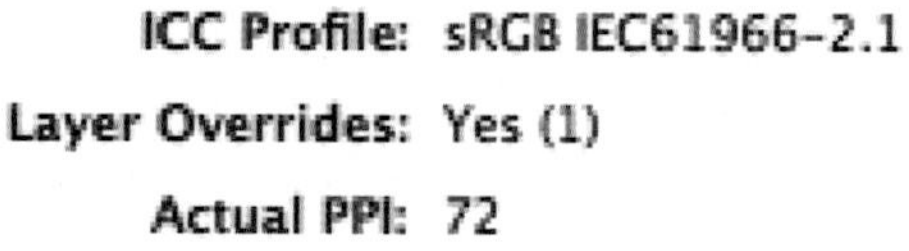

C The **Yes for Layer Overrides in the Links panel** indicates that the visibility of the layers is different from the saved state of the file.

D The transparency grid in Photoshop lets you see the **fully transparent and semi-opaque areas** of the image.

E A **transparent Photoshop file placed into InDesign** lets you see through the glass to the text behind the image.

Importing Transparent Images

InDesign offers you a special advantage when you place native Photoshop (PSD) or Illustrator (AI) files. If there is any transparency in the placed image, InDesign displays the image with the same transparency as in the original file.

To use the transparency in a Photoshop file:

1. In Photoshop, use any of the tools to silhouette or fade the edges of the image. The Photoshop transparency grid indicates which parts of the image are transparent D.

2. Save the file as a Photoshop (PSD) file.

3. Choose **File > Place** to import the file into the InDesign document.

4. Click to place the file. The areas that were transparent in Photoshop will be transparent in InDesign E.

TIP You can combine the use of a Photoshop silhouette together with transparency to create an image with a see-through transparency.

To use the transparency in an Illustrator file:

1. In Illustrator, use any of the commands to apply transparency to the artwork.

2. Save the file as an Illustrator (AI) file.

3. Make sure that the PDF Compatibility option is selected in the Save dialog box.

4. Import the file into the InDesign document. The areas that were transparent in Illustrator will be transparent in InDesign.

Viewing Images

When you have a large document with a lot of images in it, you might find that the redraw time is delayed as you move around. However, you can set preferences for how your images are displayed by lowering some of the image detail for increased speed as you move through pages. These display settings can be applied to the entire document or to individually selected objects.

TIP The display settings for images don't affect how the document will print.

To set the default appearance of previews:

1. Choose **Edit > Preferences > Display Performance** (Win).

   or

   Choose **InDesign > Preferences > Display Performance** (Mac). This opens the Display Performance Preferences dialog box 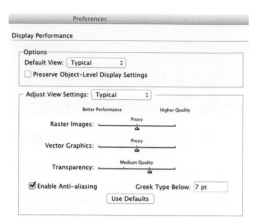.

2. Choose one of the three options from the Default View Settings menu **B**.

   - **Fast** is used when you want fast screen redraw and the best performance.

   - **Typical** is used when you want a better representation of the images.

   - **High Quality** is used when you want to see as much detail as possible onscreen. This option may cause InDesign to work slower than it will with the other choices.

TIP Each of the menu choices corresponds to one choice in the Adjust View Settings list.

3. Select Preserve Object-level Display Settings to use the display settings that have been applied to individual images **C**.

A The **Display Performance Preferences dialog box** controls how images and transparency effects are displayed.

B The **Default View Settings list** lets you choose which display performance setup is applied to images.

C Select **Preserve Object-level Display Settings** to let each object's settings override the overall document display setting.

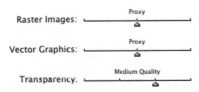

The **Adjust View Settings menu** gives you three display settings to apply to a document or individual images.

The **Raster Images and Vector Graphics slider**s let you control how those formats are displayed.

An example of the **Gray Out view setting**.

Proxy display   High Resolution display

The difference between the Proxy setting and the High Resolution setting.

The labels Fast, Typical, and High Quality are merely guides. You can customize the specific displays for raster images, vector art, and transparency effects in the Adjust View Settings area of the Display Performance Preferences.

To set the raster and vector displays:

1. Choose **Edit > Preferences > Display Performance** (Win).

   or

   Choose **InDesign > Preferences > Display Performance** (Mac).

2. Choose one of the options in the Adjust View Settings menu .

3. Drag the slider for the Raster Images or Vector Graphics as follows :

   - **Gray Out** (far left) displays a gray background instead of the image . This is the fastest performance.

   - **Proxy** (middle) displays a 72-ppi screen preview of the image . This setting provides the best performance that still shows what the image looks like.

   - **High Resolution** (far right) displays the maximum resolution for the image .

4. Repeat the process for each of the other menu settings.

TIP Raster Images and Vector Graphics settings don't have to be set for the same resolution. This allows you to have a faster redraw for large raster files, and more details in the lines of vector graphics.

You can also adjust the display for the transparency effects as well as the drop shadows and feather effects.

To set the transparency effects displays:

1. Choose one of the listings in the Adjust View Settings menu.

2. Drag the Transparency slider to each notch setting as follows **A**. (The labels appear as you drag the slider):

   - **Off** (far left) displays no transparency effects. This is the fastest performance.

   - **Low Quality** (second from left) displays basic opacity and blend modes. Drop shadows and feathers are displayed in low resolution only. Some blend modes may change in the final output.

   - **Medium Quality** (second from right) displays drop shadows and feathers in low resolution.

   - **High Quality** (far right) displays high resolution drop shadows and feathers. Blend modes appear in their correct CMYK color display.

3. Repeat the process for each of the other Adjust View menu items.

A The **Transparency slider** lets you control the display of drop shadows, feathers, and transparency effects. The setting labels appear as you move the slider.

Text Effects 9

Go back and look at the newspaper magazine advertisements created in the 1800s. (Yes, that was *way before* I worked in advertising.) In those ads, the text marches along in a straight line without swerving toward or moving around the images.

Back then, it was extremely difficult to wrap text around an image. Each line of text had to be cut and pasted around the edges of an image.

The paste-up artists never dreamed of setting text along a path so that it follows the shape of a rollercoaster — that would have been far too much work!

Adding short horizontal rules to divide paragraphs was another tedious task. In fact, if you look closely at some old advertisements, you can see that the rule isn't perfectly centered between the columns.

Fortunately, electronic page-layout programs such as InDesign make it easy to do all these special text effects with incredible precision.

Wrapping Text

One of my favorite effects to apply to text is to arrange it to flow around images and other objects. This is called *text wrap* in InDesign, a text runaround in some other programs. (InDesign doesn't give you the runaround.)

To apply a text wrap:

1. Select the object that you want the text to wrap around. This can be an imported graphic, a text frame, or an unassigned frame.

2. Choose **Window > Text Wrap.** This opens the Text Wrap panel .

3. Choose one of the following options for how the text should flow around the object 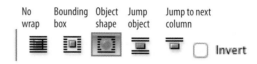. *(Options shown in the chart on the following page.)*

   • **No wrap** lets the text flow across the object.

   • **Bounding Box** flows the text around the bounding box for the object.

   • **Object Shape** flows the text around the shape of the frame or the shape of the placed graphic.

   • **Jump Object** flows the text to the next available space under the object.

   • **Jump to Next Column** flows the text to the next column or text frame.

4. Select the Invert checkbox to force the text to flow inside the object 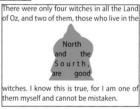.

5. Enter an amount in the offset fields to control the distance between the text and the object 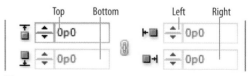.

TIP Click the Make All Settings the Same icon (chain) so that all the offsets are equal.

TIP The number of available offset fields depends on the type of text wrap you choose.

A The **Text Wrap panel** controls the settings for how text flows around an object.

B The **five different text wrap buttons** let you choose how the text wraps around objects.

Regular text wrap

C When the **Invert command** is turned on, the text wrap causes the text to flow inside, not outside, an object.

D Use the **text wrap offset controls** to set the distance between text and a graphic.

Wrap Chosen	Offset Available	Results
No Wrap	No offset options available.	
Bounding Box	Top, bottom, left, and right offset options available.	
Object Shape	Top offset option is the only one available. The amount is used as the space around the entire graphic.	
Jump Object	Top, bottom, left, and right offset options available. However, only the top and bottom offsets affect the text.	
Jump to Next Column	Top, bottom, left, and right offset options available. However, only the top offset affects the text.	

TIP Unless you change the preference setting, lines that wrap below the text wrap object skip to the next available leading increment below the object.

When you choose Object Shape for the text wrap, InDesign lets you set how the text wraps as well as the contour options for that shape.

To set the text wrap contour options:

1. Use the Direct Selection tool to select the image.

2. Click the Object Shape text wrap button in the Text Wrap panel.

3. Choose Show Options from the Text Wrap panel menu to display the Contour Options at the bottom of the Text Wrap panel **A**.

4. Use the Contour Options Type menu to choose the type of element that should be used to create the text wrap **B**:

   - **Bounding Box** uses the rectangle that contains the image.

   - **Detect Edges** uses the differences between the pixels of the image and its background.

   - **Alpha Channel** lets you choose an embedded alpha channel.

   - **Photoshop Path** lets you choose an embedded path.

   - **Graphic Frame** uses the shape of the frame that contains the image.

   - **Same As Clipping** uses whatever shape has been designated as the clipping path for the image.

5. If you choose Alpha Channel or Photo-shop Path, use the second pop-up menu to choose a specific channel or path.

6. Select the Include Inside Edges checkbox to make the text wrap inside any holes in the image, path, or alpha channel **C**.

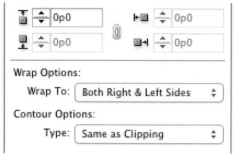

A The **Wrap Options** at the bottom of the Text Wrap panel.

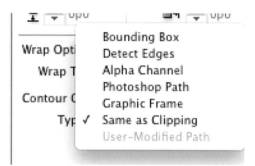

B The **Contour Options Type menu** lets you choose what type of element controls the shape of the text wrap.

Finally she picked up her basket. "Come along, Toto," she said. "We will go to the Emerald City."

C Use the **Include Inside Edges** option to have text wrap within the edges of the image, such as within the handles of the basket.

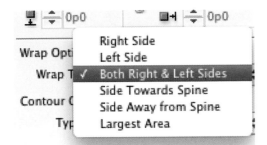

D The **Wrap To menu** lets you choose the orientation for text wraps around objects.

In the books, the origins of gruesome. Originally an name of Nick Chopper, the make his living chopping of Ox. The Wicked enchanted his axe marrying the girl | the character are rather ordinary man by the Tin Woodman used to down trees in the forest Witch of the East to prevent him from that he loved.

E The Wrap To option set to wrap the text on both sides of the object.

In the books, the origins of the character are rather gruesome. Originally an ordinary man by the name of Nick Chopper, the Tin Woodman used to make his living chopping down trees in the forest of Ox. The Wicked Witch of the

F The Wrap To option set to wrap the text on whichever side has the largest area.

Just as you can set the alignment for a paragraph, you can also set how text wraps to the object.

To set the wrap to options for a text wrap:

1. Use the Direct Selection tool to select the image.

2. Click the Object Shape text wrap button in the Text Wrap panel.

3. Choose Show Options from the Text Wrap panel menu to display the Wrap Options in the Text Wrap panel.

4. Use the Wrap To menu to choose the orientation for the text wrap **D**:

   - **Right Side** wraps only around the right side of the object.

   - **Left Side** wraps only around the left side of the object.

   - **Both Left & Right Sides** wraps to both sides of the object **E**.

   - **Side Towards Spine** wraps to either the left or right side of the object depending which side of a facing page document the object is on.

   - **Side Away From Spine** wraps to the opposite side of the object compared to the command above.

   - **Largest Area** wraps only on the side that has the most area. This may cause the text to flip from left to right **F**.

A text wrap doesn't have to be around visible objects. You can use an object with no fill or stroke as the shape to wrap text around . This creates a special effect for text around an image.

To wrap text around an invisible object:

1. Draw an object with no fill or stroke.
2. Set the Text Wrap to Object Shape.

Once you set a text wrap, you can still manipulate it so that the text reads more legibly or fits more attractively into the contour of the object. This is called a *custom text wrap*.

To create a custom text wrap:

1. Use either selection tool to select the object that has the text wrap applied to it.

TIP Apply the Object Shape text wrap button set for Graphic Frame to create a simple text wrap without a lot of points.

2. Use the Direct Selection tool to move the points on the text wrap path **B**.

TIP You can preview how the text reflows around the text wrap. Press and hold for a moment before you move the point of the text wrap. You can then see the text reflow as you move the point.

3. Click the Pen tool between points on the text wrap path to add a new point to the path **C**.

4. Click the Pen tool on a point on the text wrap path to delete the point from the path **D**.

TIP Hold the Cmd/Ctrl key to access the Direct Selection tool while using the Pen tool.

A An example of how an invisible object can be used to create a text wrap.

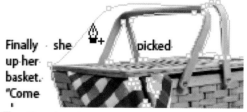

B Use the Direct Selection tool to **change the shape of a text wrap path.**

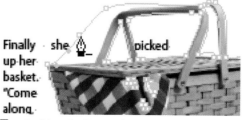

C The **plus sign next to the Pen tool** indicates that you can add a point to the text wrap path.

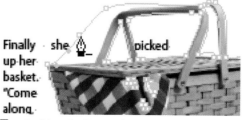

D Position the Pen tool over a point and click to **delete points from a text wrap path.**

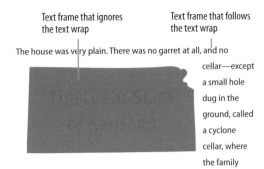

Text frame that ignores the text wrap

Text frame that follows the text wrap

The house was very plain. There was no garret at all, and no cellar—except a small hole dug in the ground, called a cyclone cellar, where the family

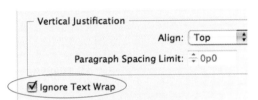

E An example of how **Ignore Text Wrap** keeps the map title from being affected by the text wrap applied to the outline of the state.

Vertical Justification

Align: Top

Paragraph Spacing Limit: 0p0

☑ Ignore Text Wrap

F The **Ignore Text Wrap checkbox** in the Text Frame Options dialog box prevents text from being affected by any text wrap settings.

You may find that you don't want some text to be affected by a text wrap. For instance, you might want to have the body text in one frame run around an image but have the text label in another frame appear over the image **E**. That's when you need to direct the text frame to ignore a nearby text wrap.

To ignore the text wrap:

1. Select the text frame that contains the text that you don't want affected by the text wrap command.

2. Choose **Object > Text Frame Options.** This opens the Text Frame Options dialog box **F**.

3. Select the Ignore Text Wrap checkbox. The text in that frame is unaffected by any objects that have a text wrap applied.

TIP Text wrap is applied even if the object that has the wrap is on a hidden layer. Use the Layer Options dialog box to change this so that hidden layers do not exert a text wrap.

Master pages *(covered in Chapter 10, "Pages and Books")* allow you to place an object on many pages at once. You can set the text wrap for an object so that it is only applied on the master page, not any document pages.

To set the text wrap for an object on a master page:

1. Place the object on a master page.

2. Choose Apply to Master Page Only from the Text Wrap panel menu. (This command is only available for objects on a master page.)

Text on a Path

When you create an object such as a text frame, the outside shape of the frame is considered the object's path. Not only can InDesign fit text inside a text frame, it also lets you position text so that it runs along the outside of the frame.

To run text on the outside of a path:

1. Choose the Path Type tool in the flyout under the Type tool in the Tools panel .

2. Move the tool so that it is near the path. A small plus sign appears next to the tool cursor **B**.

3. Click with the Path Type tool. A blinking insertion point appears on the path.

4. Type the text. Use any of the text controls to select or modify the text.

TIP Use the Direct Selection tool to select the path and change its fill or stroke to None to make the path invisible.

Once you apply text to a path, you can drag to position the text.

To position text on a path:

Drag the indicator at the start or end of the text on a path to change the start or end point of the text **C**.

or

Drag the small indicator within the text to change the center point of the text **D**.

TIP You can also drag the center point indicator to the other side of the path.

TIP You can use the Paragraph panel to change the alignment of the text between the start and end indicators.

A The **Path Type tool** in the Tools panel is used to add text to a path.

B The plus sign next to the Path Type cursor indicates that you can click to add text to a path.

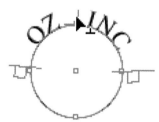

C Drag the indicator line to move the text along a path.

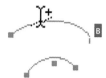

D The **center point indicator** allows you to move text or flip it from one side of the path to another.

The **Path Type Options dialog box** allows you to control how text is applied to a path.

WIZARDRY — Rainbow

WIZARDRY — Skew

WIZARDRY — 3D Ribbon

WIZARDRY — Stair Step

(Gravity)

The **five effect settings** applied to text on a path.

To apply effects to text on a path:

1. Choose **Type > Type on a Path > Options.** This opens the Path Type Options dialog box **E**.

2. Use the Effect menu **F** to control how the text is positioned in relationship to the path **G**.

   - **Rainbow** positions the text in an arc along any curves in the path.

   - **Skew** distorts the text vertically as it is positioned along curves in the path.

   - **3D Ribbon** distorts the text horizontally as it is positioned along curves in the path.

   - **Stair Step** aligns the individual baselines of each letter so that the text stays vertical as it is positioned along curves in the path.

   - **Gravity** uses the shape of the path to distort the text as it is positioned along curves in the path.

3. Select the Flip checkbox to position the text on the other side of the path.

4. If the spacing of the text is uneven, use the spacing control to tighten the character spacing around sharp turns and acute angles on the path.

TIP Higher values remove more space from between the characters.

You can also control where the letters are positioned vertically on the path.

To set the vertical alignment of text on a path:

1. Use the Align menu  to control how the text is positioned in relationship to the path 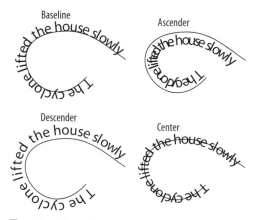.

   - **Ascender** positions the text so that the tops of the tallest letters touch the path.

   - **Descender** positions the text so that the bottoms of the lowest letters touch the path.

   - **Center** positions the text so that the middle of the text touches the path.

   - **Baseline** positions the text so that the baseline of the text touches the path.

2. Use the To Path menu to position the vertical alignment in one of the following positions **C**:

   - **Top** positions the text relative to the top of the path's stroke weight **D**.

   - **Center** positions the text in the middle of the path's stroke weight **D**.

   - **Bottom** positions the text relative to the bottom of the stroke weight **D**.

TIP If you do not see any changes between the To Path settings, try increasing the thickness of the stroke weight.

TIP You can also use the Baseline Shift controls to move the text up or down relative to the path.

A The **Align menu** controls how the text is positioned in relationship to the path.

B The **Align choices** applied to text on a path.

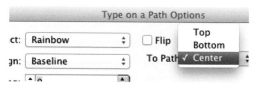

C The **To Path menu** positions the vertical alignment of the text on the path.

D The effect of the To Path settings on the **position of text on a stroked path**.

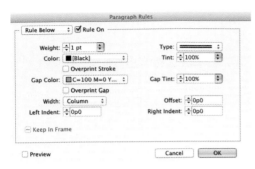

E The **Paragraph Rules dialog box** controls the settings for paragraph lines.

F Choose **Rule Above or Rule Below** to position the line above or below a paragraph.

Why Use Paragraph Rules?

If you want a line (technically called a *rule*) to appear above or below a paragraph, you might draw a line using the Pen or the Line tool. Unfortunately, if the text reflows, that line does not travel with the text. You could also paste the line into the text as an inline graphic, but you would not have much control over that line.

The proper way to create lines above or below paragraphs is to use the Paragraph Rules commands. Because the rules are applied as part of the paragraph settings, they automatically move if the paragraph moves. In addition, they can be precisely positioned in relationship to the paragraph.

Working with Paragraph Rules

The correct way to create a line above or below a paragraph is with paragraph rules. These are lines that travel with the paragraph and that can be applied as part of style sheets.

To apply paragraph rules:

1. Select the paragraph to which you want to apply the rule and choose Paragraph Rules from the Paragraph panel menu. This opens the Paragraph Rules dialog box **E**.

2. Choose Rule Above or Rule Below to specify whether the rule appears before or after the selected paragraph **F**.

3. Select the Rule On checkbox to activate the rule.

TIP If you want rules both above and below the paragraph, repeat steps 2 and 3.

Once you have turned on the rule, you can style its appearance. This is somewhat similar to styling the stroke for an object.

To style the appearance of a rule:

1. Set an amount for the weight (or thickness) of the rule .

2. Use the Type list to set a stroke style .

3. Use the Color list to apply one of the pre-defined swatch colors or gradients 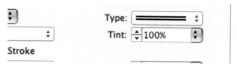.

TIP The Text Color setting sets the rule to the same color as the text.

4. If desired, select Overprint Stroke to set the ink to overprint.

5. Use the Tint control to create a shade of the color .

6. If you have chosen a rule style that has a gap, use the Gap Color list to apply a color or gradient swatch to the gap .

7. If you have chosen a gap color, use the Gap Tint controls to create a shade of the gap color 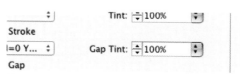.

8. If desired, select Overprint Gap to set the gap ink to overprint.

If a paragraph rule falls at the top of a paragraph, you may want to control whether the rule is displayed inside or outside the frame.

To control the position of the rule within a frame:

1. Select the paragraph with the rule.

2. Open the Paragraph Rules dialog box.

3. Select or deselect the Keep in Frame checkbox.

A Use the **Weight control** to define the thickness of the paragraph rule.

B Use the **Type list** to choose the stroke style for the paragraph rule.

C Use the **Color list** to choose the main color for the paragraph rule.

D Use the **Tint control** to set the screen for the color of the paragraph rule.

E Use the **Gap Color list** to set the secondary color of the paragraph rule.

F Use the **Gap Tint control** to set the screen for the gap color of the paragraph rule.

G The **Width list** lets you choose the length of paragraph rules.

"From the Land of Oz," said Dorothy gravely. "And here is Toto, too. And oh, Aunt Em? I'm so glad to be at home again!" Column

"From the Land of Oz," said Dorothy gravely. "And here is Toto, too. And oh, Aunt Em? I'm so glad to be at home again!" Text

H Column width fits the rule to the width of the column. Text width fits the rule to the neighboring text.

I The **Left Indent and Right Indent fields** let you modify the length of a rule.

"From the Land of Oz," said Dorothy gravely. "And here is Toto, too. And oh, Aunt Em? I'm so glad to be at home again!" No indent

"From the Land of Oz," said Dorothy gravely. "And here is Toto, too. And oh, Aunt Em? I'm so glad to be at home again!" Left and right indents

J How changing the Left and Right Indent settings changes the look of rules.

"From the Land of Oz," said Dorothy gravely. "And here is Toto, too. And oh, Aunt Em? I'm so glad to be at home again!" No offset

"From the Land of Oz," said Dorothy gravely. "And here is Toto, too. And oh, Aunt Em? I'm so glad to be at home again!" 0p8 offset

K Change the Offset amount to move a rule up or down relative to the text.

The length of a rule (called its width) can be set to cover the width of the column or the width of the text. The rule can also be set to be indented from the column or text margins.

To control the width of a rule:

1. Choose from the Width list in the Paragraph Rules dialog box as follows **G**:

   • **Column** creates a rule that is the same width as the column that holds the text **H**.

   • **Text** creates a rule that is the same width as the closest line of text **H**.

TIP If you set a rule below a paragraph that ends in a short line, the rule will be the same length as the last line.

2. Set the Left Indent to the amount that the rule should be indented from the left side of the column or text **I**.

3. Set the Right Indent to the amount that the rule should be indented from the right side of the column or text **I**.

TIP Use positive numbers to move the rule in from the margin **J**. Use negative numbers to move the rule outside the margin. The rule can extend outside the text frame.

By default the paragraph rule is positioned on the baseline of the text. You can control the position above or below the baseline **K**. This is called the *offset* of the rule.

To control the offset of a rule:

In the Paragraph Rules dialog box, enter a value in the Offset field.

   • For a Rule Above, positive numbers raise the rule above the baseline.

   • For a Rule Below, positive numbers lower the rule below the baseline.

TIP Negative numbers move rules in the opposite direction.

You can create many special effects with paragraph rules. One of the most common is to superimpose text inside paragraph rules to create the effect of reversed text. Most reversed text is white type inside a black background. However, any light color can be used inside any dark background 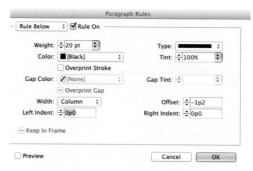.

> **TIP** Don't forget that you can also use the underline or strikethough styles to create reversed text.

To reverse text using rules:

1. Apply a light color to a line of type.

2. Open the Paragraph Rules dialog box **B**.

3. Create a Rule Below.

4. Set the weight of the rule to a point size large enough to enclose the text. For instance, if the text is 12 points, the rule should be at least 12 points.

> **TIP** If you have more than one line of text, you need to calculate the size of the leading times the number of lines.

5. Set a negative number for the offset value.

> **TIP** The offset amount should be slightly less than the weight of the rule. For instance a rule of 14 points might take an offset of minus 11 points.

6. Select the Preview checkbox so you can see the effect of the weight and offset settings you choose.

7. Adjust the weight and offset, if necessary.

8. Click OK to apply the rule.

The Guardian of the Gate

It was some time before the Cowardly Lion awakened, for he had lain among the poppies a long while.

A A paragraph rule can create the effect of reversed text.

B A dialog box showing the sample settings for a paragraph rule that create **the effect of reversed text**.

True Story

When I first started learning page layout software, I used the art director's computer at the advertising agency where I worked. I stayed after hours to explore the programs and create my own documents.

When I saw the command "Rules" in the menu, I figured that was where they kept the laws governing the program. Since I didn't want to mess up the art director's machine, I never chose the command.

It was several years later (and several horrible jobs without any paragraph rules) that I discovered what the "Rules" were.

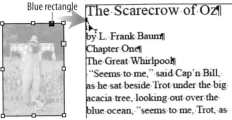
Blue rectangle

C **Drag the blue rectangle into the text** to create an anchored object outside the text frame.

Anchored object Indicator Anchored object within text indicator

D **An anchored object** positioned outside the text frame.

E **An inline object** is positioned within the text flow.

Inline and Anchored Objects

Another type of nested element is an *inline or anchored object*. These objects flow along with the text making it easy to keep the graphic in the same relative position to the text.

An *anchored object* appears outside the margins of the text frame.

To create an anchored object:

1. Position the element outside the text frame where you want it to be.

2. Use the Selection tool to drag the blue rectangle where you want the frame to be anchored **C**.

3. Release the mouse when the cursor is in the correct position. The object is now anchored to that position.

TIP The anchor indicators appear on the object that is anchored as well as within the text **D**.

TIP Use the Direct Selection tool to move the graphic within its inline frame.

An *inline object* is a frame that appears within the margins of the text frame.

To create an inline object:

1. Use the Selection tool to drag the blue rectangle to the spot in the text where you want the frame to be anchored.

2. Hold the Opt/Alt key as you drag the rectangle.

3. Release the mouse when the cursor is in the correct position. The object is now anchored within the text **E**.

TIP Use the Selection tool to select and move inline objects up or down inside the text.

You can also control the position of an inline or anchored object using a dialog box.

To use the Anchored Objects Options dialog box:

1. Hold the Opt/Alt key as you drag the blue rectangle into the text frame.

2. Release the mouse button when the cursor is in the correct position. This opens the Anchored Object Options dialog box 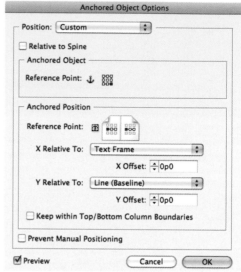.

You can choose inline or anchored object for the object position.

To set the position of the object:

Use the Position list to choose the type of positioning for the anchored object B:

- **Inline or Above Line** positions the anchored object within the text frame. This is the same as holding the Shift key as you drag the blue rectangle into the text frame.

- **Custom** allows you to position the anchored object outside the text frame. This is the same as dragging the blue rectangle into the text frame without holding any modifier keys.

If you have chosen Inline or Above Line, you can set the options for the location of the object C.

To set the options for inline objects:

1. Select the Inline radio button to specify that option for the object. This removes all the options except the Y Offset.

2. Use the Y Offset controls to move the object above or below the baseline of the text.

TIP Positive numbers move the object above the baseline. Negative numbers move the object below the baseline.

A The **Anchored Object Options dialog box** lets you control anchored and inline objects numerically.

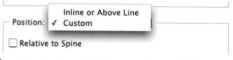

B The **Position list** lets you choose inline or custom locations for the objects.

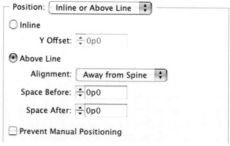

C The Position options for **Inline or Above Line anchored objects**.

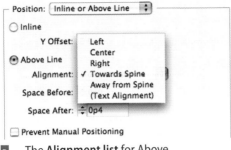

 The **Alignment list** for Above Line anchored objects.

D

To set the options for Above Line objects:

1. Click the Above Line radio button to position the object above the line that contains the anchor insertion point.

2. Use the Alignment list to position the object in the text frame as follows **D**:

   - **Left** aligns the object on the left.
   - **Center** aligns the object in the center.
   - **Right** aligns the object on the right.
   - **Text Alignment** uses whatever alignment was set for the paragraph that contains the anchored object.

3. If you have a facing-page document, you have two additional options. These options flip the anchored object depending on whether it is on a left- or right-hand page.

   - **Towards Spine** positions the object so that it is closest to the spine.
   - **Away From Spine** positions the object so that It Is furthest away from the spine.

4. Use the Space Before or Space After controls to add space above or below the object.

5. Select the Prevent Manual Positioning checkbox to stop the object from being moved with any of the selection tools.

The Custom object position creates an anchored object outside the text frame.

To set the options for custom objects:

1. Set the Position to Custom. This opens the custom settings for the anchored object .

2. Use the Anchored Object Reference Point proxy box to choose which point on the anchored object should be used as the orientation of the anchored object.

3. If the document has facing pages, you can select the Relative to Spine checkbox to allow the settings to flip depending on whether they are left- or right-hand pages.

4. Click the Anchored Position Reference Point to choose the position on the page where the object should align.

5. Use the X Relative To list to set the point from which the horizontal axis should start 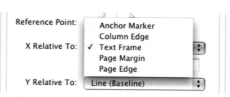.

6. Use the Y Relative To list to set the point from which the vertical axis should start .

7. Use the X Offset and Y Offset controls to move the anchored object from the X and Y reference points.

8. Select Keep Within Top/Bottom Column Boundaries to ensure that the anchored object does not move above or below the frame that contains the text.

9. Select Prevent Manual Positioning to prevent the object from being moved.

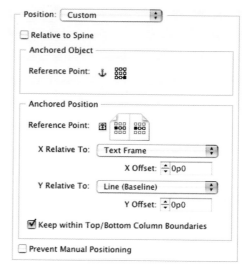

A The settings for a **custom anchored object**.

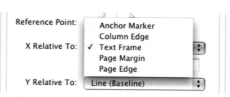

B The **X Relative To list** for custom anchored objects.

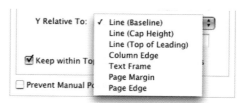

C The **Y Relative To list** for custom anchored objects.

Pages and Books 10

Most people who lay out documents work on projects that have more than one page — booklets, brochures, newsletters, menus, annual reports, magazines, books, and so on. Even a lowly business card has two pages if you design a front and back.

When you work with multipage documents, you need to add pages, flow text, apply page numbers, and force text to move to certain pages.

If you are working on very complex documents, you need to make sure all the pages have the same structure.

If you are working on a book, you will want to join individual chapters together. You may also want to automate the process of creating a table of contents or an index.

Here's where you'll learn how to automate and organize working with multipage layouts. In addition, you'll learn how to use InDesign's Book features to synchronize multiple documents in a large project. You'll also discover special features for creating a table of contents from text.

Changing the Pages Panel

You may want to change the display of the Pages panel.

To open the Pages panel:

If the Pages panel is not visible, choose **Window > Pages** to open the panel 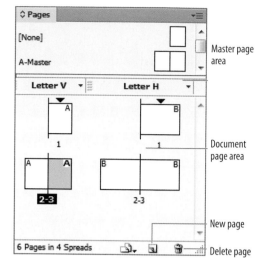.

To control the display of the Pages panel:

1. Choose Panel options from the Pages panel menu. This opens the Panel Options dialog box 🅱.

2. Use the Pages Icon Size menu to choose the size of the document pages icons.

3. Use the Masters Icon Size menu to change the size of the master page icons. These choices are the same as the Pages Icon Size menu.

4. Choose Pages on Top to position the document pages at the top of the panel.

5. Choose Masters on Top to position the master pages at the top of the panel.

6. Use the Resize list to control what happens when you resize the panel:

   - **Proportional** maintains the same relative area as you change the size of the panel.

   - **Pages Fixed** adds new space only to the masters area.

   - **Masters Fixed** adds new space only to the pages area.

🅰 The **Pages panel** is the command center for multipage documents.

🅱 The **Panel Options dialog box** lets you control the appearance of the Pages panel.

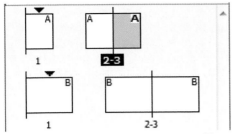

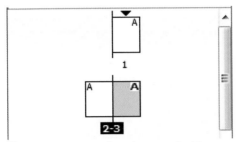

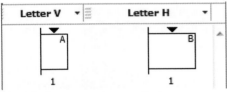

You can also change the layout of the pages in the Pages panel.

To change the layout of the pages panel:

Choose one of the following from the View Pages menu of the Pages panel menu:

- **Horizontally** arranges the pages so the spreads stack across and then down in the document page area C. This layout lets you put the most pages in the smallest panel area.

- **Vertically** arranges the pages so they stack down with only one spread in each row D.

- **By Alternate Layout** arranges the spreads so that each alternate layout is presented under its own layout area E. (*See Chapter 18, "Working with Layouts" for more information on alternate layouts.*)

The Pages panel options let you control what features you see in the panel. For instance, thumbnail previews show you representations of the pages F. This makes it easier to see which pages contain what content.

To see thumbnail previews of the pages:

Turn on Show Thumbnails in the Pages panel options.

The Pages panel also lets you know if certain features have been applied to pages. For instance, you can have an icon that indicates that a transparency effect or Photoshop transparency has been applied on that page F. (*See Chapter 19, "Printing" for more information on flattening.*)

To indicate transparency has been applied:

Turn on Transparency under the Icons area. A small grid appears next to the page F.

C The Pages panel set for a **horizontal layout**.

D The Pages panel set for a **vertical layout**.

E The Pages panel set to display the **alternate layouts**.

F The Pages panel set to display **page thumbnails and the transparency icon**.

Adding Blank Pages

If you need to add just a few pages, you can add them one by one, manually.

To manually add pages:

1. Click the New Page icon in the Pages panel to add a single page.

   or

   Drag a master page or a nonmaster page to the document area of the panel .

2. Repeat as many times as necessary until you have added all the pages you need.

If you need to add many pages, you can add them using the Insert command.

To add pages using the Insert command:

1. Choose Insert Pages from the Pages panel menu. The Insert Pages dialog box appears 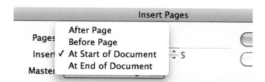.

2. Type the number of pages you want to insert in the Pages field.

3. Choose where to add the pages from the Insert menu as follows 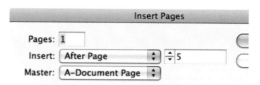:

   - **After Page** lets you insert new pages after a specific page.

   - **Before Page** lets you insert new pages before a specific page.

   - **At Start of Document** inserts new pages at the beginning of the document.

   - **At End of Document** inserts new pages at the end of the document.

4. Use the Master menu to choose the master page for the new pages.

   or

   Choose None from the Master menu to have an empty page that does not act as a master applied to the new pages.

5. Click OK. The new pages appear in the Pages panel.

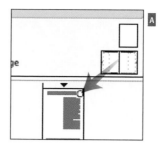

Drag a master page from the master page area of the Pages panel to the document area to add pages to a document.

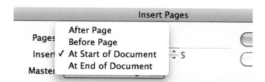

The **Polygon Settings dialog box** creates either polygons or stars.

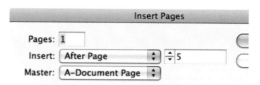

The **Polygon Settings dialog box** creates either polygons or stars.

Glossary of Page Terms

As you work with pages and the Pages panel, it helps if you understand the following:

Document pages: The main pages of your document. These are the pages that contain your project. Items that are on the document pages are *document page items*.

Master pages: The pages that contain elements that are repeated on all the document pages. Items that are on the master pages are called *master page items*.

Local Overrides: Normally you can't select or modify master page items on a document page. However, if you apply a local override to the master page items on a specific document page, they can be modified on the document page.

The colored highlight on the targeted pages (pages 4-5) shows they are not the active pages (pages 2-3).

 The highlight on both the page number and the page for the active pages (pages 2-3) shows they are both targeted and active.

Navigating and Moving Pages

As you work with pages in the Pages panel, you should understand the difference between targeting a page and working on a page. The active page is the page you are currently working on. The targeted page is the page chosen in the Pages panel.

To target a page:

Click the page in the Pages panel. A highlight appears on the page .

TIP When a page is targeted, it means you can apply a command in the Pages panel even without working on the page.

To work on a page:

Double-click the page number or name of the master page spread in the Pages panel. A highlight appears on the number or name of the page E.

TIP When you work on the page, that page or spread is centered within the document window.

InDesign has several different ways to move from page to page.

To move to a specific page using the Pages panel:

Double-click the page in the Pages panel that you want to move to. The page is centered within the document window.

or

Double-click the name of the spread to fit both pages in the document window.

TIP You can also scroll or use the Hand tool to move through the document.

You can also use the navigation controls at the bottom of the document window.

To navigate using the window page menu:

Click a page number in the window page menu to navigate through the document 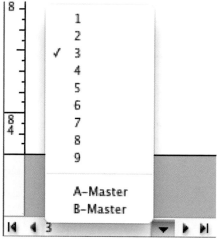.

or

Enter a number in the Page field to move to a specific page.

To use the navigation controls:

Click each of the navigation arrows to move through the document B.

You can also navigate using the commands in the Layout menu in the menu bar at the top of the application.

TIP The Layout menu commands can be applied using keyboard shortcuts. This lets you move through the document without using the mouse.

To navigate using the Layout menu:

Choose one of the following:

- **Layout > First Page** moves to the first page of the document.
- **Layout > Previous Page** moves to the previous page.
- **Layout > Next Page** moves to the next page.
- **Layout > Last Page** moves to the last page of the document.
- **Layout > Next Spread** moves to display the next spread of pages.
- **Layout > Previous Spread** moves to display the previous spread of pages.
- **Layout > Go Back** moves to the page that was previously active.
- **Layout > Go Forward** moves to the page that was active before the Go Back command was applied.

A The **pop-up page list** at the bottom of the document lets you navigate through the document.

B Use the **navigation controls** at the bottom of the document window to move through the document.

Maximum Number of Pages?

The maximum number of pages in an InDesign document is 9,999. Although most documents fall well below that number, many people do need to create books and catalogs that contain 10,000 or more pages.

If you need to create those types of super-long documents, you should break your projects into separate documents. Then, use the Book feature (covered later in this chapter) to maintain proper pagination as well as synchronize master pages and styles.

You can also use the Pages panel to duplicate and delete pages from the document.

To duplicate pages:

1. Select the page or spreads you want to duplicate.
2. Drag the pages onto the New Page icon.

   or

   Choose Duplicate Spread from the Pages panel menu.

To delete pages:

1. Use the Pages panel to select the pages.

TIP **Hold the Shift key to select contiguous pages. Hold the Cmd/Ctrl key to select noncontiguous pages.**

2. Choose Delete Pages from the Pages panel menu.

   or

   Click the Delete Page icon at the bottom of the Pages panel.

TIP **The command may change to Delete Spreads if you have a spread or spreads selected.**

3. When the confirmation dialog box appears, click OK to confirm your choice.

TIP **Hold the Opt/Alt key to bypass the confirmation dialog box.**

You can use the Pages panel to change how pages are arranged in the document.

To rearrange pages in a document:

Drag a page next to or between the pages of a spread as follows 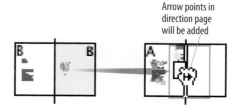:

- With Allow Document Pages to Shuffle turned on, the new page forces other pages to a new spread **B**.
- With Allow Document Pages to Shuffle turned off, the new page is added to the existing spread without moving the other pages **C**.

TIP The arrow cursor indicates which side of a spine the new page is inserted on **A**.

TIP You can drag pages between documents. When you do a dialog box appears asking where you would like the pages to appear.

To move pages in a document:

1. Choose Move Pages from the Pages panel menu. This opens the Move Pages dialog box **D**.

2. Use the Move Pages field to list the pages you want to move.

TIP Use hyphens to designate contiguous pages. Use commas to separate noncontiguous pages.

3. Use the Destination list to choose where you want the pages to move.

4. If you have chosen After Page or Before Page, enter the page number in the field.

5. Use the Move To list to choose the document location. This can be the current document or any open documents.

6. If you choose an external open document, you can select Delete Pages after Moving to delete the pages from the original file.

7. Click OK to move the pages.

Arrow points in direction page will be added

A Pages can be moved by **dragging their icons in the Pages panel.**

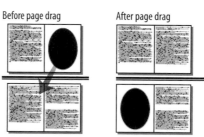

Before page drag   After page drag

B When **Allow Document Pages to Shuffle is turned on**, a page moved between two other pages forces one of the pages to the next spread.

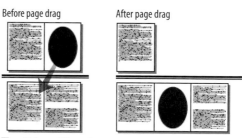

Before page drag   After page drag

C When **Allow Document Pages to Shuffle is turned off**, a page moved between other pages is added between the two pages in the spread.

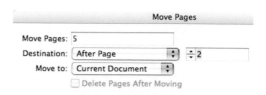

Move Pages

Move Pages: 5
Destination: After Page   2
Move to: Current Document
☐ Delete Pages After Moving

D The **Move Pages dialog box.**

E The **Page tool** in the Tools panel.

W: ▲ 28p4.157
H: ▲ 28p4.157

Compact Disc ▲

F The **page size controls** in the Control panel.

Liquid Layout Rule:
Off ▼

☑ Objects Move with Page
☐ Show Master Page Overlay

G The **Page tool options** in the Control panel.

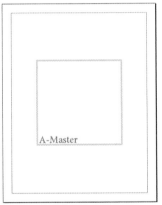

A-Master

H The **master page overlay** shows the size and name of the master page applied to a document page.

Modifying Page Sizes

Most documents contain pages that are all the same size. But there are many projects that need different-sized pages — a brochure with a return postcard, a letterhead with business card, or magazine with a foldout cover. Fortunately InDesign makes it easy to change the size of individual pages in a document.

TIP These are the basic controls for changing page sizes. *See Chapter 18, "Working with Layouts" for more information on the Liquid Layout control for resizing pages.*

To change the size of a page:

1. Select the Page tool in the Tools panel **E**.

2. Click the page you want to modify in the Pages panel or in the document window.

TIP To select multiple pages hold the Cmd/Ctrl key and click additional pages.

3. Use the W (width) and H (height) fields in the Control panel to adjust the size of the page **F**.

   or

   Choose a specific page size from the menu in the Control panel.

TIP Select a point in the proxy box to control from what position the page changes size.

4. Use the orientation icons to choose Portrait or Landscape page.

5. Choose one of the following options for the Page tool **G**:

   • Select Show Master Page Overlay to see a representation of the size of the master applied to a page **H**.

   • Select Objects Move with Page to control whether objects move with a page when the Page tool changes the position of a page.

In addition to selecting pages, the Page tool also lets you move pages around the artboard in custom positions. This is helpful if you need a special arrangement of the pages in a document.

TIP The following technique does not work when working on a facing page document. If you are working on a facing page document, choose File > Document Setup and deselect Facing Pages.

To move pages on the artboard:

1. From the Pages panel menu, deselect Allow Document Pages to Shuffle. This allows you to move all the pages in the document.

TIP You can also deselect Allow Selected Spread to Shuffle. This allows you to move just the pages in the selected spread.

2. Use the Page tool to drag a page on the artboard from one position to another  and .

TIP Pages can be moved so they overlap portions of other pages. This allows an element on one page to be printed on two separate pages.

A Use the Page tool to **drag one page away from another** on the artboard.

B Two pages separated and repositioned.

But Will It Print?

The concept of different-sized pages within one document may be difficult for your print shop to accept. If you do create a job with pages of different sizes, talk to your print shop ahead of time. Make sure they have time to test the files. Or better yet, send them a PDF to see if that will output correctly.

It doesn't help to be on the cutting edge of technology if you end up bleeding from the experience.

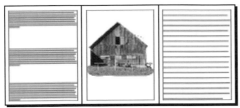

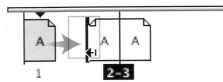

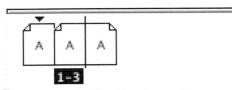

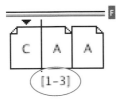

C An example of how three pages can be put together to form **an island spread**.

D The thick vertical line indicates that the new page will be added as an island spread.

E An example of **an island spread in the Pages panel**.

F The **brackets around the numbers** indicate that Allow Selected Spread to Shuffle has been turned off for the pages.

Creating and Separating Spreads

Most documents are either single-page or facing-page documents. However, you can create spreads with more than one or two pages. These are *island spreads,* like the fold-outs found in special issues of magazines **C**.

To create an island spread:

1. Deselect Allow Document Pages to Shuffle in the Pages panel menu.

   TIP This command is turned off so that the pages that are already in the spread do not move to new positions.

2. Drag a page from the pages area, or a master page, next to the spread.

3. Release the mouse button when the vertical line appears next to the spread **D**. This adds the page to the island spread **E**.

To dismantle an island spread:

1. Drag each page outside the spread.

   or

   Choose Allow Document Pages to Shuffle from the Pages panel menu. A dialog box asks if you want to maintain the current number of pages in the spread.

2. Click the No button. This dismantles the island spread into the default number of pages per spread in the document.

You can also control whether or not the pages in a spread are kept together or allowed to separate.

To keep the pages in a spread together:

1. Select the spread you want to protect.

2. Deselect Allow Selected Spread to Shuffle from the Pages panel menu. Brackets appear around the page numbers **F**. This prevents the spread from separating if you add pages.

Importing Text

If you have a short amount of text, you can easily type it directly in InDesign's text frames. However, if you are working with long amounts of text, most likely you will want to import the text from a word processing program. You will also want to place the text so that it flows from page to page.

To import text:

1. Choose **File** > **Place**. The options for placing text are at the bottom of the Place dialog box **A**.

2. Navigate to find the file you want to import.

3. Select Show Import Options to open the specific import options for that type of text file.

4. Click Replace Selected Item to replace the contents of a selected text frame with the new text.

5. Select Open to load the text into a text cursor *(also called a loaded cursor)* **B**.

TIP The text cursor also contains a preview area to show the type of object being placed. For the rest of this book, however, I will show only the text cursor itself to make it easier to see its behavior.

TIP If you hold the Shift key as you click Choose, you open the Import Options dialog box even if the checkbox is not selected.

TIP If the text file uses fonts not installed on your computer, an alert box informs you that the fonts are missing.

☑ Show Import Options
☑ Replace Selected Item
☐ Create Static Captions

A The **Import options** in the Place dialog box.

B The **loaded text cursor** indicates that you can place the imported text.

Importing Text Files

InDesign lets you import text files saved from Microsoft Word 98 or higher. You simply save the Word DOC file and import that into InDesign.

If you have an earlier version of Word, you should save the text as an RTF (Rich Text Format) document. RTF files retain most of their original formatting and can be imported by InDesign.

InDesign can also import ASCII text. *ASCII* stands for American Standard Code for Information Interchange. This is a standard character-coding scheme used by most computers to display letters, digits, and special characters. It is the most primitive computer text format. For example, when text is saved in the ASCII format, any italic or bold formatting is lost.

Although ASCII text is stripped down, it is useful for importing text from databases or Internet sites. However, you do have to reformat text imported in the ASCII format.

C The **Microsoft Word Import Options dialog box** is used to import Word files.

D The **Manual Page Breaks list** controls how Word page breaks are converted.

The options for importing text change depending on which type of text file you choose to import.

To open the import options for Microsoft Word files:

Choose Import Options to open the Microsoft Word Import Options dialog box **C**.

To set the Word import options:

1. Use the Include area to include Word's Table of Contents Text, Index Text, Footnotes, or Endnotes.

2. Choose whether dumb quotes and apostrophes (such as ' and ") should be converted into proper typographer quotes (such as ' and ' or " and ").

To control the formatting in the Word import options:

1. Select Remove Styles and Formatting from Text and Tables to remove the formatting that was applied in Word.

2. If you choose to remove styles and formatting, you can select Preserve Local Overrides to keep attributes such as italic and bold.

3. Use the Manual Page Breaks list to control how Word page break commands are handled **D**.

4. Select Import Inline Graphics to include images inserted into the Word text.

5. Select Import Unused Styles to add all styles from the Word document even if some have not been applied to text.

6. Select Track Changes to see the edits applied to the text when using InCopy.

7. Select Convert Bullets & Numbers to Text to convert Word's electronic bullets and numbers into actual characters.

If your Word document contains one or more tables, you can control how those tables are imported.

To control the formatting in the Word import options:

Use the Convert Tables To list to choose one of the following 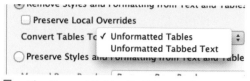:

- **Unformatted Tables** creates a table with InDesign's default settings.
- **Unformatted Tabbed Text** converts tables into tab-delimited text.

TIP The import options for RTF files contain the same options as the Microsoft Word Import Choices.

When you import a Microsoft Excel file, you can set the import options for the file. *(See Chapter 13, "Tabs and Tables," for more information on working with the tables imported from Excel files.)*

To set the options for Microsoft Excel files:

Choose Import Options to open the Microsoft Excel Import Options dialog box 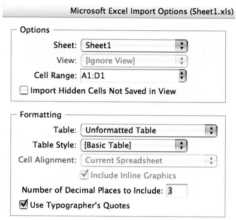.

To choose which data to import from Excel files:

1. Use the Sheet list to control which parts of the spreadsheet you want to import.

2. Use the View list to control which view information to import.

3. Use the Cell Range list to control which cells to import.

4. Select Import Hidden Cells Not Saved in View to import that data.

A The **Convert Tables To list** controls how Word tables are converted.

B The **Microsoft Excel Import Options dialog box** is used to import Excel tables.

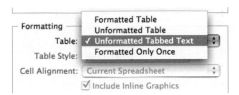

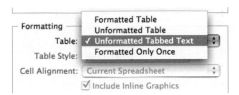

C The **Formatting Table list** controls how tables are imported.

D The **Text Import Options dialog box** is used to import raw ASCII text files.

To choose how the Excel data is formatted:

1. Use the Formatting Table list to choose how the table should be formatted **C**.

2. Use the Formatting Table Style list to apply one of InDesign's table styles.

3. Use the Cell Alignment list to choose the paragraph alignment for the information in the table.

4. Select Include Inline Graphics to include placed images along with the text.

You can also control how plain text files, such as ASCII files, are imported into an InDesign document.

To set the options for ASCII files:

1. Choose Import Options to open the Text Import Options dialog box **D**.

2. Choose the character set, platform, and dictionary to ensure that special characters are imported correctly.

3. Choose how to handle extra carriage (paragraph) returns at the ends of lines and paragraphs.

4. Choose how to delete extra spaces inserted into the text.

Flowing Text

Once you have imported the text into the loaded text cursor, you can choose how the text flows into the document.

To import text into a new frame:

Drag the loaded text cursor to create a text frame that contains the text . The straight lines indicate the text will be placed into a new frame.

or

Click the loaded text cursor on the page. InDesign creates a text frame the width of the margins of the page.

TIP To unload the text cursor, choose any tool in the Tools panel.

A primary text frame is a frame that makes it simpler to flow text from page to page.

To create primary text frames:

Choose Primary Text Frame when you first create the document . A primary text frame is indicated by its own icon **C**.

To flow text into a primary text frame:

1. Move the loaded text cursor inside the margins of the page where the primary text frame is located.

TIP Curved lines appear around the text cursor that indicate you are inserting text into the primary text frame **D**.

2. Click the loaded text cursor. The text flows onto the Page. Additional pages are created as necessary to hold all the text in the story.

A The **straight lines around the loaded text cursor** indicate that the text will be placed into a new text frame.

B Apply the **Primary Text Frame** option when you create a new document.

C The **primary text frame icon**.

D The **curved lines around the loaded text cursor** indicate that the text will be placed into a primary text frame or an existing frame.

The **autoflow cursor** indicates that the text will flow onto as many pages as is necessary.

The **white arrow in the autoflow cursor** indicates that the text will flow touching the margins of the pages.

Use the **fixed-page autoflow cursors** to flow text only onto the existing pages.

What Can You Do With a Loaded Cursor?

Once you load a cursor with text, it may seem like all you can do is click to place the text. However, there are some things you can do without losing the text loaded into the cursor. You can:

Use any of the menu or Pages panel commands to add pages to the document.

Use the keyboard shortcuts to zoom in or out.

Use the scroll bars to move through the page or the document.

Move the onscreen elements, such as the panels, to new positions.

But remember, never point a loaded cursor at anyone. It always seems funny till someone loses an icon!

You don't need a primary text frame to flow text from page to page. You can click next to the margins of the page to create ordinary text frames that hold the text.

To flow text without a primary text frame:

1. Import the text so that you have a loaded cursor.

2. Move the cursor up to the top-left corner of the margins.

3. Hold the Shift key **E**. The icon changes to the autoflow cursor.

> **TIP** Look for the cursor to change from black to white **F**. This indicates that the placed text will touch the margins.

4. Click. The text flows onto the page and creates as many pages as is necessary to place all the text.

What if you want to automatically flow text onto the existing pages of a document without adding any new pages?

To flow text onto a fixed number of pages:

1. Import the text so that you have a loaded cursor.

2. Hold the Shift+Opt/Alt keys. The cursor changes to the fixed-page autoflow cursor **G**.

3. Click the margins of the page. This flows the text automatically onto as many pages as are in the document. If there is more text, an overflow symbol appears on the last page.

You can fill a frame with dummy text instead of importing real text.

To fill a frame with placeholder text:

1. Click inside a frame.

2. Choose **Type > Fill with Placeholder Text.** The dummy text fills the frame **A**.

TIP You can use your own text for the placeholder by saving a file named placeholder.txt in the InDesign application folder.

Creating Text Breaks

InDesign has special **characters** that force the text to break to a new position.

To insert break characters:

1. Place the insertion point where you want to jump to the next location.

2. Choose **Type > Insert Break Character** or Control-click (Mac) or right-click (Win) to choose Insert Break Character from the contextual menu.

3. Choose one of the following:

Loir sends anid te mincillan me hendre an eugiat email praestio ewa with amet ip the estrud dit irn page hendignis number enim delenim ver goit velisi bla feugue delesequipit ulluptat of alis nostrud this doluptat.

A A sample of the **placeholder text** that is used to fill text frames.

Adding Pages As You Type?

Most designers import text from external files into InDesign files. But some writers type directly into InDesign text frames. What happens when the text overflows those frames? Is it possible to add pages as you type?

Yes, it is called Smart TextFlow and it is automatically turned on when you first open InDesign. For more information on setting the Smart TextFlow options, see Chapter 21, "Customizing".

Break character	Description	Symbol
Column break	Jumps text to the next column. If there is no column in the frame, the column break forces the text to the next page.	⌄
Frame break	Jumps text to the next frame.	⌄⌄
Page break	Jumps text to the next page.	●⌄
Odd page break	Jumps text to the next odd page.	▪⌄
Even page break	Jumps text to the next even page.	▪▪⌄

TIP To see a representation of the break characters, choose Type > Show Hidden Characters.

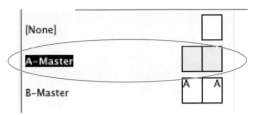

Double-click a master page in the Pages panel to view that **master page in the document window.**

Uses for Master Pages

Master pages allow you to automate page layout changes. For instance, if you have a hundred-page book, you wouldn't want to have to draw a text frame on every page and type the name of the chapter or book title.

Master pages allow you to place an object or frame on the master page and have it appear on all the document pages.

If you place an object on the master page, it will always be positioned in exactly the same spot on every page that has that master applied.

You can also use master pages to store design alternatives such as different column layouts or margin settings.

Working with Master Pages

Every new document includes a master page. When you add objects to the master page, they appear on all the document pages based on that master page.

To add objects to a master page:

1. In the Pages panel, double-click the name of the master page **B**. This opens the master page in the document window.

2. Add text boxes, graphics, or any other elements you want on the master page.

TIP If the document has been set for facing pages, there are two sides to the master page, left-hand and right-hand.
The left-hand master page governs the left-hand document pages.
Similarly, the right-hand master page governs the right-hand document pages.

3. Double-click the name of the document page to make it the active page. Any items placed on the master page now appear on the document page.

You can also add master pages from one document into another.

To import masters from one document into another:

1. Choose Load Master Pages from the Pages panel menu.

2. Use the dialog box to select the document that contains the masters you want to import.

3. If the masters contain the same name, you will be asked how to resolve the conflict.

4. An alert will tell you if the masters are not the same page size.

You can have many master pages in a document. This allows you to have different layouts for different parts of your document.

To create new master pages:

1. Choose New Master from the Pages panel menu. This opens the New Master dialog box 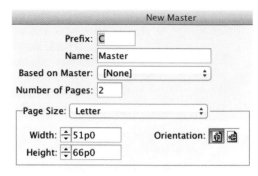.

2. Choose a letter for the prefix for the master page.

TIP The prefix is the letter that appears inside the pages that have that master page applied to them.

3. Enter a name for the master page.

4. Use the pop-up menu to set which master page, if any, the new master page should be based on.

TIP Basing one master page on another allows you to make changes on one master page that are applied to the other.

5. Enter the number of pages for the master. This allows you to create spreads that serve as master pages.

6. Use the Page Size menu to choose the size of the master pages.

   or

   Use the Width and Height controls to enter a custom size for the master page.

7. Use the orientation icons to change the pages from portrait to landscape.

TIP To create a new master page without opening the New Master dialog box, hold the Cmd/Ctrl key and click the New Page icon at the bottom of the Pages panel.

A The **New Master dialog box** allows you to set the attributes for the master page.

Strategies for Basing Master Pages on Each Other

I have three master page spreads for this book. One master — the main master — holds only the guides and page numbers for the book. The master for ordinary pages is based on that main master. The master for the chapter opener is also based on that main master.

That way, if I need to move the page numbers I only need to change the page number on the main master. The other masters update automatically.

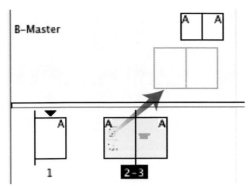

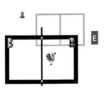

B Drag a document page into the master page area to convert the document page to a master.

C The **Apply Master dialog box** allows you to change the master that governs pages.

D The rectangle around the single page indicates that the master will be applied to that page only.

E The rectangle around the spread indicates that the master will be applied to the spread.

As you work, you might want to convert a document page into a master page. InDesign makes it easy to turn a document page into a master page.

To convert a document page to a master page:

1. Select the page or pages.
2. Drag the page or pages from the document area to the master page area **B**.

   or

   Choose Save as Master from the Pages panel menu.

New pages are based on the master page applied to the last existing page of the document. You can easily change the master page that governs pages.

To apply a new master to a page:

1. Select the page or pages.
2. Choose Apply Master to Pages from the Pages panel. This opens the Apply Master dialog box **C**.
3. Use the Apply Master menu to apply a master to the pages.
4. Use the To Pages field to change the selected pages.

TIP Selecting None creates pages that have no master page applied.

To apply masters with the Pages panel:

Drag the master page onto the document pages as follows:

- To apply to a single page, drag the master page icon onto the page. A rectangle appears around the page **D**.
- To apply to a spread, drag the master page icon onto the spread. A rectangle appears around the spread **E**.

You can also base one master page on another using the Pages panel.

To base masters on existing masters:

1. Create a new master or spread.

2. Drag one master page onto another.

   - To base the spread on the master, drag the master onto the spread.

   - To base one page on the master, drag the master onto a single page.

3. Release the mouse button. The prefix of the master appears inside the second master page 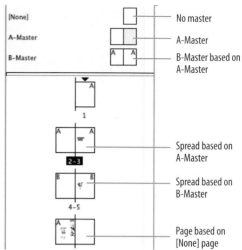. The prefix indicates that the master page governs the other master page.

Ordinarily you modify the elements of a master page only on the master page itself. The elements on the document pages are protected from being selected or modified. However, you can release that protection and modify the master elements by creating local overrides.

To modify master elements on document pages:

1. Hold Cmd/Ctrl-Shift and click the element you want to modify. This releases the protection and leaves the item selected.

2. Make any local changes to the item.

You might want to modify all the master elements on a page. Rather than release each item one by one, InDesign lets you do it with a single command.

To release all master elements on a page:

Choose Override All Master Page Items from the Pages panel menu. This releases the objects so they can be modified.

A The **letters inside the page icons** indicate what masters are applied to pages or other masters.

Labels from the figure: [None] — No master; A–Master — A-Master; B–Master — B-Master based on A-Master; Spread based on A-Master; Spread based on B-Master; Page based on [None] page

---

Overriding Master Page Elements

If you modify a master page element on a document page, the local override loses its link to the master page element. However, the element may have partial links to the master page element.

Let's say you add a stroke to an object on the document page. From that point on, the stroke of the element is removed from the control of the element on the master page.

But other attributes of the element maintain their link to the master page item. For instance, the position of the element maintains a link to the master page item. So if you move the element on the master page, the item on the document page also moves.

Similarly, the fill color of the elements on the document pages changes if you change the master page element. Only the formatting for the stroke is separated from the master page element.

How Many Master Pages?

Although it may seem like a lot of work to set up master pages, the more masters you have the easier it is to lay out complicated documents.

A weekly magazine can easily have 50 or more master pages — some for special editorial spreads and others for different types of advertising spaces.

Some publishers insist that every page must be based on a master and do not allow any modifications of the master page elements. Others let the designers override the master pages.

You decide which way best suits your work habits and the project.

Stacking Order of Master Page Items

The items on the master page are always behind any new items you may put on a page. But when you release the master page items from the master page, they always spring to the front of the document page.

If you want, you can use the Object > Arrange menu to change the stacking order of the items. However, if you release many items on many pages, it may seem cumbersome to move them backwards.

Instead, create two layers in your document (*see Chapter 11, "Layers"*). Put all the master page elements on the bottom layer, and your regular document objects on the top layer. That way when you release the master page items, they will not move in front of your regular page items.

You may want to set master page items, such as page numbers and headers, to never be modified on the document page.

To set a master page item to not be overridden:

1. Select the item on the master page.
2. Deselect Allow Master Item Overrides on Selection from the Pages panel menu.

You can also set a master page item to apply its text wrap to other master page items, and not any document page items.

To control the text wrap of a master page item:

Select the item on the master page.

1. Apply a text wrap setting.
2. Use the Text Wrap panel menu to select or deselect Apply to Master Page Only.

Once you have created a local override on a master page element, It may still have links to the original master page item. You can completely sever all ties between the master page item and the item on the document page.

To separate an item from the master item:

1. Select the object that has been released.
2. Choose Detach Selection From Master in the Pages panel menu.

Of course you can also separate all the objects on a page from their links to the master page items.

To separate all the master items on a page:

1. Use the command Override All Master Page Items to first release all the master page items from the master page.

2. Choose Detach All Objects From Master in the Pages panel menu. This severs any remaining link between the item and the master page.

You can also hide master page items on document pages so they do not print.

To change the display of master page items:

Choose Hide Master Items from the Pages panel menu or choose Show Master Items from the Pages panel menu.

InDesign also lets you quickly clear all local overrides and reapply the master page items to the document page.

To remove local overrides and reapply the master:

Choose Remove All Local Overrides in the Pages panel menu. All local override elements will be deleted and the master page items will be reapplied.

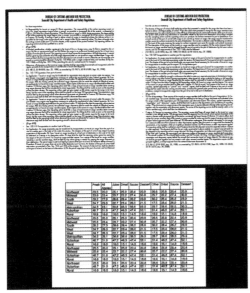

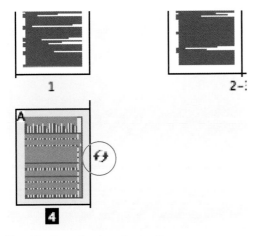

A An example of how **rotating a spread** makes it easier to read the information in a table that has been laid out horizontally.

B The **Rotation icon in the Pages panel** indicates that the page view has been rotated.

Rotating Spreads

Pages don't all have to be in the same orientation. You might have an item, such as a long table, that you want to lay out horizontally, rather than vertically. Although it's easy to rotate the text frame on the page, it's difficult to read the text when rotated. Rotating the page spread makes it easier to read the text **A**.

To rotate a spread:

1. Select the spread that you want to rotate. (Only spreads can be rotated, not single pages.)

2. Choose **Rotate Spread View** from the Pages panel menu and then choose one of the following:
   - **90° cw** (clockwise)
   - **90° ccw** (counter clockwise)
   - **180°**

   A rotation indicator appears next to the spread in the Pages panel to indicate that the spread has been rotated **B**.

To restore a spread to normal rotation:

1. Select the spread.

2. Choose **Rotate Spread View > Clear Rotation** from the Pages panel menu. The spread view is restored to the normal orientation.

Page Numbers and Text Variables

The most common element that is added to a master page is the page-number character.

To add automatic page numbering:

1. Draw a text frame on the master where you want the page number to appear.

2. Choose **Type > Insert Special Character > Markers > Current Page Number**. This inserts a special character in the text frame 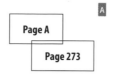.

TIP The current page number character is the prefix for the master page.

3. If the master page is a facing-page master, repeat steps 1 and 2 for the other page in the master.

You may want to change the format of page numbers or the number they start from. You do that by creating a new *section*.

To create a document section:

1. Move to the page where you want the section to start.

2. Choose **Layout > Numbering & Section Options**. The New Section dialog box appears 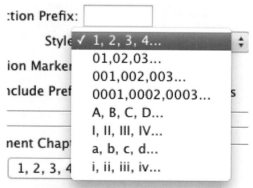.

3. Select Start Section to open the options.

4. Choose the Page Numbering options:
   - **Automatic Page Numbering** continues the count from the previous pages.
   - **Start Page Numbering At** lets you enter a specific number to start the section from.

5. Use the Style pop-up list to set the format for the automatic page numbering 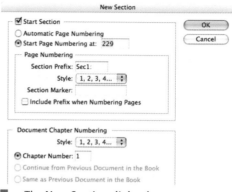.

TIP The choices for roman numerals or letters are commonly used for front and back matter in book publishing.

A The **current page number** appears as a letter on master pages but as a number on document pages.

B The **New Section dialog box** lets you change the formatting and numbering of pages.

C The **Style menu** allows you to choose different formats for page numbering of a section.

Page Numbering

Section Prefix: [ ]

Style: [1, 2, 3, 4... ⇕]

Section Marker: [#]

D The entry in the **Section Marker field** allows you to create custom labels for pages.

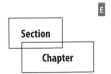

E The **section marker** appears as the word "Section" on master pages but as the label on document pages.

You can also create a section prefix that appears in front of the current page number.

To work with a section marker:

1. Choose **Layout > Numbering & Section Options** to open the New Section dialog box.

2. Type the label (up to five characters) for the section in the Section Prefix field.

3. Choose Include Prefix when Numbering Pages to add the section prefix to the page number.

4. Enter a label for the Section Marker **D**.

Once you have created an entry for the section marker, you need to insert a section marker character in the text frame to see the entry on document pages.

To add a section marker character:

1. Place the insertion point in a text frame where you want the section marker to appear.

TIP The text frame can be on a master page or a document page.

2. Choose **Type > Insert Special Character > Markers** and then choose Section Marker from the menu.

TIP If the text frame that contains the section marker character is on the master page, the word "Section" appears on the master page. If the text frame is on the document page, the label for the section marker appears **E**.

Books have more than just page numbers. They also have chapter numbers. You can specify the chapter number for your document. Then you can insert the chapter number as a text variable in a frame.

To specify a chapter number:

1. Choose **Layout > Numbering & Section Options** to open the New Section dialog box.

2. Enter a number in the Chapter Number field 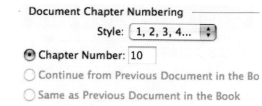.

    TIP The number can also be created automatically as part of a Book document, as covered on page 265.

3. Use the Document Chapter Numbering Style list to choose the style of the characters used for the chapter numbers .

    TIP These are similar to the styles for page numbers with the exception of the 01, 02, 03, 04 style, which is used in many textbooks.

Chapter numbers are inserted as special characters that can appear anywhere.

To add a chapter number:

1. Place the insertion point in a text frame.

2. Choose **Type > Text Variables > Insert Variable** and then choose Chapter Number from the list of preset text variables. The text variable for Chapter Number appears with a line around the display .

    TIP Other text variables include creation date, file name, last page number, modification date, output date, and running headers.

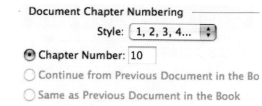

A The **Document Chapter Numbering** allows you to set the chapter number for a document.

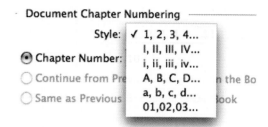

B Use the **Document Chapter Numbering Style list** to set the elements that are used for chapter numbers.

C A **text variable** is displayed with a rectangle around the information.

> Dorothy had only one other dress, but that happened to be clean and was hanging on a peg beside her bed. It was gingham, with checks of white and blue; and although the blue was somewhat faded with many washings, it was still a pretty frock. The girl washed herself carefully, dressed herself in the

Continued on page 3 ——— Overlap

D The **Next Page Number character** shows the page number that the story is continued on. The overlapping area is where the page number frame touches the story frame.

Continued from page 2 ——— Overlap

> clean gingham, and tied her pink sunbonnet on her head. She took a little basket and filled it with bread from the cupboard, laying a white cloth over the top. Then she looked down at her feet and noticed how old and worn her shoes were.

E The **Previous Page Number character** shows the page number that the story comes from. The overlapping area is where the page number frame touches the story frame.

You can also insert special characters that create jump lines that show the page where the text flow continues to or from.

To create a continued to/from page number:

1. Place the insertion point in a text frame that touches the frame that holds the story.

2. Choose **Type > Insert Special Character** and then choose one of the following:

   - **Next Page Number** inserts the number of the page that the text jumps to or continues on **D**.

   - **Previous Page Number** inserts the number of the page that the text continued from **E**.

TIP The continued to/from character needs a separate text frame so that if the text reflows, the continued to/from character doesn't move along with the text.

TIP The continued to/from characters only insert the page number that the story is linked to. You have to type the words "Continued on" or "Continued from" yourself.

Making Books

Most people who create long documents break them up so that each chapter is contained in its own document. They need a way to coordinate the page numbers, colors, and styles. An InDesign *book* is an electronic file that keeps track of all those documents.

To create an electronic book file:

1. Choose **File** > **New** > **Book**.

2. Use the dialog box to name the book document and save it in a location . The Book panel appears **B**.

TIP The tab for the Book panel contains the name of the book.

Once you have created the book file, you can then add documents that make up the book.

TIP You don't have to create the book file first. For instance, I created these chapters before I added them to a book document.

To add documents to a book:

1. Click the Add Document button at the bottom of the Book panel.

   or

   Choose Add Document from the Book panel menu.

2. Use the dialog box to find the document you want to add to the book. The name of the chapter appears in the Book panel.

3. Repeat steps 1 and 2 to add other documents to the book.

To remove documents from a book:

1. Select the documents you want to remove.

2. Click the Remove Document button at the bottom of the Book panel.

   or

   Choose Remove Document from the Book panel menu.

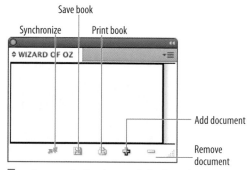

A A saved book document appears with its own document icon.

Save book

Synchronize   Print book

Add document

Remove document

B An **empty Book panel** displays the name of the book on its panel tab.

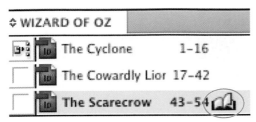

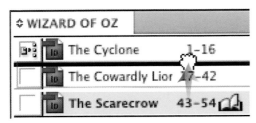

C The **open book icon** indicates that a document of the book is open.

D **Drag a listing in the Book panel** to change the order in which the documents appear in the book.

Style source icon

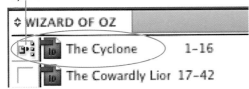

E The **style source file** is used to synchronize the style sheets and colors for other documents in a book.

You can use the Book panel and Book panel menu to open, rearrange, and control the documents that make up the book.

To open documents in a book:

Double-click the name of a document in the Book panel. The open book symbol next to the name indicates that the document is open C.

The order that documents are listed in the Book panel determines the page numbers of the book.

To change the order of the documents in a book:

Drag the name of a document in the Book panel to a new position in the panel D.

One of the benefits of creating a book document is that you can have one file (called the *style source*) control the style sheets, swatches, and master pages for the other documents in the book. If you make changes to the style source, all the other files in the book synchronize to that file.

To set the style source for a book document:

Click the Style Source box next to the name of the file that you want to control the rest of the documents in the book E.

To synchronize files to the style source:

Click the Synchronize button in the Book panel.

or

Choose Synchronize Book in the Book panel menu.

TIP The menu command says Synchronize Selected Documents if only some of the files in the book are selected.

To set the synchronizing options:

1. Choose Synchronize Options from the Book panel menu. The Synchronize Options dialog box opens **A**.

2. Choose the options that you want to apply from the style source document.

If the book is closed when you modify the files in the book, you need to update them when you do reopen the book document.

TIP This step is not necessary if you modify book files while the book document is open.

To update files in a book:

1. Choose **File** > **Open** and then navigate to the book document you want to work on.

2. Use the Book panel to open, then modify any files in the book document. An Alert icon appears next to the modified files **B**.

   or

   Use the Open command in the File menu to open, then modify any files in the book document.

3. If necessary, synchronize the files to the style source document.

You can also replace missing files in a book or swap one file for another.

TIP A Missing icon indicates that the file has been moved after being added to the book **C**.

To replace a file in a book:

1. Select the file in the Book panel that you want to replace.

2. Choose Replace Document from the Book panel menu.

3. Navigate to find the file you want to replace or relink.

4. If necessary, synchronize the files.

☑ Numbered Lists
☑ Cross-Reference Formats
☑ Text Variables
☐ Master Pages
☑ Trap Presets
▽ ☑ Styles and Swatches
  ☑ Table Styles
  ☑ Cell Styles
  ☑ Object Styles
  ☑ TOC Styles
  ☑ Character Styles
  ☑ Paragraph Styles
  ☑ Swatches
☑ Smart Match Style Groups

Style Source: C:\Users\Sandee\Desktop\Dorothy's Journey.indd

A Use the **Synchronize Options dialog box** to set which attributes of the style source file will be applied to the files in the book.

ιe	1–16
ιrow	17–28 ⚠
·dly Lion	29–54

B The **Alert icon in the Book panel** indicates that the file has been modified.

ιe Cyclone	1–16
ιe Scarecrow	17–28
ιe Cowardly Lion	29–54 ❓

C The **Missing icon in the Book panel** indicates that the file has been moved after it was imported into the book.

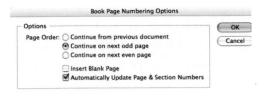

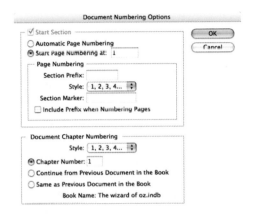

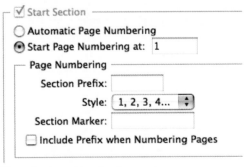

Files in a book automatically run in consecutive numbers. As you add or delete pages in one document, the page numbers in the rest of the book adjust. You can control how the page numbers are adjusted.

D Use the **Book Page Numbering Options** dialog box to set how pages will be numbered in a book.

E Use the **Document Numbering Options dialog box** to set how an individual document is numbered in a book.

F The **Page Numbering options** for a document in a book.

To set how page numbers are adjusted:

1. Choose Book Page Numbering Options from the Book panel menu to open the dialog box **D**.

2. Choose the Page Order options as follows:

   - **Continue from previous document** starts new pages sequentially from the end of the previous listing.

   - **Continue on next odd page** always starts new pages on an odd number.

   - **Continue on next even page** always starts new pages on an even number.

3. If using the odd or even options results in a skipped page, select Insert Blank Page.

4. Deselect Automatically Update Page & Section Numbers to stop InDesign from automatically numbering the files in a book.

To set the numbers for each document in a book:

1. Choose Document Numbering Options from the Book panel menu to open the dialog box **E**.

2. Choose Automatic Page Numbering to number pages as they appear in the Book panel.

   or

   Choose Start Page Numbering At to set a specific page number to start that document on **F**.

3. Set the rest of the options for styling the number as described on pages 257 and 258.

To set the chapter numbers for book files:

1. Choose Document Numbering Options from the Book panel menu to open the dialog box **A**.

2. Choose one of the following to set the number for the chapter:

   - **Chapter Number** field sets a number.

   - **Continue from Previous Document in the Book** applies the next number.

   - **Same as Previous Document in the Book** uses the same chapter number as the previous document.

3. Set the Style options for the chapter number as described on page 259.

To update the numbering in a book:

Choose one of the following from the Book panel menu's Update Numbering submenu:

   - Update Page & Section Numbers

   - Update Chapter & Paragraph Numbers

   - Update All Numbers

You can also apply output commands to the files in a book. *(See Chapter 19, "Printing," for more information on printing files.)*

To set the output options for a book:

Choose one of the following output commands from the Book panel menu:

   - **Print Book** prints the entire book.

   - **Preflight Book** preflights all the documents in the book.

   - **Package** collects the files for output.

   - **Export Book to Digital Editions** creates an eBook type of PDF.

   - **Export Book to PDF** creates a PDF of the documents in the book.

TIP Select just some of the files in the Book panel to output just those files **B**.

Document Chapter Numbering

Style: [1, 2, 3, 4... [▲▼]]

● Chapter Number: [1]

○ Continue from Previous Document in the Book

○ Same as Previous Document in the Book

Book Name: The wizard of oz.indb

A The **Document Chapter Numbering** options for a document in a book.

Preflight Book...
Package Book For Print...
Export Book for Kindle...
Export Book to PDF...
Export Book to EPUB...
Print Book...

Preflight Book...
Package Selected Documents For Print...
Export Book for Kindle...
Export Selected Documents to PDF...
Export Book to EPUB...
Print Selected Documents...

B With no files selected, the **Book panel menu** controls all the files in a book (top). However, when you select individual files in the Book, the Book panel menu commands are applied only to those selected files (bottom).

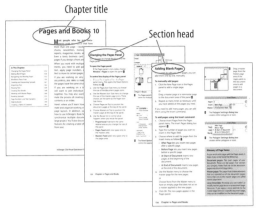

Chapter title

Pages and Books 10

Section head

The **paragraph styles applied to chapter titles and section heads in this book** can be used to create a table of contents.

The **Table of Contents dialog box** lets you select and format listings for a table of contents.

The **Save Style dialog box** lets you save the settings from the Table of Contents dialog box.

Creating a Table of Contents

InDesign creates a table of contents (TOC) by looking at the styles applied to paragraphs and then listing the text and page numbers for those paragraphs. The TOC for this book lists the chapters and the section heads **c**.

To prepare a document for a table of contents:

1. Add the page or pages that will hold the TOC.

TIP Most tables of contents are part of the front matter of a book and are numbered separately without affecting the regular page numbering.

TIP If the document is part of a book, make sure the book's pagination is current.

2. Apply paragraph styles to the paragraphs that you want to appear in the TOC.

To define the styles for TOC entries:

1. Choose **Layout > Table of Contents** to open the Table of Contents dialog box **D**.

2. Set the Title and Listing controls as described in the exercises that start on the next page.

3. Click Save Style. This opens the Save Style dialog box **E**.

4. Name the style and click OK.

To generate the TOC:

1. Choose **Layout > Table of Contents** to open the Table of Contents dialog box.

2. Set each of the controls as described in the following exercises.

3. Click OK. This closes the dialog box and creates a loaded text cursor that contains the TOC.

4. Click or drag the loaded cursor to apply the TOC text where you want it to appear in the document.

The title is the label that is applied before each entry in the table of contents. You can set the type for the title as well as the paragraph style that formats the title.

To enter the title of the table of contents:

1. Type the text for the title in the Title field .

2. Use the Style menu to the right of the Title field to choose which paragraph style is applied to format the title.

You create the entries for a table of contents by selecting the paragraph styles that are applied to those sections of your documents.

To choose the listings for the table of contents:

1. Select a paragraph style listed in the Other Styles area of the Table of Contents dialog box **B**.

2. Click the Add button. This moves the style to the Include Paragraph Styles list.

3. Repeat steps 1 and 2 for any additional styles.

If your TOC uses a style with auto numbers, you can set how the TOC styles those entries.

To set the options for numbered paragraphs:

1. Select a paragraph style listed in the Other Styles area of the Table of Contents dialog box.

2. Choose one of the options from the Numbered Paragraphs list as follows **C**:

   - **Include Full Paragraph** includes the text and the numbers.

   - **Include Numbers Only** includes just the numbers for the paragraph.

   - **Exclude Numbers** includes the text but not the numbers.

A Use the **Title field in the Table of Contents dialog box** to enter the text you want to appear before the listings.

B Move styles from the Other Styles list to the **Include Paragraph Styles list** to choose which paragraphs are added to the table of contents.

C The options in the **Numbered Paragraphs list** let you choose how paragraphs with auto numbering are handled in the table of contents.

A TOC of Nonexisting Items

The items in a TOC don't have to be from items that are visible on each page. For instance, let's say you want a list of all photographers in your book and where their pictures appear. Simply put the names of the photographers next to their photos, but set the names to not print or on a layer set to not print.

Then, run the TOC for the items. You get a list of the photographers' names, even though those names don't actually appear on the printed pages.

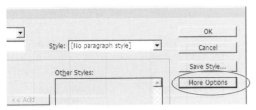

D Use the **Entry Style menu** to choose a style sheet that you have created to format the listing as it should appear in the table of contents.

E Click the **More Options button** to expand the controls in the Table of Contents dialog box.

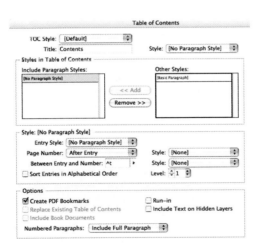

F The **Table of Contents dialog box** with all the options available.

Most likely you will want to format the entries in a table of contents with a different style than the one used within the document.

To format the entries in the table of contents:

1. Select the entry listing in the Include Paragraph Styles area.

2. Choose a paragraph style sheet from the Entry Style menu under the Style: [Name] in the Table of Contents dialog box **D**.

3. Repeat steps 1 and 2 for any additional styles.

The Table of Contents dialog box has additional controls for more advanced options such as formatting the page numbers for each entry.

To open the additional table of contents controls:

Click the More Options button in the Table of Contents dialog box **E**. This opens the advanced options at the bottom of the dialog box **F**.

TIP If the button says Fewer Options, then the dialog box already shows the advanced options.

With the advanced options open, you have additional controls for the style for each entry in the TOC . This gives you greater control over where the page numbers appear and how they are formatted.

To set the advanced Style options for each entry:

1. Choose one of the styles in the Include Paragraph Styles list. The style name appears in the Style options area.

2. If you have not already applied a listing from the Entry Style menu, do so as explained on the previous page.

3. Use the Page Number menu to choose a position for the entry's page number .

4. If desired, choose a character style for the page number from the Style list to the right of the Page Number menu.

TIP The character style lets you apply formatting to the page number for each entry.

You can also control how the entry name and the page number are separated.

To control the separator character:

1. Select one of the character options from the Between Entry and Number menu A. The character symbol appears in the field.

2. If you want, type additional text before or after the character symbol. This lets you add a label before the page number.

3. If desired, apply a style from the Style menu for the Between Entry and Number character A.

A The **Style options area** gives you controls to format how the entries are formatted and arranged in the TOC.

B The **Page Number menu** controls where the page number will appear in the TOC listings.

Other Uses for a Table of Contents

You're not limited to using the Table of Contents commands just for listings of chapters and section heads.

If you have a sales catalog, you can use the commands to create a list of all the items, which can be used as a price list. I could generate a separate file for this book that lists all the titles for sidebars such as this one. In a book of illustrations, you can use it to create a list of names of all the artists for each illustration.

The only thing you need to remember is to assign a style sheet to each item that you want to appear in the table of contents.

c   The **Options for creating TOC documents**.

Benefits of an Automatic TOC

If all this seems like too much work just to create a short table of contents, you may be tempted to create one by hand — manually entering the items in the TOC.

For instance, I could easily create the table of contents at the front of this book just by typing it out by hand.

But there is a big benefit in creating an automatic TOC. When you export PDF files with an automatically created TOC, they will have hyperlinks from the TOC to the document pages.

This means someone reading the PDF document can just click on the page number listed in the TOC to go to that specific page. Without the electronic TOC, you'd have to manually add all those links in InDesign or Acrobat.

A table of contents doesn't have to be organized in the order that the items appear.

To alphabetize the table of contents:

Select Sort Entries in Alphabetical order from the advanced options area **B**.

To indent the entries in a table of contents:

Use the Level controls to indent each table of contents entry **B**.

TIP Each entry in the Include Paragraph Styles list is automatically indented. This is for display purposes in that dialog box and does not affect the final TOC.

There are additional options you can set for a table of contents **c**.

To set the table of contents options:

Select each of the table of contents options at the bottom of the Table of Contents dialog box as follows:

- **Create PDF Bookmarks** adds bookmarks to the PDF that is created from the TOC. This is in addition to any hyperlinks within the TOC.

- **Replace Existing Table of Contents** lets you update or change the table of contents that has already been placed in the document.

- **Include Book Documents** lets you create a table of contents for all the documents in a book.

- **Run-in** creates a single paragraph table of contents with each entry divided by a semicolon (;) and a space.

- **Include Text on Hidden Layers** uses text that is on layers that are not visible.

- **Numbered Paragraphs** lets you format how paragraphs with auto numbering are formatted in the TOC.

Layers 11

When I was in advertising, we used to lay clear acetate sheets over our mechanical board as a way to create variations for our layouts. One acetate layer might have copy and prices for a test market newspaper ad. Another piece of acetate might have prices for a special Sunday-circular ad. Yet another might have copy without prices for the national magazine ads. The artwork and other graphics stayed on the bottom layer and were visible through the acetate layers.

When the mechanical was sent to be printed, the print shop workers flipped the different acetate sheets on or off the board to create the different types of ads. Because a new mechanical didn't have to be created for each variation, it saved a lot of time and effort.

InDesign gives you the same sort of flexibility with electronic layers. You may have just two layers — one for text, the other for graphics. Or you may have a document with hundreds of different layers.

For instance, if you have English and French versions of a document, you can put the text for each language on its own layer. You can then display just one version at a time.

Creating and Deleting Layers

Every InDesign document opens with a default layer in the Layers panel. You don't have to do anything special to work with this default layer. It is instantly active, and everything you do is automatically on that layer.

To open the Layers panel:

If the Layers panel is not visible, choose **Window** > **Layers** to open it 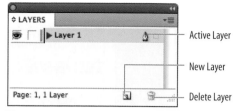.

As you work, you may want additional layers in your document.

To create new layers:

1. Choose New Layer from the Layers panel menu. This opens the New Layer dialog box.

   or

   Click the New Layer icon. This creates a new layer without opening the New Layer dialog box.

2. Set the layer options as described in the next section.

3. Click OK to create the layer.

   TIP You can open the layer options at any time by double-clicking the name of the layer in the Layers panel or by choosing Layer Options from the Layers panel menu.

It may be easier to create different versions of a document by duplicating a layer, as well as the objects on that layer.

To duplicate a layer:

Drag the layer onto the New Layer icon 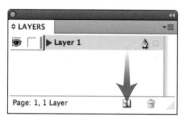. This creates a copy of the layer.

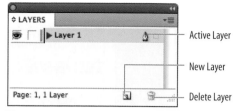

A The **Layers panel** for all new documents contains one layer.

B You can duplicate a layer by dragging it onto the **New Layer icon**.

Before paste

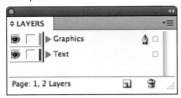

After paste

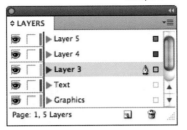

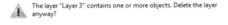 The **Paste Remembers Layers command** adds new layers when objects are pasted from one document to another.

 An alert dialog box makes sure you don't inadvertently delete artwork when you delete a layer.

You can also import the layers automatically when you paste items from one document to another. This behavior is controlled by the Paste Remembers Layers command.

To create new layers while pasting:

1. Choose Paste Remembers Layers from the Layers panel menu. If there is a check mark next to the command, then it is already turned on.

2. Drag and drop or copy and paste the items from one document into a second document. New layers are created in the second document as follows .

   - The layers from the first document are added as new layers if they do not have the same name as the layers in the second document.

   - The layers from the first document are merged with the layers if they have the same name as layers in the second document.

TIP If Paste Remembers Layers is turned off, the items are pasted onto the active layer in the second document.

As you work, you may want to delete a layer. This also deletes all objects on the layer.

To delete a layer:

1. Select the layer you want to delete.

TIP Shift-click to select multiple layers.

2. Click the Delete Layer icon. If there are items on the layer an alert box appears .

TIP Opt/Alt-click the Delete Layer icon to bypass the alert box.

You can quickly delete layers with no objects.

To delete all unused layers:

Choose Delete Unused layers from the Layers panel menu.

Setting the Layer Options

The Layer Options dialog box contains some housekeeping options that make it easier to organize and work with layers .

To name a layer:

Use the Name field to name the layer.

TIP If you have many layers, you should use descriptive names instead of the default names Layer 1, Layer 2, etc.

Each layer has a color associated with it. This is the color used to highlight object frames and paths.

To set the highlight color for a layer:

Choose a color from one of the 37 colors in the Color list 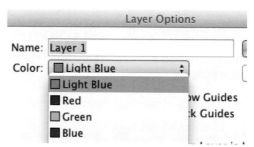.

TIP Each new layer is automatically assigned the next color in the Color list. This means you can have 37 layers without ever repeating a color.

TIP Select Custom to choose your own color for a layer.

Layers help you organize your documents. For instance, if you lock a layer you lock all the objects, so they cannot be selected, moved, modified, or deleted.

To lock a layer:

Choose Lock Layer from the Layer Options dialog box.

or

Click the Toggle Lock space in the Layers panel 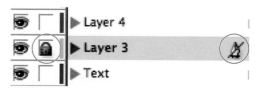. A padlock indicates that the layer is locked. A blank space indicates the layer is unlocked.

TIP Use the Lock Others command from the Layers panel menu or Opt/Alt-click the Toggle Lock space in one layer to lock all the other layers in the document 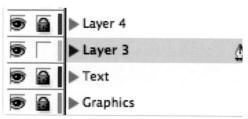.

A The **Layer Options dialog box** is the command center for all the attributes of a layer.

B The **Color list** contains all the choices for highlighting objects.

C Click the **Toggle Lock space** to lock the layer. The spotlighted icons indicate that the layer is locked.

D Opt/Alt-click the **Toggle Lock space** to lock all the other layers in the document.

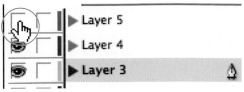

E Click the Toggle Visibility space to hide or show the layer.

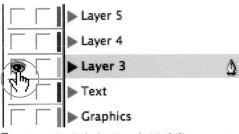

F Opt/Alt-click the Toggle Visibility space to hide all the other layers in the document.

To prevent a layer from printing:

Deselect Print Layer from the Layer Options dialog box.

TIP A layer set to not print is displayed in italic letters in the Layers panel.

You can also use layers to hide and show the information on the layer. This can make it easy to focus on certain information.

TIP Hidden layers automatically do not print.

To hide a layer:

Deselect Show Layer from the Layer Options dialog box.

or

Click the Toggle Visibility space in the Layers panel so that the space is blank **E**. When the space is blank, the layer is invisible.

TIP You cannot work on invisible layers.

TIP Use the Hide Others command from the Layers panel menu or Opt/Alt-click the Toggle Visibility space in one layer to hide all the other layers in the document **F**.

To show a layer:

Select Show Layer from the Layer Options dialog box.

or

Click the Toggle Visibility space in the Layers panel. When the eyeball is visible, the layer is visible.

To control the visibility of guides on a layer:

1. Choose Show Guides in the Layer Options dialog box to display the guides for that layer.

2. Choose Lock Guides to protect the guides on the layer from being changed.

Although hidden layers don't print, they still can affect other objects on the page. The Layer Options dialog box contains the Suppress Text Wrap When Layer Is Hidden setting, which controls what happens if you turn off the visibility for a layer that has a text wrap applied to images 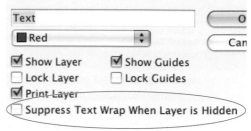.

To control the text wrap for hidden layers:

1. Apply a text wrap to an image that is on one layer.

2. Create text that is on another layer **B**.

3. Set the Layer Options dialog box as follows:

   - Turn off Suppress Text Wrap When Layer Is Hidden to maintain the text wrap when the layer is not visible **C**.

   - Turn on Suppress Text Wrap When Layer Is Hidden to discard the text wrap when the layer is not visible **D**.

A The **Suppress Text Wrap When Layer Is Hidden option** controls what happens to the text wrap for hidden layers.

> When Dorothy stood in the doorway and looked around, she could see nothing but the great gray prairie on every side. Not a tree nor a house broke the broad sweep of flat country that reached to the edge of the sky in all directions. The sun had baked the plowed land into a gray mass, with little cracks running through it. Even the grass was not green, for the sun

B An image with a text wrap is placed on one layer affecting the text on another layer.

> When Dorothy stood in the doorway and looked around, she could see nothing but the great gray prairie on every side. Not a tree nor a house broke the broad sweep of flat country that reached to the edge of the sky in all directions. The sun had baked the plowed land into a gray mass, with little cracks running through it. Even the grass was not green, for the sun

C When the layer is hidden, the wrap continues to affect text when the Suppress Text Wrap option is turned off.

> When Dorothy stood in the doorway and looked around, she could see nothing but the great gray prairie on every side. Not a tree nor a house broke the broad sweep of flat country that reached to the edge of the sky in all directions. The sun had baked the plowed land into a gray mass, with little cracks running through it. Even the grass was not green, for the sun had burned the tops

D When the layer is hidden, the wrap does not affect text when the Suppress Text Wrap option is turned on.

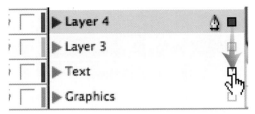

E **Drag the proxy square** to move an object from one layer to another.

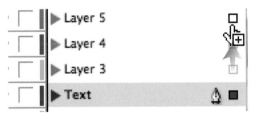

F Hold the Opt/Alt key as you drag the proxy square to **create a duplicate of an object on another layer.**

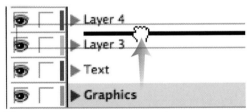

G Drag a layer up or down in the Layers panel to **change the order of the layers**.

Working with Layers

Once you've created additional layers in your document, you can move objects onto the new layers.

To apply objects to layers:

Click the layer in the Layers panel so that it's highlighted, and then create the object.

You can use the Layers panel to move the object between layers.

To move objects from one layer to another:

1. Select the object. A square object proxy appears next to the name of the layer in the Layers panel.

2. Drag the object proxy from one layer to another **E**. This moves the object to a new layer.

TIP Hold the Opt/Alt key as you drag the proxy to create a copy of the object on the new layer **F**. The original object stays on its layer.

To reorder layers:

Drag one layer above or below another to change the order in which objects appear in the document **G**.

If you have many layers in your document, you may want to combine several layers together to make it easier to work with the layers. This is called *merging* layers.

To merge layers:

1. Select the layer that you want the other layers to merge onto 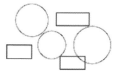.

2. Select the other layers that you want to merge.

TIP This order is important. The first layer chosen is the layer that will remain after the merge.

3. Choose Merge Layers from the Layers panel menu. The items on the layers are combined into a single layer 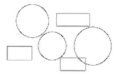.

A   Select two or more layers to be merged. Here, the Circles layer was chosen first.

B   The result of **merging two layers**. Notice that the Circle layer remains and the other layer has been deleted.

Nobody likes empty boxes and cartons taking up space in a cupboard or refrigerator. Similarly, it's confusing to have layers without content in a document. Fortunately, it is easy to delete empty layers.

To delete unused layers:

Choose Delete Unused Layers from the Layers panel menu. InDesign finds all empty layers and deletes them.

So What About Photoshop, Illustrator, and Acrobat Layers?

"Hey, Sandee, didn't I see you speak at a conference and say that InDesign can show and hide the layers in placed graphics from Photoshop, Illustrator, InDesign, and Acrobat files? How come you're not covering that topic in this chapter?"

You're right. InDesign does let you change the visibility of layers in those types of placed graphics. But the layers in those graphics aren't controlled using the Layers panel. They're shown and hidden using the Image Import Options when you first place the graphic, or later, in the Object Layer Options. *(See Chapter 8, "Imported Graphics," for how to control the layers in placed files.)*

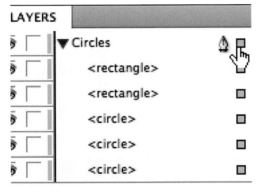

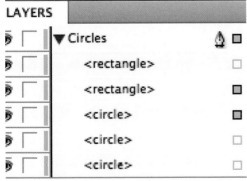

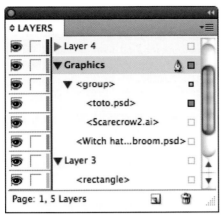

C You can **view the contents of a layer or a group** by opening the triangle next to the layer name.

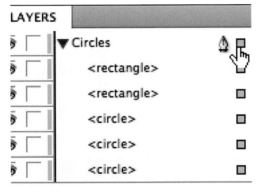

D Click the **proxy square for a layer** to select all the items on that layer.

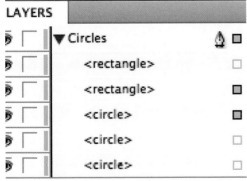

E When you select items on a layer, the proxy squares next to those items are highlighted.

Layer Contents

You can see the objects on a layer by looking at the page. But you can also see which objects are on each layer by opening the contents of the layer in the Layer panel.

To view the contents of a layer:

Click the triangle "twisty" for that layer so that the triangle points down. This reveals the items on that layer C.

To view the contents of a group:

Click the triangle "twisty" for the group so that the triangle points down. This reveals the items in that group C.

TIP You can select and delete an item in a group by selecting its proxy square and then deleting the item.

You can also use the Layers panel to select specific items on a layer or all the items on a layer.

To select all the items on a layer:

Click the proxy square placeholder to the right of the layer name. This selects all the items on that layer D. The proxy squares are highlighted with the color assigned for that layer.

TIP If the layer contents are visible, the proxy squares for each of the items will also be highlighted.

To select specific items on a layer:

1. Open the layer triangle to view its contents.

2. Click the proxy square placeholder to the right of the name of the item. This selects each specific item E.

Items on the page are named with generic names such as rectangle, group, or the name of the graphic. You can name the groups or items within a layer. This makes it easier to identify items on the layer.

To change the name of an item in the Layers panel:

1. Use a single click to select the object in the Layers panel.

2. With the object still selected, click the name of the object. This reveals the field for the name 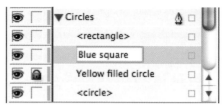.

3. Type the new name for the object.

4. Press the Return key to apply the name.

Just as you can change the order, delete, lock, and hide layers, you can do the same with the items on the layer.

To rearrange an item on a layer:

Drag the item from one position to another within the Layers panel 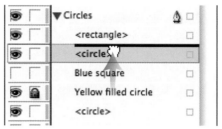. Objects at the top of the panel are in front of other objects in the document.

TIP Hold the Opt/Alt key as you drag to create a copy of the item.

To lock an item on a layer:

Click the lock area next to the item on the layer 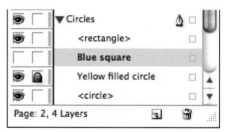. This locks the item.

TIP You can also use this technique to unlock a single item. This is very useful if you don't want to have to unlock all the items on a spread.

To hide an item on a layer:

Click the visibility icon next to the item on the layer . This hides the item.

To delete an item on a layer:

Drag the item from the list into the Layer trash icon 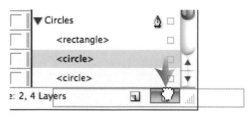. This deletes the item.

A Click to **highlight and rename** an item in the Layers panel.

B Drag **to move an object above others or to another layer.**

C A **hidden object and a locked object** on a layer.

D Drag **to delete an object from the document.**

Libraries and Snippets 12

Back when I worked in advertising, I noticed that the art directors would stick little bits and pieces of type and logos on their mechanical board, drafting table, lamp, and wall. This made it easy to grab an often-used logo or piece of art to insert into a layout.

Similarly, when you work with electronic page layouts, you use certain elements over and over. For instance, if you're working on a magazine, you might want to have a series of different-sized frames to hold frequently used ads.

Rather than copying and pasting the frames from one part of the document to another, you can use InDesign's libraries or snippets to hold the elements you use repeatedly.

Then, when you need to use an item from the library or the saved snippet file, you can simply drag it onto the page.

Storing Items in a Library

A library allows you to store elements, such as text frames, images, or empty frames. When elements are in a library, they can be dragged easily into open documents. Libraries are especially useful when you need to use the same element in many different places.

TIP Libraries appear as panels that float above the open InDesign documents. Libraries are available to use with any InDesign document.

To create a library:

1. Choose **File > New > Library**. This opens the New Library dialog box.

2. Use this dialog box to name the library file and select its location.

TIP The name of the library file appears in the tab of the Library panel.

3. Click Save. The library appears as a floating panel **A**.

To add items to a library:

1. With a library open, select the item you want to insert in it.

2. Click the Add Item button at the bottom of the Library panel.

   or

   Drag the item into the library **B**. The item appears in the Library panel.

   or

   Choose Add Item from the Library panel menu **C**.

TIP Multiple objects are always entered as a single library item. If you want individual objects, you need to select and add them to the library one by one.

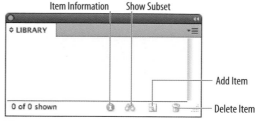

A A **new Library panel** does not contain any items.

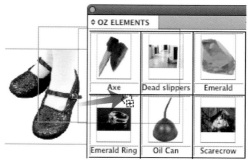

B You can **add items to a library** by dragging them from the page into the Library panel.

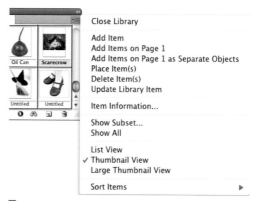

C The **Library panel menu** contains the commands for working with a library.

You can also add all the items on the current page to a library.

To add a page to a library:

1. With a library open, move to the page you want to add to the library.

2. Choose Add Items on Page [number] from the Library panel submenu.

TIP The Add Items on Page [number] command automatically labels the entry as a single page in the library Item Information dialog box.

Instead of the Add Items on Page [number] command, you may want to add all the items on a page as individual library entries. Instead of dragging them one by one into the Library panel, you can add the items as separate elements.

To add all the items on a page separately:

1. With a library open, move to the page that contains all the items that you want to add to the library.

2. Choose Add Items on Page [number] as Separate Objects from the Library panel menu.

To delete items from a library:

1. Select the item in the library.

2. Click the Delete Item icon.

   or

   Choose Delete Item(s) from the Library panel menu.

3. A dialog box appears asking for confirmation that you want to delete the items. Click Yes.

TIP Hold the Opt/Alt key to bypass the dialog box when you delete a library item.

Applying Library Items to a Page

Libraries can be opened and the elements in the libraries dragged onto any InDesign document.

To add library items to a document:

1. Select the item in the library.

   TIP Shift-click to select multiple contiguous entries in the Library panel.

   TIP Cmd/Ctrl-click to select multiple non-contiguous entries in the Library panel.

2. Drag the items from the library onto the page .

   or

   Choose Place Item(s) from the Library panel menu.

   TIP The Place Item(s) command adds the library item in the same position it was in when first defined.

You may want to modify an item in a library with a new object, text, or image. The Update Library Item command makes this easy to do.

To update an item in a library:

1. Select the item on the page that you want to use as the replacement in the library.

2. Select the item in the library that needs to be updated.

3. Choose Update Library Item from the Library panel menu. The library thumbnail updates to display the new item.

A Items can be dragged from a library onto a document.

Libraries in the Bridge

Libraries appear in the Adobe Bridge as icons, not previewed documents.

Library icons can be opened through the Bridge as you would any InDesign file.

Although you can add descriptions to the items in a library, the library items in the Adobe Bridge cannot have keywords or other XMP metadata applied to them.

EPS icon ——— Axe
Text icon ——— Caption
PDF icon ——— Dead slippers
Geometry icon ——— Emerald
Page icon ——— Emerald Ring
Image icon ——— Oil Can
Structure icon ——— Scarecrow
InDesign icon ——— Tall Scarecrow

B The **List View** shows the name of the item and an icon that shows the type of item.

Axe   Caption   Toto

C The **Thumbnail View** shows the name of the item and a preview of the item.

D The **Item Information dialog box** lets you change the information assigned to each item.

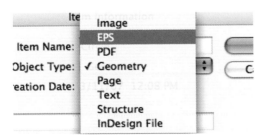

E Use the **Object Type list** to apply a label for the library element.

Setting the Library Display

If you have many items in a library, you may want to change how the items are displayed.

To change the library display:

Choose List View in the Library panel menu to see the item name and an icon that indicates the type of item **B**.

or

Choose Thumbnail View or Large Thumbnail View to see the name and a preview of the item **C**.

You can also add information such as file type and keywords that makes it easy to search for library entries.

To modify the library item information:

1. Select the item.

2. Click the Library Item Information icon.

   or

   Choose Item Information from the Library panel menu. This opens the Item Information dialog box **D**.

3. Enter the name in the Item Name field.

4. Use the Object Type list to choose one of following categories **E**:

   - **Image** contains raster images.
   - **EPS** contains EPS files.
   - **PDF** contains PDF files.
   - **Geometry** includes frames and rules that do not contain images or text.
   - **Page** is an entire page.
   - **Text** contains text frames.
   - **Structure** contains XML elements.
   - **InDesign File** contains InDesign files.

   TIP InDesign assigns a category when items are entered into a library. You can change that listing to any category you want.

5. Enter a description for the item.

Searching and Sorting Libraries

If you have many items in a library, you may find it difficult to find specific library entries. InDesign has a powerful search feature that makes it easy to locate specific items in a library.

To search within a library:

1. Click the Show Library Subset icon.

   or

   Choose Show Subset from the Library panel menu. This opens the Subset dialog box .

2. Choose Search Entire Library to search all entries in the library .

   or

   Choose Search Currently Shown Items to search through only those items currently displayed in the library.

3. Use the Parameters menu and fields to set the search criteria 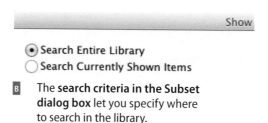.

4. Click More Choices to add up to five choices to the parameters list.

5. Choose Match All to choose only those items that match all the search parameters .

   or

   Choose Match Any One to find items that meet at least one of the search parameters.

6. Click OK to display the items that meet the search criteria.

TIP Use the Back or Forward button to move through the search settings in the Subset dialog box.

A The **Subset dialog box** lets you find specific library items.

B The **search criteria in the Subset dialog box** let you specify where to search in the library.

C The **Parameters menu** lets you choose which part of the item information is searched.

D The **match criteria** in the Subset dialog box control how the search items are matched.

Once you have sorted a library, you may need to show all the items at some other time.

To display all the library entries:

Choose Show All from the Library panel submenu.

You can also control the order in which the library items are displayed. This makes it easier to find items in large libraries.

To sort library entries:

Choose one of the Sort Items options from the Library panel menu:

- **By Name** arranges the items in alphabetical order.
- **By Newest** arranges the items in the order they were added, with the newest items first.
- **By Oldest** arranges the items in the order they were added, with the oldest items first.
- **By Type** arranges the items in groups according to their categories.

Creating and Using Snippets

Snippets are exactly what they sound like — little bits of a page that you snip off to use somewhere else.

To create snippets using the Export command:

1. Select the items on the page that you want to turn into a snippet.

2. Choose **File > Export**.

3. In the Export dialog box choose InDesign Snippet from the Format list **E**.

4. Name and save the file. The snippet icon appears in the directory.

```
Adobe PDF (Interactive)
Adobe PDF (Print)
EPS
EPUB
Flash CS6 Professional (FLA)
Flash Player (SWF)
HTML
InCopy Document
InDesign Markup (IDML)
InDesign Snippet
JPEG
PNG
XML
```

File name:

Save as type: InDesign Snippet

E The **Export dialog box** lets you save items as InDesign snippets.

To create snippets by dragging:

1. Select and drag the items that you want to turn into a snippet onto the desktop. The Snippet icon appears with a bizarre temporary name.

TIP You cannot drag portions of text as a snippet, only the entire frame.

2. Change the name to something more understandable.

Once you have created snippets, you can drag them onto a page.

To drag snippets onto a page:

1. Select the snippet on the desktop or in the file directory.

2. Drag the Snippet icon onto the InDesign document page.

TIP Use the Snippets Import setting in the Preferences > File Handling dialog to choose whether the snippet appears at its original coordinates or the cursor position .

TIP Snippets can be previewed in Bridge or Mini Bridge and dragged onto an InDesign page.

TIP You can also place snippets using the File > Place command.

A The **Snippet Import setting** in the File Handling Preferences lets you control where snippets appear when dragged onto a page.

Tabs and Tables 13

Before layouts had tabs and tables, there was chaos. Well, perhaps not chaos, but it was difficult to line up columns of text in an orderly fashion.

The word "tab" comes from the tabulator key on a typewriter. (Does anyone still use a typewriter?) The tabulator key moved the carriage a certain number of spaces.

The tabulator key was named because it allowed typists to create tabular data. Tabular data is information arranged in systematic rows and columns — otherwise known as a table.

However, mathematical information isn't the only thing arranged in tables. Resumes, menus, train schedules, calendars, and even classified ads are all arranged in some form of table.

Anytime you need to keep text or graphics aligned in either columns or rows, consider using the tabs and tables features in InDesign.

Not only can you align text using tabs, but you can create tab leaders that make it easy to read across the lines of text. You can also create tables with repeating headers and footers and add custom strokes and fills to the tables.

Inserting Tab Characters

There are two parts to working with tabs. The first part is to insert the *tab characters* that force the text to jump to a certain position.

To insert tab characters into text:

1. Position the insertion point where you want the tab character to be located.

2. Press the Tab key on the keyboard. This creates a tab character in the text **A**.

TIP Choose Type > Show Hidden Characters to see the display of the tab character within the text.

TIP InDesign recognizes tab characters in imported text.

InDesign also has a special type of tab character called a right indent tab. This tab character automatically sets the text to the rightmost position in the frame **B**.

To insert a right indent tab character:

1. Place the insertion point to the left of the text that should be shifted to the right.

2. Press Shift-Tab or choose **Type > Insert Special Character > Other > Right Indent Tab**.

Frank » Writer#

A A **tab character** is displayed as part of the hidden characters in text.

Chapter·6 ⊁ 7¶
Chapter·7 ⊁ 12#

B The **right indent tab character** automatically moves the text to the right side of the text frame.

Inserting Tabs in Text

It's actually very simple to insert a tab character into text. Just tap the Tab key on the keyboard. However, before you go tapping away, you should follow the guides for working with tabs.

Insert only one tab character for each column. Even if the text doesn't line up correctly, don't add another tab character. Use the Tab panel and tab stops to line up the columns.

If you're over a certain age, you may have been taught to put a tab at the beginning of a paragraph to indent the first line. Don't do it! As mentioned in Chapter 3, "Basic Text," you can use the first line indent to format paragraphs.

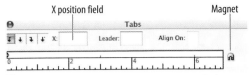

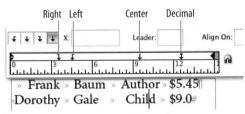

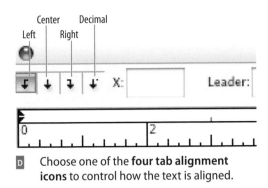

X position field   Magnet

The **Tabs panel** contains the controls for inserting tab stops and aligning the tabs.

Center   Decimal

Left   Right

Choose one of the **four tab alignment icons** to control how the text is aligned.

Right   Left   Center   Decimal

» Frank » Baum » Author » $5.45
Dorothy » Gale   »   Child » $9.0#

Examples of **how the four tab alignments** control the text.

Setting Tab Stops

The next — and most important — part to working with tabs is to set the *tab stops* or the formatting controls that set where the text should stop after it jumps to a new position. This is controlled using the Tabs panel.

To open the Tabs panel:

Choose **Type > Tabs**. The Tabs panel appears above the text frame **C**.

TIP The Tabs panel can be kept onscreen like any other panel.

TIP If the Tabs panel is not positioned above the text, click the Magnet icon in the panel to automatically move the panel to the correct position.

To set tab stops:

1. Select the text.

2. Choose the type of tab alignment from the four tab icons in the ruler **D**. The four alignments work as follows **E**:

   - **Left** aligns the left side of the text at the tab stop.

   - **Center** centers the text on either side of the tab stop.

   - **Right** aligns the right side of the text at the tab stop.

   - **Decimal** aligns the text at the decimal point or period within the text.

3. Click the ruler area where you want the tab stop to be positioned. Or type a number in the X position field. A small tab arrow corresponding to the tab type appears that indicates the position of the tab stop.

TIP The default tab stops are invisible left-aligned tabs positioned every half inch. Adding a tab stop to the ruler overrides all tab stops to the left of the new tab.

To change tab settings:

1. Select the text.

2. Open the Tabs panel.

3. To change the alignment of a tab stop, select the tab arrow and then click a new alignment icon. Or hold the Opt/Alt key and click the tab arrow in the ruler.

4. To change the position of a tab stop, drag the tab arrow to a new position.

TIP As you move a tab stop along the ruler, a line extends through the text, even if the Tabs panel is not aligned to the text frame 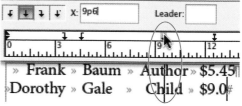. Watch for this line to help judge the position of the tab stop.

Many times you will want to have tab stops repeated at the same interval. InDesign makes it easy to set repeating tabs.

To set a repeating tab:

1. Position the first tab stop on the ruler.

2. With the tab stop still selected, choose Repeat Tab from the Tabs panel menu **B**. This adds new tab stops at the same interval along the ruler **C**.

TIP The tab stops created by the Repeat Tab command are not linked and move independently.

» Frank » Baum » Author » $5.45
Dorothy » Gale » Child » $9.0

A As you move a tab stop, **a line extends through the text** to help you position the tab stop correctly.

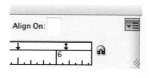

Align On:

Clear All
Delete Tab
Repeat Tab
Reset Indents

B The **Tabs panel menu** gives you several important commands for working with tabs.

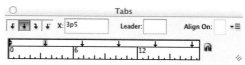

C The **Repeat Tab command** allows you to easily add tab stops at the same interval along the ruler.

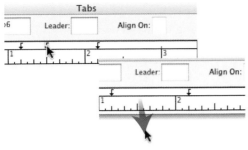

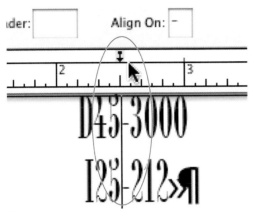

D To **remove a tab stop,** drag it off the Tabs panel ruler.

E You can enter a custom alignment character for the **Align On field**. Here the text aligns to the hyphen.

Once you have added tab stops to the Tabs panel ruler, you can remove them easily.

To remove tab stops:

1. Select the tab stop on the Tabs panel ruler.

2. Drag the tab stop off the ruler. This deletes the tab stop **D**. Or choose Delete Tab from the Tab panel menu.

TIP If there are no tab stops to the left of the one you removed, this restores the invisible default tab stops at the nearest half-inch position.

If you have many tab stops on the Tabs panel ruler, it may be easier to delete all the tab stops with a single command.

To clear all the tabs off the ruler:

Choose Clear All from the Tabs panel menu. This restores the invisible default tab stops at every half-inch mark.

The Decimal tab aligns numerical data to a decimal point. However, you may need to align text to a different character. For instance, some European currency uses a comma instead of a decimal. InDesign lets you set a custom alignment character.

To set a custom alignment character:

1. Choose the Decimal Tab icon.

2. Add a tab stop to the ruler.

3. Replace the period in the Align On field with a different character. The text aligns around that character **E**.

Creating Tab Leaders

A *tab leader* allows you to automatically fill the space between the tabbed material with a repeating character. Tab leaders are often used in the tables of contents of books. You'll find an example of tab leaders in the table of contents at the front of this book.

TIP Tab leaders are added when the reader needs to move horizontally across a wide column from one entry to another. The tab leader helps the reader's eye stay on the correct line of text. There's no need to insert tab leaders if the line of text is not wide.

To add tab leaders:

1. Select the tab stop arrow on the Tabs panel ruler.

2. Click inside the Leader field of the Tabs panel and type up to eight characters. This changes the white space between the text to a repeating leader character.

TIP I often add spaces to the period character in the Leader field to give the leader a more pleasing look 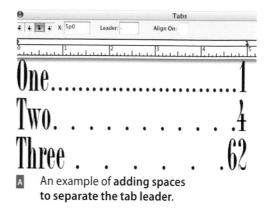.

TIP If you want to preview the characters in the Leader field, press the Tab key on the keyboard. This applies the changes.

TIP You can select the characters in a tab leader as you would ordinary text and change the point size, kerning, or other attributes.

A An example of **adding spaces to separate the tab leader.**

Choosing Between Tabs and Tables

For the longest time, designers wanted a way to create tables in page-layout documents. But the programs didn't provide tables. So we suffered with multiple frames linked together in strange groups. When InDesign first introduced tables, many designers wondered if there was any reason to still use tabs.

Absolutely! I use tabs in this book to separate numbers from the text in the exercises. I also use tabs with leaders for the listings in the table of contents.

I use tables whenever I need side-by-side paragraphs, such as in a résumé. I also use tables whenever I need to separate the information with horizontal and vertical lines.

Insert Table

Table Dimensions	
Body Rows: 4	OK
Columns: 4	Cancel
Header Rows: 0	
Footer Rows: 0	
Table Style: [Basic Table]	

B Use the **Insert Table dialog box** to create an empty table in a text frame.

Table and Cell Styles

As you read through the rest of this chapter, you may feel that it's too much work to create and format tables and the cells within tables. Relax, InDesign has powerful table and cell styles which make it easy to create very sophisticated-looking tables with just a few clicks.

However, rather than totally overwhelm you in this chapter, I'll cover the styles for tables and cells in Chapter 15, "Styles."

So, as you go through this chapter, consider this the part where you learn to bake bread from scratch. Later on I'll show you how to automate the whole process.

Creating and Using Tables

Tabs are limited to lining up only a single line of text. Tables can line up text so it extends down into several lines. Tables also let you add borders to the cell that contains the text or add fills of color behind the text.

To create a new table in a text frame:

1. Place an insertion point inside a text frame.
2. Choose **Table > Insert Table**. The Insert Table dialog box appears **B**.
3. Use the Body Rows control to set the number of rows in the table.
4. Use the Columns control to set the number of columns.
5. Use the Header Rows control to set the number of rows across the top of the table.
6. Use the Footer Rows control to set the number of rows across the bottom of the table.
7. If you have defined a table style, use the Table Style list to choose that style for the table.
8. Click OK. InDesign creates a table that fills the text frame as follows:
   - The width of the table is set to fill the width of the text frame.
   - The table columns are distributed evenly across the table.

TIP Headers and footers are special cells that are repeated when the table is divided between frames or pages.

Many times you will import text that you'd like to convert into a table. Fortunately, this is rather easy to do.

To convert text into a table:

1. Select the text.

2. Choose **Table > Convert Text to Table**. The Convert Text to Table dialog box appears 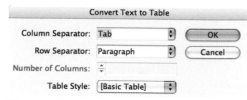.

3. Use the Column Separator menu to choose which character should be used as the marker for each column in the table. Or type the character that you would like as the marker in the Column Separator field.

   TIP **If you have imported tabbed delimited text, the marker is most likely a tab character. However, some databases will use paragraph returns or spaces as the column separators.**

4. Use the Row Separator menu to choose which character should be used as the marker for each row in the table. Or type the character that you would like as the marker in the Row Separator field.

   TIP **For most text, the row separator is the paragraph symbol.**

5. If you have chosen anything except a paragraph symbol for the Row Separator, use the Number of Columns field to choose how many columns there should be in the table.

6. If you have defined a table style, use the Table Style list to choose that style for the table.

7. Click OK to create the table .

A The **Convert Text to Table dialog box** lets you choose how text is converted to a table.

B The **Convert Text to Table command** transforms tabs and paragraphs into rows and columns.

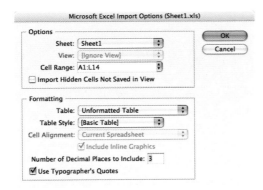

C The **Microsoft Excel Import Options dialog box** lets you choose which worksheet and cells are imported from an Excel document.

D The **Microsoft Word Import Options dialog box** lets you choose how Word tables are imported into the InDesign document.

What if you've already got a beautiful table, and some tabbed text, but they're separated from each other? InDesign lets you paste tabbed text into existing tables.

To paste text into a table:

1. Copy the tabbed text.

2. Highlight the cells in the table where you want the text to appear.

3. Choose Paste. The text will populate the cells of the table and make additional table cells if necessary.

Most people use Microsoft Word and Excel to create text and spreadsheets. InDesign lets you import the tables created by both Word and Excel.

To import a table from Word or Excel:

1. Choose **File** > **Place** and navigate to the Word or Excel file that you want to insert into your document.

2. If necessary, use the Microsoft Excel Import Options **C** or the Microsoft Word Import Options **D** to control how the file will be imported, as described on the next two pages. Click OK to close the Import Options dialog box.

3. Use the loaded text cursor to draw a text frame with the imported document. Or use any of the techniques described in Chapter 10 to flow the text onto the pages of the document.

You can also customize which Excel data is imported.

To choose the cells that should be imported:

1. Use the Sheet menu to select a worksheet.

2. Use the View menu to choose a custom view.

3. Use the Cell Range field to select cells.

4. If desired, select the Import Hidden Cells Not Saved in View checkbox.

To set the formatting for Excel cells:

1. Use the Table menu to change the formatting options as follows:

   • **Formatted Table** imports the cells with whatever formatting was applied in Excel.

   • **Unformatted Table** imports the cells with no formatting except a stroke around each InDesign cell.

   • **Unformatted Tabbed Text** converts the cells into text divided by tab characters.

2. If you have defined a table style, choose one from the Table Style list.

3. Use the Cell Alignment menu to choose:

   • **Current Spreadsheet** imports the text with the alignment that was set in the spreadsheet.

   • **Left** sets the text aligned to the left side.

   • **Center** aligns the text to the center.

   • **Right** sets the text aligned to the right.

4. Use Number of Decimal Places to Include to set how many decimal places are included in the imported cells.

5. If desired, select Use Typographer's Quotes to convert straight "quotes" (like these) into open and close "quotes" (like these).

> **Importing from Spreadsheets**
>
> Most likely, if you need to import data from Excel spreadsheets, the files have been created by accountants or others who know little about graphic design or page layout.
>
> Try to talk to them before they send you the file for layout. Explain that they should not format their document using the controls in Microsoft Excel. Most of the time you will just have to strip out that formatting in order to make the file work in your layout.
>
> You may also want to ask them for a test file so you can see how the information will be imported.

An example of how a table can be inserted inside a cell of another table.

The **Convert Table to Text command** transforms table rows and columns into tabs and paragraph returns.

You can also control how table information in Word documents is imported.

To set the formatting for Word tables:

1. Select Remove Styles and Formatting from Text and Tables in the Microsoft Word Import Options dialog box to change the original formatting applied in Word.

TIP Use this option to remove some of the hideous formatting that may have been applied to Word tables.

2. If you have set the option to remove the formatting, choose one of the following from the Convert Tables To menu:

   - **Unformatted Tables** imports the Word table with no formatting except a stroke around each cell.

   - **Unformatted Tabbed Text** converts the cells into text divided by tab characters.

To place a table in a table cell:

1. Click with the Text tool to place an insertion point inside a table cell.

2. Use the Insert Table command or a Place command to create a table within that cell .

To convert a table to text:

1. Place an insertion point in any cell inside the table.

2. Choose **Table > Convert Table to Text**.

3. Use the Convert Table to Text dialog box to choose what elements should be used to designate the column and row separators :

   - You can convert columns and rows to tabs, commas, or paragraph returns.

   - You can type your own character in the field to customize the conversion.

Navigating Through Tables

As you work with tables, you will want to add content to the cells, move from cell to cell, and select cells, rows, and columns.

To insert text into table cells:

1. Place an insertion point inside a table cell.

2. Type the text for the cell or choose **File > Place** to insert the imported text in the cell.

To move from one cell to another:

Press the Tab key to jump forward from one cell to another  or press Shift-Tab to move backward from one cell to another 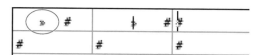.

Because you use the tab key to navigate through a table, you need special techniques to insert actual tab characters into a table.

To insert a tab character into a table:

Press Opt/Alt-Tab to insert a tab character inside a cell 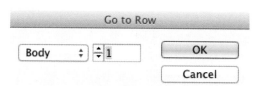 or choose **Type > Insert Special Character > Tab Character**.

To jump to a specific row:

1. Choose **Table > Go to Row**. The Go to Row dialog box appears .

2. Use the menu to move to the body, header, or footer of the table.

3. Enter the number for the row you want to move to.

A Press the Tab key to **jump forward from one cell to another** in a table.

B Press Shift-Tab to **jump backward from one cell to another** in a table.

C Press **Opt/Alt-Tab to insert a tab character** into a table.

D The **Go to Row dialog box** lets you quickly jump from one row to another.

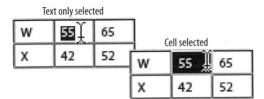

Text only selected

Cell selected

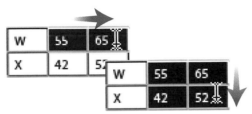

E When the text in a cell is selected, only the text is highlighted. When the entire cell is selected, the entire cell area is highlighted.

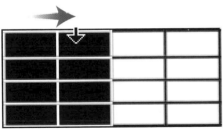

F Drag across and then down to select a specific group of cells in a table.

G Drag with the down arrow cursor to select columns in a table.

Selecting Tables

By clicking and dragging your cursor, you can select cells, columns, rows, or the entire table.

TIP When the entire cell, row, column, or combination of cells are selected, you can copy and paste cells from one part of a table to another.

To select text in a table cell:

1. Place an insertion point inside a table cell.

2. Drag across the cell until all the text in the cell is highlighted.

   or

   Choose **Edit > Select All** to select all the text within that cell.

TIP There is a difference between the highlight of a cell with just the text selected and the highlight with an entire cell selected **E**.

To select text in multiple table cells:

1. Use the Text tool to drag across to select the cells in specific columns **F**.

2. If you want, continue to drag down to select the cells in additional rows.

To select a table column:

1. Place the Text tool cursor at the top of the table. A down arrow cursor appears.

2. Click the down arrow. The entire column is selected **G**.

3. Drag across with the down arrow cursor to select any additional columns or move the down arrow to another column and Shift-click to select multiple columns.

To select a table row:

1. Place the Text tool cursor at the left side of the table. A left arrow cursor appears.

2. Click the left arrow. The entire row is selected 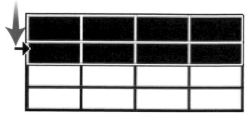.

3. Drag down with the left arrow cursor to select any additional rows or move the left arrow to another row and Shift-click to select multiple rows.

A   The left arrow cursor indicates you can click to select an entire row in a table.

To select the entire table:

1. Place the Text tool cursor at the top corner of the table. A slanted arrow cursor appears.

2. Click the slanted arrow. The entire table is selected B.

To use the table selection commands:

1. Place the insertion point in a cell in the table.

2. Choose one of the following commands:
   - **Table** > **Select** > **Cell** selects the cell.
   - **Table** > **Select** > **Row** selects the row that contains the cell.
   - **Table** > **Select** > **Column** selects the column that contains the cell.
   - **Table** > **Select** > **Table** selects the entire table.

B   Position the cursor at the upper-left corner and click to **select the entire table**.

TIP The table selection commands are helpful for applying borders and fills to cells.

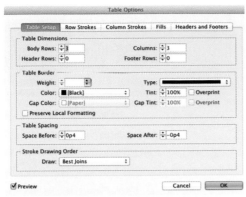

C The **Table Setup dialog box** contains the basic options for a table's appearance.

D The **Table Dimensions area** lets you set the number of rows, columns, header rows, and footer rows.

Working with Rows and Columns

Once you've created a table, you may want to change the number of rows and columns in the table.

TIP In addition to the Table menu and dialog boxes, many adjustments to tables can be made using the Table panel or Control panel. *(See the section "Using the Table or Control Panels" at the end of this chapter for more information on modifying tables with those onscreen elements.)*

To change the number of rows and columns in a table:

1. Select the entire table or any part of the table.

2. Choose **Table > Table Options > Table Setup** to open the Table Setup dialog box C.

3. Set the Body Rows controls in the Table Dimensions area to increase or decrease the number of rows in the main section of the table D.

4. Set the Header Rows controls to increase or decrease the number of rows in the header section of the table D.

5. Set the Columns controls to increase or decrease the number of columns in the table D.

6. Set the Footer Rows controls to increase or decrease the number of rows in the footer section of the table D.

TIP Use the Preview control at the bottom of the Table Setup dialog box to see the results of changing the controls.

TIP The commands in the Table Dimensions section always add rows and columns at the end of the table sections. The next exercise explains how to insert rows and columns into a specific location in the table.

You can also insert columns and rows into a specific location in a table.

To insert columns into a table:

1. Place an insertion point where you want to insert the columns.

2. Choose **Table** > **Insert** > **Column**. The Insert Column(s) dialog box appears 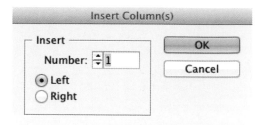.

   or

   Choose **Insert** > **Column** from the Table panel menu.

3. Use the Number field to set the number of columns.

4. Choose either Left or Right to specify where the new columns should be inserted **B**.

To insert rows into a table:

1. Place an insertion point where you want to insert the rows.

2. Choose **Table** > **Insert** > **Row**. The Insert Row(s) dialog box appears **C**.

   or

   Choose **Insert** > **Row** from the Table panel menu.

3. Use the Number field to set the number of rows.

4. Choose either Above or Below to specify where the new rows should be inserted.

TIP The Insert Row(s) dialog box inserts rows into the header, footer, or main section of a table.

To insert rows as you type:

1. Place the insertion point in the final cell of the last row of the table main body, header, or footer.

2. Press the Tab key. A new row is automatically inserted.

A Use the **Insert Column(s) dialog box** to add columns at a specific location within a table.

Original table

	A	B	C	D
Y	84	94	34	55
Z	22	33	44	55
	AA	BB	CC	DD

Selected cell

After column is inserted   New column

	A	B		C	D
Y	84	94		34	55
Z	22	33		44	55
	AA	BB		CC	DD

B An example of **how a column is added** to the left of the selected cell.

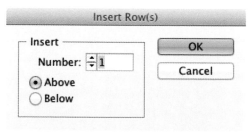

C Use the **Insert Row(s) dialog box** to add rows at a specific location within a table.

D Hold the Opt/Alt key as you drag across to **add columns to a table**.

E Hold the Opt/Alt key as you drag down **to add rows to a table**.

Selected cells   After deleting content

F An example of how you can **delete the content of selected cells**.

To add columns as you drag the table edge:

1. Drag the last column of the table.
2. Press the Opt/Alt key as you drag. This expands the size of the table by adding columns **D**.

To add rows as you drag the table edge:

1. Drag the last row of the table.
2. Press the Opt/Alt key as you drag. This expands the size of the table by adding rows **E**.

To delete table columns:

1. Select the columns you want to delete.
2. Choose **Table > Delete > Column**.

To delete table rows:

1. Select the rows you want to delete.
2. Choose **Table > Delete > Row**.

To delete the entire table:

1. Select the table.
2. Choose **Table > Delete > Table**.

You may want to delete the content inside a cell without deleting the cell itself.

To delete the content in table cells:

1. Select the cells, columns, or rows.
2. Press the Delete/Backspace key or choose **Edit > Clear**.

TIP The content is deleted but the cells themselves remain in place **F**.

You can't move cells from one place to another, but you can copy and paste cells and their content to new locations.

To copy and paste the content in table cells:

1. Select the cells, columns, or rows that you want to move to a new position.

2. Choose **Edit > Copy** or **Edit > Cut**. This puts the selected cells on the clipboard.

3. Select the new cells, columns, or rows.

TIP You should select at least the same number of cells, columns, or rows that were selected in step 1.

4. Choose **Edit > Paste**. The content on the clipboard is pasted into the selected cells A.

TIP If you selected more cells than were selected in step 1, the excess cells are not changed.

When you create a table, all the columns and rows are evenly spaced. However, you can modify the size of the rows and columns.

TIP A red dot inside a table cell indicates there is an overflow of text B. You can change the size of the cell to display the overflow text.

To change a single row height visually:

1. With the Text tool selected, place the cursor along the border of the row you want to adjust. The cursor changes to an up/down arrow C.

2. Drag to adjust the height of the row.

To change all the rows visually:

1. Place the cursor along the bottom border of the table. The cursor changes to an up/down arrow.

2. Hold the Shift key as you drag to adjust the height of all the rows in the table.

Select and copy cells

Select empty cells

Paste cells to new position

A The three-step process to **copy and move cells** from one position to another.

B A **red dot inside a table cell** indicates that there is an overflow of text inside the cell.

C The **Up/ Down arrow** indicates you can adjust the row height.

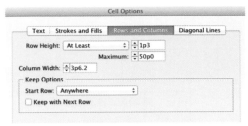

The **Rows and Columns category** of the Cell Options dialog box.

April	May	June
12	67	54
6	7	2

The **Left/ Right arrow** indicates you can adjust the column width.

The **Column Width control** of the Cell Options dialog box.

April	May	June
12	67	54
6	7	2

April	May	June
12	67	54
6	7	2

The results of using the **Distribute Columns Evenly command**.

To set the row height numerically:

1. Select the rows you want to adjust.

2. Choose **Table** > **Cell Options** > **Rows and Columns** to open the Cell Options dialog box to the Rows and Columns options **D**.

3. Set the Row Height menu as follows:

   - **At Least** sets a row height that can increase to hold text or an image.

   - **Exactly** sets a row height that does not get larger.

4. Enter an amount in the Row Height field.

5. Use the Maximum field to prevent the row from becoming too tall.

To change the column width visually:

1. With the Text tool selected, place the cursor along the border of the column you want to adjust. The cursor changes to a left/right arrow **E**.

2. Drag to adjust the width of the column.

To set the column width numerically:

1. Select the columns you want to adjust.

2. Enter an amount in the Column Width field **F**.

You can adjust columns or rows so their spacing is evenly distributed.

To automatically distribute columns:

1. Set the rightmost column to the position it should be after the adjustment.

2. Select the columns you want to adjust.

3. Choose **Table** > **Distribute Columns Evenly**. The column widths adjust **G**.

To automatically distribute rows:

1. Set the bottommost row to the position it should be after the adjustment.

2. Select the rows you want to adjust.

3. Choose **Table > Distribute Rows Evenly**. The row heights adjust so they are the same size 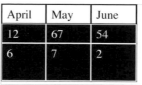.

You can control when and how the rows of a table break across text frames.

To set the keep options for rows:

1. Select the rows you want to control.

2. Choose **Table > Cell Options > Rows and Columns**.

3. Choose from the Start Row menu as follows 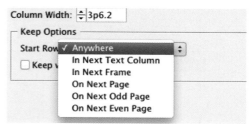:

   - **Anywhere** lets the row start anywhere in a text frame.

   - **In Next Text Column** forces the row to the next column in the frame or the next text frame.

   - **In Next Frame** forces the row to the next text frame.

   - **On Next Page** forces the row to the next page.

   - **On Next Odd Page** forces the row to the next odd-numbered page.

   - **On Next Even Page** forces the row to the next even-numbered page.

4. Select Keep with Next Row to make sure one row doesn't separate from another .

A The results of using the **Distribute Rows Evenly command**.

B The **Start Row menu** lets you choose where that row starts.

C Select **Keep with Next Row** to force one row to always stay with the next one.

Here are the dates for the Spring classes.¶

April#	May#
12#	67#

No space around table

Here are the dates for the Summer classes.¶

June#	July#
12#	22#

Space added around table

D **Add some space around a table** to keep it from colliding with text.

Table Spacing
Space Before: ⬍0p4   Space After: ⬍-0p4

E The **Table Spacing controls** let you set the amount of space before and after a table.

April#	May#	June#
12#	67#	54#
6#	7#	2#

F The text threads show how tables can flow from one frame to another.

Adjusting Tables Within a Text Frame

Tables are always contained within text frames. You can control how much space there is between the table and the text that precedes or follows it **D**.

To set the spacing around a table:

1. With the table selected, choose **Table > Table Options > Table Setup**. The Table Options dialog box appears.

2. Use the Table Spacing control for Space Before to set the amount of space between text and the top of the table **E**.

3. Use the Table Spacing control for Space After to set the amount of space between the bottom of the table and the text that follows it.

TIP A table is inserted into a text frame as an inline object in its own paragraph. This means that any space before or after the paragraph that holds the table is added to the space set by the Table Spacing controls.

If a table extends longer than a text frame, you get a text frame overflow. You can easily flow the rest of the table from frame to frame across pages.

To flow tables between frames:

1. Use the Selection tool to load the overflow cursor.

2. Click the overflow cursor inside the new frame to flow the rest of the table into the frame **F**.

Working with Headers and Footers

Tables with lots of data often flow from one location to another. To make it easier for readers to follow the table information, you can repeat the first and last rows of the table each time it appears in a new place. When the first row of a table repeats, it is called a *header*. When the last row repeats, it is called a *footer*.

To add a header or footer to a table:

1. With the table selected, choose **Table > Table Options > Headers and Footers.** The Table Options dialog box opens with the Headers and Footers tab chosen .

2. Use the Header Rows controls to set the number of repeating rows added to the top of the table 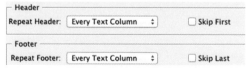.

3. Use the Footer Rows controls to set the number of repeating rows added to the bottom of the table.

TIP To turn off a header or footer, set the Header Rows or Footer Rows to zero.

To set the repeat options for headers and footers:

1. Use the Repeat Header or Repeat Footer menu as follows :

   - **Every Text Column** repeats the header or footer whenever the table appears.

   - **Once per Frame** repeats the header or footer only once in the same frame. This is useful when a table flows from one column to another.

   - **Once per Page** repeats the header or footer only once in the same page. This is useful when a table flows into multiple frames on the same page.

2. Select **Skip First** (for headers) or **Skip Last** (for footers) to display a header or footer only after the first instance of a table ▫.

A The **Headers and Footers area in Table Options** lets you control the appearance of headers and footers in the table.

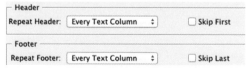

B Use the **Table Dimensions for Headers and Footers** to control the number of header and footer rows.

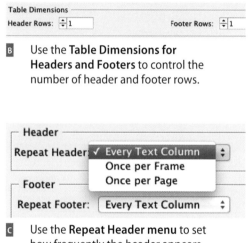

C Use the **Repeat Header menu** to set how frequently the header appears.

D The **Skip First or Skip Last** options let you repeat headers or footers after the first instance of a table.

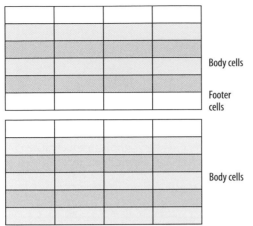

Body cells

Footer cells

Body cells

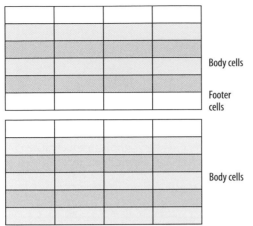 **E** An example of what happens when footer cells are converted to body cells. Notice that the footer takes on the alternating fill applied to the body cells of the table.

As you work, you may want to convert body table cells into a header or footer.

To convert cells into a table header:

1. Select the rows that you want to convert. These rows must start with the first row of the table.

2. Choose **Table** > **Convert Rows** > **To Header**. The rows are converted from the body of the table to the table header **E**.

TIP If there already is a header for the table, the cells are added to the bottom of the existing cells.

To convert cells into a table footer:

1. Select the rows that you want to convert. These rows must end with the last row of the table.

2. Choose **Table** > **Convert Rows** > **To Footer**. The rows are converted from the body of the table to the table footer.

TIP If there already is a footer for the table, the cells are added to the top of the existing cells.

Finally, you may want to convert the rows in a header or footer into the body of the table.

To convert header or footer cells into body cells:

1. Select the rows that you want to convert.

TIP The rows must include the bottom rows of the header or the top rows of the footer.

2. Choose **Table** > **Convert Rows** > **To Body**.

TIP When header or footer cells are converted into body cells, they take on the attributes of the body cells **E**.

Adding Images to Tables

Although table cells are created to hold text, you can easily add images as inline graphics to each cell.

To insert a graphic into a table cell:

1. Place an insertion point inside a table cell.

2. Choose **File** > **Place** to insert an image into the cell .

   or

   Paste a graphic copied to the clipboard into the cell.

TIP Graphics in cells are pasted as inline graphics.

If the graphic is larger than the size of the cell, some of the graphic may stick out beyond the cell. You use the Clipping setting to control whether placed graphics are seen outside a cell.

To control the display of a graphic inside a cell:

1. Place your insertion point inside the cell that contains the placed graphic.

2. Choose **Table** > **Cell Options** > **Text**. This opens the Cell Options dialog box .

3. Select Clip Contents to Cell to limit the display of the graphic to inside the cell .

   or

   Deselect Clip Contents to Cell to allow the graphic to be displayed outside the cell .

TIP In addition to allowing a graphic to appear outside the cell boundaries, you can also drag a table so that the table itself extends outside the text frame.

A An example of how a placed image can be inserted into a table cell.

B The **Clip Contents to Cell** option for inline graphics in a cell.

C With the **clip options turned on**, an inline graphic is confined to the boundaries of the cell.

D With the **clip options turned off**, an inline graphic extends outside the boundaries of the cell.

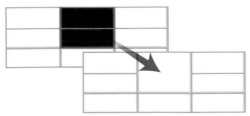

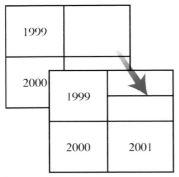

E The results of using the **Merge Cells command**.

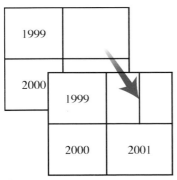

F The results of using the **Split Cell Horizontally command**.

G The results of using the **Split Cell Vertically command**.

Customizing Cells

In addition to setting the controls for the entire table, you can also make settings for individual cells. You can customize the arrangement of rows and columns by merging or splitting cells. You may want to merge cells to fit more text within a cell. You can also change the positioning of text within a cell.

To merge cells:

1. Select the cells you want to merge.

2. Choose **Table > Merge Cells**. The dividers between the cells are deleted **E**.

TIP If the merged cells contain text, the text will be divided into paragraphs.

To unmerge cells:

1. Select the cells you want to unmerge.

2. Choose **Table > Unmerge Cells**.

To split cells:

1. Select the cell you want to split.

2. Choose **Table > Split Cell Horizontally** or **Table > Split Cell Vertically** **F** or **G**.

You can also control how text is positioned horizontally and vertically within each cell.

TIP These settings also control how inline graphics are positioned within cells.

To set the cell options for text:

1. Select the cells you want to adjust.

2. Choose **Table** > **Cell Options** > **Text**. This opens the Cell Options for text controls 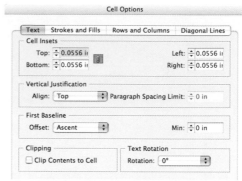.

3. Use the Cell Insets fields to adjust the space between the text and the top, bottom, left, and right sides of cells **B**.

TIP Select the link icon to make all the cell insets the same amount.

4. Choose one of the four settings from the Text Rotation menu to rotate the text in 90° increments.

You can also set the vertical alignment for where the text is positioned in the cell.

To set the text vertical alignment:

1. Select the cells you want to adjust.

2. Choose **Table** > **Cell Options** > **Text**. This opens the Cell Options dialog box for text controls.

3. Use the Vertical Justification Align menu to choose one of the four alignment options as follows:

   - **Top** positions the text at the top edge of the cell.

   - **Center** positions the text in the middle of the cell.

   - **Bottom** positions the text at the bottom edge of the cell.

   - **Justify** distributes the lines of the text evenly so that it extends from the top to the bottom of the cell.

TIP The Justify setting overrides any leading applied to the text.

A The **Text area of the Cell Options** controls how text is positioned within each cell.

B The **Cell Insets controls** let you specify how far text sits from the edge of a cell.

C When the **Justify option is chosen in the Vertical Justification Align menu**, the Paragraph Spacing Limit control is available.

D The **First Baseline controls** let you set the position of the first baseline of text within a cell.

If you choose Justify for the vertical alignment, you can then control the space between the lines or paragraphs.

To set the vertical justification spacing:

1. Select the cells you want to adjust.

2. Choose **Table > Cell Options > Text**. This opens the text controls for the cells.

3. Choose Justify from the Vertical Justification Align list.

4. Set an amount for the Paragraph Spacing Limit **C**.

TIP Increase the value for the paragraph spacing to avoid increasing the space between the lines within the paragraph.

Just as you can control where the first baseline of text appears in a text frame, you can also control the position of the text baseline within a cell.

To control the first baseline in a cell:

1. Select the cells you want to control.

2. Choose **Table > Cell Options > Text**. This opens the text controls for the cells.

3. In the First Baseline area, use the Offset menu to choose a setting **D**.

4. In the Min field, set the minimum amount of space for the first baseline.

Setting Borders, Strokes, and Fills

One of the benefits of using tables instead of tabs is how easy it is to add lines and colors to the table. (The line around a table is called the *border*. Lines around cells are called *strokes*. Colors inside the cells are called *fills* 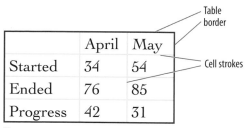.)

To add a border around the table:

1. Select at least one cell in the table.

2. Choose **Table > Table Options > Table Setup**. The Table Options dialog box opens with the Table Setup options selected **B**.

3. In the Table Border category, use the Weight field to set the thickness of the border/line **C**.

4. Use the Color menu to set the color of the border/line.

5. Use the Tint field to apply a screen to the color.

6. If desired, select the Overprint checkbox for the color.

7. Use the Type menu to set a stripe pattern for the border.

If you have applied a stroke to a cell that touches the table border, the Preserve Local Formatting checkbox controls how the table border changes the local settings to cells.

To preserve the formatting applied to cells:

1. Apply a stroke to the cells.

2. In the Table Options dialog box, select Preserve Local Formatting to maintain the appearance of the cell edges that touch the table border **D**.

   or

   Deselect Preserve Local Formatting to allow the table border to override the stroke applied to the cell.

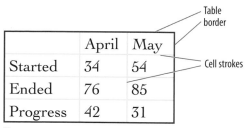

A The **table border** goes around the outside of a table. Cell strokes are within the table.

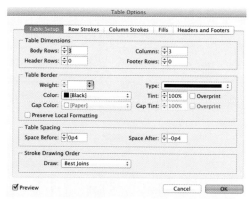

B The **Table Setup dialog box** lets you apply a border around the entire table.

C You can format the line around a table with the **Table Border controls**.

D The **Preserve Local Formatting option** maintains the appearance of cells that touch the table border.

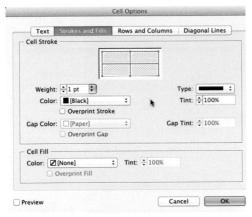

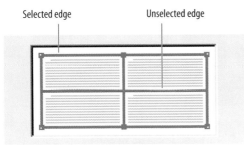

Selected edge   Unselected edge

E   The **Strokes and Fills controls** under Cell Options let you format cells in a table.

F   Click the **proxy lines for the cell stroke** to control which edges of the cell are stroked. The colored lines indicate the edge is selected.

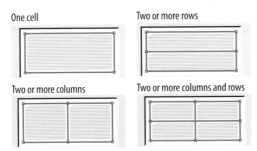

One cell

Two or more rows

Two or more columns

Two or more columns and rows

G   The **cell preview area** changes depending on how many cells, rows, or columns are selected.

Tables are automatically created with strokes around the cells. You can remove those cell strokes, apply new ones, or customize them as you see fit.

To customize the strokes around individual cells:

1. Select the cells you want to modify.

2. Choose **Table > Cell Options > Strokes and Fills**. The Cell Options dialog box appears with the Strokes and Fills options selected **E**.

3. Click the proxy lines in the cell preview to select which edges of the selected cells should be formatted **F**. The top, bottom, left, and right edges of the preview area correspond to the position of the edges in the selected cells.

TIP *Important!* Select and deselect the proxy lines in the cell preview *before* you change any of the settings in the dialog box. This avoids applying partial settings to the cells.

TIP The cell preview area changes depending on the combination of cells, rows, or columns you have selected **G**.

4. Set the controls under Cell Stroke to format the appearance of the selected edges.

5. Click OK to apply the settings.

If all your strokes are the same solid color, you don't have to worry about how the table is drawn. But as soon as you mix strokes or use nonsolid strokes, you need to set preferences for how the strokes appear when they cross each other.

To set the stacking order for the border and strokes:

1. Select at least one cell in the table.

2. Choose **Table > Table Options > Table Setup**. The Table Options dialog box appears.

3. Choose one of the following from the Draw menu 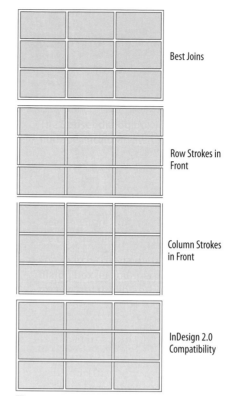:

   - **Best Joins** lets InDesign create the best possible appearance for how the strokes intersect.

   - **Row Strokes in Front** moves the strokes for the rows in front of the strokes for the columns.

   - **Column Strokes in Front** moves the strokes for the columns in front of the strokes for the rows.

   - **InDesign 2.0 Compatibility** uses a combination of the Best Joins for the table border and the rows in front of the strokes for the interior cells.

You can also fill the inside of a cell with a color or gradient.

To customize the fill inside individual cells:

1. Select the cells you want to modify.

2. Choose **Table > Cell Options > Strokes and Fills**. The Cell Options dialog box opens set to Strokes and Fills.

3. Set the controls under Cell Fill to format the color inside the selected cells **B**.

TIP If you have already defined a gradient swatch, you can fill the selected cells with a gradient.

Best Joins

Row Strokes in Front

Column Strokes in Front

InDesign 2.0 Compatibility

A Examples of **how the Draw menu settings are applied** to tables.

B The **Cell Fill controls** let you apply colors to individual cells in a table.

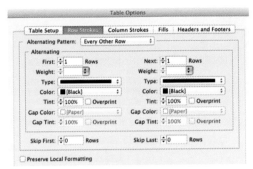

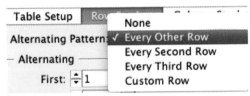

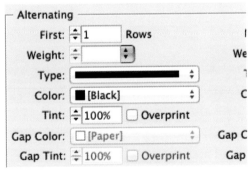

C The **Table Options for Row Strokes** allow you to apply alternating patterns for the strokes applied to rows.

D The **Alternating Pattern menu** for setting table rows.

E The **Alternating controls** allow you to choose the appearance for the alternating row strokes.

Alternating Strokes and Fills

Many people who work with tables find it helpful to set alternating strokes or fills for entire rows or columns in repeating patterns. This can help readers easily navigate down the column or across the row in lengthy tables.

TIP Even if you insert or delete rows or columns, the Alternating Pattern feature automatically reapplies the correct sequence of fills to your table.

To alternate repeating strokes for rows:

1. Select at least one cell in the table.

2. Choose **Table > Table Options > Alternating Row Strokes**. The Table Options dialog box opens set to the Row Strokes tab C.

3. Use the Alternating Pattern menu to choose how frequently the row strokes will alternate D.

4. Set the controls on the left side of the Alternating area to format the stroke appearance for the first set of rows E.

5. Set the controls on the right side of the Alternating area to format the appearance of the stroke for the next or second set of rows.

6. Use the Skip First and Skip Last fields to omit a certain number of rows at the start and end of the table from the alternating count.

TIP If you have applied custom strokes to individual cells and want to override the local formatting, deselect the Preserve Local Formatting checkbox.

To alternate repeating strokes for columns:

1. Select at least one cell in the table.

2. Choose **Table** > **Table Options** > **Alternating Column Strokes**. The Table Options dialog box opens set to Column Strokes 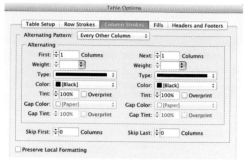.

3. Use the Alternating Pattern menu to choose how many column strokes will alternate **B**.

4. Set the controls on the left side of the Alternating area to format the appearance of the stroke for the first set of columns **C**.

5. Set the controls on the right side of the Alternating area to format the appearance for the second set of columns.

6. Use the Skip First and Skip Last fields to omit certain columns at the start and end of the table from the alternating count.

TIP If you have applied strokes to individual cells, the Preserve Local Formatting command controls whether the alternating strokes for columns override that local formatting.

A The **Column Strokes controls** under Table Options let you apply automatic alternating strokes to table columns.

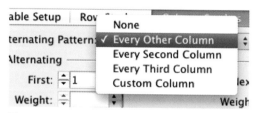

B The **Alternating Pattern menu** for table columns.

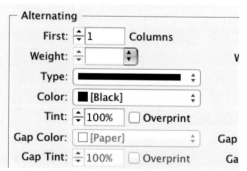

C The **Alternating controls** allow you to choose the appearance for the alternating column strokes.

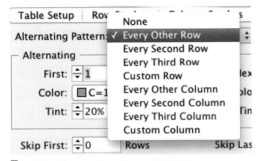

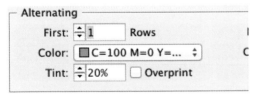

D The **Fills controls** under Table Options let you apply automatic alternating fills to table rows or columns.

E The **Alternating Pattern menu** for setting table fills.

F The **Alternating controls** allow you to choose the appearance for the alternating fills.

G An example of a table that uses the alternating fills for repeating rows.

To alternate repeating fills:

1. Select at least one cell in the table.

2. Choose **Table** > **Table Options** > **Alternating Fills**. The Table Options dialog box appears set to Fills **D**.

   or

   Choose **Table Options** > **Alternating Fills** from the Table panel.

3. Use the Alternating Pattern menu to choose how many row or column fills will alternate **E**.

4. Set the controls on the left side of the Alternating area to format the appearance of the fill for the first set of columns or rows **F**.

5. Set the controls on the right side of the Alternating area to format the appearance of the second set of columns or rows.

6. Use the Skip First and Skip Last fields to omit certain rows or columns at the start and end of the table from the alternating count.

TIP If you have applied fills to individual cells, the Preserve Local Formatting command controls whether the alternating fills override that local formatting.

TIP My own personal favorite is to set repeating fills of light and dark rows **G**.

Adding Diagonal Lines in Cells

Many people who design tables use diagonal lines to indicate empty data or corrected information. InDesign lets you apply diagonal lines inside cells.

To add diagonal lines in cells:

1. Select the cells you want to modify.

2. Choose **Table > Cell Options > Diagonal Lines**. The Cell Options dialog box opens with the Diagonal Lines options selected 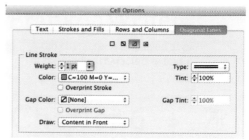.

3. Click one of the direction controls to set the direction of the diagonal lines B and their styles C.

4. Set the Line Stroke options to format the appearance of the line D.

5. Choose one of the following from the Draw menu:

   - **Content in Front** positions the diagonal line behind any text in the cell.

   - **Diagonal in Front** positions the diagonal line in front of any text in the cell.

A The **Diagonal Lines controls** under Cell Options let you add diagonal lines to cells.

B The **direction controls** for the diagonal lines in cells.

January	February	March
2,500		1,500
	3,400	

C Examples of how the diagonal lines can be used in cells.

D The **Line Stroke controls** for diagonal lines let you style the appearance of the diagonal lines inside cells.

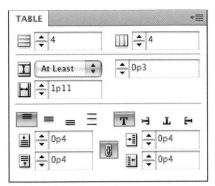

E The **Table panel** provides an onscreen panel to modify many of the table controls.

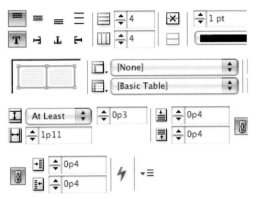

F When a table is selected, the **Control panel** displays the table controls.

Using the Table or Control Panels

You can also work with the Table panel or the Control panel to modify the number of columns and rows, their width and height, and other settings in tables.

To work with the Table panel or Control panel:

1. Select the table or cells in the table.

2. Choose **Window > Type & Tables > Table**. This opens the Table panel **E**.

   or

   Choose **Window > Control**. This opens the Control panel **F**.

3. Use the controls, fields, and icons as shown in the following table.

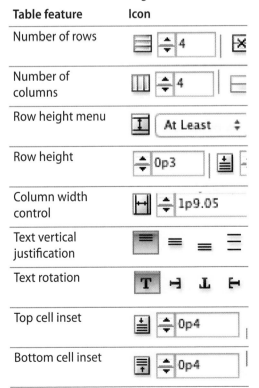

Table feature	Icon
Number of rows	
Number of columns	
Row height menu	
Row height	
Column width control	
Text vertical justification	
Text rotation	
Top cell inset	
Bottom cell inset	

Table feature	Icon
Left cell inset	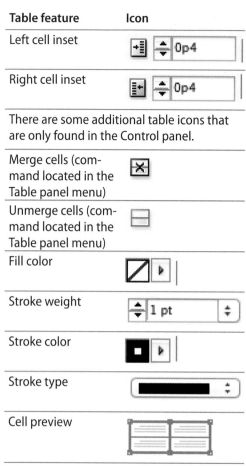
Right cell inset	

There are some additional table icons that are only found in the Control panel.

Merge cells (command located in the Table panel menu)	
Unmerge cells (command located in the Table panel menu)	
Fill color	
Stroke weight	
Stroke color	
Stroke type	
Cell preview	

TIP You can also use the commands in the Table panel menu or Control panel menu to modify the table.

TIP And if you were wondering, this table uses a header to repeat the top information from one page to another.

Automating Your Work 14

I have a general rule about working with a computer. Anytime I find myself doing the same thing more than ten times in a row, I stop. Most likely there is a command or tool that I can use to automate the process.

That's what this chapter is about — learning how to automate InDesign so the application does the dull, tedious chores for you. (Sadly, I can't apply this rule to other parts of my life, such as washing dishes, cleaning the litter box, or folding socks.)

There are many different automation features. You can use Find/Change, Spell Check, Footnotes, and Find Font to quickly change text formatting. Footnotes make it possible to simply choose the command and let InDesign do its stuff.

As amazing as these features are, they are not the ultimate in automation. Chapter 15 shows how text, tables, and object styles are even more powerful automation tools.

Of course, you're not required to learn any of these automation features. You are perfectly welcome to modify text by hand, one word at a time — especially if you don't care about doing anything else in your life.

Changing Case

InDesign gives you a command to quickly change text case.

To change text case:

1. Select the text you want to change.

2. Choose **Type > Change Case** and then choose one of the following: lowercase, Title Case, Sentence case, or UPPERCASE from the submenu.

Checking Spelling

One of the most popular features of page layout programs is the spelling checker, which searches for misspelled words.

To use the spell check command:

1. To check the spelling in a specific text frame or linked frames, click to place an insertion point anywhere within the text.

2. Choose **Edit > Spelling > Check Spelling**. The Check Spelling dialog box appears and displays the first word that needs attention .

3. Choose one of the Suggested Corrections for the word.

4. Click Change. The word is corrected and the next word is displayed. Or click Change All to change all instances of the word in the text.

5. Click Skip to continue the spelling check without changing that instance of the text.

   or

   Click Ignore All to continue the spelling check without changing any instance of that word in the text.

6. Click Done to stop the spelling check. The dialog box stays open in case you want to run more spelling checks.

A The **Check Spelling dialog box** is the command center for a spelling check.

Change To:

Whizard

Suggested Corrections:

```
Wizard
Wizards
Whizzed
Willard
Whisked
Wised
Wiser
Wiseacre
```

B InDesign gives you **a list of suggested corrections** for the unknown words found during a spelling check.

The Limitations of the Spelling Check

Every once in a while, I read an article about how the use of spelling checkers in computers is contributing to the death of proper writing and language. It's true; too many people run a spelling check and don't bother to actually read the document. Consider the following text:

Their is knot any thing wrung with using a spelling cheque on a sent tents in a doc you mint. Ewe just haft to clique the write bull ends.

Obviously the paragraph is utter nonsense. Yet InDesign's spelling checker (as well as the spelling checker in most other programs) wouldn't flag a single word as being incorrect.

A spelling checker only flags words it doesn't recognize; but because everything in the paragraph is an actual word, InDesign doesn't see any problems. So, please, don't skip a session with a proofreader just because you've run a spelling check.

Once you have opened the Spelling check, you can set which text frames should be searched.

To set the search criteria:

1. In the Search list, choose where the spelling check should be performed:
   - **All Documents** checks all open files.
   - **Document** checks the entire active file.
   - **Story** checks all the linked frames of the selected text.
   - **To End of Story** checks from the insertion point.
   - **Selection** checks only the selected text.

2. Select the Case Sensitive option to require a match for upper- and lowercase characters.

Of course, the spelling checker wouldn't be very helpful if it couldn't make changes to suspect words.

To correct the error displayed:

1. Type a correction in the Change To box.

   or

   Select a word from the Suggested Corrections list **B**.

2. Click Change to change only that instance of the word in the text.

The Ignore commands only work during a particular session of InDesign. If you use specialized words frequently, you should add them to the dictionary that InDesign uses during a spell check.

To add words to the spelling check dictionary:

Click Add when the word is displayed during the spelling check.

To edit the dictionary:

1. Choose **Edit > Spelling > Dictionary** to open the Dictionary dialog box 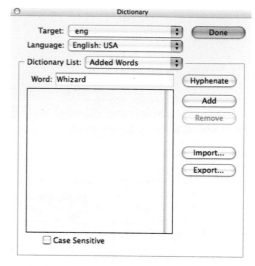.

TIP You can also open the Dictionary by clicking the Dictionary button in the Check Spelling dialog box.

2. Use the Target list to choose which dictionary you want to add the words to.

3. Choose the language from the Language list.

4. Choose Added Words, Removed Words, or Ignored Words from the Dictionary List.

5. Select the Case Sensitive checkbox to ensure that the case of the word as entered in the dictionary is used during the spelling check.

6. Type the word you want to add in the Word field.

   or

   Select the word you want to remove.

7. Click the Add or Remove button.

A The **Dictionary dialog box** allows you to add or delete words in the dictionary used during a spelling check.

dorothy and the the Munchkins

B The **wavy underlines** indicate which words have been flagged by the dynamic spelling checker.

dorothy and teh Munchkins   As typed

Dorothy and the Munchkins   After the autocorrection

C An example of how the **Autocorrect feature** corrects the capital letter and the misspelled word.

You may want to send your dictionary list to others. To do this, you can export the list.

To export entries in the spelling check dictionary:

1. Click the Export button.

2. Name the file and save it.

To import entries into a spelling check dictionary:

1. Click the Import button.

2. Find the file you wish to import.

InDesign also flags suspect words in the layout or Story Editor the same way it would in the spelling checker.

To use the dynamic spelling:

Choose **Edit > Spelling > Dynamic Spelling**. The dynamic spelling checker displays unknown words and other spelling errors with wavy underlines **B**.

You can also set InDesign to automatically correct spelling errors as you type. This is called the Autocorrect feature.

To automatically correct spelling errors as you type:

Choose **Edit > Spelling > Autocorrect**. A check mark appears in front of the command to indicate that Autocorrect is turned on.

TIP The Autocorrection feature only corrects words that are in the Autocorrect preferences or wrongly capitalized words **C**. It does not automatically correct unknown words or repeated words.

Using Find/Change

InDesign has a powerful Find/Change control panel that lets you find and replace text, font characters, or object attributes.

To choose the Find/Change mode:

1. Choose **Edit > Find/Change**. The Find/Change dialog box appears 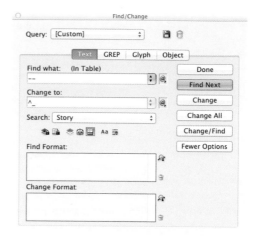.

2. Click one of the following four Find/Change categories **B**:

   - **Text** lets you search and replace strings of text as well as text formatting.
   - **GREP** lets you use codes that search for patterns within text.
   - **Glyph** lets you look for and replace specific glyphs using their Unicode or GID/CID values.
   - **Object** lets you search for and replace objects with certain formatting.

TIP Click the More Options button to see all the Find/Change controls.

The Find/Change dialog box lets you control which areas of the document are searched.

To set the search areas:

Click one of the following icons to allow a search in the area **C**.

- **Locked layers** looks on layers that have been locked. This works only for the Find field.
- **Locked stories** looks inside stories that have been checked out as part of the InCopy workflow. This works only for the Find field.
- **Hidden layers** looks on layers that have been turned off in the Layers panel.
- **Master pages** looks on master pages.
- **Footnotes** looks inside InDesign's electronic footnotes.

A The **Find/Change dialog box** allows you to set the controls for searching for and replacing text.

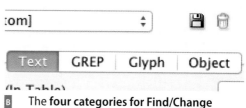

B The **four categories for Find/Change** are Text, GREP, Glyph, and Object.

C Use **the search areas** to control which part of the document the Find/Change will look at.

D The **Find/Change buttons** control the actions during a search.

Undo After a Find/Change?

I get a lot of oohs and ahhhs when I show that even after a Find/Change that has made hundreds of changes across many pages of a document, I can still undo those changes in just one **Edit > Undo** command.

Just because InDesign has done a lot of work doesn't mean that you can't undo that work.

Of course, having said that, I'm sure that if I performed some incredibly complicated routine that worked across many documents with thousands and thousands of changes, I might exhaust the memory for the undo string.

But don't let that stop you from trying an undo. The worst you'll get is a slight "beep" from InDesign.

Although all four categories look for and replace different things, the control buttons work the same for all the searches **D**.

To use the Find/Change control buttons:

1. Click Find to start the search. Once something has been found, this button changes to Find Next.

2. Click Change to make the change without moving to the next instance.

   or

   Click Change/Find to make the change and move to the next instance.

   or

   Click Change All to change all the instances in the text.

3. Click Find Next to skip to the next occurrence without changing that instance of the found text.

4. Click Done if you wish to stop the search without going through the whole document.

Using the Text Find/Change

The Text category looks for text and changes it into new text or applies formatting. A simple Find/Change works with text only.

To set the Find/Change text strings:

1. To find and change within a specific text frame or linked frames, click to place an insertion point within the text.

2. In the Find what field, type or paste the text you want to search for.

3. In the Change to field, type or paste the text to be inserted.

4. In the Search pop-up list, choose where the search should be performed 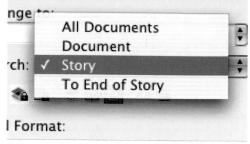:

   - **All Documents** checks all open documents.
   - **Document** checks the entire document.
   - **Story** checks all the linked frames of the selected text.
   - **To End of Story** checks from the insertion point.
   - **Selection** checks only the selected text. This option is only available if text is selected.

5. Select Case Sensitive to limit the search to text with the same capitalization . For instance, a case-sensitive search for "InDesign" does not find "Indesign."

6. Select Whole Word to disregard the text if it is contained within another word. For instance, a whole-word search for "Design" omits the instance in "InDesign."

7. Click Find. InDesign looks through the text and selects each matching text string.

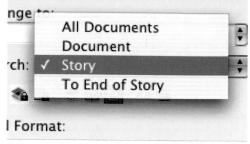

A   The **Search list** lets you choose which documents or stories should be searched.

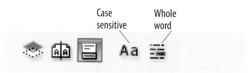

B   Use **the case and whole word controls** to modify the parameters of a text Find/Change.

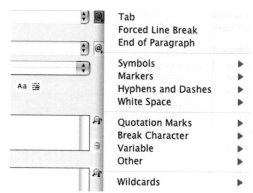

C   The **Find What list** lets you enter the special characters to look for in a search.

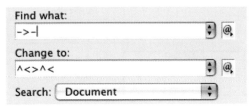

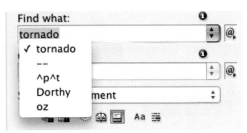

D An **example of the metacharacter codes**. Here the dashes around a > character are replaced using the codes for thin spaces.

E The **list of 15 previous search strings** is saved for each session of InDesign.

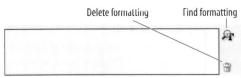

F Click the **formatting icons** to add specific formatting to the Find/Change queries.

G The **Find Format Settings** for the Find/Change search criteria.

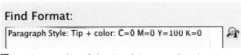

H The results of the **Find Format Settings** are displayed in the Find Format settings area.

InDesign also lets you search for special characters such as spaces, hyphens, paragraph returns, tab characters, or inline graphic markers. These are called *metacharacters*.

To Find/Change metacharacters:

1. Choose the character you want to look for in the Find what menu **C**. The codes are entered in the Find what field **D**.

2. Choose the codes you want to substitute in the Change To menu **D**.

TIP The metacharacter codes can also be entered using the keyboard.

3. Use the control buttons to run the Find/Change routine.

TIP InDesign also keeps a list of the past 15 strings for the Find what and the Change to fields **E**. You can also permanently save queries as described later in this chapter.

With the Find/Change dialog box expanded, you can set the formatting options for either the Find or Change field.

To set the Find/Change formatting options:

1. Click the Format button in the Find Format Settings area of the Find/Change dialog box. This opens the Find Format Settings dialog box **F**.

2. Choose the formatting categories on the left side of the Find Format Settings dialog box **G**.

3. Enter the criteria you want to search for in the fields for the chosen category.

4. Click OK. The search criteria are displayed in the Find Format Settings area **H**.

To delete the formatting options:

Click the Delete icon to delete all the formatting in the Find Format Settings or Change Format Settings area.

Using the GREP Find/Change

To perform GREP searches:

1. Click the GREP tab in the Find/Change dialog box 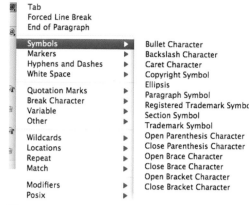.

2. Insert the GREP search codes in the Find What or Change to fields.

3. Set the rest of the dialog box controls the same way as for the Text Find/Change.

A The menu for the **GREP codes**.

Using the GREP Find/Change

Although it may sound like a rude noise heard after a full meal, GREP stands for Global Regular Expression Parser. This is a set of commands that looks for patterns in text (called regular expressions) and allows you to replace those patterns. Although a complete GREP tutorial is way beyond the scope of this book, here's a simple GREP lesson to help you automate your Find/Change routines.

Let's say you want to set all the text that is between parentheses as italic. You couldn't do it with an ordinary Text Find/Change because you don't know what text is between the parentheses.

The regular expressions in GREP let you insert symbols that stand in for the real text. For instance, to search for any text between two parentheses, you would type \([\d\l\u\s]*\) in the Find what field. Here's how that search string breaks down:

\(open parenthesis. This sets the information within the parenthesis as a group to be searched for as a single unit.

[**and**] groups the codes together.

\d any digit. This includes the numbers 0, 1, 2, 3, 4, 5, 6, 7, 8, 9.

\l any lowercase character.

\u any uppercase character.

\s any type of space.

* any of these items can appear zero or more times.

\) close parenthesis.

In ordinary talk this translates into *find any letters, numbers, or spaces that may or may not appear any number of times between two parentheses*. Once you've found the text, it's a simple matter to style it as italic.

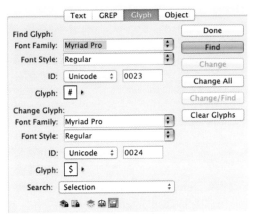

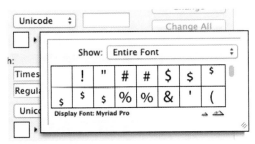

B The **Glyph category** of the Find/
Change dialog box.

C The **Glyph panel** lets you search
for specific letterforms.

Using the Glyph Find/Change

As mentioned in Chapter 3, characters can
have alternate glyphs used for fractions,
ligatures, and other letter forms. The Glyph
Find/Change area lets you search for these
alternate glyphs using special codes as well as
visual identification **B**.

TIP The Glyph Find/Change only searches and
replaces one character at a time.

To perform glyph searches:

1. Click the Glyph tab in the Find/Change
   dialog box.

2. Use the Find Glyph and Change Glyph
   areas to choose one or more of the
   following:

   • **Font Family** chooses the typeface.

   • **Font Style** chooses the style.

   • **ID** lets you choose either the Unicode
     or the CID/GID numbering system.
     Then enter that number in the
     following field.

   • **Glyph** opens a version of the Glyph
     panel, which lets you visually choose
     the letterform **C**.

3. Set the rest of the dialog box controls as
   described in the earlier section for Text
   Find/Change.

TIP The control buttons for the Glyph Find/
Change are the same as the ones for the
Text Find/Change with the exception of the
additional Clear Glyphs button. This button
clears all the information from the glyph
fields to make it easier to perform new
searches.

Using the Object Find/Change

The Object Find/Change lets you search for objects with certain attributes and change them to something else.

To perform object attribute searches:

1. Click the Object tab in the Find/Change dialog box 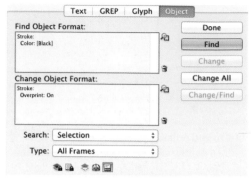.

2. Click the Find Formatting icons in the Find Object and Change Object fields. The Change Object Format Options dialog box opens **B**.

3. Click each of the categories under the Basic Attributes to choose the object style or object attributes **B**.

4. Use the Type list to choose Text Frames, Graphic Frames, or Unassigned Frames **C**. The default is All Frames.

Saving Searches

You can save your searches so you don't have to type the codes and choose the attributes over and over.

To save searches:

1. Click the Save Query icon **D**.

2. Name the search.

To apply saved searches:

Choose the saved search from the Query pop-up list.

To delete saved searches:

1. Choose the search you want to delete from the Query list.

2. Click the Delete Query icon.

A   The **Object category** of the Find/Change dialog box.

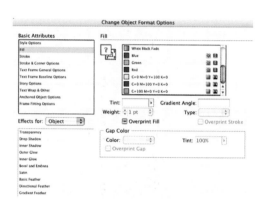

B   The **Change Object Format Options dialog box** lets you choose the attributes to search for or change.

C   Use the **Type list** to choose a specific type of object frame to search for.

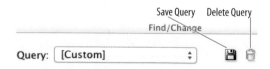

D   Use the **Query controls** list to save, apply, and delete Find/Change searches.

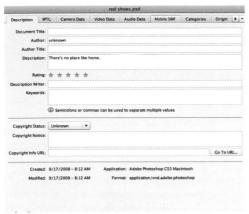

E The **File Info dialog box** lets you add custom metadata for images.

Adding Captions to Images

As you add images to your layouts, you may need to place captions along with the images. Instead of typing in those captions manually, InDesign lets you automate the process by entering captions from the image information. This image information is called *metadata*.

To add metadata to an image:

1. Open the file in Photoshop and then choose **File > File Info** to open the File Info dialog box **E**.

   or

   Select the file in Bridge and then choose **File > File Info**.

   or

   Select the file on the InDesign page and choose File Info from the Info panel menu.

2. Click the Description tab to enter metadata information such as the file name, author, document title, etc.

3. Enter information for any of the other fields.

4. Repeat steps 2 and 3 for each of the other tabs in the dialog box.

5. Click OK to add the metadata to the file.

   TIP Some fields can't be modified. For instance, the camera data for how the image was captured can't be modified.

6. Click any of the other tabs to enter the metadata information.

   TIP Using Bridge allows you to select multiple files and enter the same metadata for all the images.

Another step you need to take is to set the options for what information the caption should contain.

To set the Metadata Caption information:

1. Choose **Object > Captions > Caption Setup** to open the Caption Setup dialog box 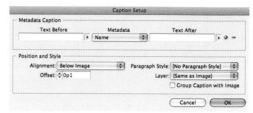.

2. Set the contents of the Metadata Caption as follows:

   - Use the Text Before or Text After fields to insert text strings that you want applied before or after the metadata.

   - Choose a field from the Metadata list.

   - Use the Symbols list to enter the codes for special items in the text fields 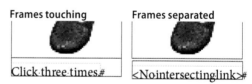.

   - Use the Add text options button to set additional text strings for the caption.

3. Click OK to apply the settings or set the Position and Style options as described in the following exercise.

To set the Position and Style of the caption:

1. Choose one of the Alignment options to set the caption frame above, below, to the right, or to the left of the image .

2. Choose an offset amount to set how close the caption frame should be to the image frame.

3. Choose a paragraph style to be applied to the caption.

4. Choose a layer on which the caption should be placed.

   or

   Choose Group Caption with Image to place the image and caption in a group together.

TIP Ordinarily the text frame must touch the graphic for a live caption to be created . However, grouping the caption and image allows the two items to be separated.

The **Caption Setup dialog box** lets you set the content of automatic captions.

The controls to set the **contents of the captions**.

The **Alignment options** for the position of the caption frame relative to the image.

The frame that contains a live caption **must touch or be grouped with the graphic it describes** in order for the caption to appear.

Live caption	Static caption

Click·three·times # | Click·three·times #

E The difference between the appearance of a live caption and a static caption.

A Workflow for Captions

Designers laying out pages are not the people who know what the metadata should be for which graphics. Those are usually the editors or authors of the text.

As a designer, you should let the editors on your project know that they can use Bridge to enter the metadata for graphics. If they have to enter metadata for large numbers of graphics, there are third-party applications that can add metadata automatically from databases.

Once the metadata has been added to the graphics, you can easily import it into the layout.

Once you have added the metadata and set up how the caption should be formatted, you can apply the caption to images. There are two types of captions. A static caption applies the information in the metadata but does not update if the metadata changes. A live caption is automatically updated if the metadata for the image changes.

To apply a static caption:

Select the image or images and choose **Object > Captions > Generate Static Caption**. The information from the metadata is inserted into a new frame positioned near the image.

To apply a live caption:

Select the image or images and choose **Object > Captions > Generate Live Caption**. The information from the metadata is inserted into a new frame positioned near the image.

TIP A light colored rectangle surrounds the live caption data. This indicates that the information changes if the metadata is modified **E**. Static captions do not have the rectangle.

TIP Live captions update when the placed image is updated in the Links panel.

TIP A live caption frame must touch the image it is associated with for the metadata to appear.

You may want to "freeze" the caption so that it no longer updates. This requires converting the live caption to a static caption.

Select the live caption text and choose **Object > Captions > Convert to Static Caption**. The caption is no longer tied to the metadata for the image.

Using the Story Editor

For people like me, one of the *good* things about electronic page layout is that I edit text as it appears on the page.

For others, one of the *bad* things about electronic page layout is that they edit text as it appears on the page. Those people like to edit text without seeing images, typefaces, sizes, and other design elements. For those people, InDesign has a Story Editor 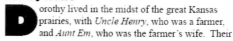.

To use the Story Editor:

1. Select the text frame that contains the text you want to edit, or place your insertion point inside the text.

2. Choose **Edit > Edit in Story Editor**. The Story Editor opens.

3. Use the right side of the Story Editor to make changes to the text. Any changes you make in the Story Editor appear on the document page.

4. Use the left side of the Story Editor to view the paragraph styles that may have been assigned to the text **B**.

5. If your text contains a table, click the small triangle next to the table to reveal the text inside the table **C**.

6. If your text is overset inside the text frame, the Overset Text indicator displays where the overset appears **D**.

TIP The Story Editor appears as a separate window from your document page. You don't have to close the Story Editor to work on the regular document page. Just click the document page to work on it; then click to move back to the Story Editor.

TIP You can change the display of the Story Editor by changing the preference settings.

A Text is displayed in the **Story Editor** without most of its special formatting.

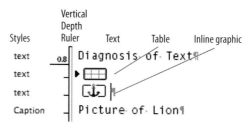

B The Story Editor displays the various elements within the story.

C Click the **Table control triangle** in the Story Editor to see the text inside a table.

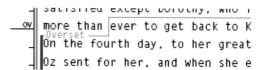

D The **Overset Text indicator** shows where the text extends outside the visible area of the text frame.

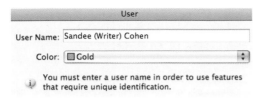

E The User dialog box allows you to identify each user with a name and a color.

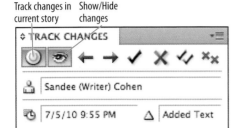

Track changes in current story   Show/Hide changes

F The **Track Changes panel** lets you move through changes and accept or reject them.

Tracking Text Changes

If you're the only one who works on a project, you know who made the changes in your text. It's you. If you work with others, you may want to see what changes each person makes. The track changes features indicate who has done what to the text.

TIP This workflow is more commonly used between InDesign and InCopy. But can be used within an InDesign document.

Before you work with Track Changes, you need to tell InDesign who you are so it knows who is making which changes. This is called setting the user.

To set the user:

1. Choose **File > User**. This opens the User dialog box **E**.

2. Enter a user name.

3. Choose a user color so that your changes stand out from others.

In order to track changes, you need to turn on the Track Changes command. You can do this for all stories in a document or for a single story.

To turn on Track Changes globally:

Choose **Type > Track Changes > Enable Tracking in All Stories** or choose Enable Tracking in All Stories from the Track Changes panel menu.

To turn on Track Changes for a single story:

1. Place your insertion point in the frame of the story you want to track.

2. Choose **Type > Track Changes > Track Changes in Current Story** or choose Track Changes in Current Story from the Track Changes panel menu.

TIP You can also click the Track Changes icon in the Track Changes panel **F**.

You can only see the changes in a document in the Story Editor . The Layout View shows the changes applied to the text.

To see the changes in a document:

1. Choose **Edit > Edit in Story Editor**.
2. Click the Show/Hide Changes icon in the Track Changes panel.

You use the Track Changes commands to move through the story to apply or discard changes.

To navigate through the changes:

1. Place your insertion point within the text in the Story Editor.
2. Click the Next Change icon to move to the first change **B**.
3. Use the Accept Change or Reject Change icons to apply or discard the changes **C**.
4. If necessary, use the Previous Change icon to move to the previous change.
5. Repeat steps 2 and 3 until finished.

TIP Hold the Opt/Alt key as you accept or reject a change and go to the next change.

To use the other Track Changes commands:

Use the following additional commands when working with tracked changes.

A **Tracked changes** displayed in the Story Editor.

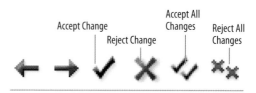

B Use the **Navigation icons to move from one change to another.**

C Use the **Accept Change and Reject Change icons** to apply or discard the changes.

Command	Location
Accept All Changes > In This Story	Track Changes icon
Accept All Changes > In This Document	Track Changes panel menu
Reject All Changes > In This Story	Track Changes icon
Reject All Changes > In This Document	Track Changes panel menu
Accept All Changes by This User > In This Story	Track Changes panel menu
Accept All Changes by This User > In This Document	Track Changes panel menu
Reject All Changes by This User > In This Story	Track Changes panel menu
Reject All Changes by This User > In This Document	Track Changes panel menu

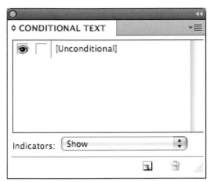

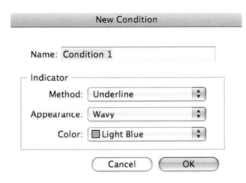

D The **Conditional Text panel** lets you define new conditions for text as well as show or hide the conditional text.

E The **New Condition dialog box** is where you name and set the indicators for conditional text.

Conditional Text

Conditional text is simply text that has been assigned with an electronic "marker." This marker can be set to make the text either visible or invisible. This allows you to have a document where some text can be set to print or not print. This is very handy for books that have teacher notes or other text that needs to be hidden at times.

To create a condition for text:

1. Choose **Window** > **Type & Tables** > **Conditional Text**. This opens the Conditional Text panel D.

2. Choose New Condition from the panel menu. This opens the New Condition dialog box E.

   or

   Click the New Condition icon at the bottom of the panel. This opens the New Condition dialog box E.

3. Give the condition a name.

4. Use the Indicator area to set the appearance of the conditional text. *(See the exercise on the following page for how to set the indicators.)*

5. Click OK to create the condition.

TIP Every document automatically contains a setting for Unconditional text in the Conditional Text panel. All text is by default set to Unconditional.

To modify a condition:

Double-click the condition in the Conditional Text panel. This opens the Condition Options dialog box which is the same as the New Condition dialog box covered above.

or

With the condition selected, choose Condition Options from the panel menu.

Conditional text can have electronic indicators that are displayed to show that a special condition has been applied. You use the Indicator area of the New Condition dialog box to set the appearance of the indicators for conditional text 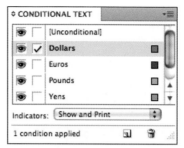.

A The **indicators for conditional text** can be set for underlines (solid, wavy, or dashed) or highlight.

To set the indicator appearance for conditional text:

1. With the New Condition dialog box open, choose one of the following from the Method menu:

   - **Underline** creates an underline for the conditional text.

   - **Highlight** creates a solid block of color over the conditional text.

2. If you have chosen Underline, use the Appearance menu to choose one of the following:

   - **Wavy** for a wavy line.

   - **Solid** for a solid line.

   - **Dashed** for a dashed line.

3. Use the Color menu to choose a color for the underline or highlight.

B Sets of conditional text in the Conditional Text panel.

Once you have created a condition, it is very simple to apply it to text.

To apply conditional text:

1. Select the text.

2. Click the Apply Condition column to display a checkmark next to the name of the condition in the Conditional Text panel **B**.

TIP You can apply more than one condition to selected text. This helps your work with conditions be more flexible.

TIP Conditional text can also be applied using the Change To attributes of the Find/Change dialog box. *(See page 332 for more information on using Find/Change.)*

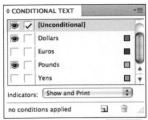

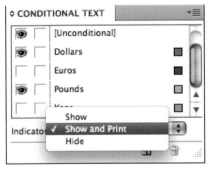

Price £2 $5

C — An example of **hiding conditional text**. Here the visibility controls for the text for Euros and Yens have been turned off.

D — The **Indicators menu** for the Conditional Text panel lets you control the display of the indicators applied to conditional text.

Once text has a condition applied to it, you can hide or show the text by changing the visibility of the condition C.

To show or hide conditional text:

Click the visibility eyeball next to a condition as follows:

- A visible eyeball indicates that the text is visible and will print.
- A hidden eyeball indicates that the text is hidden and will not print.

TIP When you hide conditional text, the space that the text occupied reflows.

You may want to change the visibility of the indicators that are applied to the condition.

To control the conditional text indicators:

1. Select the condition in the Conditional Text panel.

2. Choose one of the following from the Indicators menu D:

   - **Show** displays the indicators but they do not print.
   - **Show and Print** displays the indicators on screen and when printed or exported to PDF.
   - **Hide** turns off the visibility of the indicators.

Conditions can be imported from one document into another.

To control the conditional text indicators:

1. Open the document that you want to add the conditions to.

2. Choose Load Conditions from the Conditional Text menu.

3. Navigate to and select the document that contains the conditions.

4. Choose OK. The conditions appear in the Conditional Text panel.

Conditional Text Sets

As soon as you create a few conditions for text, you may find it easier to group those conditions into sets. These sets make it easier to turn the visibility of many conditions on and off with a single click.

To create a conditional text set:

1. Choose Show Options from the Conditional Text panel. This shows the Set menu at the bottom of the panel 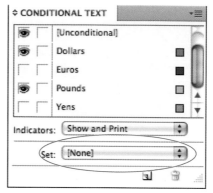.

2. Apply the visibility to the conditions as desired.

3. Choose Create New Set from the Set menu. This opens the Condition Set Name dialog box.

4. Name the set and click OK.

TIP Choose Load Conditions and Sets from the Conditional Text panel menu to add both conditions and sets to a document.

Once you have defined a set, you can choose it from the Set menu.

To apply a condition set:

Choose the set from the Set menu in the Conditional Text panel **B**.

You can easily change the definition of a condition set.

To apply a condition set:

1. Choose the set from the Set menu in the Conditional Text panel.

2. Make whatever changes you want to the visibility of the conditions. A plus (+) sign appears next to the set name.

3. Choose Redefine "[set name]" from the Set menu. The plus sign disappears and the set is changed.

A The **Set menu** for the Conditional Text panel.

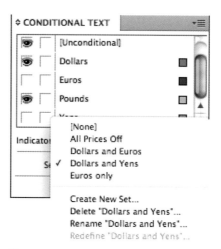

B Choose the **saved conditional sets** from the Conditional Text Set menu.

According to Littlefield, Baum wrote the book as a parable of the Populists, an allegory of their failed efforts to reform the nation in 1896.[1] Scholars soon began to find additional correspondences between Populism and The Wonderful Wizard of Oz. Richard Jensen, in a 1971 study of Mid western politics and culture, devoted two pages to Baum's story.[2]

Reference ⟶ / ⟵ Footnote

---

1 Littlefield, "Parable on Populism," 50, 58.
2 Richard Jensen, The Winning of the Midwest: Social and Political Conflict, 1888-1896 (Chicago, 1971), 282-83.

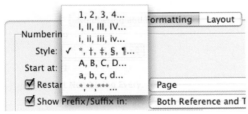

C **Footnotes within text** allow you to easily insert reference markers and the footnote text.

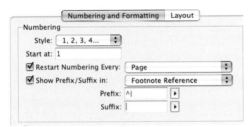

D The **Numbering controls** of the Footnote Options dialog box.

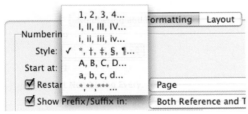

E The **Style options** for the footnote reference.

Footnotes

Footnotes are the tiny reference markers inserted into text that correspond to comments usually inserted at the bottom of that column of text. InDesign makes it easy to insert, format, and update footnotes.

To insert a footnote into text:

1. Position the insertion point where you want the footnote reference to appear.

2. Choose **Type > Insert Footnote**. The reference appears in the text and the insertion point appears in the footnote position at the bottom of the text C.

3. Type or paste the text for the footnote.

You can also format the style for the reference and the footnote.

To format the style of the footnote:

1. Choose **Type > Document Footnote Options**.

2. Click the Numbering and Formatting tab to display those options D.

3. Use the Style list to choose Roman or Arabic numerals, symbols, letters, or asterisks for the reference E.

4. Use the Start At field to set what number the footnotes should start with.

5. If desired, click the options for Restart Numbering Every and then choose Page, Spread, or Section.

6. If desired, turn on the option for Show Prefix/Suffix in and then choose Footnote Reference, Footnote Text, or Both Reference and Text.

7. Use the Prefix field to choose a special character or to type in your own prefix for the reference.

8. Use the Suffix field to choose a special character or to type in your own suffix for the reference.

You can also control the appearance of the reference and the footnote text.

To format the reference:

1. Click the Numbering and Formatting tab to open the Formatting controls 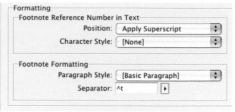.

2. Use the Position list to Apply Superscript, Apply Subscript, or Apply Normal position.

3. Use the Character Style list to apply a previously defined character style.

To format the footnote:

1. Click the Numbering and Formatting tab to open the Formatting controls A.

2. Use the Paragraph Style list to apply a previously defined paragraph style.

3. Use the Separator field to enter a tab or space between the footnote reference and the footnote text.

TIP You can enter your own character in this field, as well as have multiple characters in the field.

You can also control the appearance and position of the layout of the footnote.

To control the spacing options for the footnote:

1. Click the Layout tab of the Footnote Options dialog box to open the Layout controls B.

2. Use the Minimum Space Before First Footnote field to control how much space separates the bottom of the column and the first footnote.

3. Use the Space Between Footnotes field to control the distance between the last paragraph of one footnote and the first paragraph of the next.

A   The **Formatting controls** of the Footnote Options dialog box.

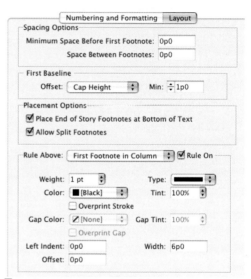

B   The **Layout controls** of the Footnote Options dialog box.

The **Rule Above controls** for footnotes.

Importing Footnotes from Microsoft Word

When you import Word documents, the Word Import Options dialog box lets you import footnotes and endnotes.

The footnotes in Word documents are converted into electronic footnotes in InDesign documents.

Endnotes, however, are imported as ordinary text. This means that although you may see the reference in the text and the note at the end of the story, there is no electronic link between the reference and the note. Unlike electronic footnotes, if you delete the reference, you won't delete the endnote at the end of the text.

You can also control the position of the first baseline of the footnote.

To set the first baseline of the footnote:

1. Use the Offset list to choose the vertical alignment for the baseline.

2. Use the Min. field to increase or decrease this setting.

To set the placement options:

1. Select Place End of Story Footnotes at Bottom of Text to force a footnote that appears at the end of a story to the bottom of the text frame.

2. Select Allow Split Footnotes to permit long footnotes to flow from their original column to the next.

To set the controls for the footnote rule:

1. Choose if a separator rule is applied to one of the following:

   - **First Footnote in Column** applies the rule to the first footnote in the text column C.

   - **Continued Footnotes** applies the rule to footnotes that are continued from previous columns or pages C.

2. Select the Rule On checkbox to apply the rule.

3. Use the rest of the controls to style the appearance of the rule.

Using Find Font

In addition to the Find/Change commands for text, InDesign lets you make global changes for font families. This helps if you open documents that contain missing fonts.

To make changes using Find Font:

1. Choose **Type > Find Font**. The Find Font dialog box appears .

2. Select the font that you want to change.

> **TIP** The icons next to each font display the type of font and its status 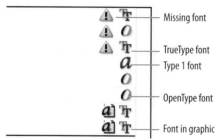.

3. Use the Replace With controls to choose a replacement for the selected font.

4. Click Find First to find the first instance of the font. InDesign highlights the first place the font is used.

> **TIP** When you find the first instance, the Find First button changes to Find Next.

5. Click one of the following options:

   - **Find Next** skips that instance.

   - **Change** replaces that instance.

   - **Change All** changes all the instances of the font.

   - **Change/Find** replaces that instance and finds the next instance.

6. Use the More Info button to find more information, such as if the fonts can be embedded in PDF documents .

7. Use the Reveal in Finder (Mac) or Explorer (Windows) button to locate where the font is on the computer.

To replace missing fonts:

1. Open the document. If fonts are missing, an alert box appears.

2. Click Find Font to open the Find Font dialog box.

3. Choose the missing font and follow the steps in the previous exercise.

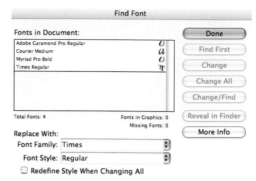

A The **Find Font dialog box** lets you make global changes to the fonts in a document.

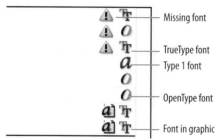

B The **Find Font icons** tell you the status and type of fonts used in the document.

C The **Info area** of the Find Font dialog box gives you more information about the font.

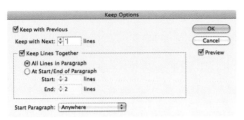

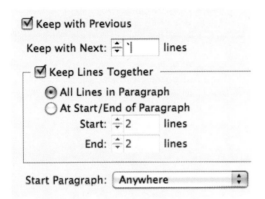

The **Keep Options dialog box** controls how paragraphs break across columns or pages.

The **Keep Lines Together controls** of the Keep Options dialog box.

The **Start Paragraph list** lets you choose where the next lines of the paragraph appear.

Keeping Lines Together

Another automation technique is to specify how many lines of text must remain together in a column or page. InDesign does this using the Keep Options controls.

To set the keep options for a paragraph:

1. Choose Keep Options from the Paragraph panel menu. This opens the Keep Options dialog box **D**.

2. Enter a number in the Keep With Next Lines field to force the last line in a paragraph to stay in the same column or page with the specified number of lines.

TIP This option ensures that subheads or titles remain in the same column as the body copy that follows.

3. Click Keep Lines Together and set one of these options **E**:

   - **All Lines in Paragraph** prevents the paragraph from ever breaking.

   - **At Start/End of Paragraph** lets you set the number of lines that must remain together for the start and the end of the paragraph.

4. Use the Start Paragraph menu to choose where the lines must jump to **F**.

   - **Anywhere** allows the text to jump anywhere.

   - **In Next Column** forces the text to the next column or page.

   - **In Next Frame** forces the text to the next frame or page.

   - **On Next Page** forces the text to the next page.

   - **On Next Odd Page** forces the text to the next odd-numbered page.

   - **On Next Even Page** forces the text to the next even-numbered page.

Using the Eyedropper on Text

The Eyedropper tool lets you quickly grab the formatting from one part of the text and apply it to another.

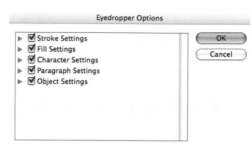

The **Eyedropper tool in the Tools panel** lets you sample and apply text formatting.

To set the eyedropper options for text:

1. Double-click the Eyedropper tool in the Tools panel **A**. This opens the Eyedropper Options dialog box.

2. Click the triangle control to open the Paragraph Settings from the list **B**.

3. Select which paragraph attributes you want the Eyedropper tool to sample.

4. Click the triangle control to open the Character Settings from the list **C**.

5. Select which character attributes you want the Eyedropper tool to sample.

B The **Eyedropper Options dialog box** contains the controls for text as well as object styling.

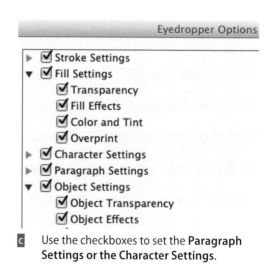

C Use the checkboxes to set the **Paragraph Settings or the Character Settings**.

The Wizard of Oz.¶

By L. Frank Baum¶

D Click the white eyedropper to sample the right alignment of the paragraph attributes.

The Wizard of Oz.¶

By L. Frank Baum¶

E Click the black eyedropper to apply the right alignment of the paragraph attributes.

The **Munchkins** and the Witch.¶

F Click the white eyedropper to sample local character attributes.

The **Munchkins** and the **Witch**.¶

G Drag the black eyedropper to apply character attributes to text.

Once you have set the eyedropper options, you can sample and apply paragraph or character attributes.

TIP Deselect the text frame as you use the Eyedropper tool to avoid styling the text frame itself.

To sample and apply paragraph attributes:

1. Choose the Eyedropper tool.

2. Click the white eyedropper inside the paragraph that you want to sample **D**. The eyedropper changes from white to black.

3. Click the black eyedropper inside the paragraph that you want to change **E**. This changes the paragraph attributes.

TIP The black eyedropper does not apply character attributes when clicked unless a paragraph style was already applied to the sampled text.

4. Click the eyedropper inside any additional paragraphs that you want to change.

To sample and apply character attributes:

1. Choose the Eyedropper tool.

2. Click the white eyedropper inside the text that you want to sample **F**. The eyedropper changes from white to black.

3. Drag the black eyedropper across the exact text you want to change. This highlights the text **G**.

4. Release the mouse button to apply the changes.

To sample new text attributes:

1. Hold the Opt/Alt key as you click the Eyedropper tool. The Eyedropper cursor changes to white.

2. Click the eyedropper inside the new text that you want to sample.

Using Scripts

Perhaps the most powerful way to automate working in InDesign is with AppleScripts on the Macintosh or VisualBasic scripts in Windows. You can also use JavaScripts, which work on both platforms. Although you need to know code to *write* scripts, it's very easy to *run* scripts in InDesign. Writing code is much too difficult for me. Running scripts is totally easy. (Honestly, if I can do it, anyone can!)

To run scripts in InDesign:

1. Place the script file or the folder containing the script file inside the following directory path:

   InDesign Application Folder: Scripts: Scripts Panel.

2. Choose **Windows** > **Utilities** > **Scripts** to open the Scripts panel A.

3. If you have placed a folder inside the Scripts directory, click the triangle controller to open the scripts in the folder.

4. Double-click the script that appears in the panel. This prompts the start of the script.

TIP Certain scripts require an object or text to be selected. Follow any onscreen prompts that occur.

TIP You can also assign keyboard shortcuts to run scripts. Choose Edit > Keyboard Shortcuts to open the dialog box.

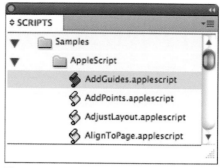

A Use the **Scripts panel** to run scripts from within InDesign.

Styles 15

A while back I taught InDesign to a group of designers that included a young woman who was responsible for a yearly 100-page catalog of her company's products. When I got to the part of the class where I showed what text styles could do, she began to cry.

I'd never had a student cry in a class, so I was concerned. "What's wrong?" I asked.

It took her a while to speak, but she eventually explained that it was "those styles." Turns out she had never been taught what styles did and she had been formatting the thousands of entries in the catalog by hand.

She now realized just how much time she could have saved by using text styles. Of course, this was before InDesign added object styles. And even more before table styles.

I dedicate this chapter to all of you who have been slaving away, working without text, object, and table styles. May the techniques you learn here bring smiles, not tears, to your faces.

Working with Paragraph Styles

InDesign has two types of text styles. *Paragraph styles* apply formatting for both character and paragraph attributes. *Character styles* apply formatting for only character attributes.

To open the Paragraph Styles panel:

Choose **Window > Styles > Paragraph Styles**.

The Basic Paragraph style is the style that is automatically applied to new text 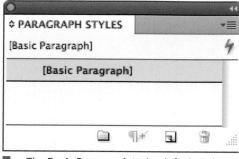. If you change the definition of the Basic Paragraph style, it automatically updates all text that has been styled with that style.

To set the Basic Paragraph by example:

1. Select some text and use any of the formatting controls to change the text attributes.

2. A plus sign (+) appears next to the Basic Paragraph listing in the Paragraph Styles panel. This indicates that local formatting has been applied to the Basic Paragraph 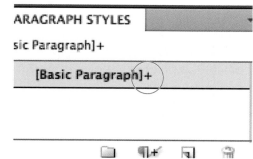.

3. Choose Redefine Style from the Paragraph Styles panel menu. This changes the definition of the Basic Paragraph to match the local formatting. The plus sign disappears.

To set the Basic Paragraph by definition:

1. Double-click the Basic Paragraph listing in the Paragraph Styles panel. This opens the Paragraph Styles Options dialog box.

2. Make whatever changes to the style definition you like as explained on the following pages.

3. Click OK to make the changes.

TIP The Basic Paragraph style can be modified but not deleted.

A The **Basic Paragraph** is the default style that appears in all new documents.

B The **plus sign (+) next to the style name** indicates that local formatting has been applied to the text.

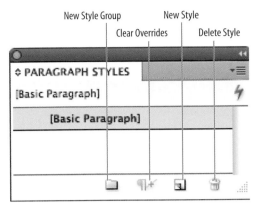

New Style Group · New Style · Clear Overrides · Delete Style

C The **Paragraph Styles panel** lets you define and apply paragraph styles.

D The **Paragraph Style Options dialog box** set to the General options.

E Click **each category in the Paragraph Styles dialog box** to set the format of the style.

You can use the Paragraph Styles panel to define new paragraph styles for a document.

To define a paragraph style manually:

1. Choose **Window > Styles > Paragraph Styles**. This opens the Paragraph Styles panel **C**.

2. Choose Paragraph Style Options from the Paragraph Styles panel menu.

   or

   Opt/Alt-click the New Style icon in the Paragraph Styles panel. This opens the New Paragraph Style dialog box set to the General options **D**.

3. Use the Style Name field to name the style.

4. Set the Based On, Next Style, and Shortcut options as described later in this chapter.

5. Click each category on the left side of the dialog box and set the criteria for each one **E**. *(These categories are the same as the character and paragraph formatting described in Chapter 3, "Basic Text.")*

6. Click OK to define the style. The name of the style appears in the Paragraph Styles panel.

The easier way to define a style is to format the selection and define the style by example.

To define a paragraph style by example:

1. Select some text.

2. Use any of the commands to format the text.

3. Leave the insertion point in the formatted text.

4. Open the Paragraph Styles panel.

5. With the insertion point blinking in the formatted text, click the New Style icon. This adds a new style to the Paragraph Styles panel.

TIP Select the Apply Style to Selection checkbox to apply the newly named style to the text originally selected.

TIP Double-click to rename the style created by the New Style icon.

The Next Style command for paragraph styles has two features. For typists who enter text directly into InDesign, it allows you to automatically switch to a new style as you type text. For instance, as I type this paragraph, I press the paragraph return after the period. This automatically switches to the next style, which is the exercise header.

To set the next paragraph style:

1. Select the General category in the Paragraph Style Options dialog box.

2. Choose a style from the Next Style list in the Paragraph Style Options dialog box **A**. The chosen style is applied to the next paragraph when you press the Return key **B**.

   or

   Choose Same Style from the Next Style list **A**. This retains the original style until you manually change the style.

Based On:

Next Style: ✓ Body Text

Shortcut:

[Same style]
[No Paragraph Style]
Body Text
Body plain
[Basic Paragraph]

A The **Next Style menu** lets you choose Same Style or an already defined style.

Checking Spelling

One of the most popular features of page layout programs is the Spelling Checker that checks a document for misspelled words.

Next style applied

To use the spell-check command:

1. To check the spelling in a specific text frame or linked frames, click to place an insertion point within the text

2. Choose Edit > Check Spelling. The Check Spelling dialog box appears ❷.

Same style applied

3. In the Search list, choose where the spelling check should be performed ❸:

B The **Next Style command** changes the paragraph style when the Return key is pressed. The Same Style command keeps the style when the return is pressed.

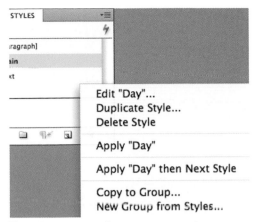

C The **contextual menu over a style name** allows you to apply a paragraph style and then the Next Style to the rest of the selected text.

STYLES

Friday

The Princess Bride (1987) Directed by: Rob Reiner

Saturday

On the Waterfront (1954) Directed by: Elia Kazan

Sunday

The Wizard of Oz (1939) Directed by: Victor Fleming, Richard Thorpe

D An example of how the **Next Style command** applies the style for the day. This changes to the movie listing and then back to the day, and so on.

The Next Style feature does even more magic when you use it to apply the next style to selected text. This allows you to format many paragraphs in one simple click.

To apply the Next Style to multiple paragraphs:

1. Highlight the text that you want to style.

   or

   Select the text frame that contains the text that you want to style.

2. Position your cursor over the name of the paragraph style that you want to apply to the first paragraph.

3. Right-click (Windows) or Control-click (Mac) the name of the style. A contextual menu appears C.

4. Choose Apply "name of style" then Next Style. This styles the text according to the Next Style controls D.

TIP The command to apply the Next Style is only available if a Next Style has been defined for the paragraph style. If the style has Same Style for the Next Style, then the contextual menu will not display the Next Style option.

Working with Character Styles

Character styles allow you to set specific attributes that override the paragraph style character attributes. For instance, **this bold text** was set by applying a character style to the paragraph style.

To open the Character Styles panel:

Choose **Window > Styles > Character Styles**.

To define a character style:

1. Open the Character Styles panel 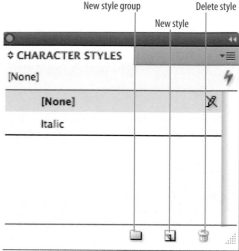.

2. Choose New Character Style from the Character Styles panel menu. This opens the New Character Style dialog box **B**.

3. Name the style.

4. Set the Based On and Shortcut controls as described later in this chapter.

5. Click each category to set the character attributes **c**.

6. Click OK to define the style. The name of the style appears in the Character Styles panel.

TIP Select Apply Style to Selection to apply the newly named style to the text originally selected.

You can also format the text and then define a character style by example.

To define a character style by example:

1. Select some sample text.

2. Format the text.

3. Leave the insertion point in the newly formatted text.

4. Choose **Window > Styles > Character Styles**.

5. Click the New Style icon. This adds a new style to the Character Styles panel.

A The **Character Styles panel** lets you define and apply character styles.

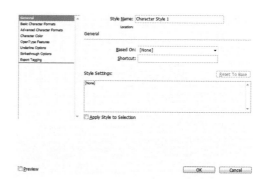

B The **New Character Style dialog box** lets you specify settings for each of the categories for character styles.

C Click each **category in the New Character Style dialog box** to set the format of the style.

Style Settings:

chapter title + next: [Same style] + color: C=0 M=20
before: 0p9

D When you base a new style on an
   existing style, you can see how they
   differ in the **Style Settings field** of the
   New Character Style dialog box.

Basing Styles

The style for the numbers of the exercises in this
book is based on the style of the subheads. If I
change the style for the subheads, the number
style and the numbers change automatically.

Similarly, the style for the exercises is based on
the style for the body copy. So if my publisher
asks me to make the copy a little smaller, I only
have to change the point size for one style.

Limit how many levels you go when you base
one style on another. Theoretically, you can
base one style on another, which is based on
another, which is based on another, and so on.
However, this can be confusing if you go down
too many levels.

I always use one style as the main one and base
others on it. I think of the main style as the hub of
a wheel, and the others are the spokes around it.

Working with Styles

The great thing about styles is that once
you understand the basics of paragraph and
character styles, you also know the basics
for object and table styles. However, rather
than wait till the end of this chapter to cover
working with styles, I'm going to cover those
techniques now. You can then use these techniques for the other types of styles.

Basing one style on another makes it easy to
coordinate multiple text styles.

TIP You can only base like styles on each other
     (paragraph on paragraph or character on
     character).

To base one style on another:

1. Start with at least one style.

2. Open the New Style dialog box to define
   a new style.

3. From the Based On pop-up menu,
   choose the style you want to use as the
   foundation of the new style.

4. Make changes to define the second style's
   attributes.

TIP The changes to the second style are displayed
     in the Style Settings area D.

TIP Any changes you make later to the original
     style also affect the second style.

If you have based one style on another, at
some point you may want to remove any
changes to the style so that it is like the first.

To reset to the base style:

Click the Reset To Base button.

You can also set the text so that it no longer is
governed by the style.

To break the link to a style:

Choose Break Link to Style from the Styles
panel menu.

Rather than create a new style from scratch, it may be easier to duplicate an existing style and then redefine it.

To duplicate a style:

1. Select the style.

2. Drag the style onto the New Style icon in the Styles panel.

   or

   Choose Duplicate Style from the Styles panel menu.

To sort styles:

Drag the style to the position where you want it to be.

or

Choose Sort by Name from the Styles panel menu.

You can also set keyboard shortcuts for styles. This makes it easy to apply styles as you type.

To set style keyboard shortcuts:

1. Open the New Style dialog box.

   or

   Double-click the name of the style to open the Style Options dialog box.

2. Click in the Shortcut field.

3. Press a keyboard modifier plus a number from the number pad. The keyboard modifiers can be a combination of one or more of the following keys:

   - Cmd (Mac) or Ctrl (Win) keys
   - Shift key
   - Opt (Mac) or Alt (Win) keys

TIP In Windows, the Num Lock key must be turned on to set and apply keyboard shortcuts.

TIP The keyboard shortcut appears next to the style name in the Styles panel **A**.

A The **keyboard shortcut for a style** is listed next to the name of the style.

Style Guidelines

I like to arrange my styles by function in the Styles panel. For instance, the styles that are applied only on master pages are grouped together; the styles for sidebars are grouped together. Rather than drag the styles all around, I use the Sort by Name command to do the work for me.

For instance, I have three different paragraph styles for the numbered lists in this book. Each style starts with the name *List* and is followed by a descriptive word, such as *List Header, List Item, List Item Bulleted,* and so on. So when I sort the styles by name, the styles automatically group together. (I haven't used the style group folders as I have some troubles remembering the proper naming conventions for working with those style groups.)

If you use keyboard shortcuts, keep them in groups. For instance, the styles for the list items all use the keypad number 2 with variations of the keyboard modifiers. So *List Item Plain* is Shift-2, while *List Item Body* is Shift-Cmd/Ctrl-2.

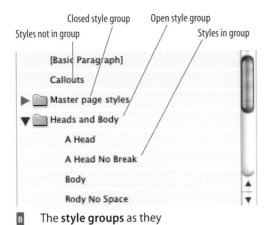

Closed style group   Open style group
Styles not in group   Styles in group

B The **style groups** as they appear in a Styles panel.

C The **Style Group Options dialog box** lets you name a style group.

D A style in a style group has a name in the **Location area** of the Styles dialog box.

Style Names in Style Groups

When you put styles in a style group, their name changes invisibly. For instance, I can have only one style named Tip at the top level of the Styles panel.

But as soon as I put the Tip style into a style group, I can now have another style named Tip at the top level of the panel. I can also have other styles named Tip in other style groups.

Each of these Tip styles is independent of the other styles and they can each have different definitions.

Creating Style Groups

Just as you can create folders to organize files on your computer, so can you create folders (style groups) that allow you to organize your styles. Style groups are available for all types of styles.

To create a style group:

1. Click the New Style Group icon in the Styles panel. A new style group folder appears **B**.

   or

   Choose New Style Group from the Styles panel. The Style Group Options dialog box appears **C**.

   or

   Opt/Alt-Click the New Style Group icon in the Styles panel. The Style Group Options dialog box appears.

2. You can double-click a style group folder to open the Style Group Options dialog box.

3. Choose a name for the style group and click OK.

TIP If a style is in a style group, the group appears next to the word Location in the Styles dialog box **D**.

To move styles into a style group:

1. Select the styles you wish to move.

2. Drag them into the style group folder.

TIP You can also select several styles and choose New Group from Styles in the Styles panel menu to create a group and put the styles in the folder at once.

TIP Select the styles and choose Copy to Group from the Styles panel menu to make copies of those styles in a style group.

Loading and Importing Styles

You can transfer or load styles from one document into another.

To transfer text styles into an InDesign document:

1. Choose one of the following from the Paragraph or Character Styles panel menus:
   - **Load Character Styles** transfers the character styles.
   - **Load Paragraph Styles** transfers the paragraph styles.
   - **Load All Text Styles** transfers both character and paragraph styles.

2. Navigate to find the document with the text styles you want to import.

3. Click Open. The text styles are added to the current document.

TIP Text style names are case-sensitive. Therefore, a paragraph style name of *Body Text* will be added as a separate style to a document that already has a paragraph style named *body text* **A**.

To transfer other styles into an InDesign document:

1. Choose Load [type of] Styles from the Styles panel menu.

2. Navigate to find the document with the styles you want to import.

3. Click Open. The styles are added to the current document.

⇧ PARAGRAPH STYLES

body text

[Basic Paragraph]

body text

Body Text

A **Style names are case sensitive,** so two styles can be listed by the same name but different character cases.

How Many Styles?

I was taught to create a unique style for each type of element in my document. For instance, I might have a paragraph that I use in these sidebars that looks identical to the paragraph I use in the regular body text.

Some people might be tempted to define only one style and apply it to both paragraphs. That's not how I work. Instead, I have a unique paragraph style for each type of element.

There are two reasons for this. The first reason is that if I ever decide to change the appearance of one type of paragraph, I have that flexibility. The other reason comes from using styles as the tags that give my document structure.

With this type of structure applied to the text, I can export the text and reuse it in an XML workflow. While XML is way beyond the scope of this book, the concept of tagging each type of element with its own style is a good practice to learn.

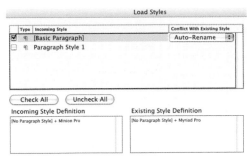

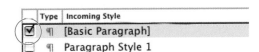

B The **Load Styles dialog box** allows you to choose how style conflicts should be resolved.

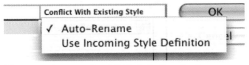

C A check mark next to the style name indicates the incoming style definition should be resolved. No check mark indicates the existing style definition should be used.

D Use the **Conflict With Existing Style menu** to resolve a style conflict.

When you load styles from one document to another, there may be times when the styles coming into the document have the same name, but different definitions. This is called a style conflict. When this happens you need to resolve the conflict between the styles.

To resolve style conflicts:

1. Choose one of the Load Styles commands. If there are conflicts, the Load Styles dialog box displays the incoming styles that have the same name as the existing styles **B**.

2. Select the styles that you want to load into the document, and resolve the conflict **C**.

   or

   Deselect the styles that you don't want to load into the document.

TIP Use the Check All or the Uncheck All button to quickly make choices in a long list of styles.

3. For all the selected styles choose one of the following from the Conflict With Existing Style menu **D**:

   • **Auto-Rename** imports the style with a suffix to differentiate it from the existing style.

   • **Use Incoming Style Definition** changes the existing style to match the imported style definition.

Importing Text Styles from Word

When you place text from word processing programs such as Microsoft Word into InDesign, the text styles from the imported text are added to the document.

To import styles in Microsoft Word text:

1. Choose **File** > **Place** and navigate to find the Word file you want to import.

2. Select Show Import Options and click Open. This opens the Microsoft Word Import Options dialog box 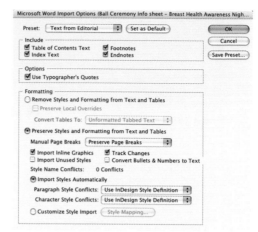.

3. Select Preserve Styles and Formatting from Text and Tables.

4. Select Import Styles Automatically or select Customize Style Import.

If you chose to import the styles automatically, you can choose how style conflicts are resolved.

To resolve style conflicts automatically:

1. To resolve paragraph style conflicts, choose one of the following from the Paragraph Style Conflicts menu **B**:

   - Choose **Use InDesign Style Definition** to have the InDesign style override the incoming style.

   - Choose **Redefine InDesign Style** to have the incoming style override the InDesign style.

   - Choose **Auto Rename** to add the incoming style to the list of styles in the InDesign Styles panel.

2. To resolve character style conflicts, choose from the Character Style Conflicts menu.

TIP A disk icon indicates the style definition came from the imported text **C**.

TIP The disk icon disappears if you modify the imported style.

A The **Microsoft Word Import Options dialog box** allows you to control how styles are imported from Word files.

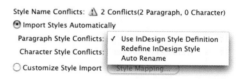

B Use the **Paragraph Style Conflicts** or Character Style Conflicts menu to resolve a style conflict.

C The **disk icon** indicates that the style definition came from an imported text file.

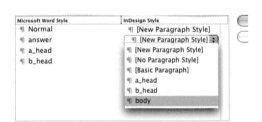

D   Choose Customize Style Import to click the **Style Mapping button**.

E   The **Style Mapping dialog box** lets you choose how each Microsoft Word style should be applied.

F   The **style choices list** lets you map one style to another. Here the Word style *answer* has been mapped to the InDesign style *body*.

What if you have a style name in Word that is totally different from the name of the style in the InDesign document? You need a way to tell InDesign which existing style to apply to the Word text. The custom style mapping controls let you change an incoming style to a specific existing style.

To map one style to another:

1. In the Microsoft Word Import Options dialog box, select Customize Style Import. This makes the Style Mapping button available **D**.

2. Click the Style Mapping button. This opens the Style Mapping dialog box **E**.

3. Under the InDesign Style column, choose one of the styles from the pop-up menu for each of the incoming Word styles **F**.

4. Click OK to close the Style Mapping dialog box.

5. Click OK in the Microsoft Word Import Options dialog box to import the text.

TIP Only paragraph styles are shown in the pop-up menu for incoming Word paragraph styles. Similarly, only character styles are shown in the pop-up menu for incoming Word character styles.

Applying Styles and Style Overrides

Defining styles is just half of the process. You reap the benefits of your planning when you apply styles.

You can apply paragraph and character styles as you type new text, or you can add the styles to existing text **A**.

To apply paragraph styles:

1. Select the paragraphs.

TIP You do not need to select entire paragraphs. As long as a portion is selected, the paragraph style will be applied to the entire paragraph.

2. Click the name of the paragraph style or type the keyboard shortcut.

You can override the paragraph style by applying a character style or local formatting.

To apply local formatting:

1. Select the text.

2. Use the Control panel or Character panel to format the text.

TIP A plus (+) sign next to the paragraph style name indicates that local formatting has been applied to the text **B**.

Rather than use local formatting, I prefer to use character styles on text. That way if I want to make changes later on, I can just redefine the character style.

To apply character styles:

1. Select the text.

TIP You must select all the text you want to format with a character style.

2. Click the name of the character style or type the keyboard shortcut.

Character styles

2. Navigate to find the document that contains the styles you want to import. —— Paragraph style

3. Click **Open**. The styles are *automatically* added to the current document.

A An example of paragraph and character styles applied to text.

.RAGRAPH STYLES

' Text+

[Basic Paragraph]

Body Text+

B A **plus sign next to the paragraph style** indicates that local overrides have been applied.

Character Style Strategies

InDesign character styles only need to be defined with a single change from the paragraph attributes.

For instance, if you want to change text to italic, define a character attribute with just italic as the definition.

You can then apply the italic character attribute to many different paragraph styles, even if they are different typefaces or point sizes.

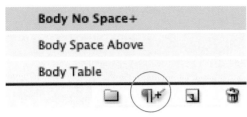

c The **Clear Overrides button** lets you remove local formatting applied to text.

Clearing Style Overrides

When you apply local formatting or character styles, you have different ways to clear those style overrides.

You can use the Clear Overrides button to clear the overrides in a text selection.

To clear the local formatting in a text selection:

1. Select the text you want to clear.

2. Click the Clear Overrides button in the Paragraph Styles panel **c**. This changes the local formatting in the selection to the underlying paragraph style.

You may find that you want to clear just the character attributes that were applied as local formatting, but you want to keep any paragraph attributes.

To clear only local character formatting in a text selection:

1. Select the text you want to clear.

2. Hold Cmd/Ctrl and click the Clear Overrides button. This changes the local character formatting in the selection to the underlying paragraph style.

A Summary for Clearing Overrides

To do this:	Do this:
Clear all the local formatting in a selection	Select the text and click the Clear Overrides button
Clear just the local **character formatting** in a selection	Hold Cmd/Ctrl and click the Clear Overrides button
Clear just the local **paragraph formatting** in a selection	Hold Cmd/Ctrl-Shift and click the Clear Overrides button
Clear **all the local formatting** applied to a paragraph	Hold Opt/Alt and click the name of the paragraph style
Clear **all the local formatting and any character styles** applied to a paragraph	Hold Opt/Alt-Shift and click the name of the paragraph style

The opposite to the previous exercise allows you to clear just the paragraph attributes that were applied as local formatting, but keep any character attributes.

To clear only local paragraph formatting in a text selection:

1. Select the text you want to clear.
2. Hold Cmd/Ctrl-Shift and click the Clear Overrides button. This changes the local paragraph formatting in the selection to the underlying paragraph style.

You can also remove all local formatting without making a specific text selection.

To override local formatting:

1. Place your insertion point in the paragraph you want to override.
2. Hold the Opt/Alt key as you click the name of the paragraph style A.

You may want to clear the character styles and local formatting applied to the text.

To override character styles and local formatting:

1. Place your insertion point in the paragraph you want to override.
2. Hold the Opt/Alt and Shift keys as you click the name of the paragraph style. This deletes both the character styles and the local formatting applied to the text B.

To break the link to a style:

1. Place your insertion point in the paragraph you want to override.
2. Choose Break Link to Style from the Paragraph Styles or Character Styles panel. This removes the style from the text, but does not change the formatting.

Original text with local formatting

Dorothy lived with **Uncle Henry**, and **Aunt Em.** Their house was small.

Opt/Alt-click removes local formatting

Dorothy lived with Uncle Henry, and Aunt Em. Their house was small.

A **Opt/Alt-click a paragraph style name** to remove any local formatting applied to text.

Original text with character style applied

Their house was small. There were four *walls*, a *floor*, and a *roof*.

Their house was small. There were four walls, a floor, and a roof.

Opt/Alt-Shift-click removes character style

B Press **Opt/Alt-Shift and click a paragraph style name** to remove character styles and local formatting.

Redefining and Deleting Styles

One of the advantages of using text or other styles is that when you redefine the style, it changes all the existing text or objects that have that style applied to it.

To redefine a style:

1. Double-click the style name in the panel. This opens the Style Options dialog box, where you can change the style attributes.

2. Click OK. The style is redefined, and text and objects that have the style applied are modified to reflect the new definition of the style.

To redefine a style by example:

1. Select the text or objects that have the style applied.

2. Use the commands to make any changes to the text or objects.

TIP A plus (+) sign appears next to the style name.

3. Choose Redefine Style from the Styles panel. The style is redefined based on the modified example.

TIP The plus (+) sign disappears.

You may have styles that you do not need in your InDesign document. You can shorten the styles list by deleting unused styles.

To delete unused styles:

1. Select the styles you want to delete.

2. Drag the styles onto the Delete Style icon.

   or

   Choose Delete Styles from the Styles panel menu.

TIP Use Select All Unused to delete all the unused styles from a document.

You can also delete styles that are being used in the document. In that case, you have a choice as to how to handle the text that has the style applied to it.

To delete paragraph styles that are in use:

1. Select the style you want to delete.

2. Delete the style as described in the previous exercise. An alert box appears .

3. Use the pop-up menu in the alert box to choose [No Paragraph Style], [Basic Paragraph], or one of the other paragraph styles.

To delete character styles that are in use:

1. Select the style you want to delete.

2. Delete the style as described in the previous exercise. An alert box appears .

3. Use the pop-up menu in the alert box to choose [None] or one of the other character styles.

4. Select the Preserve Formatting checkbox to convert the character style into local formatting.

A The **Delete Paragraph Style alert box** lets you assign another paragraph style to deleted styles.

B The **Delete Character Style alert box** lets you assign another character style to deleted styles.

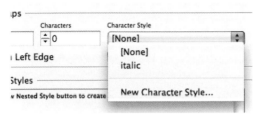

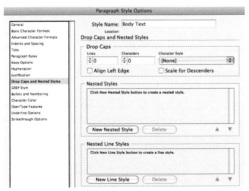

Automatic Drop Cap Styling

Each chapter of this book has a drop cap that is not the same font as the rest of the text in the paragraph. This is an example of an automatic drop cap with a character style.

To apply automatic drop cap character styling:

1. Define a character style that contains the formatting for the drop cap character.

2. Select the paragraph that you want to style with the drop cap.

3. Choose Drop Caps and Nested Styles from the Paragraph panel menu. The Drop Caps and Nested Styles dialog box appears **C**.

4. Use the Lines field to set the number of lines that the drop cap character will descend into the text.

5. Use the Characters field to set the number of characters for drop cap characters.

6. Use the Character Style menu to choose a predefined character style **D**.

TIP If you don't have a previously defined style, choose New Character Style to open the New Character Style dialog box.

7. Click Align Left Edge to force the left edge of the character to align to the left indent of the text.

8. Click Scale for Descenders to scale and adjust the drop cap so that descenders don't collide with the lines below **E**.

9. Click OK.

TIP Choose the Drop Caps and Nested Styles category from the Paragraph Style Options dialog box **F** to make the drop cap part of a paragraph style.

C The **Drop Caps area** of the Drop Caps and Nested Styles dialog box.

D Use the **Character Style menu** to assign a character style to format the drop cap character.

E An example of how the **Scale for Descenders command** avoids problems when descenders are used in drop caps.

F The **Drop Caps and Nested Styles category** for paragraph styles allows you to automate drop cap characters as you apply a paragraph style.

Using Nested Styles

Every once in a while I see a feature that is revolutionary in the field of desktop publishing. Nested styles are such a feature. Nested styles allow you to automate how character styles are applied to paragraphs.

Imagine you are formatting a phone directory. Each paragraph starts with a person's name followed by a colon. After that comes a phone number, and then a new line symbol forces the rest of the address to the end of the paragraph. These are repeating elements that you can reliably count on to use as markers for formatting using nested styles.

You want the person's name to be italic, the phone number to be bold, and the text after the new line symbol to be the regular paragraph style.

Before nested styles, you would have had to manually highlight each element in the paragraph and apply a character style. With nested styles all the formatting is applied in one fell swoop A!

TIP As you work with nested styles, remember that you need predictable elements that you can use as part of the automatic formatting. If you can't predict where the elements will be in the text, you probably can't use nested styles for that text.

To prepare to use nested styles:

Define all the character styles that will be used to apply the formatting for nested styles.

TIP You can only use character styles as part of nested styles, not local formatting from the Character panel.

Dorothy·Gale:(620)·555-5432⏎
3·Farmhouse·Lane,·Very·Small·Town,·KA,·12345¶
Scarecrow:(620)·555-5432⏎
Middle·of·Cornfield,·Very·Small·Town,·KA,·12345¶
Woodman:(620)·555-5432⏎
Deep·in·Forest,·Very·Small·Town,·KA,·12345¶

A An example of the kind of formatting that can be automated using nested styles. The predictable elements can be used to apply the automatic formatting.

Searching for Repeating Elements

It may seem difficult to find repeating elements, but they are much easier to find than you might think.

Consider the tips in my exercises. The word TIP is always separated from the rest of the text by a tab character. So I can easily set the tab as the repeating element for a nested style.

If you are formatting any text that comes from databases, it is extremely easy to have the people who create the database add tab characters to divide the different parts of the text. Then you can use the repeating tab characters to format with the nested styles.

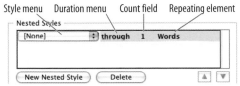

B The Nested Styles area of the **Drop Caps and Nested Styles dialog box** allows you to apply multiple character styles to predictably occurring text elements.

Style menu   Duration menu   Count field   Repeating element

C The **New Nested Style button** creates a new listing in the Nested Styles area.

D Click the **Style menu** to choose the character style that should be applied as the formatting for the nested style.

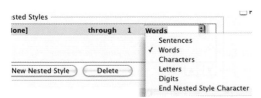

E Click the **Duration menu** to set the extent to which the formatting is applied.

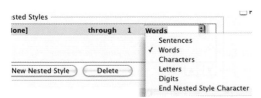

F Click the **Repeating Element menu** to choose the element that ends the nested style.

Once you have defined the character styles, you can apply them using the Nested Styles command.

To apply the Nested Styles command to text:

1. Place your insertion point inside the paragraph that you want to format.

2. Choose Drop Caps and Nested Styles from the Paragraph panel menu. The Drop Caps and Nested Styles dialog box appears **B**.

3. Click the New Nested Style button. This adds a new listing under the Nested Styles area **C**.

4. Use the Style menu to choose which character style will be applied to the repetitive element **D**.

TIP If you don't have a previously defined style, choose New Character Style to open the New Character Style dialog box.

5. Use the Duration menu to choose the extent to which the character style is applied **E**:

   • **Through** applies the style so it includes the repeating character.

   • **Up to** applies the style so it ends before the repeating character.

6. Use the Count field to set how many repeating characters should occur before the character style ends.

7. Use the Repeating Element menu to set which element controls the nested style **F**.

8. Click OK to apply the nested style.

   or

   Click the New Nested Style button to add more nested styles.

TIP Choose the Drop Caps and Nested Styles category from the Paragraph Styles dialog box to make the nested style settings part of a paragraph style.

To change the order of multiple nested styles:

1. Select the nested style you want to move.

2. Click the up or down arrow to move the nested style to a new position .

What if you know your repeating elements are going to repeat over and over? For instance, you want to change from bold to italic after every comma. Instead of setting a long string of nested styles, you can loop them.

To loop two or more nested styles:

1. Choose Repeat from the Character Style list **B**.

2. Set the number for how many styles should loop.

TIP If you type multiple characters, InDesign uses any of those characters as the repeating element.

If you don't have any repeating element in the text, you can insert the End Nested Style Here character to control the appearance of a nested style.

To manually insert the End Nested Style Here character:

1. Place your insertion point where you want the End Nested Style Here character to appear.

2. Choose **Type** > **Insert Special Character** > **Other** > **End Nested Style Here**. This inserts the End Nested Style Here character into the text **C**.

TIP The End Nested Style Here character can be seen if you choose Type > Show Hidden Characters.

TIP The End Nested Style Here character can be inserted as part of Find/Change text or GREP searches.

A Use the **up/down arrows** to change the order of nested styles.

[None]	up to	1	End Neste
Bold	through	1	End Neste
[Repeat]	last	2	Styles

B The **Repeat command in the Character Style list** is used to loop two or more nested styles.

Gale⤬Doroth

C The **End Nested Style Here character** can be inserted to end the effects of a nested style.

Using the End Nested Style Here character

When might you need to insert the End Nested Style Here character? Imagine that you want to style the last set of information in an address such as a zip code or postal code.

You can't rely on a certain number of commas appearing before the zip code appears, nor can you rely on the code to only have numbers if you have a mixture of U.S. and European addresses.

That's when you want to insert the End Nested Style Here character in front of the code.

If necessary, you can ask the editorial department that generates the text to insert a special character before the code. For instance, the zip code 10003 might appear as CODE10003. You can then use the Find/Change command to change the word CODE into the End Nested Style Here character.

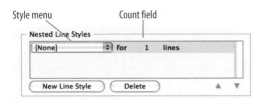

The **Nested Line Styles area** of the Drop Caps and Nested Styles dialog box.

The **controls for a nested line style** in the Drop Caps and Nested Styles dialog box.

The **Style menu** lets you choose a character style to apply to lines in a paragraph.

Creating Nested Line Styles

You can also automatically apply a character style to a certain number of lines in a paragraph. This is called a *nested line style*.

To apply the Nested Line Style command to text:

1. With your insertion point inside the paragraph, choose Drop Caps and Nested Styles from the Paragraph panel menu. The Nested Line Styles area is at the bottom of the dialog box **D**.

2. Click the New Line Style button to add a new listing to the Nested Line Styles **E**.

3. Use the Style menu to choose a character style **F**.

4. Use the Count field to choose how many lines should have the nested style.

5. Click OK to apply the nested style.

   or

   Click the New Line Style button to add more nested styles.

TIP If you don't have a previously defined style, choose New Character Style to open the New Character Style dialog box.

TIP Choose the Drop Caps and Nested Styles category from the Paragraph Styles dialog box to make the nested line style part of a paragraph style.

Like repeating nested styles, you can repeat nested line styles.

To repeat two or more nested line styles:

1. Create two or more nested line styles.

2. Create an additional nested line style.

3. Choose Repeat from the Style menu.

4. Set the number for how many styles should loop.

Creating GREP Styles

Not only can you use the power of GREP as part of Find/Change searches, you can also create GREP styles within paragraph styles. *(For more information on GREP, see Chapter 14, "Automating Your Work.")* What this does is automatically apply character styles to text whenever that text meets the GREP criteria. (Trust me, it's actually easier to do than to explain.)

To create a GREP style:

1. Place your insertion point inside the paragraph that you want to format.
2. Choose GREP Styles from the Paragraph panel menu. The GREP Style dialog box appears **A**.
3. Click the New GREP Style button. This adds a new listing.
4. Use the Apply Style menu to choose which character style will be applied to the GREP text **B**.

TIP If you don't have a previously defined style, choose New Character Style to open the New Character Style dialog box.

5. Use the To Text field to enter the GREP code for which text should be modified by the style **C**.
6. Click OK to apply the GREP style to the text **D**.

   or

   Click the New GREP Style button to add more GREP styles.

TIP Choose the GREP Styles category from the Paragraph Styles dialog box to make a GREP style part of a paragraph style.

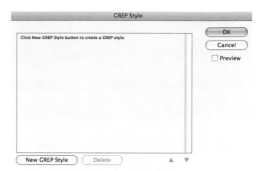

A The **GREP Style dialog box** lets you apply GREP formulas to text.

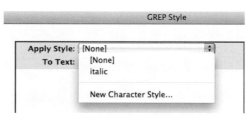

B The **Apply Style menu** lets you choose which character style should be applied to the text.

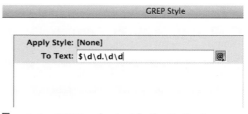

C Enter **GREP codes inside the To Text field** to control which text should be formatted by the GREP style.

The Wonderful Wizard of Oz (Hardcover)
Limited Edition (*$49.99*)
The Wizard Of Oz (Audio) (*$14.78*)
The Wonderful Wizard of Oz (Books of Wonder) Color Illustrations (*$23.89*)
Available in June

D An example of the **code $\d\d.\d\d applied as a GREP style** to automatically format prices into italic text.

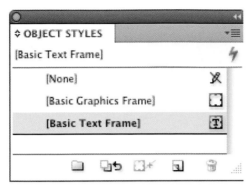

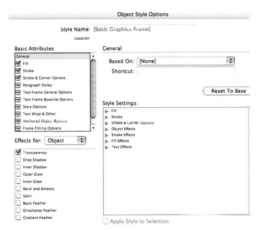

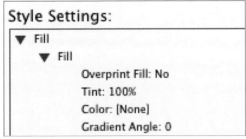

E The **three built-in object style settings** in the Object Styles panel.

F The **Object Style Options dialog box** lets you modify the object style attributes.

G Click the **Style Settings controls** to see the description of the settings for each category.

Defining Object Styles

Just as character and paragraph styles make it easy to apply formatting to text, object styles make it easy to apply formatting to objects. InDesign comes with three built-in object style settings.

TIP If you understand the principles of text styles, it will be easy to work with object styles.

To apply the built-in object styles:

1. Select the object you want to style.

2. Choose **Window > Styles > Object Styles** to open the Object Styles panel **E**.

3. Click one of the following in the Object Styles panel:

   • **[Basic Graphics Frame]** applies the default object settings for graphics frames.

   • **[Basic Text Frame]** applies the default settings for text frames.

   • **[None]** removes all formatting from the object.

To modify the default styles:

1. Double-click the Basic Graphics Frame or Basic Text Frame style. This opens the Object Style Options dialog box **F**.

TIP The [None] style can't be modified.

2. Click each of the categories on the left side of the dialog box. This displays the settings for each category.

3. Make whatever changes you like to each of the category settings.

4. Use the Style Settings controls to see a description of the settings for each category **G**.

You will most likely want to create your own object styles.

To create a new object style:

1. Choose New Style from the Object Styles panel menu. Or hold the Opt/Alt key and click the New Object Style icon in the Object Styles panel. The New Object Style dialog box appears .

2. Use the Style Name field to name the style.

3. Use the checkboxes to control which categories are part of the style **B**. Deselected categories are not part of the style.

4. Use the Based On field to base one style on another.

5. Click the Reset To Base button to remove all differences between a style and the original style it's based on.

6. Click OK to create the style.

The easier way to define an object style is to format the object and define the style by example.

To define an object style by example:

1. Select a sample object.

2. Use the panels and commands to format the object.

3. Choose New Style from the Object Styles panel menu. Or hold the Opt/Alt key and click the New Object Style icon in the Object Styles panel. The New Object Style dialog box appears.

4. Name the style.

5. Click OK to create the style.

TIP Object styles can be duplicated just like text styles.

A Use the **New Object Style dialog box** to define the attributes of an object style.

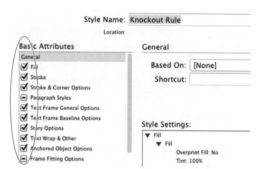

B Click the **category controls** to choose which attributes should be included in the object style.

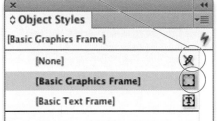

Default text frame   Default graphics frame

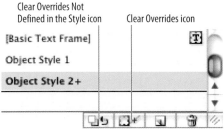

C   The **two default icons for object styles** indicate which style is the default for new objects.

Clear Overrides Not
Defined in the Style icon   Clear Overrides icon

D   There are **two ways to clear overrides** applied to object styles.

Working with Object Styles

For the most part, you work with object styles as you would text styles. However, there is a difference in how the default object style is applied. With text styles, whichever style is highlighted with no text selected will become the default style. But with object styles, you need to choose a default for either graphics frames or text frames.

To change the default object styles:

Drag the Default Graphics Frame icon to a new object style.

or

Drag the Default Text Frame icon to a new object style C.

Like text styles, a plus (+) sign next to an object style name indicates that local formatting changes have been made to the object. However, you may also have made changes to the object in categories that were not selected in the object style. This local formatting is not indicated by a plus sign.

To clear local formatting not defined in the style:

1. Select the object that has the modifications to the object style.

2. Click the Clear Overrides icon to clear all local formatting applied to the object. This applies to formatting applied to the style as well as formatting that was not checked for the object style.

3. Click the Clear Overrides Not Defined in the Style icon to clear the local formatting that was not selected in the object style D.

TIP   The only way to know if that local formatting has been applied to the object is if the icon is visible in the Object Styles panel.

Defining Table and Cell Styles

If you create just one or two tables in a document, you most likely won't have to worry about table and cell styles. But anyone who creates a lot of tables will enjoy how these features automate their work. As you work with table and cell styles, it is best to start by defining cell styles.

To define cell styles:

1. Choose New Cell Style from the Cell Styles panel menu. The New Cell Style dialog box appears .

2. Name the style and set the Style Info controls.

3. If you want, you can use the Paragraph Style list to choose a default paragraph style for table cells.

4. If desired, choose each of the Cell Styles categories to select the attributes of the style 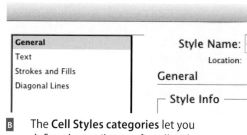.

TIP Unlike the relationship between paragraph and character styles, the formatting of cell styles is not duplicated by a table style. This means you must define a cell style if you want the cells in a table to be controlled by a style.

TIP The Style Settings area displays a description of the attributes for the cell style **C**.

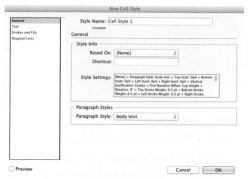

A Use the **New Cell Style dialog box** to define the attributes of cells.

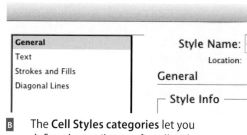

B The **Cell Styles categories** let you define the attributes of a cell style.

C The **Style Settings area** shows you the attributes of a cell style.

D Use the **New Table Style dialog box** to define the attributes of tables.

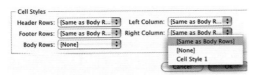

E Use the **Cell Styles pop-up lists** to apply a cell style to the cells in the various positions of the table.

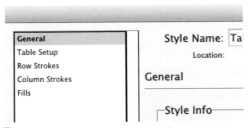

F The **Table Styles categories** let you define the attributes of a table style.

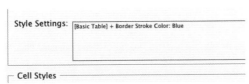

G The **Style Settings area** shows you the defined attributes of a table style.

Once you have defined your cell styles, you can then "move up the ladder" to define table styles.

To define table styles:

1. Choose New Table Style from the Table Styles panel menu. The New Table Style dialog box appears **D**.

2. Use the Cell Styles pop-up lists to apply a cell style to the cells in each position of the table **E**. (That's why you needed to define the cell styles first.)

3. If desired, choose each of the Table Styles categories to select the attributes of the style **F**.

TIP The Style Settings area displays a description of the attributes for the table style **G**.

TIP Unlike paragraph styles, table styles do not have to have all their attributes defined. This is why the Style Settings area displays only a description of the defined attributes for the table style.

Using the Quick Apply Feature

Once you have defined your text, table, and object styles, there is a very easy way to quickly apply them. The Quick Apply feature works entirely from the keyboard — no mouse required!

To use Quick Apply to apply styles:

1. Select the text, table, or object that you want to apply the style to.

2. Press Cmd/Ctrl and then press Return/Enter to open the Quick Apply panel.

   or

   Click the Quick Apply icon on any of the Style panels or the Control panel 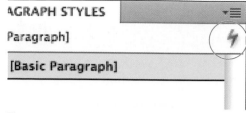.

   TIP The panel can be moved to other positions on your screen.

3. Type a few of the letters that appear in the name of the style. As you type, the Quick Apply area shows just those styles that contain the letters .

   TIP The letters you type do not have to appear in sequence in the name of the style.

4. Keep typing until you have the style you want **B**.

   or

   Use the up and down arrow keys to move to the style you want.

5. Press the Return/Enter key to select the style.

   TIP Quick Apply remembers the last selected style, so you can open Quick Apply and simply press Return/Enter to apply the same style to another selection.

   TIP Press Shift-Return/Enter to apply the Quick Apply entry without closing the Quick Apply panel.

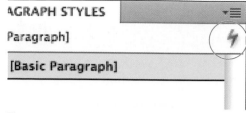

A The **Quick Apply icon** appears in all the Style panels as well as the Control panel.

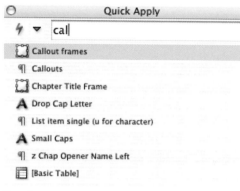

B As you type in the **Quick Apply field**, the list shows just the styles that contain those letters.

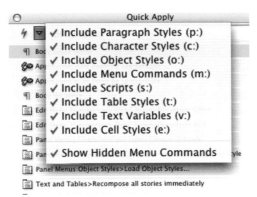

Use the **Quick Apply menu control** to open the list of items that will be displayed as part of Quick Apply.

Quick Apply on Macintosh Notebooks

The keyboard shortcuts for text styles require you to use the numbers on the keyboard number pad.

However, Macintosh notebooks don't have a keyboard number pad. Older models, such as my 15-inch MacBook Pro, let you use the fn key to get the numbers from some of the keys on the keyboard. But the newer models, such as my 13-inch MacBook Pro, don't have that feature.

That's why I use QuickApply's keystrokes to assign keyboard shortcuts to my styles. It does require a few more keystrokes, but this way I can apply the same keyboard shortcuts without having to worry on which model of Mac I am working.

You can even use Quick Apply to edit the styles dialog box for the selected Quick Apply style.

To edit a style through Quick Apply:

1. Open the Quick Apply panel.

2. Type or navigate to get to the style that you want to edit.

TIP This technique only works with styles, not the menu commands, scripts, or text variables.

3. Press Cmd-Return (Mac) or Control-Enter (Windows). This opens the dialog box for that style.

In addition to paragraph, character, object, table, and cell styles, Quick Apply can also apply menu commands, text variables, and scripts. However, you may not want to wade through hundreds of menus and scripts before getting to your own style. That's when you can customize the settings for Quick Apply.

To customize the results for Quick Apply:

1. Open the Quick Apply panel.

2. Press the menu control to open the list of items that Quick Apply will apply .

3. Select those items you want to have displayed using Quick Apply. Deselected items are not displayed using Quick Apply.

You can also use the prefix letters for each of the styles, commands, or scripts that are part of a Quick Apply display.

To use the letter commands with Quick Apply:

1. Open Quick Apply.

2. Type one of the following prefixes before the name of the item you want to apply:

   - **p:** for paragraph styles
   - **c:** for character styles
   - **o:** for object styles
   - **m:** for menu commands
   - **s:** for scripts
   - **t:** for table styles
   - **v:** for text variables
   - **e:** for cell styles

3. Type the rest of the command or style name.

TIP **Don't put a space after the colon when you type the rest of the name. For example, to apply a paragraph style called Callouts, you would type p:Callouts.**

4. Press Return/Enter to apply the Quick Apply item.

Typography 16

The one thing that truly separates the amateurs from the experts in page layout is the control they take over their text. Amateurs are pleased if they can apply simple formatting such as fonts, sizes, alignment, tracking, and so on.

Experts, though, want more from a page-layout program. They want sophisticated control over kerning. This includes the ability to move one character in so that it tucks under the stroke of another.

They want to control how lines are justified within a text frame. This means that if one line looks too crowded and the next has big gaps between the words, the experts tell the program to reapportion the spaces.

The experts also want to work with the newest typefaces that give more choices for how letters look and act together.

These are advanced text effects. Once you apply these features, you move from being an ordinary designer to a typographer.

Optical Margin Alignment

One of the most sophisticated text effects in InDesign is the ability to apply hanging punctuation to justified text, in which a slight adjustment of the margin creates a more uniform appearance for the edge of the text. Hanging punctuation is applied by setting the *optical margin alignment*. This moves punctuation characters slightly outside the text margin . In addition, optical margin alignment moves the serifs of letters outside the margin .

Optical margin alignment is set using the Story panel.

To set optical margin adjustment:

1. Select the text.

2. Choose **Window** > **Type & Tables** > **Story**. This opens the Story panel .

3. Select the Optical Margin Alignment checkbox. The text reflows so that the punctuation and serifs lie outside the margin edges.

4. Enter a size for the amount of overhang.

TIP As a general rule, set the overhang to the same size as the text.

Off
"From the Land of Oz.
On
"From the Land of Oz.

A To create the effect of a straight edge, **optical margin alignment** moves punctuation outside the margin edges.

The Lion shook the dust out of his mane, and the Scarecrow patted himself into his best shape.

B The **Optical Margin Alignment setting** also moves the serifs of letters slightly outside the margin.

C The **Story panel** lets you set the Optical Margin Alignment to hang punctuation in the margin.

The road was still paved with
yellow brick, but these were much
covered by dried branches and
dead leaves from the trees, and the
walking was not at all good.

Off

The road was still paved with yellow
brick, but these were much covered
by dried branches and dead leaves
from the trees, and the walking was
not at all good.

On

D Turn on **Adobe Paragraph Composer** to
improve the spacing between words.

Using Adobe Paragraph Composer

InDesign has two ways of composing (laying
out) text. Single-line composition looks at the
current line and evaluates the best place to
break the line or apply hyphenation. Paragraph composition looks at all the text in a
paragraph — forward and backward — when
it evaluates the best place to break lines.
When paragraph composition is turned on,
the result is more even spacing for the text
and fewer hyphens **D**.

To apply paragraph composition:

1. Select the text.

2. Choose **Type** > **Paragraph** to open the
Paragraph panel.

3. Choose Adobe Paragraph Composer
from the Paragraph panel menu. The text
reflows.

TIP Adobe Paragraph Composer is a paragraph
attribute and is applied to all the text in a
paragraph.

TIP Adobe Paragraph Composer is turned on by
default when you first open InDesign.

TIP Choose Adobe Single-line Composer to apply
standard line-by-line composition.

Applying Justification Controls

Justification determines how lines fit between margins. *(See the sidebar below for information on how justification affects text.)* InDesign provides three different ways to control justification: word spacing, letter spacing, and glyph scaling. *Word spacing* changes the space between words.

To set word spacing:

1. Select the text.

2. Choose **Type** > **Paragraph** to open the Paragraph panel.

3. Choose Justification from the Paragraph panel menu. This opens the Justification dialog box .

4. Set the Word Spacing options as follows :

   - **Minimum** controls the smallest amount of space you want between words. For instance, a value of 80% means that you are willing to allow the space to be 80% of the normal space.

   - **Desired** controls the preferred amount of space between words. A value of 100% indicates that you want the same amount that the designer of the typeface created.

   - **Maximum** controls the largest amount of space you want between words. A value of 120% means that you are willing to allow the space to be 120% of the normal space.

5. Click OK to apply the changes .

TIP The Minimum, Desired, and Maximum settings apply only to text that is set to one of the Justified settings. Other alignments, such as left-aligned text, use only the Desired setting.

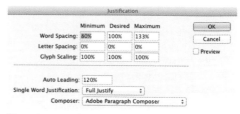

A The **Justification dialog box** controls word and letter spacing.

	Minimum	Desired	Maximum
Word Spacing:	80%	100%	133%
Letter Spacing:	0%	0%	0%
Glyph Scaling:	100%	100%	100%

B The **spacing controls** in the Justification dialog box.

Welcome, my child, to the Land of Oz
Min: 80, Desired: 100, Max: 120

Welcome, my child, to the Land of Oz
Min: 80, Desired: 100, Max: 100

C The effect of changing the **word spacing**. Notice the change in the amount of space between the words.

Understanding Justification

The text in this paragraph is justified — that is, both ends of the line are aligned with the paragraph margins. Not all the words can fit evenly between the margins, so some lines have a bit more space between the words and others have less.

The Justification settings control how much space is added to make the lines fit between the margins.

Welcome, my child, to the Land of Oz — Min: 0, Desired: 0, Max: 0

Welcome, my child, to the Land of Oz — Min: -4, Desired: 0, Max: 4

D The effect of changing the **letter spacing**. Notice how there is less space between the characters within the words.

What Are the Best Justification Settings?

Perhaps the most debated issue in desktop publishing is what the best settings are for the Justification controls. The answer depends on a variety of factors. The typeface, width of the columns, even the type of text all need to be considered in setting the Justification controls.

For body text, such as the text here, I use word spacing of 70%, 100%, and 110%. (Here in New York City, most designers like to set copy tightly.) For headlines, I fit letters tighter, with word spacing of 60%, 90%, and 100%.

I keep all the letter spacing values at 0%. I set the glyph scaling values at 100%. I don't like to scrunch up the space between letters, and I definitely don't like to change the shape of the text, which happens with glyph scaling *(see the next page)*.

But that's just me. And that's why they call them preferences!

The space between letters is *letter spacing,* sometimes called character spacing. InDesign lets you change the letter spacing for text whether justified or not.

To set letter spacing:

1. Select the text.
2. Choose **Type > Paragraph** to open the Paragraph panel.
3. Choose Justification from the Paragraph panel menu.
4. Set the Letter Spacing options as follows:
    - **Minimum** controls the smallest amount of space between letters. A value of –5% allows the space to be reduced by 5% of the normal space.
    - **Desired** controls the preferred amount of space between letters. A value of 0% indicates that you do not want to add or subtract any space.
    - **Maximum** controls the largest amount of space between letters. A value of 5% allows the space to be increased by 5% of the normal space.
5. Click OK to apply the changes **D**.

TIP **If a paragraph cannot be set according to the Justification controls you choose, InDesign violates the settings by adding or subtracting spaces. Set the Composition preferences to have those violations highlighted.**

Another way to control justification is to use *glyph scaling*. (*Glyph* is the proper term for all the letters, numbers, punctuation marks, and other parts of text.) Glyph scaling applies horizontal scaling to the letters themselves so that the text takes up more or less space within the line.

To set glyph scaling:

1. Select the text.

2. Choose **Type** > **Paragraph** to open the Paragraph panel.

3. Choose Justification from the Paragraph panel menu.

4. Set the Glyph Scaling options as follows:

    *   **Minimum** controls the smallest amount of scaling that you are willing to apply to the text. A value of 98% means that you are willing to allow the characters to be reduced by 2% of their normal width.

    *   **Desired** controls the preferred amount of scaling. A value of 100% indicates that you do not want to apply any scaling to the character shape.

    *   **Maximum** controls the amount that you are willing to expand the space between words. A value of 105% means that you are willing to allow the characters to be increased by 5% of their normal width.

5. Click OK to apply the changes A.

TIP Glyph scaling distorts the shape of letters. Most people say you can't see the slight distortion. However, typographic purists (such as this author) try to avoid distorting the letterforms whenever possible B.

The road was still paved with yellow brick, but these were much covered by dried branches and dead leaves from the trees, and the walking was not at all good.

Min: 100
Desired: 100
Max: 100

The road was still paved with yellow brick, but these were much covered by dried branches and dead leaves from the trees, and the walking was not at all good.

Min: 80
Desired: 100
Max: 120

A   The effects of changing the **glyph scaling.**

B   The black area shows the original shape of the character. The gray area shows the effects of 80% glyph scaling.

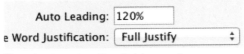

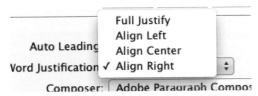

C The **Auto Leading field** controls how InDesign calculates the leading when set to Auto.

D The **Single Word Justification menu** controls what happens when a single word occupies a line of justified text.

Full Justify

Align Left

Align Center

Align Right

E The effects of the **Single Word Justification settings**.

The Auto Leading field controls how much space is put between the lines whenever automatic leading is chosen.

To set the Auto Leading percentage:

1. Choose Justification from the Paragraph panel menu.

2. Enter an amount in the Auto Leading field **C**.

TIP The Auto Leading percentage is based on the point size of the text. So an Auto Leading of 120% applied to 12-point text creates a leading of 14.4 points (12 × 1.20 = 14.4).

TIP Most professional designers use an absolute amount for leading by entering a specific number, rather than relying on the automatic leading.

Have you ever seen a paragraph of justified text where a single word stretched out along the entire line? InDesign lets you control what happens to a single word in a justified paragraph.

To set the single word justification:

1. Choose Justification from the Paragraph panel menu.

2. Choose a setting from the Single Word Justification menu **D**. Any text that is set to Justify in the Paragraph panel will be set according to the menu command **E**.

Controlling Hyphenation

InDesign lets you turn on hyphenation in the Paragraph panel. Once hyphenation is turned on, you can then control how the hyphenation is applied.

To turn on hyphenation:

1. Select the text.

2. Select the Hyphenate checkbox in the Paragraph panel 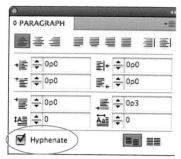.

To control the hyphenation:

1. Choose Hyphenation from the Paragraph panel menu. The Hyphenation Settings dialog box appears 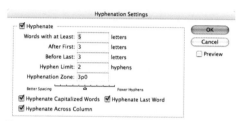.

2. Select the Hyphenate checkbox to set the following controls 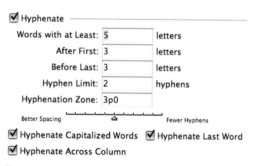:

   - **Words with at Least** controls the minimum number of letters a word must contain before it can be hyphenated.

   - **After First** sets the minimum number of letters before the hyphen.

   - **Before Last** sets the minimum number of letters after the hyphen.

   - **Hyphen Limit** sets how many consecutive lines can end with hyphens.

   - **Hyphenation Zone** controls the amount of whitespace at the end of a nonjustified line.

3. Select Hyphenate Capitalized Words to allow those words to be hyphenated.

4. Select Hyphenate Last Word to let the last word in a paragraph be hyphenated.

5. Select Hyphenate Across Column to let words that break across a column be hyphenated.

6. Adjust the hyphenation slider to control the total number of hyphens in the paragraph.

A Select the **Hyphenate checkbox** to turn on automatic hyphenation for a paragraph.

B The **Hyphenation Settings dialog box** lets you control how hyphenation is applied.

C The Hyphenation controls let you enter values for how words are hyphenated.

Hyphenation Units are Nigels

The units in the hyphenation slider are called Nigels in honor of Nigel Tufnel (Christopher Guest), the Spinal Tap guitarist, whose amplifier went to 11.

Behold! I am the great and mighty, all-pow-erful Oz.

Behold! I am the great and mighty, all-powerful Oz.

D   In the bottom example the word **powerful** was selected and the **No Break command** was applied to prevent the text from hyphenating.

A·document· can·not·be· completed#

E   A **discretionary hyphen** appears within the word but prints only when it appears at the end of a line.

Setting Hyphenation Controls

My own preference is to set "Words with at Least" to six or more. This allows a word such as *person* to be hyphenated. I also prefer a minimum of three letters before the hyphen and three letters after. This avoids breaking words as *un-excited* or *reluctant-ly*.

Hyphenate Capitalized Words?

Some people automatically turn this off so that capitalized words do not hyphenate. I don't. The command doesn't distinguish between proper nouns and words that begin a sentence. So I would rather selectively control how proper nouns break by using the No Break command or by inserting a discretionary hyphen before the word.

Sometimes you may want to prevent words or phrases from being hyphenated or break-ing across lines. For instance, you might not want the words *Mr. Cohen* to be separated at the end of a line. You might not want a com-pound word such as *self-effacing* to be broken with another hyphen D.

To apply the No Break command:

1. Select the text.

2. Choose **Type** > **Character** to open the Character panel.

3. Choose No Break from the Character panel menu.

You can also control hyphenation by inserting a *discretionary hyphen,* which forces the word to hyphenate at that point if it breaks at the end of a line.

To use a discretionary hyphen:

1. Place the insertion point where you want the hyphen to occur.

2. Press Command/Ctrl-Shift-(hyphen) or Control-click (Mac) or right-click and choose **Insert Special Character** > **Hyphens and Dashes** > **Discretionary Hyphen** from the contextual menu.

TIP   The discretionary hyphen prints only when it appears at the end of the line E.

TIP   Insert a discretionary hyphen before a word to prevent that instance of the word from being hyphenated.

You can control where a word is hyphenated.

To edit the hyphenation in the dictionary:

1. Choose **Edit** > **Spelling** > **Dictionary**.

2. Type the word you want to modify in the Word field as follows 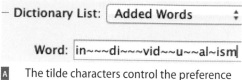:

   - **One tilde (~)** indicates the best possible hyphenation position.

   - **Two tildes (~~)** indicates the next best possible position.

   - **Three tildes (~~~)** indicates the least acceptable position.

   - **A tilde before the word** prevents the word from being hyphenated.

3. Click Add to add the new hyphenation preferences to the dictionary.

Baseline Grid

InDesign has an electronic grid that you can force text to align to. This ensures that text lines up correctly in two separate frames **B**.

To set the baseline grid:

1. Choose **Edit** > **Preferences** > **Grids (Win)** or **InDesign** > **Preferences** > **Grids (Mac)**. This opens the Baseline Grid settings in the Preferences dialog box **C**.

2. Use the Color menu to set the grid color.

3. Use the Start field to control where the grid should start vertically in the document.

4. Use the Relative To menu to choose between the top of the page or the top margin **D**.

5. Use the Increment Every field to control the space between the gridlines.

6. Set View Threshold for the magnification amount above which the grid is visible.

A The tilde characters control the preference for where hyphenation should occur.

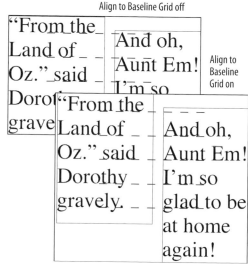

B When **Align to Baseline Grid** is turned on, the text in two different frames lines up.

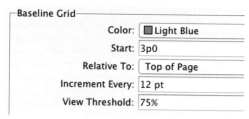

C The **Baseline Grid settings** in the Grids preferences.

D The **Relative To menu** lets you choose where the baseline grid should start.

Do not align to baseline grid

Align to baseline grid

E The **Align to Baseline Grid buttons** in the Paragraph panel.

Align to Baseline Grid off

Chapter Two: The Council with the Munchkins¶

She was awakened by a shock, so sudden and severe that i soft bed she

As it was,

Align to Baseline Grid on

Chapter Two: The Council with the Munchkins¶

She was awakened by a shock, so sudden and severe that if Dorothy had not been lying on the soft bed she might have been hurt.¶

As it was, the jar made her catch her breath

F When text is **aligned to the baseline grid**, the leading may increase. Also, the space between paragraphs may adjust.

Align all lines to grid

As it was, the jar made her catch her breath and wonder what had happened; and Toto put his cold little nose into her face and whined dismally. Dorothy sat up and noticed that the house was not moving; nor was it dark, for the bright sunshine came in at the window, flooding the little room.

This sou very mu like the opening the movi

Only align first line to grid

As it was, the jar made her catch her breath and wonder what had happened; and Toto put his cold little nose into her face and whined dismally. Dorothy sat up and noticed that the house was not moving; nor was it dark, for the bright sunshine came in at the window, flooding the little room.

This sounds very much like the opening for the movie

G Use the **Only Align First Line to Grid command** to align just the first line of a paragraph without affecting the leading.

To align text to a baseline grid:

1. Select the text.
2. Click the Align to Baseline Grid button in the Paragraph panel **E**. The text aligns to the grid.

TIP When you align to the baseline grid, the grid setting overrides the leading. Most designers set the baseline grid to the same amount as the leading for the text **F**.

TIP Aligning to the baseline grid may also change the space between paragraphs.

In addition to setting the baseline grid, you can choose to set just the first line of a paragraph to the baseline grid.

To align just the first line to the baseline grid:

1. Select the text.
2. Click the Align to Baseline Grid icon in the Paragraph panel. All the lines in the paragraph will be aligned to the baseline grid.
3. Choose Only Align First Line to Grid in the Paragraph panel menu or choose First Line Only from the Align to Grid menu in the Indents and Spacing area of the Paragraph Style Options dialog box.

TIP This forces the first line of a paragraph to align to the grid but allows the other lines in the paragraph to be controlled by the leading **G**.

You can also set a custom baseline grid for a text frame. This is especially helpful for formatting margin notes alongside text .

To create a custom grid for a text frame:

1. Select the text frame.

2. Choose **Object > Text Frame Options** and then click Baseline Options. This opens the text frame baseline controls **B**.

3. Select the Use Custom Baseline Grid checkbox to set the options.

4. Use the Start field to control where the grid should start vertically in the document.

5. Use the Relative To menu to choose between the top of the page or the top margin.

6. Use the Increment Every field to control the space between the gridlines.

7. Use the Color controls to set the color of the grid.

8. Don't forget to set the text to align to the baseline grid.

Document grid   Custom frame grid

"All the same," said the Scarecrow, "I shall ask for brains instead of a heart; for a fool would not know what to do with a heart if he had one."

Is the Scarecrow actually smart here? Does the Tin Woodman show feeling? What does this tell you?

"I shall take the heart," returned the Tin Woodman; "for brains do not make one happy, and happiness is the best thing in the world."

A A **custom frame grid** allows you to have multiple grids in a document.

B The **Baseline Grid settings** in the Text Frame Options.

C The **Balance Ragged Lines command** rearranges text so there is a more equal number of words in the lines.

Kin

King

Kingd

Kingdom

D As you add more letters to an OpenType font, the previous letters change.

What Is OpenType?

OpenType is a type format that was developed by Adobe and Microsoft. OpenType fonts have many advantages over previous type formats. In addition to containing thousands of glyphs, OpenType fonts are also cross-platform. This means you can use the same font on Mac or Windows without any document reflow.

Adobe sells different types of OpenType fonts. "Pro" versions of a font, such as Minion Pro, contain the extended character sets that give you access to fractions, ligatures, and other special effects. "Standard" versions, such as Futura Std, contain only the basic characters.

Balancing Ragged Lines

Another nuance for good typography is to make sure that there are no uneven line breaks, especially in headlines or centered type. InDesign's Balance Ragged Lines command makes this easier **C**.

To balance uneven line breaks:

1. Select the text.

2. Choose Balance Ragged Lines from the Paragraph panel menu or choose Balance Ragged Lines in the Indents and Spacing area of the Paragraph Style Options dialog box.

Using OpenType

Instead of the paltry 256 glyphs (characters) in ordinary fonts, OpenType fonts can have thousands of glyphs. InDesign has special commands that help you get the most out of OpenType fonts. For instance, you can set the commands to automatically swap ordinary characters with special OpenType glyphs.

To set automatic OpenType alternate characters:

1. Select the text.

TIP OpenType features can be applied to all the text in a document or just part of the text.

2. Choose **Type** > **Character** to open the Character panel.

3. Choose the options from the OpenType submenu in the Character panel menu. InDesign automatically swaps characters with the alternate glyphs in each category **D**.

You can also manually choose alternate glyphs for each character in the font.

To choose the alternate glyphs:

1. Select the character in the text.

2. Choose **Type** > **Glyphs** to open the Glyphs panel.

3. Press the triangle next to the selected character in the panel 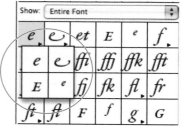. The alternate glyphs for the selection appear.

4. Choose one of the alternate characters. This replaces the selected text with the alternate character in the Glyphs panel.

You can also set the Glyphs panel to display just certain categories of glyphs.

To view certain categories in the Glyphs panel:

1. Press the Show list in the Glyphs panel.

2. Choose the category of OpenType characters that you want to display **B**.

TIP Not all OpenType fonts contain all the possible glyph features. So the Show list will display different categories depending on the OpenType font chosen.

A Press a character or letter that has a triangle to see the alternate glyphs.

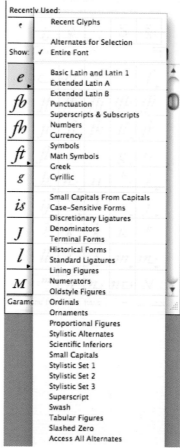

B The **Show list** in the Glyphs panel lets you choose to see the categories of specialized glyphs.

OpenType Categories

Feature name	Comments	Examples	
All Caps	Changes text to uppercase letters. Also changes punctuation and spacing. Notice how the question marks and hyphen are raised in the OpenType all caps formatting.	Manually typed all caps	¡MAMMA-MEXICO?
		OpenType all caps	¡MAMMA-MEXICO?
Small Caps	Changes lowercase text to small capital letters. More appropriate weight for the letters compared to the fake small caps created electronically.	Electronic small caps	SMSOLUTIONS
		OpenType small caps	SMSOLUTIONS
All Small Caps	Changes all text, including uppercase characters, to small capital letters. Use for acronyms such as FBI, CIA, and PDF. The advantage to this setting is that you do not have to retype uppercase characters to make the conversion.	Without small caps	The FBI and CIA opened the IRS PDF.
		With small caps	The FBI and CIA opened the IRS PDF.
Ligatures	Applies the special letter combinations such as fi and fl. Other ligatures, such as ffi, ffl, and ff may be present in most Adobe Pro OpenType fonts.	No ligatures	difficult flush fish
		With ligatures	difficult flush fish
Discretionary Ligatures	Applies both discretionary ligatures and historical ligatures. These ligatures should be used sparingly as they are not common in contemporary text.	No discretionary ligatures	reaction burst
		With discretionary ligatures	reaction burst
Fractions	Converts numbers around a slash into numerator and denominator characters and changes the slash to a virgule. Settings for Numerator and Denominator also use the fraction glyphs.	Manually styled	$3\frac{1}{2}$ $4\frac{3}{4}$
		OpenType formatted	$3\frac{1}{2}$ $4\frac{3}{4}$
Ordinals	Converts the characters to the superscript position. Like fractions, the OpenType version is faster to apply and has a better weight than electronic styling.	Manually styled	1st 2nd 3rd 4th
		OpenType formatted	1st 2nd 3rd 4th
Swash	Substitutes a stylized alternative for the ordinary glyphs. Swashes are usually found in the italic version of a font. They are contextual and are inserted at the beginning or end of a word.	Without swash	Quick Awesome
		With swash	Quick Awesome
Stylistic Sets	Substitutes sets of characters that are applied depending on their context in relationship to other letters. Visible in the Glyphs panel.	Without stylistic set	Huddled
		With stylistic set	Huddled

continues on next page

Feature name	Comments	Examples	
Contextual Alternates	Substitutes specially designed characters that are applied depending on their context in relationship to other letters.	Without contextual alternates	*bogged who fish stall look lodge*
		With contextual alternates	*bogged who fish stall look lodge*
Stylistic Alternates	Created by the type designer, these alternatives are inserted as alternate choices to the selected glyphs.	Original character	&
		Stylistic alternate	&
Superscript/ Superior	Substitutes proper superscript or superior characters for ordinary glyphs. Limited to numbers, punctuation, and a selected set of letters.	Manually styled	x^2 $\$4.00$ 2^e
		OpenType formatted	x^2 $\$4.00$ 2^e
Subscript/Inferior	Like superscript, this substitutes proper subscript characters for ordinary glyphs. Limited to just numbers and punctuation, not letters.	Manually styled	H_2O
		OpenType formatted	H_2O
Slashed Zero	Substitutes a slashed zero for the normal character. Used in scientific and mathematical writing.	No slashed zero	x-0=y
		Slashed zero	x-∅=y
Figure (number) types	There are two main categories for figures: Tabular and Proportional. *Tabular figures* have fixed widths and are used particularly where the numbers need to line up under each other. *Proportional figures* have variable widths. Use these unless it is necessary to line figures up into columns of tabular data. Tabular figures and Proportional figures each come in two varieties: Lining and Oldstyle. *Lining figures* have a uniform height. Use them with all cap text or for a contemporary look. *Oldstyle figures* have unequal heights. Use them with mixed-case text or when a more traditional look is desired. *Default figure* is the category that the type designer has designated as the default. This is usually tabular lining.	These are the four types of figures:	
		Tabular lining	12: 09/11/2001 34: 07/22/2008
		Tabular oldstyle	12: 09/11/2001 34: 07/22/2008
		Proportional lining	12: 09/11/2001 34: 07/22/2008
		Proportional oldstyle	12: 09/11/2001 34: 07/22/2008

Interactive and Multimedia 17

At the risk of sounding like an old codger, I can remember when a page-layout program only laid out print files. The idea of creating "push buttons" that sent you flying to other pages — or even other documents — was totally unfathomable. After all, how was someone supposed to press on a weather summary on the front page of a newspaper to jump to the full weather map on the last page?

So it is with some amazement that I write this chapter. Page layout no longer refers to just printed pages. InDesign has a wealth of features that let you create interactive elements for electronic documents.

Types of Interactive Elements

There are five types of interactive elements you can add to InDesign documents: Hyperlinks, Cross-References, Bookmarks, Buttons and Forms. Each has its own particular uses, but some of the features may overlap. Before you start work, decide which type of interactive element is right for you.

Feature	Description	Advantages	Limitations
Hyperlink	Adds a hotspot area to text or objects where you can click to move to other parts of the document, other documents, or Web pages.	Can be applied directly to the text inside a story. Hyperlinks can also be automatically applied to the entries in a table of contents or index using those InDesign features.	Provides only very primitive visual indications of the linked area.
Cross Reference	Adds a hotspot area to text that is linked to other parts of the document.	Also adds dynamic text that indicates the position of the cross-reference.	Provides only primitive visual indications of the linked area.
Bookmark	Adds a navigational element that is visible in the Bookmarks pane of Adobe Reader or Adobe Acrobat.	The Bookmark pane can be set to be visible at all times in the PDF document. Can be created automatically using the Table of Contents feature.	Requires some education to teach the reader how to use the Bookmarks pane in the Reader. Is not directly on the document page. No special visual indication in the document.
Button	Adds a hotspot area that can contain text or graphics. This hotspot can be set to invoke a wide variety of behaviors including navigation as well as movie or audio playback.	Offers the most navigational and design choices.	Buttons can't be created automatically from text or styles. Requires the most work to create.
Form	Adds an area that can be used in Acrobat to enter information or mark checkboxes or radio buttons.	These forms can be filled out in the PDF and the information then sent back to the creator for tabulation.	Forms can't be created automatically. Requires the most work to create.

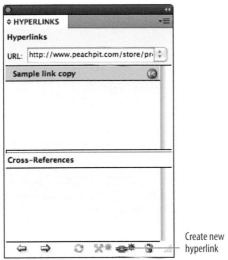

Create new
hyperlink

A The **Hyperlinks panel** is used to define both hyperlinks and cross-references.

B The **New Hyperlink dialog box** lets you set the destination and appearance of a hyperlink.

Defining Hyperlinks

A hyperlink is an area of a page that can be clicked to send the reader to a new page, open a new document, move to a Web page, or send an email message. There are two parts to a hyperlink. The *source* is the object or text that you click to trigger the hyperlink. The *destination* is the page or Web link you go to.

To create a hyperlink:

1. If the Hyperlinks panel is not visible, choose **Window > Interactive > Hyperlinks** to open the panel **A**.

2. Select the text or object that you want to make the hyperlink source.

3. Click the Create New Hyperlink icon in the panel or choose New Hyperlink from the panel menu. This opens the New Hyperlink dialog box **B**.

4. Set the options for Link To, Destination, Character Style, and Appearance as described in the following exercises.

There are several types of destinations for hyperlinks. You can, for instance, choose to link to a specific place in the document or you can link to a Web page. The type of link you choose determines the destination options that appear in the New Hyperlink dialog box.

To choose the type of link:

Use the Link To menu to choose one of the following types of links :

- **URL** creates a link to a Web page.
- **File** creates a link that opens a file in another application. Note: the file must be accessible to anyone choosing the link.
- **Email** creates a link that opens the default email application. You can also set the email address and subject line.
- **Page** creates a link that opens a new page in the document.
- **Text Anchor** creates a link to a point in the text that was defined as a text anchor.
- **Shared Destination** creates a link to a previously defined hyperlink. This is particularly helpful if you want several different hyperlinks to go to the same destination.

As you define hyperlinks, they appear in the Hyperlinks panel. Different types of hyperlinks display different icons.

To see the types of hyperlinks in the Hyperlinks panel:

Click each hyperlink in the Hyperlinks panel. An icon next to the link shows the type of link **B**.

TIP A selected hyperlink also displays its URL or other link information in the Hyperlinks panel.

A The **Link To menu** lets you choose the type of destination for the hyperlink.

York   URL, file, or email link

usiness and becom   Text anchor link

                                        Page link

B The **icons for hyperlinks** in the Hyperlinks panel.

Character Style

☑ Style: hyperlinks

C Use the **Character Style menu** to apply a text style to a hyperlink.

Appearance
Type: Visible Rectangle
Highlight: None   Width: Thin
Color: ■ Black   Style: Solid

D Use the **Appearance settings** to format the display of hyperlinks.

Character Styles for Hyperlinks

The Appearance settings for hyperlinks add rectangles around the hyperlink. But you may want your hyperlink to look more like the links on Web pages: blue text with a blue underline.

Once you have created a character style you can easily apply it as part of defining the hyperlink.

Of course all hyperlinks and other interactive elements also display the pointing finger symbol when you move the cursor over the link in the interactive document.

In addition to setting the destinations for hyperlinks, you can also control how the hyperlink appears on the page.

To set a character style to text hyperlinks:

1. Select the text that you want as a hyperlink.

2. In the New Hyperlink dialog box, click the Character Style menu **C**.

3. Choose a predefined character style. Or choose None to apply no style to the selected text.You can also create visual indicators around all hyperlinks. This is controlled using the Appearance settings **D**.

To set the appearance of a hyperlink:

1. Use the Type menu in the Appearance area to choose a setting for the visibility of the rectangle around the hotspot.

2. Use the Highlight menu to choose the appearance of the hotspot area when clicked.

3. Use the Width menu to choose the thickness of the visible rectangle.

4. Use the Style menu to choose a solid or dashed line for the visible rectangle.

5. Use the Color menu to choose a color for the rectangle.

The easiest way to create a hyperlink destination is to create it as you define the hyperlink. However, it's also possible to define destinations without defining the hyperlink. This is helpful if you have a lot of destinations that you want to define before you know where you will create the hyperlinks.

TIP Destinations don't appear in the Hyperlinks panel, but are available when you define new hyperlinks.

To create a page destination:

1. Choose New Hyperlink Destination in the Hyperlinks panel menu.

2. Choose Page from the Type menu. This sets the Page destination controls 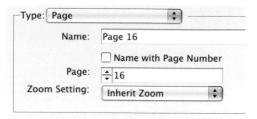.

3. Use the Page number control to set the page destination.

4. Enter a name for the page destination

   or

   Click the option for Name with Page Number. This forces the destination name to the name of the page and the zoom setting.

5. Use the Zoom setting menu to set the magnification for the jump to that page.

You can set destinations for a URL. These are the links that are used to open Web pages.

To create a URL destination:

1. Choose New Hyperlink Destination in the Hyperlinks panel menu to open the New Hyperlink Destination dialog box.

2. Choose URL from the Type menu .

3. Enter a name for the destination.

4. Enter the URL information.

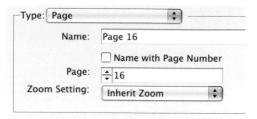

A The New Hyperlink Destination dialog box set for a **Page destination**.

B The New Hyperlink Destination dialog box set for a **URL destination**.

Tips for Hyperlinks

Hyperlinks don't have to be ordinary text or plain frames. You can use placed images, text inside tables, or even inline graphics as the source objects for hyperlinks.

If you use text as the source object for a hyperlink, you may not want to display the clunky rectangle as the link indicator. Instead, consider using an underline with colored text (applied as a character style) to indicate where the hyperlink is located. This changes the link so it is more similar to links in Web pages.

Go to source	Go to destination		New hyperlink	Delete hyperlink

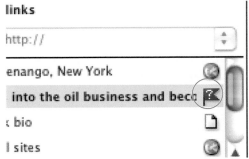

C The **Hyperlinks panel** contains controls for working with hyperlinks.

links

http://

enango, New York

into the oil business and beco

bio

sites

D The **missing destination icon** indicates that the hyperlink needs to be fixed.

Testing Hyperlinks

You can use the SWF Preview panel to test your hyperlinks without having to export the file. This option allows you to see the pointing finger as well as move to the destination.

As you work, you can edit the settings for the hyperlink source.

To edit hyperlinks:

1. Double-click the hyperlink entry in the Hyperlinks panel or choose Hyperlink Options in the Hyperlinks panel menu.

2. Make changes in the Hyperlink Options dialog box.

To delete a hyperlink:

1. Select the hyperlink you wish to delete.

2. Click the Delete icon in the Hyperlinks panel **C** or choose Delete Hyperlink/ Cross-Reference from the Hyperlinks panel menu.

To move to a hyperlink:

1. Select the hyperlink in the Hyperlinks panel.

2. Choose Go to Source from the Hyperlinks panel menu or click the Go to Source icon in the Hyperlinks panel **C**.

To move to a hyperlink destination:

1. Select the hyperlink in the Hyperlinks panel.

2. Choose Go to Destination from the Hyperlinks panel menu or click the Go to Destination icon in the Hyperlinks panel **C**.

TIP If the destination is a URL, the default Web browser will be launched.

To fix a missing hyperlink:

1. Select the hyperlink that displays the missing destination icon **D**.

2. Double-click the hyperlink to open the Edit Hyperlink dialog box.

3. Set the new destination for the hyperlink.

Creating Cross-References

Cross-references are a subset of hyperlinks and are found at the bottom of the Hyperlinks panel. Like hyperlinks, cross-references create an electronic link from one part of a document to a destination in the same or different document. But cross-references go further than hyperlinks in that they also insert a reference to the page number or text. So you can automatically create a cross-reference on one page that says, "for more information see page ###."

To define a cross-reference:

1. Place your insertion point in the text where you want the cross-reference to appear.

2. Click the Create New Cross-Reference icon A in the Hyperlinks panel. This opens the New Cross-Reference dialog box B.

3. Choose one of the following from the Link To menu:

   • **Text Anchor** sets the controls to a previously defined text anchor.

   • **Paragraph** sets the controls to text defined with a paragraph style.

4. Set the Text Anchor controls or set the Paragraph controls.

5. Use the Cross-Reference Format menu to control what text is placed inside the cross-reference.

6. Set the Appearance controls for the cross-reference.

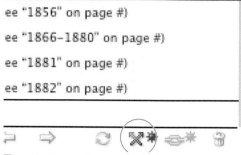

A   The **Create New Cross-Reference icon** in the Hyperlinks panel.

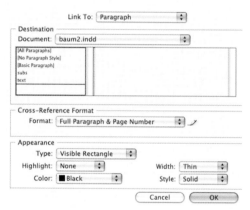

B   The **New Cross-Reference dialog box**.

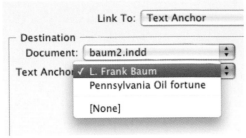

C The New Cross-Reference dialog box **set to link to a text anchor.**

Paragraph styles list   Text display

D The New Cross-Reference dialog box **set to link to paragraph styles.**

To set a text anchor as a cross-reference:

1. With the New Cross-Reference dialog box open, use the Link To menu to choose Text Anchor C.

2. Use the Document menu to choose the current document.

   or

   Choose the Browse command at the bottom of the Document menu to choose a different document.

3. Use the Text Anchor menu to choose a previously defined text anchor.

To set a paragraph style as a cross-reference:

1. With the New Cross-Reference dialog box open, use the Link To menu to choose Paragraph.

2. Use the Document menu to choose the current document.

   or

   Use the Browse command to choose a different document.

3. Click one of the paragraph styles from the paragraph options D.

4. Choose one of the paragraphs shown in the text display.

A cross-reference can be formatted to include the paragraph text, a page number, a file name, and other aspects of the text. You use the Cross-Reference Formats.

To set the cross-reference text:

Choose one of the pre-made Cross-Reference Formats from the Format menu .

TIP InDesign ships with these pre-made cross-reference formats already installed. So, for example, the format labeled "Page Number" will insert the cross-reference text "page #" into the text.

Cross-references are a type of hyperlink. So just like you can style hyperlinks, you can also format the appearances of cross-references.

To set the appearance of a cross-reference:

1. Use the Type menu in the Appearance area to choose a setting for the visibility of the rectangle around the hotspot 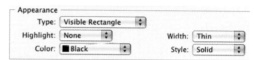.

2. Use the Highlight menu to choose the appearance of the hotspot area when clicked.

3. Use the Width menu to choose the thickness of the visible rectangle.

4. Use the Style menu to choose a solid or dashed line for the visible rectangle.

5. Use the Color menu to choose a color for the rectangle.

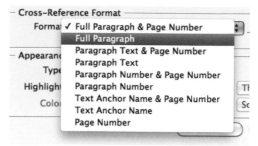

A The **Cross-Reference Format menu** lets you choose the pre-made building blocks that insert the text in a cross-reference.

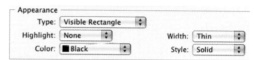

B The **Appearance controls** for styling cross-references.

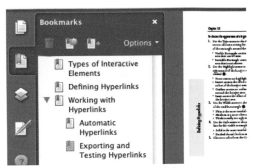

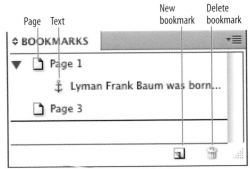

The **Bookmarks pane** in Adobe Reader or Acrobat displays the bookmarks created in InDesign.

New bookmark   Delete bookmark

Page   Text

The **Bookmarks panel** holds the bookmarks created for the document.

Working with Bookmarks

Bookmarks provide a different way to navigate within a document. Instead of elements on the page, bookmarks are displayed in the Acrobat or Reader Bookmarks pane **C**. The reader clicks each bookmark to move to that position in the document. One of the advantages to using bookmarks is that the Bookmarks pane can be always visible next to the area being read.

To create a bookmark:

1. Choose **Window** > **Interactive** > **Bookmarks** to open the Bookmarks panel **D**.

2. Do one of the following to create the destination for the bookmark:

   - Place the insertion point within the text. This creates a text bookmark.

   - Select the text. This creates a text bookmark named with the selected text.

   - Select a frame or graphic. This creates a page bookmark.

   - Double-click a page in the Pages panel. This creates a page bookmark.

3. Click the New Bookmark icon in the Bookmarks panel.

   or

   Choose New Bookmark from the Bookmarks panel menu. The bookmark is added to the Bookmarks panel.

   TIP Icons show the difference between text and page bookmarks, although there are no such differences in Acrobat.

   TIP If you already have bookmarks in the Bookmarks panel, the new bookmark is created directly under whichever bookmark is selected in the panel.

New bookmarks are created with the name *Bookmark 1*, *Bookmark 2*, and so on. You can rename the bookmark with a more descriptive name to help readers know what is located there.

To rename a bookmark:

1. Select the bookmark in the Bookmarks panel.

2. Choose Rename Bookmark from the Bookmarks panel menu. This opens the Rename Bookmark dialog box .

3. Enter a new name in the field and click OK.

You can also rename a bookmark directly in the list area of the Bookmarks panel.

To rename a bookmark in the list area:

1. Click once to select the bookmark in the Bookmarks panel.

2. Click again to open the field that contains the bookmark name **B**.

3. Type the new name.

4. Press Return/Enter or click a different bookmark to apply the new name.

You can also delete bookmarks you no longer want in the document.

To delete a bookmark:

1. Select the bookmark in the Bookmarks panel.

2. Choose Delete Bookmark from the Bookmarks panel menu.

   or

   Click the Delete Bookmark icon in the Bookmarks panel.

A Use the **Rename Bookmark dialog box** to change the bookmark names.

B Click the bookmark name to type a new name directly in the Bookmarks panel.

Loads of Bookmarks?

What if you want to quickly make lots of bookmarks? Rather than doing it manually, you can cheat by creating a table of contents using InDesign's Table of Contents command. As you create the TOC, InDesign can automatically create bookmarks for all the elements in the TOC.

While you do need to keep the TOC in the document in order to export the bookmarks into a PDF, the TOC doesn't have to stay visible. Put the TOC on a non-printing layer to keep the bookmarks in the exported PDF.

BUTTONS ‖ BOOKMARKS

- 📄 Chapter Two
- 📄 Chapter Three
- 📄 Chapter Four
- 📄 Chapter Five
- 📄 Chapter Six
- 📄 Chapter Seven
- ⚓ The Great Whirlpool
- ⚓ The Ork   ⟨ʔ⟩
- ⚓ The Cavern Under the Sea

C Drag a bookmark **between two bookmarks** to put it in a new position in the panel.

BUTTONS ‖ BOOKMARKS

- ▶ 📄 Chapter One
- 📄 Chapter Two
- 📄 Chapter Three
- 📄 Chapter Four
- 📄 Chapter Five
- 📄 Chapter Six
- 📄 Chapter Seven
- ⚓ The Cavern Under the Sea

D Drag the bookmark **onto the name** to nest it under another bookmark.

Bookmarks don't have to appear in the order that you create them. You can move important bookmarks up to the top of the list, even if they refer to pages that are at the end of your document.

To move bookmarks to new positions:

1. Drag the bookmark up or down the list to the new position.

2. When you see a black line appear, release the mouse button. The bookmark moves to the new position **C**.

TIP Use the Sort Bookmarks command in the Bookmarks panel menu to rearrange the bookmarks into the order they occur in the document.

You can also *nest*, or move bookmarks so they are contained within others. The top bookmark is called the *parent*; the nested bookmark is called the *child*.

To nest bookmarks:

1. Drag the bookmark you want to nest onto the name of the parent bookmark.

2. When the name is highlighted, release the mouse button **D**. The child bookmark is indented under the parent. A triangle controller appears that lets you open or close the parent bookmark.

TIP When you delete a bookmark, you also delete any bookmarks that are nested within that bookmark.

TIP You can continue to nest bookmarks through as many levels as you want.

To unnest bookmarks:

1. Drag the child bookmark out from the parent so that the black line is no longer indented below the parent bookmark **D**.

2. Release the mouse button. The child bookmark is no longer nested.

Adding Sounds

Despite the mind-bending concept of adding sound to a page layout, it's actually very simple to add sounds to an InDesign document. My favorite use for sounds is to add click effects that play when a button is pushed. I also might add short bits of music that play when a document is first opened.

If you know how to place an image into InDesign, you already know how to place a sound in a document.

To add a sound to a document:

1. Choose **File** > **Place**, and then choose the sound file you want to import. The cursor changes into the Sound Clip cursor A.

    TIP You can also click the Place a Video or Audio File button at the bottom of the Media panel to place a sound file.

2. Click or drag the Sound Clip cursor to add the sound clip to the document.

    TIP The sound clip contains a special icon within its frame that identifies it as a sound item B. This icon and stripes within the frame take their color from the layers panel they are on.

The **Sound Clip cursor** indicates the loaded cursor contains a sound clip.

The **sound icon inside a frame** indicates the frame contains a sound.

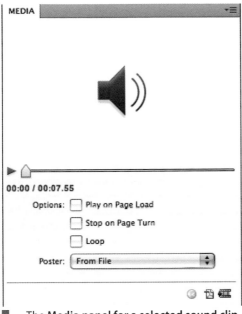

c The **Media panel for a selected sound clip**.

Once you have the sound on the page, you use the Media panel to modify and set the options for how the sound plays.

To open the Media panel:

Choose **Window > Interactive > Media**. The Media panel appears **c**.

TIP The Media panel controls are unavailable until a media file is selected.

To set the sound options:

1. Select Play on Page Load to have the sound automatically play when the page is visible.

2. Select Stop on Page Turn to have the sound automatically stop when the page is no longer visible.

3. Select Loop to have the sound repeat until manually stopped.

TIP Without this option selected, the sound will continue until it finishes its run time.

The Media panel also lets you play the sound from start to finish or select specific portions of the sound.

To play a sound using the Media panel:

1. Select the sound. The media panel shows the controls and poster image for the sound .

2. Click the Play button to hear the sound. The play head moves along the sound play line to show how far into the sound length the sound has played.

3. As the sound plays, the Play button is replaced by a Stop button. Click the Stop button to stop the playback.

TIP The two time indicators show how far along the playback is and the total length of time that the sound plays.

TIP You can also use the SWF Preview panel to hear sounds.

If a sound file is going to be used in a PDF document, there are some additional controls you can set.

To set the PDF sound options:

1. Click the Export Interactive PDF icon on the Media panel or choose PDF Options from the Media panel menu. This opens the PDF Options dialog box 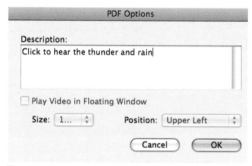.

2. Enter the text that will be used as a tool tip for the sound clip. This lets sight-impaired users hear a description of what the sound contains so they can choose to activate the sound.

TIP The rest of the options are for video files and are not available for sound clips.

Play/Pause   Play head

A Use the **Media panel** to listen to a sound and control how it plays in the exported document.

B The **PDF Options dialog box** for items that are exported to interactive PDF files.

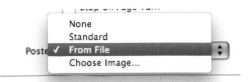

C The **Poster options menu** for a placed sound clip.

D A sound with **no poster image**.

E The **standard sound poster image**.

F A sound with a **custom poster image**.

When a sound is included on a page, it acts like a button that can play the sound when clicked. Therefore you might want to include a *poster*, or visual indicator, that lets people know that there is a sound on the page.

To set the sound poster:

Use the Poster menu to choose an image that will be used to show where the sound is in the document **C**:

- **None** leaves the sound clip frame empty **D**.
- **Standard** uses the standard sound poster image **E**.
- **From File/Choose Image** lets you import a custom image to use as the sound poster **F**. Use the Choose button to choose the custom image.

TIP The standard sound icon is actually the image *StandardSoundPoster* stored in the Presets > Multimedia folder in the InDesign application folder. You can open this file and make changes to it. This will then become your standard sound file poster.

Movies and Animations

One of the more exciting multimedia features is the ability to add movies to your electronic documents.

To add a video to a document:

1. Choose **File > Place** and then choose the movie file you want to import. The cursor changes into the Video Clip cursor .

2. Click or drag to place the video on the document. This adds a video object to the document. Video objects are identified by the Video Clip icon .

TIP You can also click the Place a Video or Audio File button at the bottom of the Media panel to place a video file.

Once you have the video on the page, you use the Media panel to modify and set the options for how the video plays.

To open the Media panel:

Choose **Window > Interactive > Media**. The Media panel appears 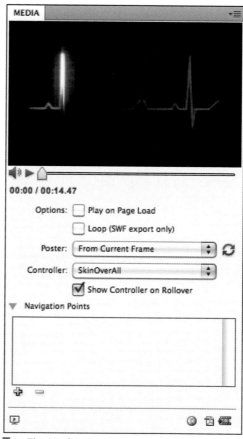.

TIP The Media panel controls are unavailable until a media file is selected.

To set the video options in the Media panel:

1. Select Play on Page Load to have the video automatically play when the page is visible.

2. Select Loop (SWF export only) to have the video repeat until manually stopped. This option will not apply if the file is exported as a PDF.

TIP If you need a video to loop, but are exporting as a PDF, you can apply a loop setting in the program, such as Adobe Premiere, that creates the video.

The loaded cursor for **video clips**.

The **Video Clip icon** inside a frame.

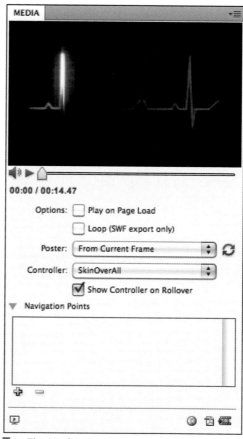

The **Media panel controls** for a selected video.

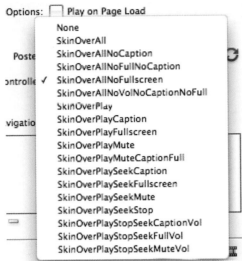

D The **standard movie poster image**.

E Use the **Controller menu** to choose which controller features you want for a movie.

F The **SkinOverAll controller** contains all the controller features for placed movies.

Like sound files you can set poster options for movies. However, since they are movies, they have more options than sounds.

To set the movie poster options:

1. Use the Poster menu to choose an image that will be used to show where the movie is in the document **D**:

   - **None** leaves the frame empty.

   - **Standard** uses the standard video file icon.

   - **From Current Frame** uses the frame currently displayed in the Media Panel.

   - **Choose Image** lets you import a custom image to use as the movie poster.

2. Use the Controller menu to apply a controller that can be used to control the playback of the movie as well as play it in full screen and show captions **E**.

TIP The name of each controller explains which features it has. For instance, SkinOverAll contains all the features **F**. SkinOverPlay contains only the Play button.

3. Select Show Controller on Rollover to have the controller appear and disappear when the mouse moves inside and outside the area of the video.

TIP When Show Controller on Rollover is not selected, the controller appears throughout the video playback.

The Media panel also lets you play a movie from start to finish or move to specific portions of the movie 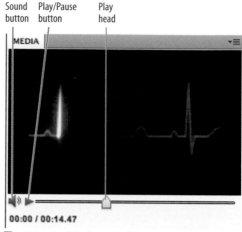.

To play a movie using the Media panel:

1. Click the Play button to play the movie within the preview area of the Media panel **A**.

2. As the movie plays, the Play button is replaced by a Pause button. Click the Pause button to stop the playback.

3. Click the Sound button to mute the sound during the playback **A**.

TIP The two time indicators show how far along the playback is and the total length of time that the movie plays.

If a movie file is going to be used in a PDF document, there are some additional controls you can set.

To set the options for a video in a PDF document:

1. Click the Export Interactive PDF icon on the Media panel **B** or choose PDF Options from the Media panel menu. This opens the PDF Options dialog box **C**.

2. In the Description field, enter the text that will be used as a tool tip for the video clip. This lets sight-impaired users hear a description of what the video contains.

3. Click Play Video in Floating Window to have the video display in a separate window above the PDF file.

4. If you have the video play in a floating window, you can set a size for the display. Use the Size list to choose a size for the video.

Sound button Play/Pause button Play head

A Use the **Media panel video controls** to control the playback of a movie file.

B The **Export Interactive PDF icon** in the Media panel.

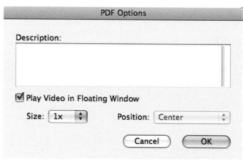

C The additional **PDF Options dialog box** for videos to be played in PDF files.

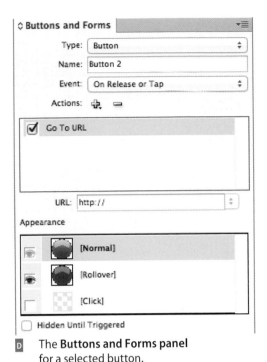

The **Buttons and Forms panel** for a selected button.

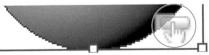

The **Convert Object to Button** icon at the bottom of the Buttons and Forms panel.

The **Button icon** appears inside an object that has been converted into a button.

The **Convert Button to Object** icon at the bottom of the Buttons and Forms panel.

Creating Buttons

Buttons are more powerful than simple hyperlinks. Buttons contain the code that can send you to destinations, flip pages, open Web pages, play movies, show and hide other buttons, and other tricks.

You use the Buttons and Forms panel to create and apply actions to Buttons.

To view the Buttons and Forms panel:

Choose **Window > Interactive > Buttons and Forms** to open the Buttons and Forms panel D.

To create and name a button:

1. Select an object. Any object, except media files, can be used as a button.

2. Choose **Object > Interactive > Convert to Button** or click the Convert Object to Button icon in the Buttons and Forms panel E. The object displays the button icon F.

3. Use the Name field in the Buttons and Forms panel to change the default name to something more descriptive.

TIP I usually name my buttons with their function. So, for example, buttons that move to the previous page and the next page are labeled *Previous Page* and *Next Page*.

TIP When a button is selected, the Buttons and Forms panel displays all the interactive options for the button.

If you need to, you can remove the button properties from an object.

To remove the button properties:

1. Select the button object.

2. Choose **Object > Interactive > Convert to Object** or click the Convert Button to Object icon in the Buttons and Forms panel G.

A button without an action is like a light switch that's not connected to a lamp. You can click the button all you want, but nothing's going to happen. There are two parts to setting actions. First you choose the type of event that will prompt the action.

To choose the event for a button action:

Use the Event menu to choose what type of mouse or keyboard action should prompt the button to perform the action .

- **On Release or Tap** applies an action under two circumstances: when the mouse button is released after a click or when a tablet screen is tapped.

- **On Click** applies an action as the mouse button is pressed down.

- **On Roll Over** applies an action when the mouse cursor is moved over the button's bounding box.

- **On Roll Off** applies an action when the mouse cursor is moved away from the button's bounding box.

- **On Focus (PDF)** applies an action when the button is prompted by the Tab key. This event only works for buttons in PDF documents.

- **On Blur (PDF)** applies an action when the Tab key takes the focus off the button. This event only works for buttons in PDF documents.

TIP You can set multiple events for a button. For example, a button can play a sound when the mouse rolls over the button but open a Web page when the same button is clicked.

A Use **the Event list** to choose which mouse actions will prompt a button action.

A Button Trick

My favorite use for buttons is to use the On Roll Over and On Roll Off events to show and hide other buttons.

Usually I set the button to show the image on roll over and then hide it on roll off. Or I show the image on the mouse click and hide it on the mouse release.

Add new action   Delete action

Event: On Release or Tap

Actions:

☑ Show/Hide Buttons and Forms

Visibility: ⊗ R15
            ⊗ Button 2

B The **Actions area** displays the actions for each mouse event.

Go To Destination
Go To First Page
Go To Last Page
Go To Next Page
Go To Previous Page
Go To URL
Show/Hide Buttons and Forms
Sound
Video
HTML5 and SWF Only
Animation
Go To Page
Go To State
Go To Next State
Go To Previous State
PDF Only
Clear Form
Go To Next View
Go To Previous View

C The **Actions menu** in the Buttons and Forms panel.

Once you have chosen the mouse event, you then choose the action that follows the event.

To choose the action for a button event:

1. Click the Add New Action icon from the Actions area of the Buttons and Forms panel **B**. This displays the Actions menu **C**.

2. Choose the action that you want to apply. The action appears in the Actions area of the Buttons and Forms panel.

3. Depending on the action, additional controls may appear in the Buttons and Forms panel. Set those controls as necessary.

4. If desired, you can apply more actions to the button by repeating steps 1–3.

To delete the action for a button event:

1. Select the action in the Actions area.

2. Click the Delete Action icon.

TIP Instead of deleting an action, you can disable it by clicking its check mark. This keeps the action available, but it does not export with the button.

If you have multiple actions for an event, the actions are applied in the order that they appear in the list. You can change this order of how the actions are applied.

To change the position of an action:

Drag the action up or down in the Actions list.

TIP The order that the actions appear can be important when playing sounds and movies. For instance, you might want the action for a click sound to play before the action to play a movie.

One of the benefits to working with buttons is the ability to change the appearance so that the button itself responds to the actions of the user. When you create a button, it only has one appearance called the Normal state. You need to create new appearances for the Rollover and Click button states.

To set the appearances of a button:

1. Select the button. Unless you have already modified it, only the [Normal] state is active in the Buttons and Forms panel .

TIP The [Normal] state displays the appearance of the button when the mouse is not near it.

2. Click the [Rollover] state listing in the Buttons and Forms panel. This activates the state.

TIP The Rollover state displays the appearance of the button when the mouse cursor enters the button area.

3. Click the [Click] state listing in the Buttons and Forms panel. This activates the state.

TIP The [Click] state displays the appearance of the button when the mouse presses down on the button.

To make changes to each appearance state:

1. Select the button you want to modify.

2. In the Buttons and Forms panel, select the state that you want to modify.

3. Use any of InDesign's styling features to add a fill, stroke, or effect to the object. Use the Type tool to insert text as a label. You can also insert different images for each state.

To delete button states:

1. Select the state you want to delete.

2. Click the Delete State icon .

TIP You cannot delete the [Normal] state.

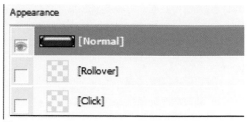

A The **States** in the Buttons and Forms panel.

B The **Delete State icon** in the Buttons and Forms panel.

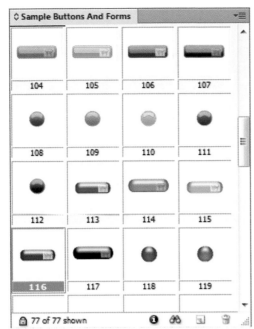

104 105 106 107

108 109 110 111

112 113 114 115

116 117 118 119

🔒 77 of 77 shown

C A portion of the **sample buttons** in the Sample Buttons And Forms library.

Instead of deleting states, which tosses out their content, it may be better to change whether or not the state is exported.

To change the visibility of a state:

Click the eyeball next to the name of the state. If the eyeball is visible, it means the state is enabled and will export. If the eyeball is not visible, it means the state is disabled and will not export.

Sample Buttons

In addition to creating your own buttons, Adobe has generously provided a library of pre-made buttons that already have rollover states as well as actions to go to pages and Web addresses.

TIP The Sample Buttons And Forms library also contains forms objects which can be used to create interactive PDF forms. *(See "Creating PDF Forms" on page 428.)*

To access the Sample Buttons And Forms library:

Choose Sample Buttons And Forms from the Buttons and Forms panel menu. The library appears **C**.

Once you have the sample buttons visible, you can easily add buttons to a document.

To place buttons from the Sample Buttons And Forms library:

Drag the buttons onto your document page. Or, select the buttons in the library and choose Place Item(s) from the panel menu.

TIP The sample buttons can be customized with new states, actions, and events like any other button.

Creating PDF Forms

Most likely you've gotten a PDF where you click inside the areas of the form and fill it out with the information requested. InDesign lets you add form fields to your documents so you can create these interactive PDF files without having to open Acrobat.

You use the Buttons and Forms panel to create forms.

To view the Buttons and Forms panel:

Choose **Window > Interactive > Buttons and Forms** to open the Buttons and Forms panel.

To create and name a form:

1. Select an object. Any object, except media files, can be used as a form.

2. Choose **Object > Interactive > Convert to [form name]** or choose one of the types of forms from the Type menu in the Buttons and Forms panel 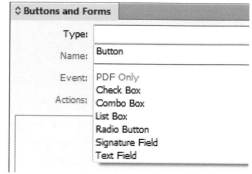. The form icon appears in the object.

TIP The form icons change depending on the type of form chosen.

3. Use the Name field in the Buttons and Forms panel to change the default name to something more descriptive.

4. Leave the Event menu as On Release or Tap.

5. Use the Action controls to apply actions as described on page 425.

6. If you have chosen a check box or radio button, style the Appearance states as described on page 426.

7. Fill in the PDF options  as described in the next exercise.

A The **Type field for forms** in the Buttons and Forms panel.

B The **PDF Options** for form objects. Not all forms contain all these PDF options.

Description:

Enter your name

C The **Description field** is used to enter a tool-tip of the field for sight-impaired users.

List Items: Tin Man

Good Witch

Scarecrow

Font Size: 12

D The List Items area displays items that will be used in List Box and Combo Box menus.

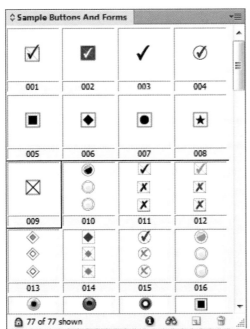

Sample Buttons And Forms

001 002 003 004
005 006 007 008
009 010 011 012
013 014 015 016

🔒 77 of 77 shown

E A portion of the **sample forms** in the Sample Buttons And Forms library.

To set the options for a PDF form:

1. Fill in the Description field with the text that will be used as a tool tip for the form field **C**. This lets sight-impaired users hear a description of what the form field does.

2. Check the options as follows:

   - **Printable** allows the field to be printed.

   - **Required** means the form can not be submitted unless that field is filled.

   - **Password** hides the field's content as a series of asterisks.

   - **Read Only** prevents the contents of the field from being modified.

   - **Multiline** allows text to wrap to multiple lines.

   - **Scrollable** applies scroll bars if the contents exceed the depth of the field.

   - **Selected by default** applies the selection when the form is first opened.

   - **Sort Items** arranges the list items alphabetically or numerically.

TIP Some forms contain different options than others.

3. If you have chosen List Box or Combo Box, use the List Items controls to select the menu items for the form **D**.

4. If you have chosen List Box or Combo Box, set the Font Size for the menu items.

Sample Forms

Like the sample buttons, you can use the Sample Buttons And Forms library to drag out pre-made forms **E**. See page 427 for how to access the library for the sample forms.

TIP The sample forms consist primarily of radio buttons and check boxes with one set of combo boxes for the numbers 1–12 and 1 31.

Animating InDesign Objects

Instead of having to go to Flash or some other animation program, I can animate the items on the InDesign page and export the result as a SWF video. This section will show you the controls that let you create this type of animation.

The primary controls for working with animated objects require the use of the Animation panel.

To open the Animation panel:

Choose **Window** > **Interactive** > **Animation**. The Animation panel appears 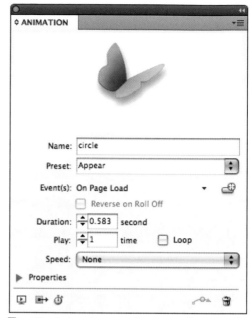.

To add animation to an object:

1. With the object selected, choose one of the motion presets from the Preset list **B**. This applies an animation to the object as indicated by the Animation icon.

TIP The butterfly image in the Animation panel displays a preview of the action of the animation.

2. If desired, use the Name field to change the generic name of the object into something more descriptive. This is especially helpful if you have many animated objects on the spread.

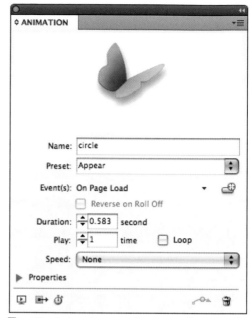

A **The Animation panel** contains the controls for applying motion to objects on a page.

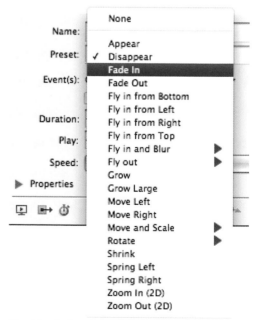

B **The Animation Preset menu** contains the preset motions and effects you can apply to objects.

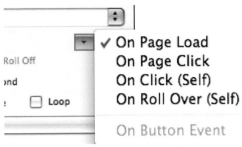

C Use the Event(s) menu to set what **mouse or page actions trigger the animation**.

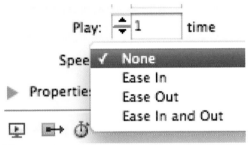

D Use the Speed menu to set choose **how the motion accelerates or decelerates**.

To set the events that prompt the animation:

Use the Event(s) list to choose what mouse or page actions trigger the animation **C**:

- **On Page Load** starts the animation when the page is visible.
- **On Page Click** starts the animation when the mouse clicks anywhere on the page.
- **On Click (Self)** starts the animation when the object is clicked.
- **On Roll Over (Self)** starts the animation when the mouse moves over the area of the object.

TIP If you choose On Roll Over (Self), you can select Reverse on Roll Off to play the animation backwards when the mouse moves away from the object.

TIP The menu item for On Button Event is applied by using the Create Button Trigger icon or by setting a button action in the Buttons panel.

To set the timing and speed settings:

1. Use the Duration field to choose for how long (in seconds) the animation plays.

2. Use the Play field to choose how many times the animation repeats. Select Loop to have the animation repeat endlessly.

3. Use the Speed list to choose how the motion accelerates or decelerates **D**.

   - **None** keeps a constant speed throughout the animation.
   - **Ease In** starts slowly and speeds up.
   - **Ease Out** starts at a constant speed and slows down at the end.
   - **Ease In and Out** starts slowly, remains constant for a while, and then slows down.

The InDesign team figured (rightly) that people would want to quickly make buttons that can play animated objects.

To create a button to control an animated object:

1. Select the animated object.

2. Click the Create button trigger icon in the Animation panel .

3. Click the object that you want to act as a button to play the animation. The object is converted into a button (if necessary) and the controls to play the animation are applied.

TIP You can then make any modifications to the button in the Buttons panel.

If you no longer want an object to be animated, you can convert it back into an ordinary object.

To remove the animation applied to an object:

1. Select the animated object.

2. Click the Remove Animation icon in the Animation panel B.

A Use the **Create Button Trigger icon** to quickly set a button to prompt an animated object.

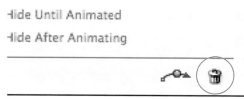

B Click the **Remove animation icon** to delete any animations applied to an object.

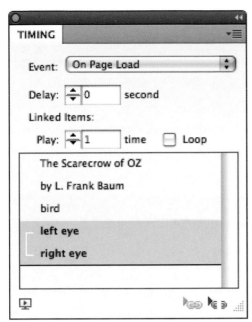

C The **Timing panel** contains the timing controls for all the animations on a spread.

Timing

Just as in comedy, when working with animation timing is everything. So in addition to the duration controls in the Animation panel, the Timing panel gives you additional control over how an animation plays. There are two main features for what the Timing panel does. The first allows you to set a delay for when animated objects start their animation.

To set the delay for animated objects:

1. Open the Timing panel (**Window > Interactive > Timing**). All the animated objects for that spread are listed in the Timing panel area **C**.

TIP You don't add items to the Timing panel. They appear automatically when you create animated objects.

2. In the Timing panel, not on the page itself, click the name of the object you want to control.

3. If you have applied an event to control the animated object, use the Event list to choose the event that triggers the object.

4. Use the Delay field to set the amount (in seconds) that the object's animation will be delayed.

The Timing panel also lets you control the order that objects are animated.

To change the order that objects are animated:

Drag the name of the object up or down in the list in the Timing panel. Objects are played from the top of the list down.

Each object in the Timing panel plays individually. However, you can link objects so they play at the same time.

To set objects to animate together:

1. Select the names of the objects in the Timing panel.

2. Click the Play Together icon in the Timing panel. A bracket appears around the selected items indicating they will play together.

3. If you have items linked to play together, you can use the Play field and Loop control to control how many times they play.

TIP Click the Play Separately icon to release the items from playing together.

Timing Is Everything!

Even the slightest change in timing can make an enormous difference in the effectiveness of an animation. While I can't anticipate every timing situation, here are some general rules I try to follow.

Take a moment. When items are set to play on the loading of a page, you may want to set a slight delay before they play. This gives your viewers a moment to get accustomed to the setting.

Keep the pacing up. Nothing is more boring than elements that move too slowly on the page. This means that the speed of the animation as set in the Animation panel as well as the Timing panel should be short. Your audience can anticipate where an object is moving. So don't bore them by making them watch it happen.

Don't loop unless you mean it. Setting something to endlessly play on a page is distracting. But that doesn't mean you can't loop objects such as wheels on a car that moves across a page. The wheels should loop in that situation.

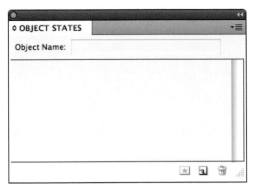

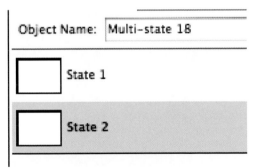

A The **Object States panel** with no states visible.

B The **New State button** in the Object States panel.

C The **Object States panel with two states** applied to an object.

Multi-State Objects

Instead of cluttering up my bookshelf with hundreds of pictures of my family, friends, and pets, I have an electronic screen that displays all my pictures in a single picture frame. That's what a multi-state object is like. A regular InDesign frame displays only a single image or text content. But multi-state objects are special frames that can display more than one image or text content. You can then cycle through the multi-state object in a presentation to show many different items.

TIP Multi-state objects don't work when exported to PDF documents.

To create a multi-state object:

1. Choose **Window > Interactive > Object States**. This opens the Object States panel **A**.

2. Select the object that you want to convert into a multi-state object.

3. Click the New State button **B**. This adds a multi-state name to the object and adds a second state to the object.

TIP Multi-state objects are identified by the Multi-state Object icon.

To change the name of the multi-state object:

1. Double-click the name in the Object Name field.

2. Type a new name.

3. Press Return to apply the new name.

To add states to a multi-state object:

1. Click the New State button.

2. Repeat to add as many new states as you want **C**.

Adding and modifying multi-states one at a time takes too much time. What you want to do is select a whole bunch of objects and convert them into a multi-state object.

To create a multi-state object from existing frames:

1. Select all the objects that you want to use in the multi-state object 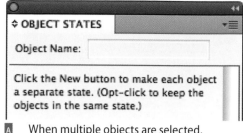.

2. Click the New State button in the Object States panel. This converts each object into a new state within a multi-state object.

TIP Hold the Opt/Alt key to convert all the objects into a single state of the multi-state object.

TIP The objects appear in the multi-states in the same stacking order that they were on the page.

Once you have a multi-state object, you can modify the object as a whole or change the contents of a particular state.

To modify the content of a state:

1. Select the multi-state object with the Selection tool.

2. Double-click the name of the state that you want to modify. This selects the state.

3. Switch to the Direct Selection tool. The icon changes to indicate the content of the state has been selected 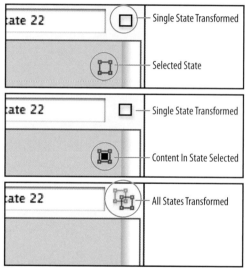.

4. Make whatever changes you want to the content of the multi-state.

TIP Click with the Direct Selection tool to select the last active state in the object in the content mode.

5. Click the Paste Copied Content icon in the Object States panel . The pasted content is added to the state.

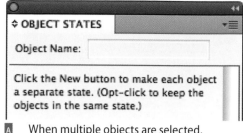

A When multiple objects are selected, you can create **multiple states in the Object States panel**.

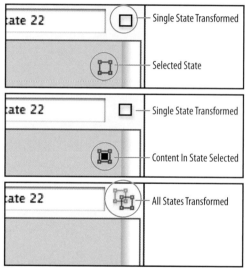

B The **icons that show the status of the multi-states** of a multi-state object.

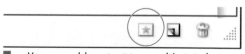

C You can add content to a multi-state by using the **Paste Copied Content icon**.

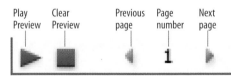

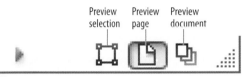

D The **Preview panel** lets you see and interact with the elements in the document.

E The **preview selections controls** of the SWF Preview panel.

F The **play controls** of the SWF Preview panel.

Working with the SWF Preview Controls

Interactive elements don't react on the InDesign page. Fortunately, you can preview if your elements are set correctly.

TIP The previews of the interactive documents are for SWF output. If you want to see the PDF attributes, you need to view the PDF in Acrobat.

To use the SWF Preview panel:

1. Choose **Window > Interactive > SWF Preview**. This opens the SWF Preview panel **D**.

2. Choose one of the preview selection mode buttons **E**:
   - **Preview Selection** sets the Preview panel to display just the selected object. Use this when you have many interactive elements on a page and need to test just one or two elements.
   - **Preview Page** sets the Preview panel to display the spread currently selected.
   - **Preview Document** sets the Preview panel to display the entire document.

3. Click the Play Preview button **F**.

4. If you edit the document, use the Clear Preview button to delete the previous version of the document from the Preview panel.

5. Use the Next Page and Previous Page buttons to move through the document.

6. Move your mouse over the preview area of the Preview panel. Interactive elements react with the mouse cursor as they would in the exported SWF.

TIP Drag the corners or edges of the Preview panel to increase the size of the preview area in the panel. This makes it *much* easier to control small interactive items.

Setting Page Transitions

Transitions are the effects that are applied when the viewer moves from one page to another when viewing the document in Acrobat or the Flash Player.

To set the transitions using the Page Transitions panel:

1. Select the pages in the Pages panel to which you want to apply a transition.

2. Choose **Window** > **Interactive** > **Page Transitions**. This opens the Page Transitions panel 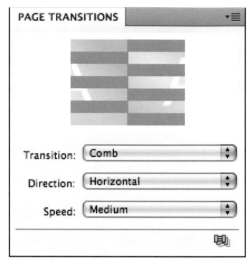.

3. Choose one of the transitions from the Transition menu **B**.

4. If applicable, set the Direction **C** and Speed **D** for the transition.

TIP Click the Apply to All Spreads icon **E** or choose Apply to All Spreads from the panel menu to apply the transition to all the spreads in the document.

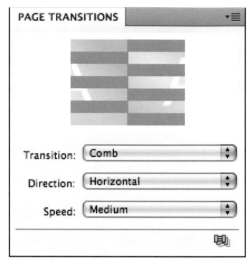

A The **Page Transitions panel** displays the preview of each page transition.

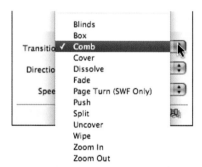

B Choose a transition from the **Transition menu** in the Page Transitions panel.

C If needed, use the **Direction list** to apply the direction to a page transition.

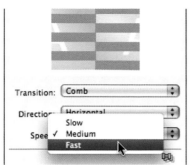

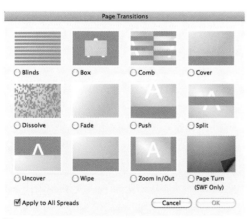

D If needed, use the **Speed list** to set the speed of a page transition.

E The **Apply to All Spreads icon** sets a page transition to all the spreads.

F The **Page Transitions dialog box** displays previews of the transition between pages and lets you assign those transitions.

To set the transitions using the Pages panel:

1. Select the pages in the Pages panel to which you want to apply a transition.

2. Choose **Page Transitions** from the Pages panel menu. The Page Transitions dialog box appears **F**.

3. Select one of the transitions.

TIP Click Apply to All Spreads to apply the transition to all the spreads in the document.

You may need to clear all the transitions applied to pages.

To clear all the page transitions:

1. Choose Clear All from the Page Transitions panel menu or **Page Transitions** > **Clear All** from the Pages panel menu.

Page Turn or Page Curl?

The Page Turn is a page transition that allows any button to trigger the effect of turning a page. The Page Turn also is applied when the arrow keys on the keyboard are invoked to move from page to page.

When you export the document as a SWF, you have the option of adding a Page Curl. The Page Curl is an interactive effect that allows the reader to move the mouse to any corner and P-U-L-L the page to the next or previous page.

Working with Layouts 18

Once you have created a basic layout, most likely you will want to create variations of that layout. For instance, you might have multiple page sizes for different versions of an ad or for designing for various tablet devices.

You might also need the same text in multiple documents—but want to edit one version and have it update in the others. This is where the linked content and layout adjustment tools come into play.

The idea behind linked content is to be able to make edits or modifications to text and images and have those changes reflected elsewhere in the document.

Layout adjustment means you can change the size and shape of a page and the elements on the page can change their shape and move into new positions.

These features are very helpful for anyone who needs several versions of a file—especially for those who are designing digital publications for different size tablets such as the iPad or Kindle Fire.

Even if you don't feel you need these features right away, you need to know that InDesign has them.

Collecting and Placing Content

Most of the time you use copy/paste to create copies of text, images, and other objects. However when you use copy/paste, the duplicated object has no link to the original object. The content tools—the Content Collector, Content Placer, and Content Conveyer—allow you to copy objects that can be linked to the original object. So when you make a change to the original, the linked object updates.

TIP You have the choice to duplicate an object with or without a link to the original source object.

To collect content:

1. Choose the Content Collector from the Tools panel **A**. The Content Collector cursor appears **B**.

TIP There are two content tools. When you select either one, the Content Conveyer appears. This shows a representation of the items that have been collected.

TIP If you want to hide the Content Conveyer but still use the Content tools, press Cmd/Ctrl-Opt/Alt-B. Press the keystroke again to reshow the Content Conveyer.

2. Click the item that you want to duplicate. The item appears in the Content Conveyer **C**.

3. Click to continue to collect other items. Each item appears in the Content Conveyer. A number appears in the Content Collector cursor indicating the number of collected items **D**.

A The **Content Collector tool** in the **Tools panel**.

B The **Content Collector cursor** indicates you can collect objects.

C The **Content Conveyer** stores the content collected by the collection tools.

D The **number in the Content Collector cursor** indicates how many objects have been collected.

The **Content Placer tool** in the Tools panel.

Content Collector   Content Placer

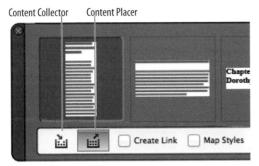

F The **Content Conveyer controls**.

Place/   Place/   Place/
Remove/   Reload/   Keep/
Load   Keep   Load

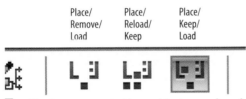

G The icons to control how objects are **placed and loaded** from the Content Conveyer.

Once you have collected content, you can place it in a different area of the page, a different page, or even a different document.

To place content:

1. Choose the Content Placer from the Tools panel **E** or the Content Conveyer **F**.

2. Move to the new area, page, or document where you want the content to be placed. A preview of the content appears in the cursor.

TIP If there is more than one item in the Content Conveyer a number appears in the preview indicating how many items are in the Conveyer.

3. Click or drag to place the text or image.

TIP Use the right or left keyboard arrow keys or the Previous/Next controls to move to different items in the Conveyer.

You can control whether items in the Content Conveyer are kept or deleted as they are placed. This is helpful for those times you want to keep the items for placement elsewhere.

To control the placement of items:

1. With at least one item in the Content Conveyer, switch to the Content Placer tool.

2. Choose one of the following from the Content Conveyer area **G**:

   • **Place/Remove/Load** places the content, removes it from the Content Conveyer, and then loads the next item.

   • **Place/Reload/Keep** places the content, keeps it in the Content Conveyer, and then reloads the item.

   • **Place/Keep/Load** places the content, keeps it in the Content Conveyer, and then loads the next item.

You can also add items to the Content Conveyer using the Load Conveyer dialog box. This gives you more options than using just the Content Collector tool.

To use the Load Conveyer command:

1. Click the Load Conveyer icon . This opens the Load Conveyer dialog box.

2. Choose one of the following 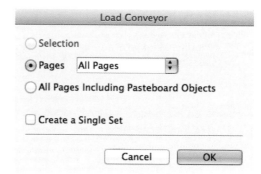:

   - **Selection** adds whatever content was selected on the page.

   - **Pages** allows you to choose a specific set of pages.

   - **All Pages Including Pasteboard Objects** adds the items from all the pages, including any items on the pasteboard.

3. Check Create a Single Set to load all the items as a single group instead of individual items.

To quickly place linked content:

1. Select the item.

2. Choose **Edit > Place and Link**. This loads the item into the Content Conveyer and switches to the Content Placer tool.

Load Conveyer

A The **Load Conveyer icon** in the Content Conveyer.

B The **Load Conveyer dialog box** lets you load items to the Content Conveyer automatically.

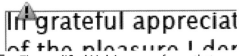

C   The **Link icon** on a frame that indicates the item is linked back to a source document.

D   The **modified Link icon** on a frame that indicates the source has been changed.

Making Changes to Linked Content

Most people only make changes to the source item and then update the linked items to reflect those changes. However, there are some times where you might edit the linked item. Watch out!

You can make whatever changes you want to the linked item. However, if you then click the yellow icon to update the linked item, the changes you made to the linked item will be discarded.

If you need to make changes to the linked content, it is better to unlink that item from the source and treat it as its own text story. See the next page for how to unlink items.

Linking Items

As you place items with the Content Collector tool, the items are added to the Content Conveyer. You can link duplicated items back to their original source object. This allows you to make edits in the source object that are applied to the duplicated object.

To link objects with the Content Placer tool:

1. With at least one item in the Content Conveyer, switch to the Content Placer tool.

2. Check Create Link option in the Content Conveyer to link the placed item to the original source item.

3. Click or drag to place the text or image. If the Create Link option is chosen, an icon appears on the frame indicating that the item is linked C.

TIP If the Create Link option is not checked, the duplicated object has no relationship to the source object.

Once you have linked content on the page, you can update the content across pages or document.

To modify linked content:

1. Select the original item.

2. Make whatever changes you want to the original item. A yellow alert icon appears on the frame of the linked item indicating that the source for that item has been modified D.

To update linked content:

Click the yellow alert icon on the linked item. This updates the item.

You can also use the Links panel to update modified links.

To use the Links panel to update links:

1. Open the Links panel (**Window > Links**). A yellow icon appears next to the items that have been modified 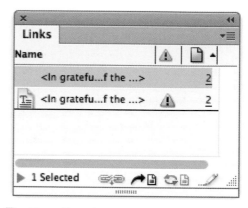.

2. Double-click the yellow icon. This updates the item.

TIP Linked items are listed twice in the Links panel. One listing controls the content of the linked item such as the text or image **B** and **C**. The second listing controls the formatting of the frame that holds the text and image.

You can also unlink an item so that it is no longer governed by the source item.

To unlink items:

1. Select the item you want to unlink.

2. Choose Unlink from the Links panel menu. The link icon disappears from the frame indicating that it is no longer linked to the source item.

A The **yellow alert icon** in the Links panel indicates that modifications have been made to the original source item.

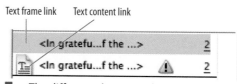

B The difference between the link for a text frame and the link for the text content.

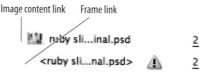

C The difference between the link for an image frame and the link for the image content.

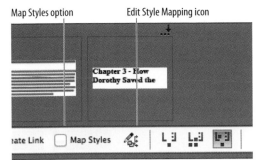

Map Styles option   Edit Style Mapping icon

Chapter 3 - How Dorothy Saved the

ate Link   ☐ Map Styles

D   The controls for **mapping styles**.

Style "body text" in first document

In grateful appreciation of the pleasure I derived from association with them, and in recognition of their sincere endeavor to uplift humanity through kindness, consideration and good-fellowship. They are big men--all of them--and all with the generous hearts of little children.

Style "body text" in second document

In grateful appreciation of the pleasure I derived from association with them, and in recognition of their sincere endeavor to uplift humanity through kindness, consideration and good-fellowship. They are big men--all of them--and all with the generous hearts of little children.

E   An example of how **a style with the same name but two different definitions in two separate documents** is changed when the text is duplicated between the documents.

Mapping Styles

When you duplicate content from one place to another, you have a choice as to how the styles from the source are handled in the destination. This is important if the names or definitions of the styles in one document are different from the names or definitions of the styles in the other.

To map styles with the same name:

1. Use the Content Collector to select text that has character, paragraph, table, or cell styles applied.

2. Switch to the Content Placer tool and turn on the Map Styles option **D**.

TIP The Map Styles option is not available until you switch to the Content Placer tool.

3. Switch to the place where you want to duplicate the text. This document should have paragraph styles with the same name as the first document but can have different definitions for those styles.

4. Click or drag to place the styles into the new document. The text takes on the style formatting of the new document **E**.

TIP Styles with the same name are automatically mapped between documents.

TIP If you have two styles with different names, you can click the Edit Style Mapping icon to customize how styles are mapped. However, custom mapping of styles is beyond the scope of this book.

Creating Alternate Layouts

When I started with InDesign you could only have one page size for the documents. Now you can have different sized pages within one document. That feature allows you to create two different layouts for the same set of information.

To create an alternate layout:

1. Choose Create Alternate Layout from the Pages panel menu or **Layout > Create Alternate Layout**. This opens the Create Alternate Layout dialog box **A**.

2. Set the options as described in the following exercises.

To set the name and source page for the alternate layout:

1. Use the Name field to enter a name for the alternate layout.

TIP A default name is entered based on a previous layout, such as iPad V (vertical) from an iPad H (horizontal). But you can change it to reflect any device and orientation.

2. Use the From Source Pages to choose which layout you want to use as the starting point for the alternate layout. The text and images from the source pages will be duplicated on the alternate layout.

To set the page size for the alternate layout:

1. Use the Page Size menu to choose one of the preset page sizes **B**. These choices change depending on the intent that was chosen in the New Document dialog box.

2. Use the Width and Height controls to apply custom dimensions to the new layout.

3. Click the horizontal or vertical icons to flip the orientation of the alternate layout **C**.

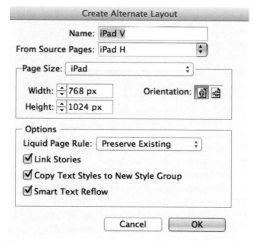

A The **Create Alternate Layout dialog box**.

B The **Page Size menu** for the Create Alternate Layout dialog box.

Vertical   Horizontal

C The **Vertical and Horizontal orientation** icons.

D The **paragraph style groups** created for alternate layouts.

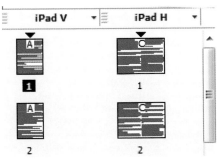

E The Pages panel set to **View Pages By Alternate Layout**.

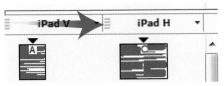

F Drag to move one layout to a different position in the Pages panel.

To set the options for the alternate layout:

1. Use the Liquid Layout Rule menu to set how the items and text will be modified to fit the alternate layout. Liquid Layout is a complex topic, so it is covered in the next section, "Applying Liquid Layout Rules."

TIP Unless you choose Use Existing, the setting in the Create Alternate Layout dialog box overrides the settings applied to the individual pages.

2. Check Link Stories to link the text from the source layout to the alternate layout.

3. Check Copy Text Styles to New Style Group to take the styles from the source document and make a duplicate of them in the Paragraph Styles panel **D**.

TIP The new style group allows you to have different style definitions depending on the page size of the alternate layout.

4. Check Smart Text Reflow to automatically add pages to the alternate layout If an overset is created.

TIP When you create an alternate layout, the Pages panel changes the display to the View Pages By Alternate Layout setting **E**.

You may want to move layouts around in the Pages panel so that similar devices or orientations are grouped together.

To rearrange layouts in the Pages panel:

Drag the gripper for one layout to move the layout from one position to another **F**.

Applying Liquid Layout Rules

When you create alternate layouts, most likely you will need to adjust the size and shape of text and image frames to fit the size of the new pages. Liquid Layout Rules are electronic settings that control how these elements change.

To set the Liquid Layout Rules:

1. Choose the Page tool from the Tools panel.

2. If it is not already selected, click the page to which you want to apply a Liquid Layout Rule.

3. Choose a Liquid Layout Rule from the Control panel 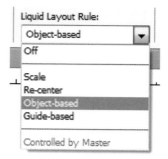. These choices are explained in the chart on the following page.

You can also use the Liquid Layout panel to set the Liquid Layout Rules.

To use the Liquid Layout panel:

1. Choose **Layout** > **Liquid Layout** to open the Liquid Layout panel **B**.

2. Choose one of the choices from the Liquid Layout Rule menu. *(See the next page for a chart of what each Liquid Layout Rule does.)*

To apply the Scale rule:

1. Choose Scale from the Liquid Layout Rule menu. There are no additional settings.

2. Create the alternate layout. Objects are scaled to fit the new layout.

To apply the Re-center rule:

1. Choose Re-center from the Liquid Layout Rule menu. There are no additional settings.

2. Create the alternate layout. Objects are repositioned so they appear in the center of the layout.

A The **Liquid Layout Rules menu** in the Control panel.

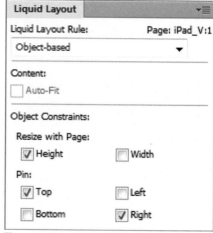

B The **Liquid Layout panel**.

Liquid Layout Rule	Description	Comments	When to use
Off	Turns off the Liquid Layout Rules for the page. Objects do not change their size or shape.		
Scale	Objects are scaled to the same change in proportions as the page changes. Text and images are scaled to fit within the new frame size and shape.	This is the only rule that scales text and images.	Use when it is not important if the text and images change their size for the new layout.
Re-center	Objects do not resize but are kept in the center of the page. If the page is made bigger than the original layout, white space is added around the objects.	No white space is added if the page size is made smaller than the elements. Elements are repositioned to the center of the layout.	Use when the layout is made bigger and you don't mind adding white space around the elements.
Object-based	Allows you to set if the width or height of the object should change. Also allows you to maintain the relative space between the object's side and the sides of the page.	Requires individual settings for each object.	Use when you want the most control over how objects are resized. This is the only setting that controls the relationship of the space between an object and the edge of the page.
Guide-based	Uses guides to set if an object's width or height should change. The position of the guides controls which objects are affected.	Requires slightly less work than the object-based rule to individual objects.	Use when you only need to control the width or height of an object, not the space between the object and the edge of the page.
Controlled by Master	Uses the setting that has been applied to the master page governing the page.	Allows you to quickly apply a Liquid Layout Rule to multiple pages in the layout.	Use when you don't want to have to apply settings to each individual page. This allows you to set the Liquid Layout Rule to just the master and have it applied to other pages.
Use Existing	Uses the setting that has been applied to each page.	Is only available in the Create Alternate Layout dialog box.	

TIP You can only apply one Liquid Layout Rule for each page.

To set the Object-based rule:

1. With the Object-based setting applied, use the Page tool to select the object you want to control. The object-based controllers appear.

2. Click the controllers to set how the item changes its size, shape, and position 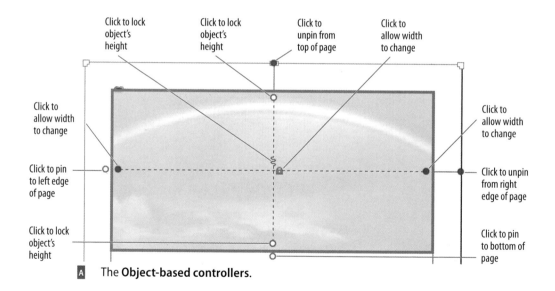.

TIP Some of the controllers duplicate commands. For example, there are three controls to change or unlock an object's height or width.

3. Repeat for other objects on the page.

TIP You can also set the controllers using the options in the Liquid Layout panel. This is easier than clicking the small controllers on the page.

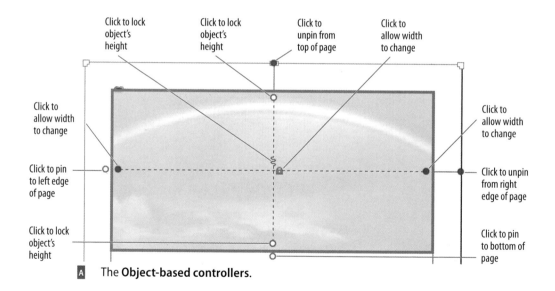

Click to lock object's height

Click to lock object's height

Click to unpin from top of page

Click to allow width to change

Click to allow width to change

Click to allow width to change

Click to pin to left edge of page

Click to unpin from right edge of page

Click to lock object's height

Click to pin to bottom of page

A The **Object-based controllers**.

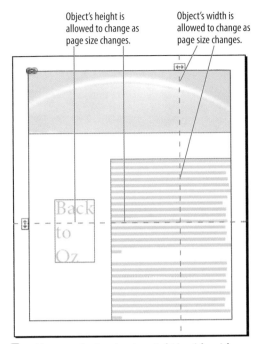

Object's height is allowed to change as page size changes.

Object's width is allowed to change as page size changes.

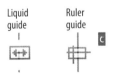

B How **vertical or horizontal Liquid guides** affect the Guide-based changes.

Liquid guide

Ruler guide

C The **guide icons** to distinguish Ruler guides from Liquid guides.

To set the Guide-based rule:

1. With the Page tool chosen, drag a vertical or horizontal guide from the ruler. This creates a Liquid guide instead of a Ruler guide.

2. Position the guides so that they cross whatever objects you want to control **B**.

   - A vertical guide allows the object's width to change as the page size changes.

   - A horizontal guide allows the object's height to change as the page size changes.

TIP It doesn't matter at what position the guide crosses the object. It just has to touch.

TIP A Liquid guide is displayed with a dashed line instead of the solid line of a Ruler guide.

TIP If you select a guide, an icon appears that indicates what type of guide it is **C**. Click the icon to convert from one type of guide to another.

Testing the Liquid Layout Rules

It's not always easy to anticipate how the Liquid Layout Rules will affect objects. You may try guide-based rule and then see you need the additional precision of the Object-based rule.

One way I have found to test how the settings will work is to drag with the Page tool to change the size of the page. This way I can judge how the objects will change.

I then release the drag and the page snaps back to its original position.

Auto-Fit Commands

As you add graphics and text to frames, you may want the frames to automatically adjust to fit the content. That's where the auto-fit commands can help.

TIP The auto-fit commands can be used in conjunction with the Liquid Layout Rules or alone as you add images or text to frames.

To use the auto-fit image command:

1. Select the graphic frame that you want to set to auto-fit.

2. Choose **Object** > **Fitting** > **Frame Fitting Options**. This opens the Frame Fitting Options dialog box .

To set the auto-fit image options:

1. In the Frame Fitting Options dialog box, check Auto-Fit to turn on auto-fit for the selected frame.

2. Use the Fitting menu to choose how the image should fit within the frame 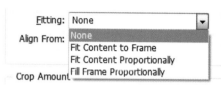:

   - **None** imports the image with no adjustments. You can then manually adjust the size of the image.

   - **Fit Content to Frame** forces the image to fit the frame which may cause the image to be distorted.

   - **Fit Content Proportionally,** which may create some empty space in the frame.

   - **Fill Frame Proportionally,** which may crop one or more sides of the graphic.

3. Use the Align From reference box to set from what point the image fitting and cropping appears .

4. Use the Crop Amount settings to specify position of the image in relation to the frame.

   - **Positive numbers** crop the image.

   - **Negative numbers** add space between the image and the frame.

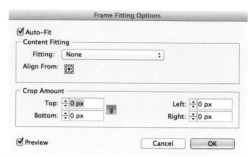

A The **Frame Fitting Options dialog box** controls the auto-fit options for graphics.

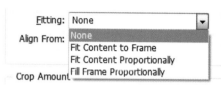

B The **Fitting menu** of the Frame Fitting Options dialog box.

C The **Align From reference box** for the frame fitting options.

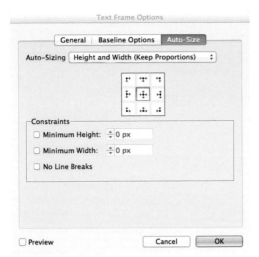

D The **Auto-Size controls** of the Text Frame Options dialog box.

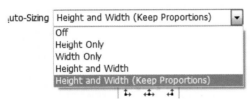

E The **Auto-Sizing menu** of the Auto-Size tab of the Text Frame Options dialog box.

To use the auto-fit text command:

1. Select the text frame that you want to set to auto-fit.

2. Choose **Object > Text Frame Options.** This opens the Text Frame Options dialog box.

3. Click the Auto-Size tab to display the auto-fit text settings **D**.

To set the auto-fit text commands:

1. In the Auto-Size area of the Text Frame Options, use the Auto-Sizing menu to choose how the text frame should expand to fit the text **E**.

   - **Off** turns off any auto-sizing for the frame.

   - **Height Only** expands the height dimension of the frame.

   - **Width Only** expands the width dimension of the frame.

   - **Height and Width** expands both dimensions of the frame.

   - **Height and Width (Keep Proportions)** expands both dimensions of the frame, but keeps the proportions of the frame.

2. Use the reference settings to control whether the frame expands from a corner, a side, or the center of the object.

3. Check Minimum Height and enter an amount to maintain a minimum height for the frame.

4. Check Minimum Width and enter an amount to maintain a minimum width for the frame.

5. Check No Line Breaks to force the text to continue to expand the frame horizontally.

Printing 19

There are two types of printing from InDesign. Some people print only to a desktop printing machine connected by cord or wirelessly to their computer. They are not concerned with color separations or other high-end print settings.

Others create their Indesign files as part of the professional prepress process. They need to know more than just how to print to a desktop printer. They need to know how to make sure their documents have been set up correctly. They need to know what files are necessary to send to a print shop.

So "Printing" refers to preparing documents and printing them — either with an ordinary desktop printer or with a high-end printing device such as an imagesetter.

Printing a Document

When a document is printed, many different instructions are sent to the printing machine. You need to set those instructions correctly.

TIP Adobe recommends using only the controls inside the InDesign Print dialog box — not the Page Setup (Mac) dialog box or the Printer Properties (Win) dialog box.

To print a document:

1. Choose **File** > **Print**. This opens the Print dialog box 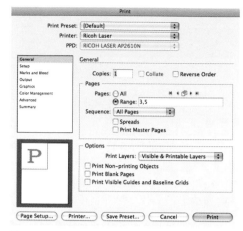.

2. Click each of the categories **B** on the left side of the dialog box to set the options as described in the chart on the following page.

TIP You do not need to set all the controls every time you print unless you need to change a specific setting.

3. Click the Print button to print the document according to the settings.

Before you print a document, you may want to set some objects (such as private notes or alternate designs) to not print.

To set elements to not print:

Select the object and turn on Nonprinting in the Attributes panel.

or

Turn off the visibility of the layer in the document. This suppresses the printing for all objects on the layer.

A The **Print dialog box** contains all the settings for printing documents.

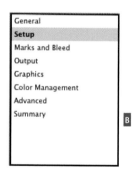

B Click each of the categories to display those settings in the Print dialog box.

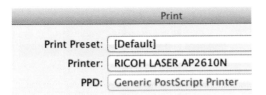

Print

Print Preset: [Default]

Printer: RICOH LASER AP2610N

PPD: Generic PostScript Printer

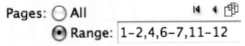

C The **Printer list** lets you choose the printer to print a document.

Copies: 1 ☐ Collate ☐ Reverse Order

Pages

Pages: ○ All

● Range: 1-7

Sequence: All Pages

☐ Spreads

☐ Print Master Pages

D The **Copies and Pages** area of the General controls for printing.

Pages: ○ All

● Range: 1-2,4,6-7,11-12

E Use a **combination of hyphens and commas** to print both individual pages and a range of pages.

Setting the General Print Options

If you are printing to a desktop printer, the options in the General category may be all you need to set to print a document.

To choose the printer:

Choose the printer from the Printer menu at the top of the dialog box **C**.

To control the copies:

1. Set the number of copies in the Copies field **D**.

2. Choose Collate to print multiple copies organized as complete sets.

3. Choose Reverse Order to print the copies back to front.

To control the pages:

1. Choose All to print all the pages or choose Range to print a single page or a group of pages **E**. (*See the next exercise for how to specify both individual pages and page ranges.*)

2. Use the Sequence menu to choose All Pages, Even Pages, or Odd Pages.

3. Select the Spreads checkbox to print spreads together.

4. Select Print Master Pages to print the master pages in the document.

To print specific pages or page ranges:

Use the following controls in the Range field to print specific pages:

- Use a comma to separate individual pages.

- Use a hyphen to specify a range of pages.

If you have different-sized pages, you can use the Select Same-Sized Pages icons to select specific pages for printing.

To select specific page sizes for printing:

1. In the Pages panel, select one of the pages that is the size you want to print.

TIP This page does not have to be one of the pages that you want to print.

2. In the Pages area of the Print dialog box, click the Select Same-Sized Pages icons as follows :

   - **First Range icon** enters the page numbers for the first range of pages that are the same size as the selected page.

   - **Previous Range icon** enters the page numbers for the preceding range of pages that are the same size as the selected page.

   - **All Pages icon** enters the page numbers for all individual pages as well as page ranges that are the same size as the selected page.

   - **Next Range icon** enters the page numbers for the next range of pages that are the same size as the selected page.

   - **Last Range icon** enters the page numbers for the last range of pages that are the same size as the selected page.

To set the general options:

1. Use the Print Layers menu to choose which layers to print 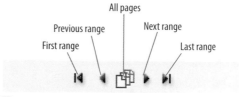.

2. Select Print Non-printing Objects to print objects set to not print 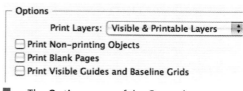.

3. Select Print Blank Pages to print pages that have no visible items .

4. Select Print Visible Guides and Baseline Grids to print the guides and grids .

All pages
Previous range   Next range
First range   Last range

A The **Select Same-Sized Pages icons** in the Print dialog box.

Print Master Pages
Options
All Layers
Visible Layers
Print Layers: ✓ Visible & Printable Layers
Print Non-printing Objects

B The **Print Layers menu** in the Options area of the General controls for printing.

Options
Print Layers: Visible & Printable Layers
Print Non-printing Objects
Print Blank Pages
Print Visible Guides and Baseline Grids

C The **Options area** of the General controls for printing.

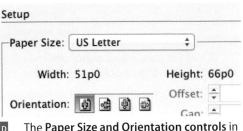

The Setup options contain the controls to set the paper size and orientation.

To set the paper size and orientation:

1. Use the Paper Size menu to choose the size of the paper on which to print the document .

TIP This menu changes depending on the type of printer chosen.

2. Click one of the Orientation buttons. This changes the rotation of the document on the printed page.

To choose the setup options:

1. Set the Scale amount for either Height or Width to change the size of the printed document on the paper .

2. Click the Scale to Fit button to have the document automatically resized to fit the chosen paper size.

3. Use the Page Position menu to choose where to position the document on the printed page 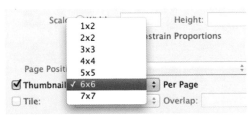.

4. Select Thumbnails to print small versions of the pages on a single page.

5. If you have chosen Thumbnails, use the Thumbnails menu to choose how many pages are printed on each page .

TIP See the next section for information on how to use the Tile controls.

D The **Paper Size and Orientation controls** in the Setup category of the Print dialog box.

E The **Options controls** in the Setup category of the Print dialog box.

F The **Page Position menu** in the Setup category of the Print dialog box.

G The **Thumbnails menu** in the Setup category of the Print dialog box.

Tiling Pages

If your document is larger than the paper in the printer, you can print portions of the document on different pages. You can then assemble the pages together. This is called *tiling*. Auto tiling automatically divides the page into smaller segments.

To set automatic tiling:

1. Select Tile in the Setup category of the Print dialog box.

2. Choose Auto from the Tile menu .

3. Set the amount in the Overlap field. This controls how much of one page is repeated on the tile for a second section of the page.

TIP The Preview area in the lower-left portion of the Print dialog box shows how the page will be tiled 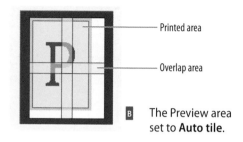.

Auto justified tiling divides the pages so that the right edge of the document lies on the right side of a printed page and the bottom edge of the document lies on the bottom edge of a printed page 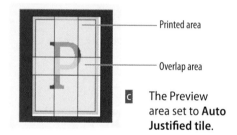.

TIP The Auto setting ensures that there is no white space on the right side and bottom of the tiled pages.

To set auto justified tiling:

1. Select Tile in the Setup category of the Print dialog box.

2. Choose Auto Justified from the Tile menu.

A The **Tile menu** in the Setup category of the Print dialog box.

Printed area

Overlap area

B The Preview area set to **Auto tile**.

Printed area

Overlap area

C The Preview area set to **Auto Justified tile**.

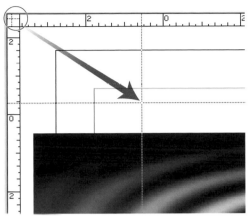

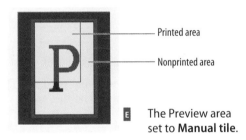

D **Move the zero-point crosshairs** to set the area to print as a tile on one page.

Printed area

Nonprinted area

E The Preview area set to **Manual tile**.

You can also tile pages manually. This lets you make sure that the edge of the paper does not cut across an important portion of the document.

To set manual tiling:

1. Use the zero-point crosshairs on the ruler to set the upper-left corner of the area you want to print **D**. *(See Chapter 2, "Document Setup," for more information on setting the zero point of the ruler.)*

2. Choose **File > Print**.

3. Click the Setup category of the Print dialog box.

4. Choose Manual from the Tile menu.

TIP The Preview area of the Print dialog box shows the area that will be printed **E**.

5. Click Print to print that one page.

6. Reposition the zero-point crosshairs to set a new area to be printed.

7. Follow steps 2 through 5 to define and print the second tile.

8. Repeat the process until the entire page has been printed.

Setting Marks and Bleed

You can also add information that shows where the page is to be trimmed, the document name, and so on. This information is sometimes called printer's marks or page marks.

To set the page marks:

1. Select All Printer's Marks to turn on all the marks, or use the checkboxes to set each one individually 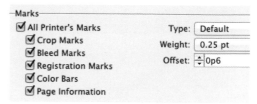 and B.

   - **Crop Marks** indicates where the page should be trimmed.

   - **Bleed Marks** shows how far outside the crop marks you must put graphics so that they are trimmed correctly.

   - **Registration Marks** adds crosshair targets that are used to line up pieces of film.

   - **Color Bars** provides boxes that display the colors used in the document as well as the tint bars that can be used to calibrate the printing press for correct tints of colors.

   - **Page Information** prints the name of the file, the page number, and the time the document was printed.

2. Use the Type menu to choose a custom set of marks such as those used in Japanese printing.

3. Enter an amount in the Weight menu for the thickness of the crop marks.

4. Enter an amount in the Offset field to determine how far away from the trim the page marks should be positioned.

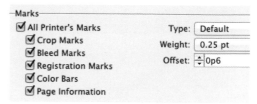

A The **Marks settings** in the Marks and Bleed category of the Print dialog box.

B The **page marks and information** as they appear on the printed page.

Bleed area

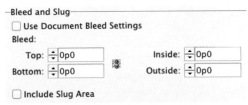

An example of an object that bleeds off a page.

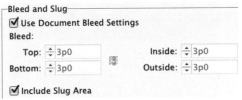

Select the checkbox for **Use Document Bleed Settings** to have the bleed use the same settings as in the Document Setup dialog box.

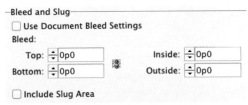

The **Bleed controls** allow you to define a custom bleed in the Print dialog box.

You can also control the bleed, or the area that allows objects that extend off the page to print ⧉.

To set the bleed area:

To use the bleed set in the Document Setup dialog box, select Use Document Bleed Settings ⧉.

or

Deselect Use Document Bleed Settings and then set the custom amounts for the bleed around each side of the page ⧉.

TIP These custom bleed controls make it easy for print shops to set a uniform bleed as part of a print preset.

If you have set a slug for the document, you can choose whether that slug area prints or not.

To set the slug area:

To print items in the slug area, select Include Slug Area ⧉.

Setting the Output Controls

You may need to set the color controls to choose how color documents are printed.

To control how colors are printed:

1. Choose one of the following from the Color menu :

   - **Composite Leave Unchanged** prints without converting colors to either RGB or CMYK.

   - **Composite Gray** prints all the colors as a gray image. Use this when printing on one-color laser printers.

   - **Composite RGB** prints all the colors as an RGB image. Use this when printing on RGB ink-jet printers.

   - **Composite CMYK** prints all the colors as a CMYK image. Use this when printing on PostScript CMYK printers.

   - **Separations** prints all the colors onto separate plates or pages.

   - **In-RIP Separations** prints all the colors onto separate plates using the separation controls in the RIP.

2. If you choose one of the composite settings, you can select the Text as Black checkbox.

   TIP The Text as Black command is helpful if you have color text that you want to be more readable when printed on a one-color printer.

3. Use the Flip menu if you need to flip the orientation of the page 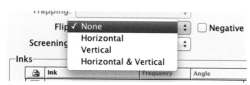 and 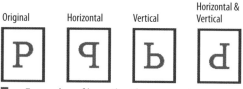.

4. Select the Negative checkbox in the Output category of the Print dialog box.

   TIP These last two options are not commonly used for desktop printers, but are used by print shops when they create film separations.

A The **Color menu** in the Output category of the Print dialog box.

B The **Flip menu** in the Output category of the Print dialog box.

C Examples of how the **Flip menu** changes the readability of a document.

| Frequency: | 70 | lpi | ☐ Simulate Overprint |
| Angle: | 45 | ° | Ink Manager... |

D The **Frequency and Angle fields** in the Output category of the Print dialog box.

What Does RIP Stand For?

You may hear people use the term RIP when they talk about printing. RIP stands for *raster image processing*.

RIP is simply a fancy term for what happens when a file is processed for output by a high-resolution imagesetter. In addition, RIP also refers to the device that does the processing.

You can also change the screen frequency and angle of halftones in the image.

To change the screen settings:

1. Use the Screening menu to set the frequency and angle for the screen applied to images.

2. Select a color in the Inks area and then use the Frequency and Angle fields **D**.

TIP Always talk to your print service provider for the correct settings.

Trapping refers to the various techniques that are used to compensate for the misregistration of printing plates. However, if you don't understand trapping, you should consult with the service bureau that will print your file before you set the trapping.

To turn on basic trapping:

Choose Application Built-In or Adobe In-RIP from the Trapping menu.

Working with Separations Preview

When a document is printed with more than one color, each color is called a plate. Printing the different colors onto separate plates is called making separations. You use the Separations Preview panel to view the different color plates onscreen. This makes it possible to gauge how a document will look on press.

To turn on separations preview:

1. Choose **Window > Output > Separations Preview**. The Separations Preview panel appears.

2. Choose Separations from the View menu . This displays the controls for the colors in the document 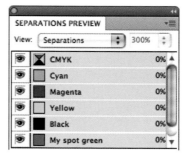.

3. Click each Show/Hide icon next to the color name to change the display of the colors on the page 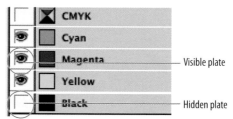.

TIP Click the Show/Hide icon next to the CMYK listing to show or hide all those plates together.

A Use the **View menu** in the Separations Preview panel to turn on the separations preview.

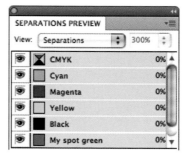

B The **colors in the document** are displayed in the Separations Preview panel.

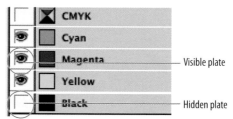

Visible plate

Hidden plate

C Click the **Show/Hide icons** in the Separations Preview panel to change the display of the colors on the page.

My Favorite Childhood Book

One of my favorite books I had as a kid was a *World Book Encyclopedia* that had acetate pages that you could flip to see how colors built up to a full-color image. (It's true! At the age of 13 I was into page production and color separations.)

When I worked in advertising we called these color breakdowns *prog proofs* (for progressive proofs). But during many years of working with computer graphics, we had no way to see how colors combine on the page. The best we could do was print color on individual laser prints and then hold them up to the window to see how the colors would separate.

With InDesign, I am thrilled to use the separations preview — an electronic version of my *World Book* acetate pages. Instead of flipping pages, I click ink colors on and off. I can spend hours doing it. It makes me feel like a kid again!

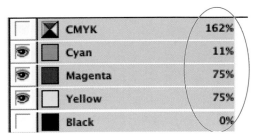

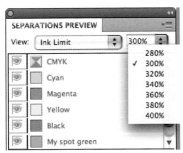

The Separations Preview panel also lets you view the total amount of ink for each plate.

To view the inks for each plate:

1. Choose Separations from the View menu.

2. Move the cursor around the page. The ink percentages appear next to the name of each color .

The Separations preview also shows you the areas of the page that exceed a certain ink limit. For instance, many print shops will request that you not define colors totaling more than 300% of all the inks combined. The Ink Limit setting lets you see if there are any areas that exceed this limit.

To check the ink limit:

1. Select Ink Limit from the View menu in the Separations Preview panel.

2. Use the amount menu to set the ink limit amount **E**.

TIP When you switch to the Ink Limit view, the document preview changes to a grayscale image. Any areas that exceed the ink limit are shown in red **F**. The deeper the red, the more the color is over the ink limit.

TIP You can also enter your own custom amount in the Ink Limit field.

D The Separations Preview panel displays the **ink percentages next to each color plate**.

E Use the **Ink Limit controls** to check the total ink applied in areas of the layout.

F The Ink Limit setting shows red areas where the **ink is too dense to print properly**.

Color Separations and Ink Manager

The Inks area of the Output category also lets you control how the inks are separated and printed.

To set the inks to be printed:

Click the printer icon next to the name of each color. Each click changes how the ink will print as follows 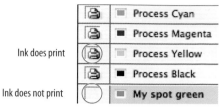:

- If the icon is visible, the color will print.
- If the icon is not visible, the color does not print.

Sometimes you find yourself with a document that contains spot colors that should be process colors. The Ink Manager lets you convert the spot colors to process inks.

To convert spot colors to process:

1. Open the Ink Manager by clicking the Ink Manager button in the Output area of the Print dialog box **B**.

TIP You can also open the Ink Manager from the Swatches panel menu or the Separations Preview panel menu.

2. Click the color icon next to the name of each color. Each click changes how the ink will print as follows **C**:
   - A CMYK symbol indicates that the color will separate as a process color.
   - A spot color symbol indicates that the color will separate on its own plate.

3. Select the All Spots to Process checkbox to convert all spot colors to process **B**.

4. If desired, select Use Standard Lab Values for Spots. This converts the spot colors to process using their built-in Lab color values **B**.

Ink does print

Ink does not print

A The **printer icon next to an ink color** indicates whether that ink will print or not.

B The **Ink Manager dialog box** gives you control over how inks are separated or printed.

Process color

Spot color

C Click the **color icons** in the Ink Manager to convert spot colors to process.

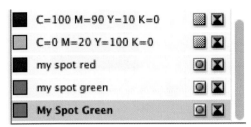

When you import artwork that contains spot colors, those spot colors are added to the document and the Swatches panel. There are no problems if the imported colors are named exactly the same as existing colors. But if the name of the imported color differs from the color you have defined, you can wind up with two separate color plates instead of one . Thankfully, InDesign lets you map one color to be an alias of another.

To map one color to be the alias of another:

1. Select the color you want to change in the Ink Manager.

2. Use the Ink Alias menu to choose a different color to map to the selected one **E**. The color is listed in the Ink Manager as mapped to the other color **F**.

TIP You can map the selected color to a spot or process color.

TIP Colors that are mapped to another color are not listed in the Inks area of the Output category. They are also not listed in the Separations Preview panel.

D An example of how names typed in different cases can create **too many spot colors** in a document.

E Use the **Ink Alias menu** to have one color map to a different one.

F An example of how **one color is used as the alias** for another.

Setting the Graphics Options

The Graphics options control how much information is sent to the printer. You can control the data that is sent for placed images.

To control the data sent for images:

Choose one of the following from the Send Data menu 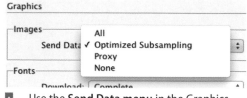:

- **All** sends all the information for the image. This is the slowest setting.

- **Optimized Subsampling** sends only the amount of information necessary for the chosen output device. Use this option if you're proofing high-resolution images on a desktop printer.

- **Proxy** sends only a 72-ppi version of the image.

- **None** replaces the image with crosshairs within the frame. Use this option when you want to proof only the text in the file.

You can also control how much of the font information is sent to the printer.

To control the font information sent for printing:

1. Choose one of the following from the Download menu 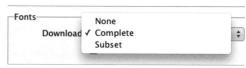:
   - **None** sends only a reference to the font that you can replace in the PostScript data stream.
   - **Complete** sends the entire set of glyphs for the font. This is the longest option.
   - **Subset** sends only those glyphs used in the document.

2. Choose Download PPD Fonts to send all fonts, even if they have been installed on the printer . This option is helpful if you use a variation of the fonts installed on the printer.

A   Use the **Send Data menu** in the Graphics category to control how images are printed.

B   Use the **Download menu** in the Graphics category to control how much of a font is sent to the printer.

C   Choose **Download PPD Fonts** to send printer fonts as part of the print information.

Setting the Color Management Options

Rather than go into details of color management, it is better for me to recommend that you ask your print shop how to set the color management options.

Not only is the field of color management way beyond the scope of this book, it's probably way beyond what you want to read in this book.

Suffice it to say there is no "QuickStart" for color management. It's a deep topic and deserves much more than a section in my book. See *Real World Color Management 2nd Edition* by Bruce Fraser, Chris Murphy, and Fred Bunting (Peachpit Press) for the best information on the topic.

D Set the **OPI Image Replacement options** to control how images are handled during prepress.

E Use the **Preset menu** in the Transparency Flattener area to set the resolution for converting transparency effects into rasterized images.

Setting the Advanced Options

The Advanced category lets you set the options for OPI and choose a transparency preset. OPI stands for *Open Prepress Interface*. The OPI controls are used when files are sent to Scitex and Kodak prepress systems.

TIP The OPI workflow is considered an outdated output system and is not used by modern print houses.

To set the OPI controls:

1. In the OPI area, select the OPI Image Replacement checkbox **D**.

2. Choose which types of images should be replaced during an OPI workflow. (An OPI workflow uses low-resolution images for the layout and swaps them with high-resolution images just before printing.)

When you use any of the transparency features, InDesign needs to flatten or convert those effects into vector and raster images as they are sent for output. The Transparency Flattener section of the Advanced category controls how InDesign flattens the image.

To set the flattener preset:

1. Use the Preset menu to choose one of the flattener settings **E**.

2. If you have used the Pages panel to flatten individual spreads, you can select the Ignore Spread Overrides checkbox (located just below the Preset menu) to override that setting. This means that the setting you choose in this dialog box will be used no matter what flattener settings you have applied to the individual pages.

Flattener Presets and Preview

The transparency flattener presets control how the transparency effects, drop shadows, and feathers are handled during output.

To create a transparency flattener preset:

1. Choose **Edit** > **Transparency Flattener Presets**. This opens the Transparency Flattener Presets dialog box 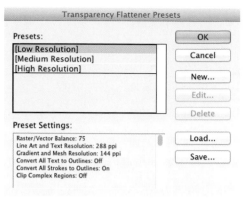.

2. Click the New button. The Transparency Flattener Preset Options dialog box appears **B**.

3. Use the Name field to name the preset.

4. Move the Raster/Vector Balance slider to create more vector or more rasterized artwork **C**.

5. Set an output resolution in the Line Art and Text Resolution field.

TIP A setting of 300 PPI is sufficient for most output.

6. Set an output resolution for gradient objects in the Gradient and Mesh Resolution field.

TIP A setting of 150 PPI is sufficient for most gradients.

7. Select Convert All Text to Outlines to convert the text to paths.

TIP If this checkbox is not selected, only transparent portions of the text may be converted to outlines. This option makes the text width consistent.

8. If you have strokes that pass through different transparencies, you may want to select Convert All Strokes to Outlines to convert the strokes to filled paths.

9. Select Clip Complex Regions to ensure that any differences in raster and vector objects always fall along existing paths.

TIP This can result in complex clipping paths, which may not print on some devices.

A The **Transparency Flattener Presets dialog box** lets you define new presets for handling transparency effects.

B The **Transparency Flattener Preset Options dialog box** contains the settings for a custom transparency flattener preset.

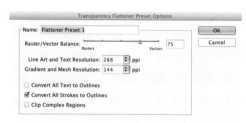

C The controls in the Transparency Flattener Preset Options dialog box.

Presets:

[Low Resolution]
[Medium Resolution]
[High Resolution]
My presets

D The **three default transparency flattener presets** in brackets cannot be edited or deleted.

Preset Settings:

Raster/Vector Balance: 100
Line Art and Text Resolution: 288 ppi
Gradient and Mesh Resolution: 144 ppi
Convert All Text to Outlines: Off
Convert All Strokes to Outlines: On
Clip Complex Regions: N/A

E The **Preset Settings area** displays a readout of the settings for a particular transparency flattener preset.

To edit a transparency flattener preset:

1. Choose the preset you want to edit.

TIP The three default presets, surrounded by brackets, cannot be edited **D**.

2. Click the Edit button.

3. Edit the preset in the Transparency Flattener Presets dialog box.

TIP The Preset Settings area displays a readout of the settings for each preset **E**.

To delete transparency flattener presets:

1. Choose the presets you want to delete.

TIP The three default presets, surrounded by brackets, cannot be deleted **D**.

TIP Use the Shift key to select multiple adjacent presets. Use the Cmd/Ctrl key to select multiple nonadjacent presets.

2. Click the Delete button.

You can also save transparency flattener presets to share among others. Once saved, the presets can then be loaded onto other machines.

To save a transparency flattener preset:

1. Choose the presets you want to save.

TIP Use the Shift key to select multiple adjacent presets. Use the Cmd/Ctrl key to select multiple nonadjacent presets.

2. Click the Save button.

3. Name the file.

To load a transparency flattener preset:

1. Click the Load button.

2. Navigate to find the file that contains the presets.

3. Click Open. The presets appear in the Transparency Flattener Presets dialog box.

You can apply a flattener preset to the document in the Advanced category of the Print dialog box. However, you may have one page that requires special flattener controls. InDesign lets you apply flattener presets to each specific spread.

TIP Flattening must be handled on a per spread, not per page, basis.

To apply a flattener preset to an individual spread:

1. Move to the spread.
2. In the Pages panel menu, choose one of the following from the Spread Flattening menu:
   - **Default** leaves the spread flattening at whatever setting is applied to the document.
   - **None (Ignore Transparency)** prints the spread without any transparency effect. This setting is useful for print shops that need to troubleshoot during output.
   - **Custom** opens the Custom Spread Flattener Settings dialog box. These settings are identical to ones in the Transparency Flattener Preset Options dialog box 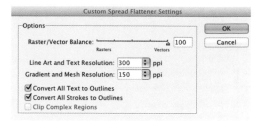.

A The **Custom Spread Flattener Settings dialog box** lets you apply different flattener controls to a specific spread.

A Short Course in Flattening

You may feel a little overwhelmed by all the controls for flattening transparency. Don't panic: Most of the flattening options are best set by the print house that will output your files.

However, there are some simple rules that can make it easier to get successful results when flattening artwork.

Unless you absolutely want text to be part of a transparency effect, keep your text above any transparency effects. For instance, instead of putting text underneath a drop shadow, move it above. If the text is black, you won't see any difference in the final output. If it's a color, set it to overprint.

Try to avoid overlapping two gradients with transparency effects. That combination creates objects that are much too complex.

Run tests. The first time I used transparency and blend modes, I sent ten sample pages to my publisher, who had them output at the print shop. We looked to make sure none of the text had changed and there were no problems with the images. It saved us a lot of worry when the book went to press.

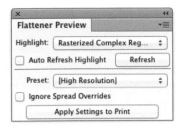

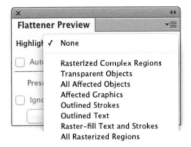

B The **Flattener Preview panel** lets you see the effects of the flattener presets on your document.

C Use the **Highlight menu** to choose which objects will be displayed in the flattener preview.

Text below shadow   Text above shadow

D The **flattener preview highlights** the objects affected by transparency. Here the text below the shadow is highlighted whereas the text above the shadow is not.

Instead of waiting for your file to be printed, you can preview how the flattening will occur with the Flattener Preview panel.

To preview the flattener settings:

1. Choose **Window > Output > Flattener Preview**. This opens the Flattener Preview panel **B**.

2. Choose one of the options from the Highlight menu **C**. This controls which objects will be displayed in the flattener preview.

3. Use the Preset menu to choose which flattener preset is used to control the flattener preview.

4. Click the Refresh button to update the screen preview. The page displays the highlighted objects in red against other grayscale objects **D**.

   or

   Select Auto Refresh Highlight to have the screen update automatically.

5. Select Ignore Spread Overrides to use only the setting in the Preset menu.

6. If you want, click the Apply Settings to Print button to apply the settings to the Advanced category of the Print dialog box.

TIP You can open the Transparency Flattener Presets dialog box using the Flattener Preview panel menu.

Transparency Resources

This book can hardly cover all the aspects of setting transparency and flattening. For more information see the InDesign online Help pages.

Also, download the document *Getting Started with Transparency Using Adobe Creative Suite Software* on the Adobe Web site.

Finally, if you are a service provider, you should look at the Print Service Provider Resources page of the Adobe Solutions Network (ASN).

Working with Print Presets

With all the areas in the Print dialog box, you wouldn't want to have to set all the controls each time you have a new document. InDesign lets you save the print settings so you can easily apply them later.

To save a print preset:

1. Set all the categories in the Print dialog box to the settings you want to save.

2. Click the Save Preset button at the bottom of the Print dialog box . This opens the Save Preset dialog box .

3. Enter a name for the preset.

4. Click OK. This saves the preset.

To apply a print preset:

Choose a saved preset from the Print Preset menu at the top of the Print dialog box 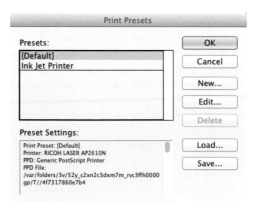.

You don't need to go through the Print dialog box to create and save a print preset.

To define a printer preset:

1. Choose **File > Print Presets > Define**. The Print Presets dialog box appears 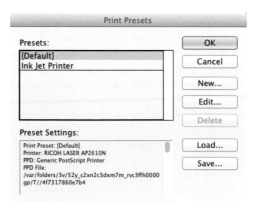.

2. Click the New button to define a new preset. This opens a version of the Print dialog box that lets you set the various print categories.

   or

   Click the Edit button to make changes to the selected print preset.

To delete a printer preset:

1. Select the presets you want to delete in the Print Presets dialog box.

2. Click the Delete button.

A Click the **Save Preset button** to save the current Print settings as a print preset.

B Use the **Save Preset dialog box** to name your own printer preset.

C A saved preset can be applied using the **Print Preset menu** at the top of the Print dialog box.

D Saved presets are listed in the **Print Presets dialog box**.

```
Summary
─────────────────────────────────────────
Print Preset: Ink Jet Printer
Printer: RICOH LASER AP2610N
PPD: Generic PostScript Printer
PPD File: /var/folders/3v/52y_c2xn2c3dxm7m_rvc3ffh0000gp/T//4f9d921f58a70

General
   Copies: 1
   Collate: N/A
   Reverse Order: Off
   Pages: N/A
   Sequence: All Pages
   Spreads: Off
   Print Master Pages: Off
   Print Layers: Visible & Printable Layers
   Print Non-printing Objects: Off
   Print Blank Pages: Off
   Print Visible Guides and Baseline Grids: Off

Setup
   Paper Size: US Letter
   Paper Width: 51p0
   Paper Height: 66p0
   Page Orientation: Portrait
   Paper Offset: N/A
   Paper Gap: N/A
─────────────────────────────────────────
       [ Save Summary... ]
```

E   Use the **Summary area** to see all the print settings applied to a document.

One of the benefits of working with printer presets is that you can export them so others can print documents with the same settings.

To export printer presets:

1. In the Print Presets dialog box, select the presets you want to export.

TIP Use the Shift key to select adjacent multiple presets. Use the Cmd/Ctrl key to select nonadjacent multiple presets.

2. Click Save. A dialog box appears where you can name the document that contains the exported presets.

Your service bureau can provide you with printer presets that you can import to use for printing or packaging documents.

To import printer presets:

1. In the Print Presets dialog box, click Load.

2. Use the dialog box to select the document that contains the presets exported from another machine.

3. Click OK. The presets appear in the Print Presets dialog box.

Creating a Print Summary

With all the settings in the Print dialog box, you may want to keep track of how a document has been printed. The Summary area gives you a report of all the print settings.

To use the Summary area:

Scroll through the Summary area to see all the settings applied to a print job **E**.

or

Click the Save Summary button to save a text file listing all the print settings.

Creating Printer's Spreads

When you work on an InDesign document, you view the pages in what are called *reader's spreads*. However, when documents are printed, they need to be arranged in what are called *printer's spreads*. (This is also called *imposing* pages in position.)

For example, in an eight-page brochure, page one would be paired up with page eight. Page two would be next to page seven. Manually creating printer's spreads is a nightmare. Fortunately, you can easily arrange your document into printer's spreads using the Print Booklet command.

To impose a document into printer's spreads:

1. Choose **File** > **Print Booklet**. The Print Booklet dialog box appears 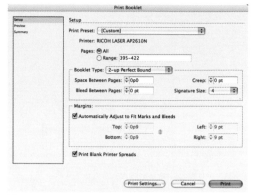.

2. Click the Setup category. The Setup controls appear 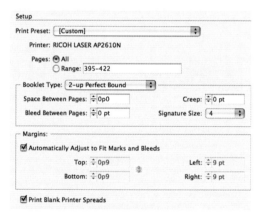.

3. Choose a print preset from the Print Preset menu 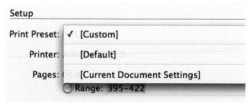. If you have no preset available, choose [Current Document Settings] to use whatever printer is chosen in your Print dialog box.

TIP This setting allows you to choose the Adobe PDF printer to impose as a PDF file.

4. Use the Pages control to choose which pages should be imposed.

5. Choose the Booklet Type and Margins controls as explained in the following exercises.

A The **Print Booklet dialog box** lets you create printer's spreads.

B The **Setup controls** of the Print Booklet dialog box.

C The **Print Preset menu** lets you choose which print preset should be used.

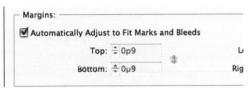

D The **Booklet Type menu** of the Print Booklet dialog box.

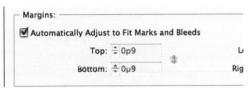

E Choose **Automatically Adjust to Fit Marks and Bleeds** to set the booklet margins automatically.

Please! Think Before You Impose!

At least once a month I read about someone who thinks they need to send printer's spreads in to their service bureau before their job (brochure, book, pamphlet, or other document) can be printed.

This is not a safe road to go down. Creating printer's spreads is not something the average designer is trained to do. Even I wouldn't have the foggiest idea of how to make the settings for my jobs. There are too many variables.

I have no idea what the signature size is going to be or how many pages will be imposed together.

Even worse, I don't know what to choose for the creep size as I don't know how thick the folds in my paper will be.

Having said that, if all you want to do is set up a job to be run on your office printing machine, or send the job to the local copy shop for a simple booklet, then the Print Booklet command is perfect for you!

There are different types of booklets. Each one requires separate controls. If you are unsure of which type of booklet you are creating, ask your print shop.

TIP Check with your printer for the correct settings for all of these controls.

To set the type of booklet:

1. Choose the orientation and binding for the booklet from the Booklet Type menu **D**.

2. Depending on the orientation and binding, you may need to set any or all of the following controls:

   - **Space Between Pages** is the amount of space between the pages.
   - **Bleed Between Pages** is the amount of space added around the pages.
   - **Creep** is an adjustment for the thickness of the pages as they are folded.
   - **Signature Size** is how many pages are bound together.

You also need to set the margins for the pages that are imposed.

To set the margins:

Select Automatically Adjust to Fit Marks and Bleeds **E** to set the amount necessary to fit any printer's marks and bleeds on the original layout.

or

Deselect that option and manually set the margins.

To print blank spreads:

Select Print Blank Printer Spreads (at the bottom of the Print Booklet dialog box) to include those spreads that don't contain any items on the pages.

You can gauge if you're setting things up correctly by checking the Preview option in the Print Booklet dialog box.

To preview the imposed pages:

1. Choose Preview from the Print Booklet dialog box. The pages as they will be imposed appear in the Preview window 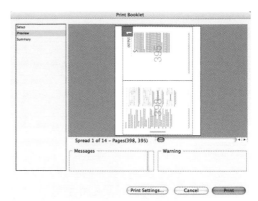.

2. Use the page controls to scroll through a preview of all the imposed pages **B**.

3. Check the Messages area to see if there is any information that you should know about regarding the imposition **C**.

4. Check the Warning area to see if there are alerts for any problems in the final imposed document **D**.

You can also see a summary of all the settings for an imposed document.

To see the summary of the imposed settings:

Choose Summary from the Print Booklet dialog box. The summary appears.

A The **Preview window** of the Print Booklet dialog box shows how the pages will be imposed.

B Use the **page controls** to scroll through previews of the imposed pages.

C The **Messages area** of the Print Booklet dialog box gives you information about the imposed document.

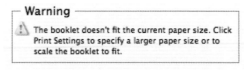

D The **Warning area** of the Print Booklet dialog box alerts you to any problems that may occur in the imposed document.

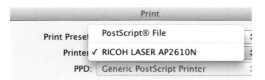

Choose **PostScript® File** from
the Printer menu to create a file
that contains all the information
necessary to print the document.

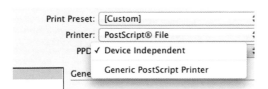

Choose **Device Independent** from the
PPD menu to create a PostScript file
that can be printed to any printer.

Creating PostScript Files

Instead of sending the InDesign document to
a service bureau, you can create a PostScript
file that contains all the information necessary to print the file. (This is sometimes called
printing to disk.) A standard PostScript file
contains all the information needed for printing the file as well as the specific information
about the printer.

To create a standard PostScript file:

1. Choose **File > Print**.
2. Choose PostScript® File from the Printer
   menu **E**.
3. Choose the type of printer that will print
   the file.
4. Set all the options in the print categories
   in the Print dialog box.

TIP Check with the service bureau that will print
your file for the correct options.

5. Choose a name and location for the file.
6. Click Save.

A device-independent PostScript file does not
contain any information about the type of
printer or output device.

TIP This lets you create a PostScript file even if
you don't know the type of printer that your
document will be printed on.

To create a device-independent
PostScript file:

1. Choose **File > Print**.
2. Choose Device Independent from the
   PPD menu **F**.
3. Follow steps 3 through 6 in the previous
   exercise.

Preflighting Documents

Before you send your document out to be printed, you need to know if there could be any problems printing your job. Fortunately, InDesign can *preflight* the elements in your document. (The name comes from the list that pilots complete before they take off.)

To run a preflight check:

1. Choose **Window > Output > Preflight**. The Preflight panel opens .

2. Choose Pages: All to check all the pages in the document.

   or

   Click the button next to the Pages field to enter a specific page or range of pages.

3. Click the On button. InDesign lists problems in the Error area.

4. Click on a specific error, and then open the Info triangle to reveal any additional information about the errors B.

5. Choose Save Report from the Preflight panel menu to create a PDF file that summarizes all the items in the Preflight panel.

Once you find a preflight error, you will want to fix it. This can be easily handled through the Preflight panel.

To fix errors in the Preflight panel:

1. Open the Error list so you can see the specific error in the panel.

2. Click the page number link in the Preflight panel C. This moves you to the errant object or text.

3. Follow the steps in the Info area to fix the error or handle it any other way you can.

TIP When the error is resolved, it disappears from the Errors list.

A The **Preflight panel** lets you check to find problems with your document.

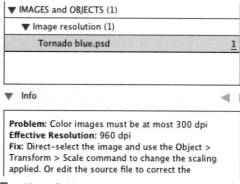

B The **Info area** gives you specifics as to why an error is listed and how to fix it.

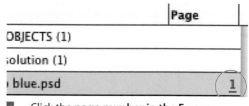

C Click the **page number in the Errors list** to go to the specific errant object or text in the document.

D The **Preflight Profiles dialog box** lets you select errors that should be flagged by the Preflight panel.

Creating Preflight Profiles

The Preflight panel only searches for those items that it has been told are errors. InDesign ships with a Basic profile that flags the most common document errors. But it is very simple for you to create your own profile that highlights the errors you need to find.

To create your own preflight profile:

1. Choose Define Profiles from the Preflight panel menu. The Preflight Profiles dialog box appears **D**.

2. Click the plus sign to create a new profile.

3. Enter a name in the Profile Name field.

4. Click the triangle to open the General category and enter a description that explains the purpose of the profile.

5. Use the triangle to open each of the categories and choose the errors as described in the chart that follows this exercise.

6. Click Save to save your settings as you work.

   or

   Click OK to finish the profile.

TIP The table on the next page contains the preflight categories and a list of the profile items and what each profile flags as an error.

Categories and Errors for Preflight Profiles

Category	Profile Item	Flags as an Error
Links	Links Missing or Modified	Files labeled missing or modified.
	Inaccessible URL links	Hyperlinks that have broken or missing URL links
	OPI Links	OPI tags on images.
Color	Transparency Blending Space Required	Transparency blend space not defined as CMYK or RGB.
	Cyan, Magenta, or Yellow Plates Not Allowed	Presence of non-black plates.
	Color Spaces and Modes Not Allowed	Presence of RGB, CMYK, Gray, Lab, or Spot Color plates.
	Spot Color Setup	Number of spot colors exceeds maximum.
		Spot colors using Lab values or CMYK equivalents.
	Overprinting Applied in InDesign	Colors set to overprint.
	Overprinting Applied to White or Paper Objects	White or [Paper] colors set to overprint.
	[Registration] Applied	Objects have color [Registration] applied.
Images and Objects	Image Resolution	Minimum and maximum resolutions outside the defined values for color, grayscale, and 1-bit images.
	Non-Proportional Scaling of Placed Object	Horizontal and vertical scaling are not identical.
	Use Transparency	Presence of transparency effect or transparent image.
	Image ICC Profile	Profile that checks to see if image has an ICC profile.
		Searches for images that have their ICC profiles modified. Exception can be made for images with no embedded profiles.
	Layer Visibility Overrides	Images with layers turned on or off in InDesign.
	Minimum Stroke Weight	Stroke weights exceed amount set by the user. Can be limited to just multiple inks or white.
	Interactive Elements	Interactive objects such as buttons or hyperlinks.
	Bleed/Trim Hazard	Elements that exceed a certain amount outside the specified bleed area. Can also look for elements near the spine.
Text	Overset Text	Text frames with overset text.
	Paragraph Style and Character Style Overrides	Style overrides applied to text. Exceptions can be made for styles, language, kerning/tracking, or color.
	Font Missing	Missing fonts.

Categories and Errors for Preflight Profiles

Category	Profile Item	Flags as an Error
	Glyphs Missing	Glyphs that are missing from a font.
	Dynamic Spelling Detects Errors	Words flagged by the Dynamic Spelling feature.
	Font Types Not Allowed	A choice of protected fonts, TrueType, Bitmap, Type 1 Multiple Master, OpenType CFF CID, OpenType TT, Type 1 CID, ATC (Adobe Type Composer).
	Non-Proportional Type Scaling	Unequal horizontal and vertical text scaling.
	Minimum Type Size: [amount]	Text set below a certain user-defined amount. Can be limited to text with multiple inks or white.
	Cross-References	Cross-references that are out of date. Cross-references that are unresolved.
	Conditional Text Indicators Will Print	Conditional text that has been set to print its conditional set indicators
	Unresolved Caption Variable	Variable text for caption does not have information
	Span Columns Setting Not Honored	Span setting for text across columns not correct
	Tracked Changes	Tracked changes not accepted and still visible
Document	Page Size and Orientation	Page size not a specified size. Incorrect orientation can be ignored.
	Number of Pages Required	Too many or too little number of pages.
		Not a certain number of pages.
		Number of pages are not a multiple of an amount.
	Blank Pages in Document	Pages that contain no objects.
		Pages that contain only master page items.
		Pages that contain only nonprinting items.
	Bleed and Slug Setup	Bleed amounts that are not a minimum size, a maximum size, or exactly a certain size.
		Slug amounts that are not a minimum size, a maximum size, or exactly a certain size.
	All Pages Must Use Same Size And Orientation	Multiple page sizes or different orientations

To delete a preflight profile:

1. With the Preflight Profiles dialog box open, select the profile you want to delete.

2. Click the minus sign from the Preflight Profiles menu to delete the profile.

3. Click Save or OK when prompted.

You can export a profile from one document so that it can be used by other documents.

To export a preflight profile:

1. With the Preflight Profiles dialog box open, select the profile you want to export.

2. Choose Export Profile from the Preflight Profiles menu 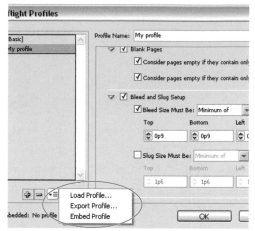.

3. Name the profile document and navigate to store it in the proper folder (directory).

4. Click Save or OK to save the profile.

Preflight profiles are saved as part of the InDesign application. However, you can embed a profile so that it is always available even if the document is moved to another person's copy of InDesign.

To embed a preflight profile:

1. With the Preflight Profiles dialog box open, select the profile you want to embed.

2. Choose Embed Profile from the Preflight Profiles menu.

   or

   Click the Embed Profile icon in the Preflight panel .

A The **Preflight Profiles menu** lets you export, add, or embed preflight profiles.

B The **Embed Profile icon** in the Preflight panel lets you embed a profile in a document.

C The **Preflight Options dialog box** controls which objects and layers should be included as part of a preflight.

Setting the Preflight Options

You can set how preflight profiles should be applied as part of a preflight check.

To set the preflight options:

1. Choose Preflight Options from the Preflight panel menu. This opens the Preflight Options dialog box **C**.

2. Use the Working Profile menu to choose which profile should be used as part of the preflight.

3. Set the When Opening Documents options to choose to use the embedded profile or the working profile.

4. Use the Layers menu in the Include area to choose which of the following items should be part of the preflight:

    • All layers in the document

    • Visible layers only

    • Visible and printable layers only

5. Select the Objects on Pasteboard checkbox to include objects not on the document pages.

6. Select the Non-printing Objects checkbox to include objects not set to print.

Packaging a Document

Instead of manually collecting files needed to print, you can use the Package command to assemble the files for you.

To package files for printing:

1. Choose **File** > **Package** to open the Package dialog box. This gives you a final overview of the document where you can spot any obvious errors 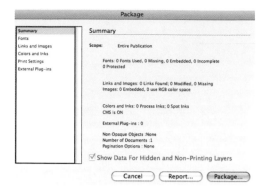.

2. Click the Package button to open the Printing Instructions dialog box.

3. Fill out the contact and file information.

4. Click Continue. This opens the Create Package Folder dialog box .

5. Name the folder that will hold the files.

6. Select the following options for the package:

   • **Copy Fonts (except** CJK**)** copies the fonts used in the document except double-byte fonts such as those for Asian languages.

   • **Copy Linked Graphics** copies placed images that are not embedded in the file.

   • **Update Graphic Links in Package** automatically updates any modified graphics.

   • **Use Document Hyphenation Exceptions Only** limits the hyphenation exceptions to only those added to the document.

   • **Include Fonts and Links From Hidden and Non-Printing Content** adds the fonts and graphics from layers that are not visible.

   • **View Report** launches a text editor to open the report created with the document.

7. Click Save to assemble all the necessary files in the package folder.

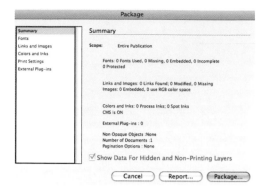

A The **Package dialog box** shows the fonts, images, links, colors, print settings, and plug-ins in the document.

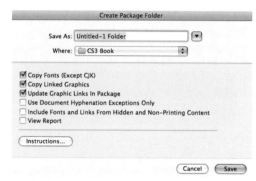

B The **Create Package Folder dialog box** lets you set options for the contents of the package that InDesign creates.

Package As You Work

I routinely package documents as I work. Most of the time this is because I've got screen shots and illustrations scattered all over my hard disk.

Another reason to package is that when you do you're doing a Save As for the file. This reduces the file size and can make the file save faster.

Exporting 20

Printing a document on paper isn't the only way in which your InDesign files can be published. Exporting gives you many options for publishing documents.

For instance, you might want to publish your document as an ebook. Or you might want a client to see the exact InDesign layout — even if they don't have the InDesign application. Or you might want to take a design that you created with InDesign and use it as the graphic in another page-layout program. Or you may want to turn your InDesign document into Web pages. You may even want to display your InDesign pages on mobile phones!

When you convert your InDesign files into other formats, you use the export features of the program. Using the Export command lets you change InDesign documents into other types of publications such as Portable Document Format (PDF) files or Extensible Hypertext Markup Language (XHTML) pages.

Setting the Export File Options

InDesign gives you many export options. In each case you choose a file format, name the file, and save it to a location.

To choose a file format:

1. Choose **File > Export**. The Export dialog box appears 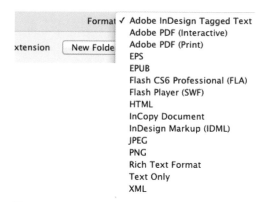.

2. Give the file a name and set the location.

3. Use the Format menu (Mac) or Save as type menu (Win) to choose one of the formats from the table below.

4. Click Save. If necessary, this opens an options dialog box for the format.

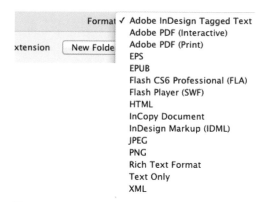

A The **options for exporting** InDesign documents.

File format	Function	Notes
Adobe InDesign Tagged Text	Creates a text file that contains the codes used for formatting text.	An insertion point must be inside a text frame for this option to appear in the Export Format list.
Adobe PDF (Interactive)	Allows you to create a PDF with interactive and multimedia features.	
Adobe PDF (Print)	Brings up the export options for creating a static PDF for print and editorial review.	
EPS	Creates a file that can be placed as a graphic. PDF files are preferred over EPS files.	
EPUB	Creates a document that can be displayed by ebook readers.	
Flash CS6 Professional (FLA)	Creates a file that can be opened by Adobe Flash CS6.	
Flash Player (SWF)	Creates a Flash movie (SWF) that can be played in a Web browser or added to a Flash (FLA) presentation.	
HTML	Exports the document in a format that can be formatted using Adobe Dreamweaver or any CSS-capable HTML editor.	

File format	Function	Notes
InCopy Document	Creates a text file that can be opened using InCopy.	A text frame must be selected or an insertion point must be inside a text frame for this option to appear in the Export Format list.
InDesign Snippet	Creates a small file that contains the instructions for recreating InDesign elements.	An object or objects must be selected for this option to appear in the Export Format list.
InDesign Markup (IDML)	Creates a file that can be opened by the InDesign CS4 or later applications. It also can be used to clean up CS6 files that are behaving strangely.	This creates the same file format as the Save As InDesign CS4 or later command. Honest, it's the exact same format. So you can use either command.
JPEG	Converts the page, pages, or selected elements into a raster image that can be used in a Web page.	
PNG	Converts the page, pages, or selected elements into a raster image that can be used in a Web page.	
Rich Text Format	Exports selected text with formatting that can be read by most word processing applications.	An insertion point must be inside a text frame for this option to appear in the Export Format list.
Text Only	Exports selected text without any formatting.	An insertion point must be inside a text frame for this option to appear in the Export Format list.
XML	Creates text formatted with the Extensible Markup Language, which offers customizable definitions and formatting tags.	

Creating Print PDF Files

Adobe has provided two types of PDF files—Print and Interactive. However, you can use the print files for onscreen work. And you can print out the interactive files

To set the PDF (Print) export options:

1. Choose Adobe PDF (Print) from the Export dialog box. The Export Adobe PDF dialog box appears.

2. Click each of the categories on the left side of the Export Adobe PDF dialog box 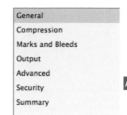 to display the options.

> **TIP** You do not need to set all the controls every time you print unless you need to change a specific setting.

3. Click the Export button to create the PDF file.

Setting the PDF General Controls

These are the various areas in the General category for exporting as a PDF 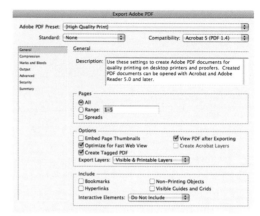.

To set the PDF version and standard:

1. Use the Compatibility menu to choose which version of PDF files you want to save 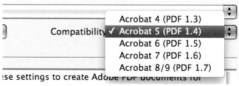.

> **TIP** Higher versions allow you to save a PDF with more options.

2. Use the Standard menu to choose one of these five recognized ISO (International Organization for Standardization) standards for PDF/X files 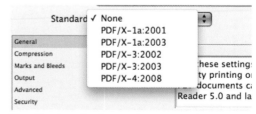.

> **TIP** Check with your print shop or publication for which PDF/X file they require.

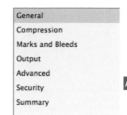

A The Export Adobe PDF (Print) **categories list**.

B The **General category** of the Export Adobe PDF (Print) dialog box.

C The **Compatibility menu** lets you choose which PDF version you export.

D The **Standard menu** lets you apply an ISO printing standard for PDF documents.

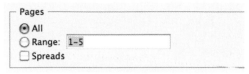

Pages
- ⊙ All
- ○ Range: 1–5
- ☐ Spreads

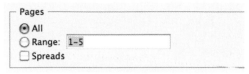

E The **Pages area** in the General category of the Export Adobe PDF (Print) dialog box.

Options
- ☐ Embed Page Thumbnails   ☑ View PDF after Exporting
- ☑ Optimize for Fast Web View   ☐ Create Acrobat Layers
- ☑ Create Tagged PDF
- Export Layers: [Visible & Printable Layers ▼]

F The **Options controls** in the General category of the Export Adobe PDF (Print) dialog box.

To specify which pages to export:

1. In the Pages area, select All to export all the pages in the document **E**.

   or

   Select Range to enter specific pages.

   TIP Use the hyphen to select a range of pages such as *4–9*, or use commas to enter individual pages such as *3, 8*.

2. Select the Spreads checkbox to keep pages that are within spreads together in the Acrobat file.

To set the general options:

1. Choose one of the following from the Options area in the General category **F**:

   - **Embed Page Thumbnails** adds a thumbnail image for each page. It is not necessary for Acrobat 5 and higher.

   - **Optimize for Fast Web View** prepares for downloading from Web servers.

   - **Create Tagged PDF** adds tags that allow the PDF to be read by screen readers.

   - **View PDF after Exporting** opens the finished Adobe PDF file in Acrobat.

   - **Create Acrobat Layers** is available for PDF 1.5 and higher. It converts the InDesign layers into Acrobat layers.

2. Choose which layers to include from the Export Layers list **F**.

ISO Standards?

The ISO (International Organization for Standardization) has created standards for PDF documents. When you use these standards you are choosing settings that are relied on as working properly for many publishers. This eliminates many of the color, font, and trapping variables that may create printing problems.

You may be asked to use a PDF/X standard if you are creating PDF documents that will be placed in magazines or newspapers.

To control what to include in the PDF:

Choose one of the following from the Include area in the General category **A**:

- **Bookmarks** creates bookmarks for table of contents entries, preserving the TOC levels.

- **Hyperlinks** creates Acrobat hyperlinks from InDesign hyperlinks, cross-references, table of contents entries, and index entries.

- **Non-Printing Objects** exports objects that have the nonprinting option applied.

- **Visible Guides and Grids** exports the guides and grids currently visible in the document.

If you have interactive elements, such as rollover buttons, you need to control how to handle those elements during PDF export.

To handle interactive elements:

Choose one of the following from the Interactive Elements menu **A**:

- **Do Not Include** deletes the interactive elements from the PDF output. Use this option when you want no trace of the interactive element in the PDF file.

- **Include Appearance** leaves the visible artwork for the interactive elements, but deletes the interactivity.

A The **Include settings** in the General category of the Export Adobe PDF (Print) dialog box.

Creating PDF Files for Both Print and Interactivity

So what should you do if you need a PDF for print as well as an interactive presentation? The answer is simple, just export once using the Adobe PDF (Print) controls and then again using the Adobe PDF (Interactive) settings.

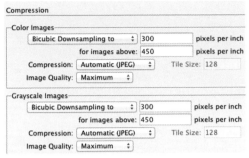

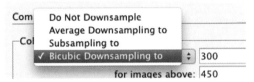

B The **Compression controls** in the Export Adobe PDF (Print) dialog box for color and grayscale bitmap images.

C The **Sampling menu** for color and grayscale bitmap images.

D The **resolution fields** for color and grayscale bitmap images.

> **Talk to Your Print Shop**
>
> If you create PDF files for onscreen viewing or to be downloaded from the Web, you can use the compression settings to reduce the file size.
>
> However, if you create PDF files to be output by a print shop, you should not apply too much downsampling or compression.
>
> Ask your print shop for the correct settings. Better yet, ask them to create a PDF preset that you can load onto your machine.

Setting the PDF Compression Options

One of the benefits of creating PDF files is that they can be compressed to take up less space. You use the same controls for compressing color and grayscale bitmap images **B**.

To set the color and grayscale images:

1. Choose one of the following from the Sampling menu **C**:

   - **Do Not Downsample** does not throw away any pixel information. Use this to maintain all information in the image.

   - **Average Downsampling to** averages the pixels in a sample area.

   - **Subsampling to** reduces processing time compared to downsampling, but creates images that are less smooth.

   - **Bicubic downsampling to** is the slowest but most precise method, resulting in the smoothest tonal gradations.

2. Enter an amount in the resolution field **D**.

   TIP For print work this setting is usually 1.5 times the line screen of the printing press.

   TIP For onscreen viewing this setting is usually 72 pixels per inch.

3. Enter an amount in the field for images above a certain resolution **D**.

   TIP This helps you downsample only high-resolution images without losing information in lower-resolution images.

To set the color and grayscale compression:

1. Choose one of the following from the Compression menu :

   - **None** applies no compression.

   - **Automatic (JPEG)** lets InDesign automatically determine the best quality for color and grayscale images.

   - Use **JPEG** for images with tonal changes.

   - Use **ZIP** for images with large areas of flat color.

   - Use **JPEG** 2000 for tonal images for Acrobat 6 or higher.

   - Use **Automatic** (**JPEG 2000**) for color and grayscale images for Acrobat 6 or higher.

2. Choose an Image Quality setting :

   - **Maximum** sets the least amount of compression.

   - **Minimum** sets the most.

There are different compression options for monochrome bitmap images (such as 1-bit scanned art).

To set the monochrome bitmap downsampling:

Choose one of the following from the Sampling menu 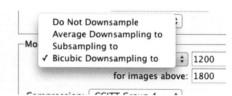:

- **Do Not Downsample** does not throw away any pixel information. Use this setting if you want to maintain all the information in the image.

- **Average Downsampling to** averages the pixels in a sample area.

- **Subsampling to** is faster than downsampling, but creates images that are less smooth.

- **Bicubic downsampling to** is the slowest but most precise method, resulting in the smoothest tonal gradations.

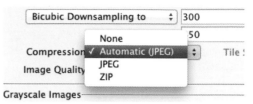

A   The **Compression menu** for color and grayscale bitmap images.

B   The **Image Quality menu** for color and grayscale bitmap images.

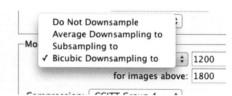

C   The **Sampling menu** for monochrome images.

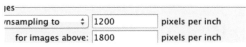

D The **resolution fields** for monochrome images.

E The **Compression menu** for monochrome images.

> ### Marks and Bleeds PDF Options
>
> The options for setting the Marks and Bleeds category for PDF documents are the same as the options when you print the file. *See Chapter 19, "Printing," for how to work with those settings.*

To set the monochrome bitmap resolution:

1. When you have set a downsampling method, enter an amount in the resolution field **D**.

TIP For print work, this setting is usually the resolution of the output device, with a limit of 1500 dots per inch.

2. Enter an amount in the field for images above a certain resolution **D**.

TIP This helps you downsample only high-resolution images without losing information in lower-resolution images.

To set the compression for monochrome images:

1. Choose one of the following from the Compression menu **E**:

   • **None** applies no compression to the image.

   • **CCITT Group 3** is similar to the compression used for faxes.

   • **CCITT Group 4** is a general-purpose method that produces good results for most monochromatic images.

   • **ZIP** works well for black-and-white images that contain repeating patterns.

   • **Run Length** produces the best results for images that contain large areas of solid black or white.

2. Select Compress Text and Line Art to further reduce the size of the file.

3. Select Crop Image Data to Frames to delete the image outside the frame.

Exporting Interative PDF Files

The Export PDF (Interactive) dialog box is where you can control the settings for interactive documents. This dialog box omits the controls for high-end print production.

TIP Once you have created an interactive PDF, you can still print it to a desktop printer.

To export as an interactive PDF:

1. Choose **File > Export** and then choose Adobe PDF (Interactive) as the format.

2. Name the file and click the Save button. The Export to Interactive PDF dialog box appears **A**.

You can set the options for how the page opens in Acrobat.

To set the page view options:

1. Choose one of the options from the View menu **B**. This sets the magnification for how the PDF file opens.

2. Use the Layout menu to choose how the pages are arranged when the document is opened **C**.

3. Click Presentation: Open in Full Screen Mode to have the PDF file cover the entire screen.

4. If you choose the full screen mode, you can set the timing to have the pages automatically flip every certain number of seconds.

5. Use the Page Transitions menu to choose the transitions already in the document or to override them with new transitions. (*For more information, see "Setting Page Transitions" on page 438.*)

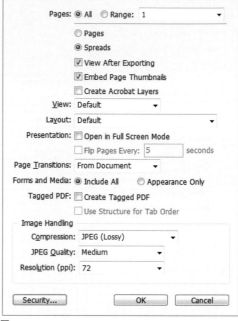

A The **Export to Interactive PDF dialog box**.

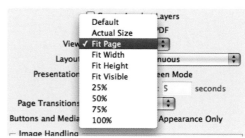

B The **View menu** of the Export Interactive PDF dialog box.

C The **Layout menu** of the Export Interactive PDF dialog box.

D   The **Compression menu** of the Export Interactive PDF dialog box.

E   The **JPEQ Quality menu** of the Export Interactive PDF dialog box.

To set the options for tagged PDF files:

1. Select Create Tagged PDF to apply the electronic tags that help screen reader devices convert the text to speech for visually impaired readers.

2. If you have set a Tagged PDF you can choose Use Structure for Tab Order for the order in which tabbing moves through the document.

Finally, you can choose how any bitmapped images or effects (such as drop shadows and glows) are compressed when exported.

To set the Image Handling options:

1. Use the Compression menu to choose how images are converted .

2. Use the JPEG Quality menu to control the amount of detail in the exported image . The higher the quality, the larger the file size.

3. Use the Resolution (ppi) field to set the output resolution. Use 72 ppi for most work. Set a higher resolution if your viewers will zoom in to see images at higher magnification.

Setting the PDF Security Options

You can also set security options for both types of PDF files to restrict who can open the file or to limit what they can do to it.

To set the Security options:

Click the Security choice in the Export Adobe PDF categories list or click the Security button in the Export to Interactive PDF dialog box. This opens the Security dialog box.

The Document Open Password area allows you to set the password that readers must enter in order to open the file.

To set the document password:

1. Select Require a Password to Open The Document 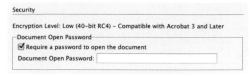.

2. Type a password in the Document Open Password field.

The Permissions area sets up what modifications people can make to the PDF. A password is needed in order to change the settings in the Permissions area.

To set the permissions password:

1. Select Use a Password to Restrict Printing, Editing, and Other Tasks **B**.

2. Type a password in the Permissions Password field.

TIP The Permissions Password can't be the same as the Document Open Password.

A The **Document Open Password area** of the Security category of the Export Adobe PDF dialog box.

B The **Permissions area** of the Security category of the Export Adobe PDF dialog box.

Limits of Security

Even when you set security options, there are some additional things to remember.

First, if you email a PDF document, send the password in a separate email. That makes it less likely that the password will be found if your email is hijacked.

Next, passwords are case sensitive. Use a combination of uppercase and lowercase letters as well as numbers to make the password more secure. Don't use ordinary words as passwords.

Finally, if you feel that you would lose your entire livelihood if the PDF were to fall into the wrong hands, then don't distribute it as a PDF. There are plenty of people who take it as a challenge to break into password-protected PDF documents.

C The **Printing Allowed menu** of the Security category of the Export Adobe PDF dialog box.

D The **Changes Allowed menu** of the Security category of the Export Adobe PDF dialog box.

E The other permissions you can set in the **Security category** of the Export Adobe PDF dialog box.

To set the printing permission:

Choose one of the following from the Printing Allowed menu **C**:

- **None** turns off all printing from the document.
- **Low Resolution (150 dpi)** prints only low-resolution versions of the images.
- **High Resolution** prints the full resolution of the images.

To set the changes that are allowed:

1. Choose one of the following from the Changes Allowed menu **D**:
   - **None** allows no changes whatsoever.
   - **Inserting, deleting and rotating pages** allows the user only to add, remove, or change the position of pages in the document. It does not allow changing the content of the pages.
   - **Filling in form fields and signing** allows changes to form fields or applying a security signature to the document.
   - **Commenting, filling in form fields, and signing** allows adding comments, changing form fields, or applying a security signature to the document.
   - **Any except extracting pages** allows all changes except removing pages from the document.

2. Select any of the following as desired **E**:
   - **Enable copying of text, images and other content.**
   - **Enable text access of screen reader devices for the visually impaired.**
   - **Enable plaintext metadata.**

Using InDesign Markup Files

The InDesign Markup export command creates an IDML file. This IDML file can then be opened using InDesign CS4 or later. This is the same as the using the Save As InDesign CS4 or later (IDML) command. (*For more information see page 38.*)

Exporting for InCopy

InCopy is InDesign's sister program that is used for word processing. At about one-third the cost of InDesign, InCopy is the best way to create an editorial and design workflow between the two users. InCopy documents are then automatically linked to the InDesign file.

To export as an InCopy file:

1. Place your insertion point inside the story that you want to export.

2. Choose **File > Export** and then choose the InCopy Document format.

3. If prompted, choose a User Name, which is used to identify each person working on an InCopy document **A**.

4. Name and save the document. An icon appears on the frame indicating that the story is linked to an external InCopy file **B**.

TIP A pencil icon indicates that the story has been checked out for editing **C**.

A The **User dialog box** lets you assign a distinct user name to each person who works on the InCopy document.

B The **linked file icon** means that the story is linked to an external InCopy file.

C The **pencil icon** means that the InCopy story is currently checked out.

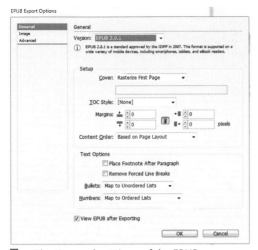

D The **General settings** of the EPUB Export Options dialog box.

E The **Image settings** of the EPUB Export Options dialog box.

Exporting EPUB Files

EPUB files are special versions of HTML that can be read by ereader devices such as the Amazon Kindle or Apple iPad. For an in-depth coverage of creating and exporting EPUB files, see *Digital Publishing with Adobe InDesign CS6* by Sandee Cohen and Diane Burns, published by Adobe Press.

To export as an EPUB file:

    Choose **File > Export** and then choose the EPUB format.

There are three sections to exporting EPUB documents from InDesign.

To choose the general controls of the EPUB Export Options:

1. Click the General category of the EPUB Export Options dialog box **D**.
2. Choose the version of the EPUB.

TIP At the time of writing these instructions, most devices only support version 2.0.1.

3. Choose the options for the Setup controls.
4. Choose the setup for the Text Options.
5. Choose to view the EPUB after Exporting.

TIP You can download the Digital Editions application from Adobe to preview the EPUB.

You use the Image controls of the EPUB Export Options dialog box to set the options for the images in the EPUB.

To choose the Image controls of the EPUB Export Options:

1. Click the Image category of the EPUB Export Options dialog box **E**.
2. Set the options for the resolution, alignment, and conversions for the images.
3. Set the options for creating GIF or JPEG images.

Finally, you can set the the Advanced controls of the EPUB Export Options dialog box 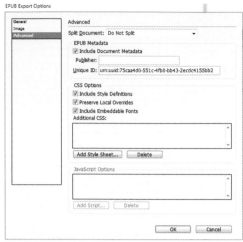.

To choose the Advanced controls of the JPEG Export Options:

1. Click the Advanced category of the EPUB Export Options dialog box.

2. Set the metadata options for the publisher and unique identifier of the publication.

TIP If you leave the identifier field empty, a unique identifier will automatically be created for the EPUB.

3. Set the CSS Options to control the cascading styles applied to the text.

4. Set the Javascript Options to control what scripts run within the document.

A The **Advanced Settings** of the EPUB Export Options dialog box.

Exporting HTML Files

InDesign lets you export files in the HTML format. However, these files are not complete Web pages. You need to open the HTML in a program such as Dreamweaver that can convert these HTML files into fully formed Web pages.

To export as an HTML file:

Choose **File** > **Export** and then choose the HTML format.

B The **General settings** of the HTML Export Options dialog box.

HTML Export Options

C The **Image settings** of the HTML Export Options dialog box.

D The **Advanced settings** of the HTML Export Options dialog box.

There are three sections to exporting HTML files from InDesign.

To choose the general controls of the EPUB Export Options:

1. Click the General category B.

2. Set the options to export the document or the selection.

3. Set the options for the order in which items are arranged on the page.

4. Choose the format options for bullets or numbered list.

5. Check the option to view after exporting.

To choose the image controls of the HTML Export Options:

1. Click the Image category C.

2. Set the options for the formatting, resolution, alignment, and conversions for the images.

3. Set the options for creating GIF or JPEG images.

To choose the Advanced controls of the HTML Export Options:

1. Click the Advanced category D.

2. Set the CSS Options to control the cascading styles applied to the text.

3. Set the Javascript Options to control what scripts run within the document.

Exporting JPEG Files

You might want to convert an InDesign document into a JPEG file that can be posted on the Web. This can be done using the Export JPEG dialog box 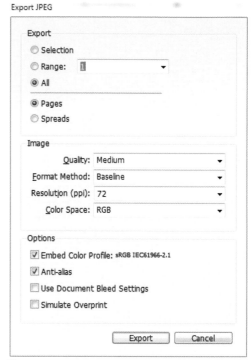.

To export as an JPEG file:

Choose **File** > **Export** and then choose the JPEG format.

To set the JPEG export controls:

1. Use the Export area to choose what pages or objects are exported:

2. Use the Image area to set the qualiy, format, resolution, and color space.

3. Use the Options to embed a color profile to maintain the color of the image.

4. Choose Anti-alias to add grayscale smoothing of text and vector art.

5. Check Use Document Bleed Settings to add the bleed space to the image size.

6. Check Simulate Overprint to combine colors set to overprint.

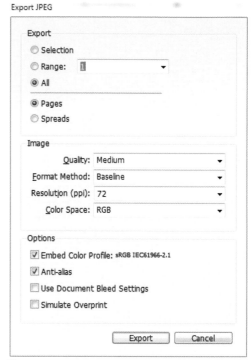

A   The **Export JPEG dialog box**.

Export PNG

B The **Export PNG dialog box**.

Exporting PNG Files

PNG is another file format that is used on the web as well as in programs such as Microsoft Power Point. You can export InDesign files in the PNG format using the Export PNG dialog box **B**.

To export as a PNG file:

Choose **File** > **Export** and then choose the PNG format.

To set the PNG export controls:

1. Use the Export area to choose what pages or objects are exported.

2. Use the Image area to set the qualiy, format, resolution, and color space.

3. Use the Options to set the background as transparent.

4. Choose Anti-alias to add grayscale smoothing of text and vector art.

5. Check Use Document Bleed Settings to add the bleed space to the image size.

6. Check Simulate Overprint to combine colors set to overprint.

Exporting as SWF Files

One of the coolest features for exporting InDesign documents is the ability to convert the entire file into a SWF document. Not only is the SWF file smaller than a similar PDF, but it also has special effects not available in a PDF document. For an in-depth coverage of creating SWF files, see *Digital Publishing with with Adobe InDesign CS6* by Sandee Cohen and Diane Burns, published by Adobe Press.

To export as a SWF document:

1. Choose **File** > **Export** and then choose Flash Player (SWF) as the format.

2. Click the General to set the General options 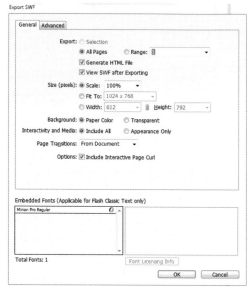.

3. Click the Advanced tabs to choose the different settings B.

4. Apply the SWF options.

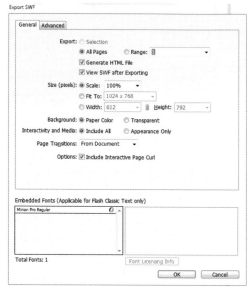

A The **General options** of the Export SWF dialog box.

B The **Advanced options** of the Export SWF dialog box.

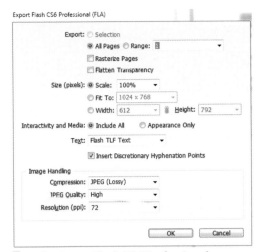

C The **Export Flash CS6 Professional (FLA) dialog box**.

What to Do with Flash Files

I'm not an expert with Adobe Flash Professional, but even I know how limited the SWF animation tools are in InDesign. Fortunately I have a few friends who I can cajole into helping me finish off a project that I start in InDesign CS6. The way I can do this is work in InDesign, and then export the file as a FLA file. (FLA is the native file format for Adobe Flash.) The Flash expert can then open this file in Flash CS6 Professional and make changes, add new animations, and then export it as a finished SWF.

The benefit of this is that I create the rough layout in a program I am familiar with while the finished SWF gets all the bells and whistles of Adobe Flash.

Exporting as FLA Files

InDesign also lets you export files in the native Flash (FLA) format that can be opened in Adobe Flash. These files can then be modified and enchanced for final output.

To export as a FLA file:

1. Choose **File > Export** and then choose Flash CS6 Professional (FLA) for the format C.

2. Set the Export options to control what pages are exported.

3. Use the Size area to set the size of the exported document.

4. Use the Interactivity and Media area to set how interactive elements are exported.

5. Set the type of text for the Flash file.

6. Use the Image Handling area to choose how images are converted into JPEP files.

Exporting Text

You may find it necessary to export text from InDesign. For instance, you may want to send the text to someone who works with Microsoft Word. You can send them a text file by exporting the text.

To export text:

1. Place an insertion point inside the frame that contains the text. All the text within that story will be exported.

TIP Select an area of text to export only that portion of the text.

2. Choose **File** > **Export**. This opens the Export dialog box.

3. Choose a text export format:
   - **Rich Text Format** keeps all the styles and text formatting. This format can be opened by most word processors, especially Microsoft Word.
   - **Text Only** exports only the characters of the text and discards any styles and text formatting. Use this option only if you want to strip out the text formatting or if the application you are working with does not support Rich Text Format.
   - **Adobe InDesign Tagged Text** format exports the text with special codes for local character formatting and styles.

4. Name the file and choose a destination.

5. Click Save to export the file.

Customizing 21

Working with computer software is a personal thing. I'm always impressed with how emotional my students are (maybe *too* emotional) about how their software should work. One student tells me she hates the way a certain feature works; yet another insists it's his favorite thing in the entire program.

The InDesign team recognizes that some people want the program to work one way, and others want it exactly the opposite. That's why there are many ways to customize the program.

You can change the keyboard shortcuts so that they are similar to other software you use. You can modify the settings for the display of images and onscreen elements. You can control how text wraps around other objects. You can even throw away all your own customized settings and start back at the out-of-the-box settings.

It's all your choice.

Modifying Keyboard Shortcuts

Keyboard shortcuts are the fastest way to invoke program commands. However, if you are used to working with other programs, your fingers may be trained to use those other shortcuts. You may also want to assign a shortcut to a command that doesn't have a shortcut. InDesign lets you change the keyboard shortcuts to keystrokes that match your preferences.

InDesign ships with three sets of shortcuts. The default set is the one that the Adobe engineers created. This set uses most of the shortcuts found in Adobe products such as Adobe Illustrator or Adobe Photoshop. The second set contains the shortcuts used in PageMaker 7.0. The third set contains the shortcuts used in QuarkXPress 4.0.

To change the shortcut set:

1. Choose **Edit > Keyboard Shortcuts**. The Keyboard Shortcuts dialog box appears **A**.

2. Choose one of the shortcuts from the Set menu **B**.

3. Click OK. The new shortcuts appear in the menus **C**.

TIP Some keyboard shortcuts are "hard-wired" to the program and do not change to match the keystrokes in PageMaker or QuarkXPress. For instance, the Zoom tool does not change to the XPress Control key (Mac) or Ctrl-Spacebar (Win) shortcuts.

A The **Keyboard Shortcuts dialog box** lets you change the shortcuts used for commands, tools, and panels.

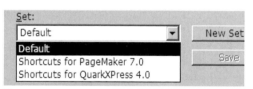

B The **Set menu** lets you choose a set of keyboard preferences.

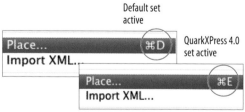

C You can switch the InDesign default shortcuts to the set for other applications.

D The **New Set dialog box** lets you name a new shortcut set and choose which set it should be based on.

Creating Your Own Keyboard Shortcuts

I use quite a few programs from many different software companies. I taught QuarkXPress for more than 17 years. I work with both Adobe Illustrator and Acrobat. I also know Adobe Photoshop and Adobe Fireworks. And I use InDesign to lay out all my books.

With all those programs in my head, I find it easier to teach my fingers just one set of shortcuts. That's InDesign because I use it the most.

I don't change InDesign's keyboard shortcuts to follow all those other programs. I find it easier to concentrate on learning InDesign's shortcuts. It's the primary program I use when working on a book — so I'd rather remember its shortcuts.

New Shortcuts for Commands

My primary use for new shortcuts is to add shortcuts to commands that I use a lot, but don't have a keyboard command.

For instance, the Change Case commands under the type menu don't have any shortcuts. But I'm constantly applying the Lowercase command to text that has been typed with the Caps Lock key on. That's why I set a keyboard shortcut for that command.

If you work with other programs, you may want to create your own shortcut set to match it.

To create a new shortcut set:

1. Choose **Edit > Keyboard Shortcuts**.
2. Choose New Set. This opens the New Set dialog box **D**.
3. Enter a name for the set.
4. Choose a set that the new set will be based on.

TIP A set must be based on another set so that it starts with some shortcuts. However, If you later change something in the original set, the one that was based on it does not change.

5. Click OK. You can now edit the set as described on the next page.

If you want a list of keyboard shortcuts to print out and post next to your computer, you can create a file with all the shortcuts.

To create a list of the keyboard shortcuts:

1. Choose **Edit > Keyboard Shortcuts**.
2. Use the menu to choose the set.
3. Click the Show Set button. This opens the list of shortcuts in Notepad (Win) or TextEdit (Mac).
4. Print the text file.

TIP I can't always remember where a specific shortcut is located. So I create the text file of shortcuts and then use the text editor Find command to search for the location of the shortcut.

You can change the shortcut applied to a command. However, not all commands have shortcuts assigned to them. So you can also assign a shortcut to commands.

To change or assign a shortcut:

1. Choose a shortcut set in the Keyboard Shortcuts dialog box.

   or

   Create a new set.

2. Use the Product Area menu to choose the part of the program that contains the command to which you want to assign a shortcut 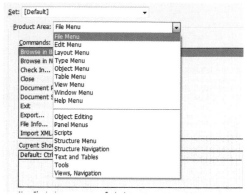.

3. Choose a command from the list under the Product Area menu 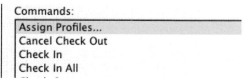.

4. Use the Context menu to choose in what portion of the program the keystroke will work .

5. Click inside the New Shortcut field to make that field active.

6. Press the keys on the keyboard that you want to assign to invoke the command.

   TIP If the keystroke is already assigned to another command, the command that uses the shortcut is listed in the Currently Assigned to area .

7. Change the keys if necessary by selecting them and typing a new combination.

   or

   Click Assign to apply the new shortcut.

8. Click Save to save the set as modified.

To delete a set:

1. Use the Set menu to choose the set you want to delete.

2. Click the Delete Set button.

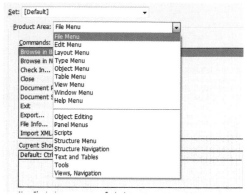

A The **Product Area menu** lets you choose which parts of the program you want to change.

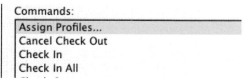

B The **Commands field** contains a list of the commands available for a specific product area.

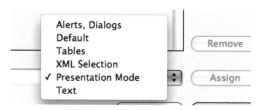

C The **Context menu** lets you choose in which context a keyboard shortcut is applied.

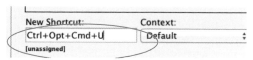

D The **Currently Assigned to area** shows what command a keystroke is assigned to.

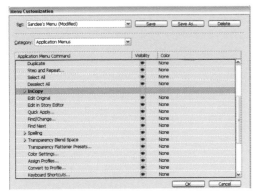

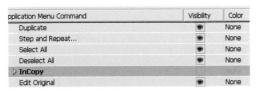

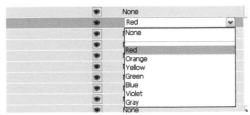

E The **Menu Customization dialog box** lets you modify the appearance of menu commands.

F The **Category list** lets you choose between the Application menus or the Context & Panel menus.

G Click the **Visibility icon** to change the menu display. When the icon is hidden, the menu command does not show.

H Use the **Color menu** to highlight a command with a color in the menu.

Modifying the Menu Commands

You may feel that the menus in InDesign are too long for you to easily find the command you want to choose. Or you would like one menu command to stand out from the others. You can easily customize the menus to highlight or hide certain commands.

To highlight menu commands:

1. Choose **Edit > Menus**. This opens the Menu Customization dialog box **E**.

2. Use the Category list to choose the Application menus or the Context & Panel menus **F**.

3. Click the command you wish to customize.

4. Click the Visibility icon to cause the command to be hidden or visible in the menu **G**.

5. Use the Color menu to choose a background color to highlight the command in the menu **H**.

6. Use the Save or Save As buttons to save the custom set of menus.

As you are working, you may want to invoke a command that has been hidden. Rather than turn off the custom menu configuration, you can temporarily restore the command.

To restore a hidden command to a menu:

1. Click the menu that ordinarily contains the command.

2. Choose Show All Menu Items from the bottom of the menu. This temporarily restores all hidden commands to that menu.

Choosing the Preferences Categories

InDesign has 18 categories that let you customize how the program works.

TIP Change the preferences with no document open to create the defaults for all new documents.

To choose a preference category:

1. Choose **Edit** > **Preferences** > **[category]** **(Win)**. This opens the Preferences dialog box 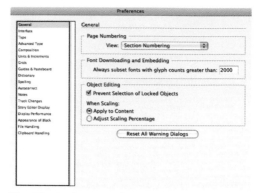. Or choose **InDesign** > **Preferences** > **[category]** **(Mac)**.

2. Click the categories on the left side of the dialog box to open a new category.

General Preferences Controls

The General category lets you control several types of preferences .

If you have several sections in the same document, they could all have a page number of 1. The page numbering preferences change how the page numbers are displayed.

To set the page number preferences:

Choose one of the following from the Page Numbering View menu 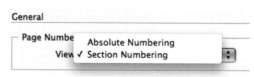:

- **Absolute Numbering** uses the physical placement number of the page in the document **D**.
- **Section Numbering** uses the numbers set from the section options **D**.

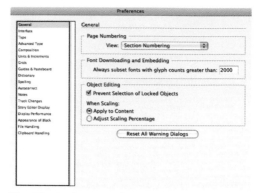

A The **Preferences dialog box**.

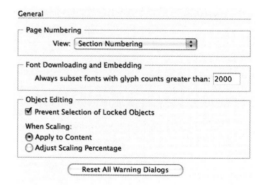

B The **General settings** of the Preferences dialog box.

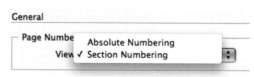

C The **Page Numbering View menu** lets you choose the section numbers or absolute numbers.

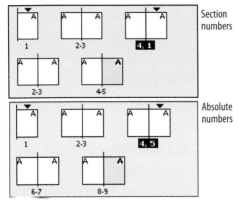

Section numbers

Absolute numbers

D The difference in the Pages panel between using absolute numbers and section numbers. The black triangles indicate the start of a new section.

```
┌─ Font Downloading and Embedding ──────────────┐
│  Always subset fonts with glyph counts greater than: 2000 │
└───────────────────────────────────────────────┘
```

E The **Font Downloading and Embedding** area lets you control whether fonts are embedded or subset.

```
┌─ Object Editing ──────────────────────────────┐
│  ☑ Prevent Selection of Locked Objects        │
```

F Deselect **Prevent Selection of Locked Objects** to use them as the anchored objects for alignment.

```
When Scaling:
 ⦿ Apply to Content
 ○ Adjust Scaling Percentage
```

G Choose one of the **When Scaling options** to set how the point size of text changes when the frame is scaled.

```
┌──────────────────────────────┐
│     Reset All Warning Dialogs │
└──────────────────────────────┘
```

H Click the **Reset All Warning Dialogs button** to bring back those annoying alert messages when you perform certain actions.

The Font Downloading and Embedding section controls the threshold below which a font is subset.

To choose the threshold for font subsetting:

Enter an amount in the Always Subset Fonts With Glyph Counts Greater Than field **E**.

TIP The number 2000 ensures that fonts with large character sets are always subset, creating smaller files. Custom fonts with a few characters are set in their entirety.

To select locked objects:

Deselect Prevent Selection of Locked Objects to use them as the anchored objects for alignment **F**.

To set the scaling preferences:

Choose one of the following from the When Scaling area **G**.

- **Apply to Content** scales text so that the point size changes.

- **Adjust Scaling Percentage** scales text so that the original point size is displayed with the new size in parentheses.

Every once in a while you may see a dialog box that warns you about doing something. These alerts have checkboxes you can select so you never see the warning again. If you've turned them off, you can reset them all to turn back on.

To reset the warning dialog boxes:

Click the Reset All Warning Dialogs button at the bottom of the General preferences **H**. An alert box informs you that you will now see the warnings.

Interface Preferences

The Interface preferences control how some aspects of the program appear 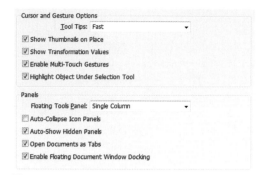. Tool tips are notes that appear when you pause the cursor over an onscreen element .

To control how quickly the tool tips are displayed:

Use the Tool Tips menu to choose one of the following:

- **Normal** waits a moment before displaying the tip.
- **None** turns off the display of the tips.
- **Fast** displays the tool tips almost immediately.

The Cursor Options let you change how the mouse cursor behaves.

To change the place cursor preview:

Deselect the option Show Thumbnails on Place to see only the cursor, and not the thumbnail preview, for placed text and images .

To change transformation preview:

Deselect the option Show Transformation Values to see only the cursor, and not the transformation values as you draw and modify objects .

You can also control whether InDesign allows you to use the multi-touch gestures for track-pads and mice.

To control trackpad gestures:

Deselect the option Enable Multi-Touch Gestures to avoid input by two or three fingers on trackpads and mice that use that feature.

A   The **Interface settings** of the Preferences dialog box.

B   An example of a **tool tip** that appears when you pause over an interface element.

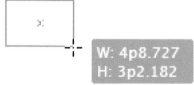

C   The **thumbnail preview** next to the Place cursor.

D   The **transformation values** that appear as you create or modify objects.

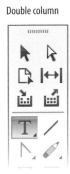
Double column

Single column

Single row

E The **arrangements for the Tools panel.**

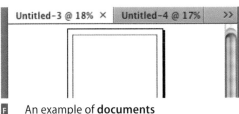

F An example of **documents arranged in tabs**.

The default for the Tools panel is a single column. But you can change that setting.

To change the display of the Tools panel:

Use the Floating Tools Panel menu to choose how the Tools panel is displayed **E**:

- **Double column** shows the tools vertically in two columns.
- **Single column** shows the tools vertically in a single column.
- **Single row** arranges the tools horizontally in a single row.

TIP Click the two arrows in the Tools panel title bar to shift between the three settings *when it is not docked.*

You can also change how the panels and documents behave.

To change how docked panels collapse:

Select Auto-Collapse Icon Panels to cause selected docked panels to automatically close when you move back to a document.

To change how hidden panels are displayed:

Select Auto-Show Hidden Panels to display any panels that were hidden by pressing Tab or Shift-Tab when the cursor moves over the hidden panel area.

To change how new documents appear:

Select Open Documents as Tabs to combine the windows for new documents into a tabbed display **F**.

To change how documents can be docked to others:

Select Enable Floating Document Window Docking to allow floating document windows to dock as tabs into other windows while being dragged.

Type Preferences

Use the Type Preferences controls for working with text 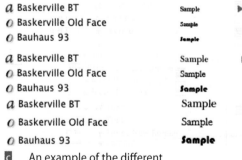 A.

To set the Type Options preferences:

1. Use Typographer's Quotes automatically changes typewriter quotes into the proper curly quote characters B.

2. Type Tool Converts Frames to Text Frames lets you double-click inside a frame to change from the selection tools to the Type tool.

3. Automatically Use Correct Optical Size sets the correct value for the optical size of Multiple Master fonts.

4. Select the Triple Click to Select a Line checkbox so that three clicks selects a line, four clicks selects a paragraph, and five clicks selects the story.

TIP If this option is deselected, three clicks selects the paragraph and four clicks selects the story.

5. Apply Leading to Entire Paragraphs lets InDesign work more like QuarkXPress.

6. Adjust Spacing Automatically When Cutting and Pasting Words avoids adding two spaces when pasting text.

7. Font Preview Size lets you choose the size of the preview in the Type menu C.

TIP Deselect this option to turn off the font preview and make the menu display faster.

You can also control whether or not drag-and-drop text is activated.

To turn on drag-and-drop text:

1. Select Enable in Layout View to drag selected text when working within frames.

2. Select Enable in Story Editor to drag selected text within the Story Editor.

A The **Type settings** of the Preferences dialog box.

"The Wizard of Oz" Off
"The Wizard of Oz" On

B An example of using **typographer's quotes**.

a Baskerville BT — Sample ▶
o Baskerville Old Face — Sample
o Bauhaus 93 — Sample

a Baskerville BT — Sample ▶
o Baskerville Old Face — Sample
o Bauhaus 93 — Sample

a Baskerville BT — Sample
o Baskerville Old Face — Sample
o Bauhaus 93 — Sample

C An example of the different font preview sizes.

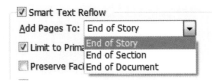

 Use the **Add Pages To menu** to control where new pages are added for Smart Text Reflow.

The Smart Text Reflow options control how new pages and frames are created when text overflows a frame.

To set the Smart Text Reflow options:

1. Turn on Smart Text Reflow to automatically add pages when a story spans at least two pages.

2. Use the Add Pages To menu to choose where the new pages will be added as follows :

   - **End of Story** adds pages directly after the page that contains the story.

   - **End of Section** adds pages to the last page in that section of the document. This can cause the story to skip pages.

   - **End of Document** adds pages after the last page in the document. This can cause the story to skip pages.

3. Choose Limit to Master Text Frames to only add pages when copy overflows master text frames.

4. Choose Preserve Facing-Page Spreads to ensure that the number of right- or left-hand pages remains constant when new pages are added.

5. Select Delete Empty Pages to have InDesign automatically delete any pages where the linked text frame no longer contains text.

TIP Pages are deleted only if the text frame is the only object on the page.

My Preferences for Smart Text Reflow

I'm a typist. So the idea of being able to type in InDesign and add or delete pages as I work is very appealing. However, I have modified the default settings for Smart Text Reflow.

First, I have turned off the setting for Limit to Master Text Frames. This way I can place text directly onto a page without using master text frames.

Next, I always add pages at the end of the story. It is too confusing to go find linked pages that might appear way at the end of the document or section.

Next, I have Preserve Facing-Page Spreads turned off. I don't mind adding another right-hand page to my document as I add pages.

Finally, I always select Delete Empty Pages. It's so cathartic to watch InDesign delete empty pages that I no longer need.

My Preferences for Drag and Drop Text

I grew up using computer word processing programs that have drag and drop text features. So I always have Drag and Drop Text turned on for both Story Editor View as well as Layout View.

However, I understand that many designers find drag and drop gets in the way when they work. So I suggest turning it on for the Story Editor and off for the Layout View.

You get the benefits of drag and drop without messing up your layouts.

Advanced Type Preferences

Don't let the term "Advanced Type" throw you off. These are settings that you may want to change depending on the typefaces you work with.

The Character Settings control the size and position of superscript, subscript, and small cap characters 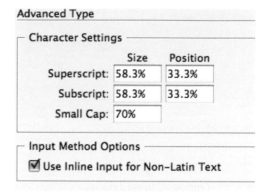.

To set the Character Settings preferences:

1. Enter amounts in the Size fields to control the size of the characters.

2. Enter amounts in the Position fields to control how far above or below the baseline the characters are positioned.

TIP The percentage amount is based on the total space between the two lines.

A non-Latin typeface is one that uses 2-byte and 4-byte characters. Japanese, Korean, and Chinese are examples of non-Latin typefaces. If you work with non-Latin typefaces, you may need to use features in the operating system to enter characters instead of the keyboard 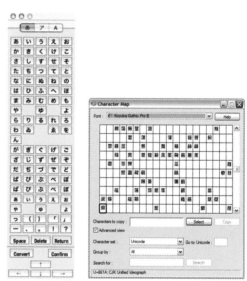.

To use the operating system to enter non-Latin text:

Select the option **Use Inline Input For Non-Latin Text** to allow you to input text using the electronic keyboards built into the computer operating system.

A The **Advanced Type settings** of the Preferences dialog box.

B The **non-Latin input controls** for the Macintosh and Windows operating systems.

Highlight

- ☐ Keep Violations   ☑ Substituted Fonts
- ☐ H&J Violations   ☐ Substituted Glyphs
- ☐ Custom Tracking/Kerning

Text Wrap

- ☐ Justify Text Next to an Object
- ☑ Skip by Leading
- ☐ Text Wrap Only Affects Text Beneath

C The **Composition settings** of the Preferences dialog box.

that Trot and Cap'n
he Land of Oz, where
society of Dorothy, B

D An example of text with a **highlight** applied.

Composition Preferences

The Highlight settings let you control which parts of the text are highlighted to indicate composition or typographic violations or substitutions **c**.

To set the highlight options:

Set the Highlight options as follows:

- **Keep Violations** displays lines that have been broken in violation of the Keep With settings that you chose for the paragraph settings.

- **H&J Violations** highlights those areas that violate the hyphenation or justification settings.

TIP H&J Violations occur when InDesign has no other way to set the text except to break the H&J controls.

- **Custom Tracking/Kerning** highlights the text with tracking or kerning applied to it.

- **Substituted Fonts** highlights characters that are substituted for a font that is not installed in the computer system.

TIP This is the famous pink highlight for a missing font that many people see when they import text or change typefaces.

TIP If the shape of the uninstalled font exists in the Adobe Type Manager database, the shape of the font is approximated. If not, a default font is used.

- **Substituted Glyphs** highlights OpenType characters that have been substituted with alternate glyphs.

You can also control the effect of the Text Wrap settings and how text wraps around objects.

To set the text wrap options:

Choose one of the following from the Text Wrap options:

- **Justify Text Next to an Object** forces text next to an object to be justified if it wraps around an object inside the frame 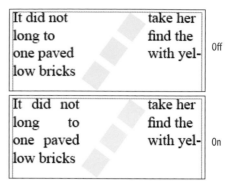.

- **Skip by Leading** forces text that has wrapped around an object to move to the next available leading increment. This avoids problems where text may not line up across columns or frames .

- **Text Wrap Only Affects Text Beneath** causes InDesign text wrap to work only on text below the object, rather than text above and below the object.

Units & Increments Preferences

Units and Increments refer to the units of measurement and how much things change when you apply keyboard shortcuts .

To set where the ruler starts:

Use the Origin menu to select one of the following:

- **Spread** sets the horizontal ruler to stretch across the pages in a spread.

- **Page** sets the horizontal ruler to reset for each individual page in a spread.

- **Spine** sets the horizontal ruler to stretch across the spine of the document.

A The effect of setting the **Justify Text Next to an Object** option.

B When **Skip By Leading** is turned off, the text does not line up across columns. When it is turned on, the text does line up.

C The **Units & Increments settings** of the Preferences dialog box.

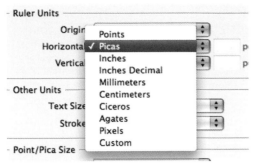

D The units of measurement for the **horizontal and vertical rulers.**

E The units of measurement for **text sizes.**

F The units of measurement for **stroke sizes.**

Point/Pica Size

Points/Inch: PostScript (72 pts/inch)

G Use the **Points/Inch field** to choose between the PostScript measurement for points per inch or the Traditional measurement.

eyboard Increments

| Cursor Key: 0p1 | Baseline Shift: 2 pt |
| Size/Loading: 2 pt | Kerning/Tracking: 20 /1000 em |

H The **Keyboard Increments** area lets you choose how the arrow keys move objects and change text controls.

To set the ruler units:

Use the Horizontal and Vertical menus to select the unit of measurement for each of the rulers **D**.

TIP Set an amount, in points, for a custom unit of measurement.

To set the units for text sizes:

Use the Text Size menu to choose points or pixels for how text is measured **E**.

To set the units for stroke sizes:

Use the Stroke menu to choose Points, Millimeters, or Pixels for how text is measured **F**.

To set the number of points per inch:

Use the Points/Inch field to choose between the PostScript or the Traditional numbers of points per inch **G**.

The keyboard increments control how much the objects move or the text changes **H**.

To set the keyboard increments:

Enter an amount in the fields as follows:

- **Cursor Key** lets you choose the amount that the arrow keys move objects.
- **Size/Leading** controls the amount that the type size and leading change.
- **Baseline Shift** lets you set the amount that the baseline shift changes.
- **Kerning/Tracking** controls the amount that the kerning or tracking changes.

Grids Preferences

Designers just love to set up lines that stretch up and down and across their pages to help keep text and graphics lined up correctly. The Grids preferences control those lines 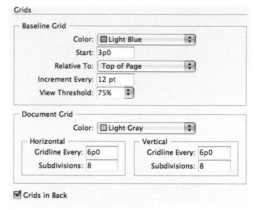.

To set the baseline grid options:

1. Use the Color menu to choose a color for the baseline grid.

2. Use the Start field to position where the grid should start on the page.

3. Use the Relative To menu to position the start of the grid relative to the top of the page or the top margin.

4. Use the Increment Every field to set the distance between the lines of the grid.

5. Use the View Threshold field to set the lowest magnification at which the grid is visible.

TIP Set this for something like 75% to make it easier to see the entire page when you zoom out.

To set the document grid preferences:

1. Use the Color menu to choose a color for the document grid.

2. Enter a value for the Horizontal and Vertical fields as follows:

   • **Gridline Every** sets the distance between the major lines of the grid.

   • **Subdivisions** sets the number of secondary lines of the grid.

To set the positioning of the grids:

Select Grids in Back to position the grids behind graphics and text .

A   The **Grids settings** of the Preferences dialog box.

B   An example of setting the **Grids in Back option** in the Grids category.

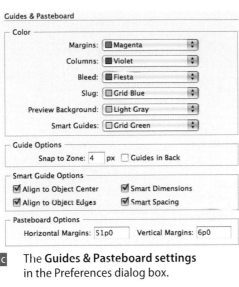

Guides & Pasteboard

Color

Margins: ☐ Magenta

Columns: ■ Violet

Bleed: ■ Fiesta

Slug: ☐ Grid Blue

Preview Background: ☐ Light Gray

Smart Guides: ☐ Grid Green

Guide Options

Snap to Zone: 4 px ☐ Guides in Back

Smart Guide Options

☑ Align to Object Center ☑ Smart Dimensions

☑ Align to Object Edges ☑ Smart Spacing

Pasteboard Options

Horizontal Margins: 51p0 Vertical Margins: 6p0

C The **Guides & Pasteboard settings** in the Preferences dialog box.

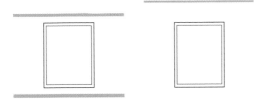

D The effect of increasing the minimum vertical offset.

Guides & Pasteboard Preferences

You can customize the appearance and size of your ruler guides and the pasteboard.

The Color area is a rainbow of choices for how to color onscreen guides and areas **C**.

To set the onscreen elements colors:

Use the menus to set the colors for the margins, columns, bleed, slug, Smart Guides, and the area that surrounds the page in the Preview Mode.

To set the Guide Options:

1. Use the Snap to Zone field to set how close the objects should be when they snap to guides. This amount is set in pixels.

2. Select Guides in Back to hide the guides when they appear behind objects.

To set the Smart Guide Options:

Select each of the display settings to indicate whether Smart Guides should appear at the object centers, object edges, similar sizes, or spacing.

To set the Pasteboard Options:

1. Enter an amount in the Horizontal Margins field to increase or decrease the amount of pasteboard space to the left and right sides of the page.

2. Enter an amount in the Vertical Margins field to increase or decrease the amount of pasteboard space above and below the page **D**.

Dictionary Preferences

The Dictionary preferences work with whichever languages and dictionaries are used for InDesign documents .

The Language setting is used to choose which language dictionary should be used to check whether words are correctly spelled. Consider that the word *cinema* is correctly spelled if English is the chosen language. However, the word is incorrectly spelled if French is chosen as the language. In that case the word should be *cinéma*.

To set the dictionary preferences:

1. Use the Language menu to set the default language.

2. Select the dictionaries in the User Dictionary area. *(See the next exercise for how to add a user dictionary.)*

3. Choose a preference from the Hyphenation menu.

4. Choose a preference from the Spelling menu.

5. Use the Double Quotes menu to choose the characters for double quotation marks **B**.

6. Use the Single Quotes menu to choose the characters for single quotation marks **B**.

TIP The Quotes menus list the marks used for different languages, such as Spanish and French. Or you can enter your own characters in the field.

A The **Dictionary settings** in the Preferences dialog box.

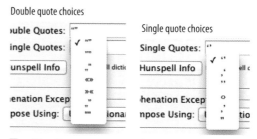

B The **Quote menus** in the Dictionary preferences.

New Dictionary   Delete Dictionary

Relink Dictionary   Add Dictionary

C The **Dictionary buttons** in the Dictionary preferences.

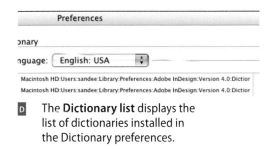

D The **Dictionary list** displays the list of dictionaries installed in the Dictionary preferences.

E The **Missing icon in the Dictionary list** indicates that you need to relink to the dictionary.

You use the dictionary management tools to create, link to, add, and delete new user dictionaries. This allows you to create several dictionaries for InDesign.

To create a new user dictionary:

1. Click the New Dictionary button in the Dictionary preferences **C**.
2. Name and save the dictionary file (UDC) to a location. The new dictionary appears in the Dictionary list **D**.

You don't have to create your own new dictionary. You can use the dictionary management tools to add someone else's dictionary to your version of InDesign.

To add a dictionary:

1. Click the Add Dictionary button in the Dictionary preferences.
2. Navigate to select the new dictionary. The dictionary appears in the Dictionary list.

To delete a dictionary:

1. Select the dictionary that you want to delete in the Dictionary list.
2. Click the Delete Dictionary button in the Dictionary preferences.

To relink a dictionary:

1. Select the dictionary that has a missing or modified icon next to its name in the Dictionary list **E**.
2. Click the Relink Dictionary button in the Dictionary preferences.
3. Navigate to find the missing dictionary.

The hyphenation exceptions let you choose whether to apply the hyphenations created by editing the Dictionary or those built into the application.

To set the hyphenation exceptions:

Choose one of the following from the Compose Using menu 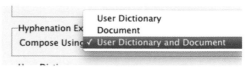:

- **User Dictionary** uses only the hyphenation exceptions set by editing the Dictionary.

- **Document** uses the hyphenation exceptions list stored inside the document. *(See the next exercise for how to add the user dictionary hyphenation exceptions to a document.)*

- **User Dictionary and Document** merges the exceptions in both the document and the user dictionary. This is the default setting.

The User Dictionary options let you merge hyphenation exceptions into a document and create new hyphenation exceptions that affect the document 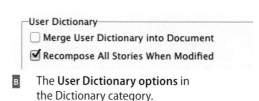.

To set the user dictionary preferences:

1. **Merge User Dictionary into Document** adds the hyphenation exceptions in the user dictionary to the document. This is on by default.

TIP This is especially useful if you send the native InDesign document to a service bureau for output.

2. **Recompose All Stories When Modified** applies the new exceptions in the user dictionary to all the stories in the document.

A The **Compose Using menu** in the Dictionary category.

B The **User Dictionary options** in the Dictionary category.

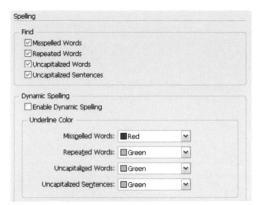

C The **Spelling settings** in the Preferences dialog box.

D Use the **Dynamic Spelling controls** to turn on dynamic spelling and specify colors for each of the error categories.

Spelling Preferences

The Find section of the Spelling preferences controls what types of problems the spelling checker flags during a spelling check C.

To set the Find options for Spelling:

1. Select **Misspelled Words** to find words that are not known in the spelling dictionary.

2. Select **Repeated Words** to find instances of words that are repeated, such as "the the spelling checker."

3. Select **Uncapitalized Words** to find words that are listed in the dictionary as capitalized. For instance, proper names of countries are capitalized in the dictionary.

4. Select **Uncapitalized Sentences** to flag uncapitalized words that begin sentences.

Dynamic spelling highlights errors right on your page. If you want to work with dynamic spelling, you have a choice as to which colors the errors are underlined with.

To set the Dynamic Spelling options:

1. Select Enable Dynamic Spelling in the Spelling preferences D.

2. Use the Underline Color menus to specify the color used to highlight misspelled words, repeated words, uncapitalized words, and uncapitalized sentences.

Autocorrect Preferences

The Autocorrect preferences not only turn on the Autocorrect feature, they allow you to add or remove those words that you want to have automatically corrected.

To turn on autocorrection:

1. Choose Enable Autocorrect to turn on the basic correction for words 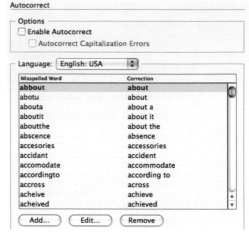.

2. Choose Autocorrect Capitalization Errors to also automatically correct errors in uppercase and lowercase words.

The Autocorrect list contains the words that are commonly mistyped. In addition to the words the Adobe engineers felt you would mistype, you can easily add your own.

To add words to the Autocorrect list:

1. Use the Language menu to choose the language for the autocorrection **B**.

2. Click the Add button at the bottom of the Autocorrect Preferences. This opens the Add to Autocorrect List dialog box **C**.

3. Type the typical misspelling in the Misspelled Word field **C**.

4. Type the correct spelling in the Correction field.

5. Click OK to add the word to the list.

To delete words from the Autocorrect list:

1. Select the word in the list that you want to delete.

2. Click the Remove button.

A The **Autocorrect settings** in the Preferences dialog box.

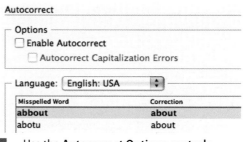

B Use the **Autocorrect Options controls** to turn on autocorrection for word errors and for capitalization errors.

C The **Add to Autocorrect List dialog box** lets you enter the misspelling for a word and its correction.

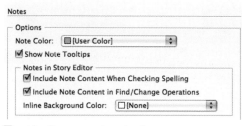

D The **Notes settings** in the Preferences dialog box.

Notes Preferences

Notes are primarily used in an InDesign/InCopy workflow. The Notes preferences control how the notes appear in the InDesign or InCopy stories **D**.

To set the Notes options:

1. Use the Note Color list to set a color for the user. This color should be unique.

2. Select Show Note Tooltips to display the text for the note when the user hovers over the note display **E**.

You can also set the preferences for how notes are handled when working in the Story Editor.

E A **note tooltip** that is revealed when the cursor pauses over the note.

To set the options for notes in the Story Editor:

Select the following as desired:

- **Include Note Content When Checking Spelling** to apply a spelling check to the note text.

- **Include Note Content in Find/Change Operations** to include the note text in the results of a Find/Change routine.

To set the background color for the note:

Use the Inline Background Color list to choose a color for the area behind the note when viewed in the Story Editor **F**.

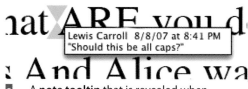

F The **note background color** as displayed in the Story Editor.

Track Changes Preferences

You can customize how the changes for Track Changes are displayed. There are three types of text changes that are displayed as the tracked changes. Each one can be turned on or off individually.

To select which text changes are displayed:

Select or deselect one of the following from the Show area of the Track Changes preferences 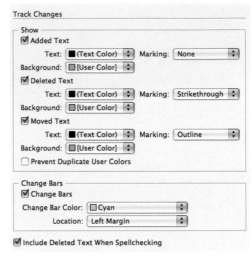:

- **Added Text** displays text that has been inserted.

- **Deleted Text** displays text that has been cut.

- **Moved Text** displays text that has been moved from one location to another.

Each type of tracked text change can have its own display.

To set the display for the types of changes:

1. Use the Text menu to set the color for the changed text 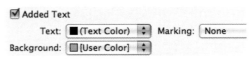.

2. Use the Background menu to set the color behind the changed text .

3. Use the Marking menu to choose one of the indicators for the changed text .

   - **None** applies no indicator to the changed text.

   - **Strikethrough** adds a line through the changed text D.

   - **Underline** adds a line under the changed text D.

   - **Outline** draws a rectangle around the changed text D.

A   The **Track Changes settings** in the Preferences dialog box.

B   The **three menu controls** for the display of changed text.

C   The **marking choices menu** for the display of changed text.

D   The **strikethrough, underline, and outline markings** for the display of changed text.

The **menu controls** for the change bars that run along the side of the tracked changes.

Change bar

F The **change bar** positioned on the left margin of the Story Editor.

☑ Include Deleted Text When Spellchecking

G The command **Include Deleted Text When Spellchecking** controls whether deleted text is included when the spelling check runs.

The user color, defined in the User dialog box, allows each person to have his or her own color for the tracked changes. But it is possible that two people will pick the same user color. So you may want to ensure that two people don't have the same user color.

To prevent changes appearing with the same user colors:

Select Prevent Duplicate User Colors.

If you have a lot of text, it is helpful to display the change bars. These are vertical lines on the side of the Story Editor text that indicate that a tracked change has been applied to the text.

To set the display for the types of changes:

1. Select the Change Bars option to display the change bars **E**.

2. Use the Change Bar Color menu to choose a color **E**.

3. Use the Location menu to choose where the change bar appears **F**. Your choices are Left Margin or Right Margin.

One of the most common reasons for changing text is for spelling errors. If you run a spelling check on a document, you might not want to go through all the deleted text with the original spelling errors.

To prevent the spelling check from going through delected text:

Deselect Include Deleted Text When Spellchecking **G**.

Story Editor Display Preferences

If you work in the Story Editor, you can choose the preferences for its display 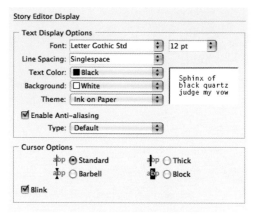.

TIP None of these settings affect the appearance of the text in the layout.

To set the preferences for text display:

1. Use the Font menu to set the typeface.

2. Use the point size menu to set the size.

3. Use the Line Spacing menu to choose the leading between the lines **B**.

4. Use the Text Color menu to set the color of the text.

5. Use the Background menu to set the color of the Story Editor window background.

   or

   Use the Theme menu to select a preset text and background color scheme **C**.

6. Choose Enable Anti-aliasing to soften the edges of the text.

7. If you choose Enable Anti-aliasing, choose an anti-aliasing Type option.

   • **Default** is the typical anti-aliasing.

   • **LCD Optimized** works best on light-colored backgrounds with black text.

   • **Soft** produces a lighter, fuzzier appearance than Default.

You can also change how the cursor, or insertion point, is displayed within the Story Editor.

To set the preferences for cursor display:

1. Choose **Edit > Preferences > Story Editor Display** (Win) or **InDesign > Preferences > Story Editor Display** (Mac).

2. Choose one of the Cursor Options **D**.

3. Select Blink to make the cursor turn on and off within the text.

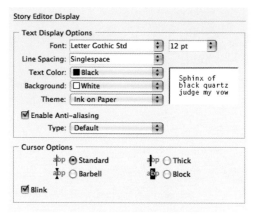

A The **Story Editor Display settings** of the Preferences dialog box.

B The **Line Spacing menu** of the Story Editor preferences controls the space between the lines of text.

C The **Theme menu** lets you quickly change the text and background colors in the Story Editor.

D The **Cursor Options** change the display of the cursor within the text.

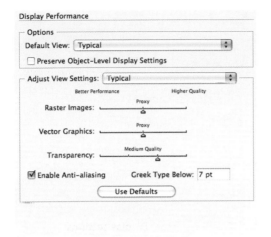

E The **Display Performance settings** in the Preferences dialog box.

Dorothy On

Dorothy Off

F The effect of applying **anti-aliasing** to type.

Display Performance Preferences

The default view is the view that is used when documents are first opened.

To set the default view:

1. Use the Default View menu to choose which of the display performance settings is automatically applied to new documents **E**.

2. Select Preserve Object-Level Display Settings to maintain any individual settings applied to graphics.

The Adjust View Settings control how images appear onscreen for each of the three view choices.

To choose the options for Adjust View Settings:

1. Choose one of the options from the Adjust View Settings menu.

2. Drag the slider controls to set the quality for raster images, vector graphics, and the transparency effects.

3. Repeat for the other two view settings.

TIP It takes longer for the screen to redraw if you choose the highest-quality previews.

Anti-aliasing is the term used to describe the soft edge applied to either text or graphics.

To control the anti-aliasing of text and graphics:

Select Enable Anti-aliasing to add a soft edge to the type and graphics displayed on the monitor **F**.

Greeking is the term used to describe the gray band that is substituted for text characters .

To set text to be greeked:

Enter an amount in the Greek Type Below field. This sets the size below which the text characters will be replaced with gray bands onscreen.

When you use the Hand tool to scroll around a document, InDesign needs to determine how text and images that were not originally in the window appear when you move them into view. You use the Hand Tool preferences to control how the images appear or how fast you can move while scrolling.

To set the scrolling preferences:

Drag the Hand Tool slider to one of the following:

- The left position greeks both text and images. This is the fastest setting but it loses the appearance of the page as text and images come into view .

- The middle position greeks images but maintains text visibility .

- The right position turns off all greeking of text and images. This is the slowest setting but it maintains the appearance of the page as text and images come into view .

On

Off

The Wizard of Oz by L. Frank Baum

A The effect of applying **greeking** to type.

Left position   Middle position   Right position

B The appearance of text and images for each of the Hand Tool slider settings.

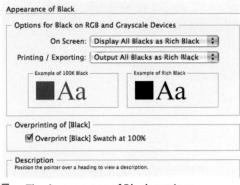

The **Appearance of Black settings** in the Preferences dialog box.

Appearance of Black Preferences

As many designers have discovered, when a color-corrected black is displayed on a computer screen, 100% black ink winds up looking very washed out. The Appearance of Black preferences allow you to choose how 100% black ink is displayed and printed .

To control the appearance of black onscreen:

Choose one of the following from the On Screen menu:

- **Display All Blacks Accurately** displays 100%K as dark gray. This setting allows you to see the difference between pure black and rich black.

- **Display All Blacks As Rich Black** displays 100%K as jet black (RGB=000). This setting makes pure black and rich black appear the same onscreen.

You can also control how 100%K appears when printing to a non-PostScript desktop printer or exporting to an RGB format. This helps control the appearance of blacks in PDF and JPEG files.

To control the appearance of black when printing or exporting to an RGB format:

Choose one of the following from the Printing/Exporting menu:

- **Output All Blacks Accurately** outputs 100%K using the color numbers in the document. This setting allows you to see the difference between pure black and rich black in the finished document.

- **Output All Blacks As Rich Black** outputs 100%K as jet black. This setting makes pure black and rich black appear the same.

File Handling Preferences

If InDesign crashes or the computer is shut down before you can save the InDesign documents, a file is created that contains the recovered document. The Document Recovery Data area lets you choose where that recovered document is located.

TIP Although most people will use the same drive that contains the application, this option lets you specify a folder on a drive that has more space than the one that contains the InDesign application folder.

To set the temporary folder:

1. Click the Browse (Win) or Choose (Mac) button in the Document Recovery Data area 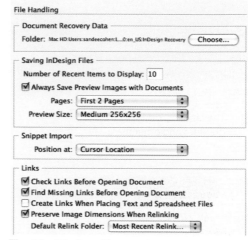.

2. Use the dialog box to choose the location of the recovered documents.

The Saving InDesign Files area lets you set how many files appear in the Open Recent menu. You can also add a thumbnail preview to the file as well as control the size of the preview.

To set the number of files in the Open Recent menu:

Enter a number in the Number of Recent Items to Display field.

To create a preview with saved documents:

1. In the Saving InDesign Files area, choose Always Save Preview Images with Documents.

2. Use the Pages menu to choose how many pages will be displayed in the preview 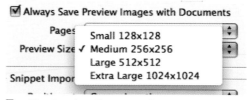.

3. Choose one of the sizes from the Preview Size menu .

TIP More pages and larger previews increase the file size and the time it takes to save the document.

A The **File Handling settings** in the Preferences dialog box.

B The **Pages menu** of the Always Save Preview Images with Documents area lets you choose how many pages are displayed as part of the preview.

C The **Preview Size menu** lets you choose the size for the preview image that is saved with the file.

Links

☑ Check Links Before Opening Document
☑ Find Missing Links Before Opening Document
☐ Create Links When Placing Text and Spreadsheet Files
☑ Preserve Image Dimensions When Relinking
Default Relink Folder ✓ Most Recent Relink Folder
                        Original Relink Folder

D The **Links options** for placed graphics and other files.

You can control the position where snippets appear when you drag them onto a page.

To control the location of snippets:

Select the Snippet Import options as follows:

- **Position at Original Location** places the snippet at its original coordinates.
- **Position at Cursor Location** ignores the original coordinates and places the snippet where the cursor is located when the mouse button is released on the page.

Use the Links options to control how placed graphics and other links are handled.

To set the Links options:

Choose the Links options as follows:

- Choose Check Links Before Opening Document to have InDesign look at the links in the document.
- Choose Find Missing Links Before Opening Document to have InDesign try to relink any missing links in the previously linked folder.
- Select the option Create Links When Placing Text and Spreadsheet Files to link those styles back to the original files.

TIP All local formatting you have applied will be discarded when the text is updated.

- Choose Preserve Image Dimensions When Relinking if you want images to appear at the same size as the images they're replacing; deselect this option to have relinked images appear at their actual size.
- Use the Default Relink Folder to choose what folder should be used when automatically relinking missing links.

Clipboard Handling

You may need to change the options for what type of information is included in the clipboard 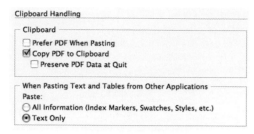.

To set the clipboard format:

Select the Clipboard options as follows:

- **Prefer PDF When Pasting** adds graphics as self-contained pdf files that retain effects.
- **Copy PDF to Clipboard** copies data as pdf files. Select this in order to paste paths into Illustrator or Photoshop.
- **Preserve PDF Data at Quit** maintains any copied pdf information on the clipboard for use in other applications.

To set the attributes for pasting text:

Select When Pasting Text and Tables from Other Applications as follows:

- **All Information** maintains formatting.
- **Text Only** strips out all formatting.

Trashing Preferences

Sometimes InDesign may start to act strangely. This may mean that the files that hold all your preferences and settings have become corrupt. In that case you need to trash those files and let InDesign start over with the factory settings.

To restore all preferences and default settings:

1. As you launch InDesign, immediately press Ctrl-Alt-Shift (Win) or Cmd-Opt-Shift-Control (Mac).
2. Click Yes when asked if you want to delete your preference files .

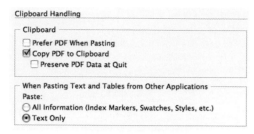

A The **Clipboard Handling settings** in the Preferences dialog box.

B The **Delete InDesign Preference files dialog box** lets you start from scratch with factory-fresh default settings.

Index

typography
  balancing ragged lines, 399
  controlling hyphenation, 394–396
  justification controls, 390–393
  OpenType categories, 401–402
  optical margin alignment, 388
  overview of, 387
  using Adobe Paragraph Composer, 389
  using baseline grid, 396–398
  using OpenType, 399–400

U

unassigned frames
  creating, 80
  overview of, 43–44
  placing artwork into existing, 187
  selecting, 112
Underline styles, 52–53
underline styles, 226
Undo command, 39, 331
uneven line breaks, balancing, 399
Units and Increments preferences, 19, 526–527
unlinking items, 446
unlocking guides, 24, 26
unlocking objects, 111
unnamed colors, 119, 121, 127
unnamed gradients, 134
unnesting bookmarks, 415
unused colors, 126
updating
  files in book, 262
  item in library, 283
  modified links, 206, 446
Up/Down arrow, 306
URL, hyperlinks, 406–409
Use Existing rule, 451
user, tracking text changes, 341
User Dictionary preferences, 532

V

vectors, 193, 211
vertical alignment, 222, 314–315
vertical distribute icons, Align panel, 102
vertical justification, 74, 314–315
vertical layout, Pages panel, 233
vertical Liquid guides, 453
vertical scale controls, text distortion, 56
video, adding to document, 420–422
View Pages menu, Pages panel, 233
views
  changing with Application bar, 36–37
  Display Performance preferences, 539–540
  document, 35
  document grid, 28
  ruler guides, 26

visibility
  button state, 426
  changing menu display, 517
  controlling guides on layer, 276

W

Warning
  customizing preferences, 519
  in Print Booklet dialog box, 482
weight, 144, 224, 316
Welcome Screen, 10
white eyedropper, 167, 353
white precision eyedropper, 168
white space characters, 77, 78, 294
Window menu, 2
Word. *see Microsoft Word*
words
  adding to spell check dictionary, 328
  selecting single, 46
  spacing, 390
  text Find/Change controls for, 332
workflow
  for captions, 338
  creating with InCopy, 504
  totally style-driven, 371
  tracking text changes, 341
workspace, 4–5, 37
wrapping text, 214–219

X

XPress. *see QuarkXPress*

Z

zero point, positioning document ruler, 20
ZIP files, PDF compression options, 498
zoom
  changing magnification, 29–30
  creating page destination, 408
  modifying keyboard shortcuts for, 501
  setting image handling options, 501
  setting view threshold in baseline grid for, 528
  using Hand tool for power, 34
  using loaded cursor for, 247
  using Zoom tool for, 33

THREE WAYS TO QUICKSTART

The ever popular Visual QuickStart Guide series is now available in three formats to help you "Get Up and Running in No Time!"

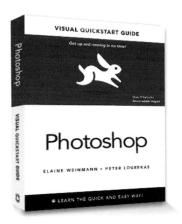

Visual QuickStart Guide Books

The best-selling Visual QuickStart Guide series is available in book and ebook (ePub and PDF) formats for people who prefer the classic learning experience.

Video QuickStart

Video QuickStarts offer the immediacy of streaming video so you can quickly master a new application, task, or technology. Each Video QuickStart offers more than an hour of instruction and rich graphics to demonstrate key concepts.

Enhanced Visual QuickStart Guide

Available on your computer and tablet, Enhanced Visual QuickStart Guides combine the ebook with Video QuickStart instruction to bring you the best of both formats and the ultimate multimedia learning experience.

Visit us at: Peachpit.com/VQS

VISUAL QUICKSTART GUIDE